NEW SOARING PILOT

NEW
SOARING
PILOT

Ann and Lorne Welch
and Frank Irving

THIRD EDITION
REVISED AND ENLARGED

JOHN MURRAY

Printed in Great Britain by The Pitman Press, Bath
0 7195 3302 3

To the memory of
FRED SLINGSBY

AUTHORS' NOTE

The Preface, Chapters 1, 9 and 15 – 20, and Appendices 1, 3 and 5 – 8 were written by Frank Irving. Chapters 2 – 8 and 10 – 14 and Appendices 9 – 12 and 14 were written by Ann and Lorne Welch. The remaining Appendices were written jointly or were contributed. The diagrams were drawn by the authors.

ACKNOWLEDGEMENTS

We are grateful to the following for their help in preparing this book: G. E. Burton, H.C.N. Goodhart, P.M. Tunbridge, the late Dr D.W. Wilks.

We are also indebted to those numerous gliding friends whose comments contributed to this latest revision.

Contents

Illustrations

TABLES

PLATES

Preface

This book is largely concerned with technology, for the glider
is essentially a product of this technological age. The pilot
must therefore learn the appropriate mechanical skills which,
as we try to show, probably encompass a greater proportion
of the process of soaring than the newcomer to the sport
might imagine. But this is not to say that soaring has been
reduced to a drill for operating the controls and pressing
buttons: these are merely means to an end, and since soaring
occurs in a very variable and subtle element—not without its
dangers—there is plenty of scope for art and inspiration. Our
object is to try to render soaring a little easier, by demonstrating that all the actions involved in a given situation are
amenable to a logical approach.

However, the pilot has a large element of choice in arranging the situations, since he is not just a passive spectator. Each
small section of a flight is usually a fairly straightforward
matter, but inspiration is often involved in taking advantage
of the weather or the terrain. The successful pilot conducts
his flight with the inspired logic of a composer making
splendid music from a series of simple phrases.

In such circumstances, the technology becomes quite
unobtrusive. As Antoine de Saint-Exupéry wrote: '...precisely
because it is perfect, the machine dissembles its own existence
instead of forcing itself upon our notice. And thus, also, the
realities of nature resume their pride of place. It is not with
metal that the pilot is in contact. Contrary to the vulgar
illusion, it is thanks to the metal and by virtues of it, that the
pilot rediscovers nature. As I have already said, the machine
does not isolate man from the great problems of nature but
plunges him more deeply into them.' This was written in
the context of flying powered aeroplanes, but those who love
soaring will recognize its general truth.

This, then, is the glider: a machine of great elegance, cleverly fashioned from wood, metal or fibres so as to cause the least possible disturbance to the air it traverses. Its behaviour is quite complicated and to exploit it to the full is not particularly easy. In this book, we try to explain most of those characteristics which are of interest to the pilot, indicating their relevance to the process of soaring. It is as well to point out at this stage that soaring is essentially a practical matter: there is no substitute for flying and putting the book-learning into practice until the control of the machine becomes instinctive and 'it dissembles its own existence'. It also follows that, whilst the designer of a good glider is unlikely to achieve great riches on earth, he can be content in the knowledge that he has contributed something to the sum of human happiness.

Each individual has his own idea of the enjoyable soaring flight: for some it is the exercise of a somewhat esoteric logic with the aim of surpassing others in speed or distance; or it may be the solitude and beauty; or simply, escape from a desk. But all satisfying flights have one feature in common: they involve taking decisions. As Dr Johnson might have said: 'Nothing concentrates a man's mind so wonderfully as the knowledge that he is ten minutes from a forced landing.' We hope that this book will be of some help in making the right decisions and thus contribute to the enjoyment of soaring.

Soaring Progress

Soaring as a sport is less than sixty years old, and represents as yet an infinitesimal fragment of human experience. Various writers have observed that perhaps man's age-old yearning to fly has been overrated in that the construction of a glider was technically feasible some two centuries ago but did not come to fruition until quite recently. Be that as it may, many thousands of people have now experienced the unique pleasures, beauties, triumphs and frustrations of soaring, finding satisfaction in its subtle blend of art and science.

This book is primarily concerned with the science (or, more exactly, the technology) of soaring but first it is useful to consider how soaring has developed, not so much in terms of personalities and outstanding flights but rather in terms of the techniques which made these flights possible.

A little soaring occurred towards the end of the nineteenth and at the beginning of the present century, not so much as an end in itself, but as incidental to the development of flying machines. The names of Lilienthal, Wright, Pilcher and many others are rightly venerated as befits brave pioneers of flying. The first sporting gliding took place just before the First World War at the Wasserkuppe, but no real soaring occurred. However, it demonstrated the value of the site, and when Oskar Ursinus put on his famous hat in 1920 and started a campaign to stimulate soaring, it was there that it developed. The first few annual meetings produced rapid progress in pure slope soaring, from flights of a few seconds in 1920, of twenty minutes in 1921, to over three hours in 1922. By then, soaring was being attempted at other hill-sites in Germany and the celebrated meeting took place at Itford, Sussex, which saw comparable flights but produced little real result.

The requirements for a suitable glider were now becoming clear and machines were built, which, although crude by modern standards, were far cleaner than the contemporary aeroplanes. Stagnation then rapidly set in since enthusiasm for pure hill-soaring tended to flag despite improvements in glider design. In some measure declining interest was due to the prevailing meteorological opinion on thermals; one writer declared that '. . . the wind varies so much in speed and direction that, owing to the resultant turbulence, the extent to which we can make use of up-currents is very limited. The vertical wind forces are also not strong enough to enable one to soar by means of vertical currents alone. . . . Tests usually show a lift of only 1 metre/sec. . . . The skill of our pilots and the manoeuvrability of our sailplanes are not, however, such that we are able to stay in the narrow columns of rising air and gain height by means of tight circles as the birds seem able to do. In view of this, it appears that man will never be able to soar for any length of time with the help of thermal up-currents. . . .' Thus scientifically discouraged, soaring pilots remained hill-bound and frustrated, their outlet being occasional short cross-country flights performed by hopping from one hill to the next.

The first major technical development which effectively set soaring free from hills was the variometer of Lippisch and Kronfeld in 1928. A reasonably skilled pilot of today can soar in thermals without instruments, but usually only because he can relate the feel of the glider in the thermal to his previous experience with a variometer, and he has considerable understanding of the nature of a thermal. In the absence of such experience, the variometer became a key to an understanding of all types of vertical motion in the atmosphere. In 1929, Kronfeld climbed to over 6000 ft in a thunderstorm, landing 90 miles away. His glider, the Wien, was highly refined by any standards, but the lack of blind-flying instruments and airbrakes rendered such a flight dangerous. Progress was then rapid: Wolf Hirth flew in clear-air thermals at Elmira, N.Y.; in 1930 and by 1932 German pilots had carried out enough cloud flying, often indulging in spiral dives, to realize that machines specially designed for cloud flying were vital. Enthusiasm in other countries was greatly stimulated by such feats. In England, the British Gliding

Association was formed in 1929, and Kronfeld made some excellent demonstration flights in 1930. By 1933 pilots at the London Gliding Club at Dunstable were regularly soaring in thermals.

About this time, a third and unexpected form of useful upcurrent was discovered: the standing wave. Nehring had flown in an 'evening thermal' in 1926, a phenomenon which was misunderstood for another twenty years or so, and may well have been the beginning of a wave. In 1933, Deutschmann and Hirth flew Grunau Babys to 4600 ft in the Moazagotl wave in Silesia, and in 1939 a height of 11,000 ft was attained by Noel McClean above Cross Fell, Cumberland. Waves are now known to be very common in this country and, following the experiences of glider pilots, have been the subject of intensive study by meteorologists.

During the few years before the Second World War, skill in thermal soaring and cloud flying progressively improved; distances became hundreds of miles and heights tens of thousands of feet. Broadly speaking, the exterior appearance of gliders did not alter greatly during the 1930s, although they became much stronger in order to withstand large gust loads and stability and control were improved. They were no longer designed to give the lowest minimum sinking speed, but to travel as fast as possible on thermal cross-country flights, so that wing loadings became higher. Reliable blind-flying instruments also became available. There was another outstanding technical development: speed-limiting air-brakes. The terminal velocity of a clean glider is about 300 or 350 knots, a quite impossible speed for it to withstand. Given speed-limiting brakes which would reduce the terminal velocity to 100 knots or so, the spiral dive lost much of its danger and pilots could go cloud flying with infinitely greater security. The Second World War bequeathed three assets to post-war soaring in the form of synthetic waterproof glues, a vast fund of knowledge of the properties and design of low-drag aerofoils, and a generation of pilots who were accustomed to the handling qualities of powered aircraft or who had gained experience of modern test-flying methods. There were also minor pickings in the form of cheap instruments and parachutes.

Shortly after the war, a large number of Olympias were built by Elliotts of Newbury, by redesigning the pre-war Jacobs Meise to satisfy British Civil Airworthiness Requirements. Some of these machines are still in use. There was a similar reliance on pre-war German designs elsewhere in Europe, and variants of the Meise and Weihe were built in several countries.

The next generation of glider designs also relied on the example of pre-war Germany. Types such as the Slingsby Sky and the French Air 100 were recognizably descended from the Weihe, although with higher wing loadings and more effective air-brakes. A major stimulus to glider design came from the USA, in the form of the Ross-Johnson RJ-5 of 1950. By the use of the then novel low-drag NACA wing sections, and careful attention to detailed finish, a glide angle of nearly 1 in 40 was achieved. This machine was the subject of detailed investigation by Dr August Raspet who continued to pursue 'low-loss aerodynamics' until his untimely death. Following the example of the RJ-5, other designers were quick to adopt low-drag wing sections and more accurate profiles. In the UK, the Skylark series (Fig. 1.1) were typical of this trend, using thick gaboon plywood as wing covering in an attempt to reduce the waviness commonly associated with the thinner birch used in earlier structures.

The low-drag NACA wing sections were not specifically designed for low-speed operation, although the thicker members of the series had useful properties for glider application. The next revolution came from Germany, where R. Eppler and F. X. Wortmann designed sections particularly suited to gliders. In particular, they were intended to operate at high lift coefficients (see Chapter 16) without an undue increase in drag. One of the earlier machines to embody these ideas was the Phönix of 1957 designed by Hänle. In the interests of maintaining accurate profiles, this machine was largely built from glass fibre and resin. Although not particularly successful as a contest aircraft, it displayed the merits of these special aerofoils and the advantage of accurate

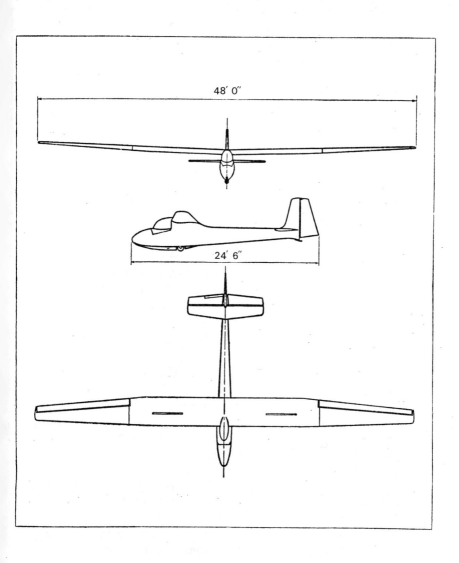

48' 0"

24' 6"

Fig 1.1 General arrangement of Slingsby Skylark II

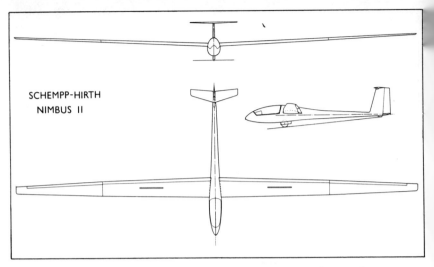

Fig 1.2 The Nimbus II, designed by Klaus Holighaus and built by Schempp-Hirth in glass-fibre. Span 20.3 m; aspect ratio: 26.6; empty weight: 340 kg; max. AUW: 530 kg; max. L/D: 49 at 90 km/h (49 knots); min. sink: 0.48 m/s (0.93 knots) at 75 km/h (40 knots). The performance relates to an AUW of 460 kg.

contours. Its successors, such as the Nimbus (Fig. 1.2), ASW-17 (Fig. 1.3) and the Kestrel (Plate I), are production aircraft which represent the current development of these themes. They also illustrate a further trend, that of reducing the extra-to-wing drag as much as possible. This drag arises from the fuselage and the tail, and is associated with the need to house the pilot in adequate comfort and to provide acceptable longitudinal stability and control. Ideas on 'adequate comfort' were radically revised when the Polish Zefir and Foka appeared in 1960, demonstrating that a very reclining posture was, surprisingly, quite acceptable even if initially somewhat disconcerting. Likewise, it is not too difficult to arrange the size of the tail surfaces and the centre of gravity position of the aircraft so as to keep the 'trim drag' as low as possible.

The outcome of such endeavours is that the extra-to-wing profile drag of a modern machine is about 60% of that of the wing (again, see Chapter 16), and there is doubtless room for further improvement by arranging for extensive laminar boundary layer on the front fuselage and suitable shaping of

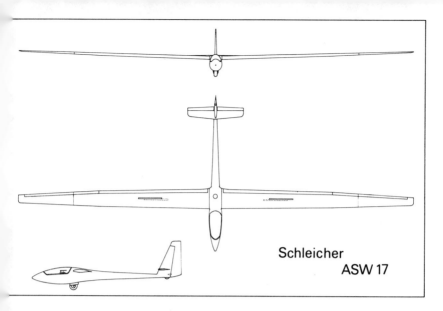

Fig 1.3 The ASW-17. Designed by Gerhard Waibel of Schleicher, Germany. Holder of World Goal record of 1231 km in 1974, flown by Hans Werner-Grousse

the rear fuselage to minimize the drag due to the turbulent boundary layer.

Glass-fibre construction is now widely used; it gives a superb finish and the difficulties introduced by its low stiffness have been largely overcome. Gliders such as the Caproni A21 Calif 2-seater have shown that an excellent finish can also be obtained on a metal structure.

The evolution of gliders has been greatly stimulated by competitive flying, particularly in World Gliding Championships, and the introduction of classes. In 1956, discussions were initiated which produced the 'Standard Class', initially intended to consist of straightforward 15-m gliders without expensive gadgets such as flaps and retracting landing gear. Typical contemporary examples were the K-6CR and the Skylark II. Designers applied themselves with great enthusiasm to the challenge presented by these limitations and a new generation of 15-m gliders, exemplified by the Polish Foka, soon appeared. The Foka really represented the end-product of the wooden glider era, and was soon supplanted

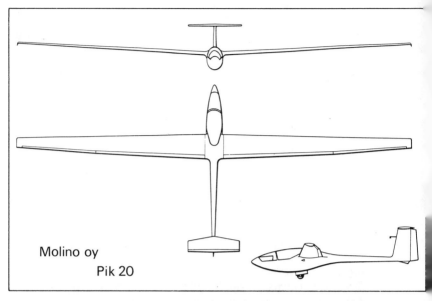

Molino oy
Pik 20

*Fig 1.4 The Pik–20. Glass-fibre built in Finland. Span
15 m; aspect ratio 22.5; empty wt 518 lb; water ballast
176 lb; max. all-up wt 880 lb. Performance at 816 lb;
best L/D at 53 knots 1:40; min. sink at 44 knots 1.30
knots*

by glass-fibre Standard Class machines such as the Libelle
(Fig. 1.5), ASW-15, Standard Cirrus and LS-1. At the same
time, the Standard Class rules were gradually modified to
permit retractable landing gear and then water ballast and
flaps provided that they were also airbrakes.

It rapidly became apparent that a consequence of the
15-m span limitation was to encourage designers to exploit
almost every other performance-increasing feature apart
from increased span. The Standard Class gliders evolved far
beyond the original concept of the inexpensive club aircraft, but new rules, coming into force in 1978, reintroduce
a class similar to that defined in 1972, thus prohibiting
purely performance-improving flaps and establish a new
'Open 15-m' Class where the only limitation is the span. Designs for this new Class (ASW-20, etc.) are already appearing.

At the same time, Open Class gliders, with no restrictions
at all, have been steadily getting bigger in the interests of

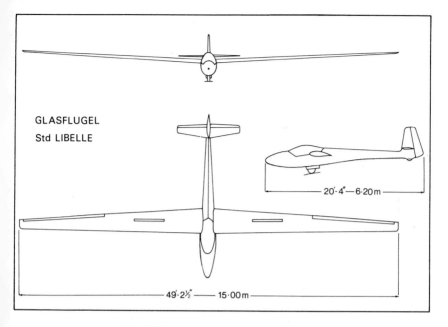

GLASFLUGEL
Std LIBELLE

20′·4″—6·20 m

49′·2½″ —— 15·00 m

Fig 1.5 The Standard Libelle. Glass-fibre built in Germany. Span 15m; aspect ratio 22; empty wt 407 lb; water ballast 77 lb; max. all-up wt 772 lb. Performance at 695 lb: best L/D at 52 knots 1:35; min. sink at 45 knots 1.39 knots

increased performance. Spans between 20 and 22 m are now commonplace, leading to very expensive and heavy machines. In an attempt to keep costs within reasonable bounds, an Open sub-class of 19-m span has been defined, of which the Kestrel 19 (Plate I) is a typical example.

The result of these advances is that, if we regard the best gliding angle as a good measure of overall aerodynamic efficiency, gliders have been improving at a rate of somewhere between two and three per cent per annum. As is usual in any technology, it has not always been clear how the next improvement can be achieved. At present, one can argue that without discovering some new law of nature there is little prospect of reducing the drag of wings much further and fuselages cannot be made much slimmer unless high performance gliding is restricted to the wee folk. Obviously, there is

Plate 1 The Kestrel 19 built by Slingsby Sailplanes in glass-fibre. Winner of the 19 metre World Cup, 1972, flown by A. Haemmerle, Austria. Span: 19 m, aspect ratio: 28, empty weight: 321 kg, max. AUW with water ballast: 472 kg, max. L/D: 44 at 97 km/h (52 knots), min. sink: 0.52 m/s (1.01 knots) at 74 km/h (40 knots)

some minor cleaning-up to be done, but what then? As Chapter 17 indicates, the design of a glider involves a compromise between the ability to perform slow circles when climbing in thermals and the ability to cruise at high speeds in straight flight. It seems very likely that the machine can be caused to perform more efficiently in both regimes of flight by using a variable-chord and variable-camber wing. The British experimental design Sigma embodied this concept and showed that the principle worked, although the performance was degraded by poor fits and leaks. A great deal of mechanical ingenuity is required to make such a system practicable, coupled with painstaking detail work. The end-product is very expensive but there seem to be few other possibilities of making significant performance improvements.

A relatively small improvement in the pilot's ability to find and use thermals has a much more significant effect on cross-country performance than hard-won aerodynamic and structural advances. Over the last few years, various instruments for locating thermals and displaying rates of climb have been proposed, but none has reached a practical stage other than the electric variometer and various types of computer. Thermal location by means of temperature or electrical charge gradients has been singularly unsuccessful. One possibility, within the scope of current technology, is the infra-red location of thermal sources, and another is the detection of thermals by laser techniques. At present, both developments are costly and not readily available even to the well-endowed experimenter, but this situation could change quite quickly.

All things considered, there is still much scope for technological advance, even if one eschews ideas such as building solar cells into the wing surfaces. With the possible exception of variable-chord wings, we seem to be getting into the realms of diminishing returns, and it is becoming debatable whether pilots, outside World Championships, will regard expensive electronic aids as contributing enough to the fun. In the nature of things they probably will.

Figure 1.6 illustrates the progress in soaring, in terms of significant distance flights. Some very meritorious flights have been omitted if they have no noticeable effect on the

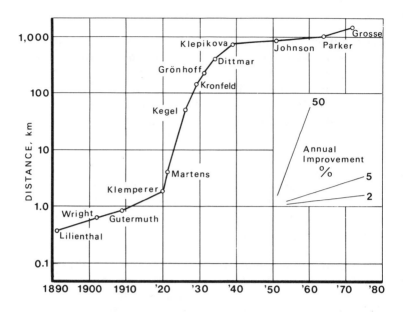

Fig 1.6 Progress in soaring as illustrated by significant distance flights

overall trend. The distance scale is logarithmic, and hence any straight line sloping upwards to the right represents a constant percentage rate of improvement per year on a compound-interest basis as indicated by the lines on the right of the diagram. The spectacular rate of improvement in the '20s and '30s is immediately apparent, as is the relatively slow rate thereafter. It is probably fair to say that the greatest advances were associated with a rapidly increasing knowledge of how to put soaring weather to good account, particularly after the invention of the variometer, rather than to improvements in the gliders themselves. It is very significant that the considerable improvements in glider design since the war are quite invisible on the basis of this diagram. Of course, one has to be careful in looking at logarithmic plots: a considerable improvement in distance, measured in kilometres, looks very small towards the upper end of the diagram. Moreover, distance is not the only measure of progress in soaring. The pursuit of ultimate performance has led to the production of a wide range of magnificent gliders with maximum lift/drag ratios near the magic 50:1 figure. Given the skill and knowledge to fly them really well, pilots derive immense satisfaction and exhilaration from these beautiful and sophisticated machines. The occasional weekender is unlikely to find them so rewarding: if he cannot afford the time to practise, he will be unable to exploit their full performance potential and may well find himself worried by the prospect of a field landing, all to the detriment of his enjoyment.

High-performance gliders are inherently expensive and recent world-wide economic trends have pushed prices beyond the reach of all but a few prospective owners. By the same token, development costs are now so high that the rate of future progress is likely to be fairly slow, with successive improvements of existing machines rather than radical innovations.

The more sophisticated machines are generally inappropriate for club use and designers are coming to recognize that clubs have not been well served in recent years. Interest in lighter, less expensive gliders is reviving and types such as the Club Libelle, K-18 and Astir are intended to provide safe flying for fun at reasonable cost. Various competitions for such Club Class gliders are being established.

Even a Club Class glider costs about twice as much as an average car, so there are plenty of people who cannot afford to start conventional gliding, however much they yearn to get airborne. Curiously enough, their salvation has come in the form of spin-off from the most expensive endeavour of all: NASA's manned space-flight program. Francis Rogallo designed the delta sailwing, originally conceived as a capsule recovery device, and it has become a cheap and simple glider controlled by movements of the pilot's body weight. The Rogallo has a maximum lift/drag ratio of about 4:1, an order of magnitude worse than a good conventional glider. But its wing loading is so low that it can slope-soar for as long as the wind blows or the pilot's muscles permit him to retain control. Hang-gliding exponents are by no means devoid of the desire for higher performance, so higher aspect-ratio sailwings and rigid-aerofoil ultralight gliders soon appeared, with maximum lift/drag ratios of 8:1 or 10:1 and capable of thermal soaring and cross-country flights.

A whole spectrum of motorless aircraft is now available, from the basic hang glider, exploring the air over a hill slowly and gently, to the big expensive sailplane, capable of traversing a noticeable fraction of a continent at over 60 mile/h. There is no lack of challenge: the further development of light, simple structures and safer operating techniques at one end of the scale will be essential if hang gliding, the fastest-growing sector of amateur aviation, is to prosper; at the other extreme, breaking the new world record for speed around a 1000-km triangle will exercise the best intellects in soaring for decades to come.

Chapter 2

Introduction to Soaring

People start flying gliders for a variety of reasons. Some never learn to do it well, and drift away to other activities, but some reach the soaring stage, and become so enthusiastic with its fascinations that they will spend nearly all their time, energy and money on it. To those who have done some soaring there is no need to explain where this fascination lies, but for those who have not yet climbed high in a glider or flown across country it may be useful to attempt a description.

From watching a glider soaring, effortlessly it seems, it might be supposed that the pilot would be in a state of delightful repose drifting silently from cumulus to cumulus without a care in the world. This is far from the truth, and if it were so, soaring would soon become boring. In reality the attractions of soaring lie not in effortlessness, but in the results of skill, decision-taking and hard work. There is the obvious satisfaction to be derived from accurate control of the aircraft, and from the beauty of the scene and the sky, enhanced to a surprising extent by the quietness. But even more important is the satisfaction to be obtained from understanding the air itself; from knowing where upcurrents can be found and downdraughts avoided, to the knowledge of the incredible power of a thunderstorm, and the ability to search out lift in an unexplored wave.

If the exact answer to the conditions which the glider pilot meets were known, gliding would lose much of its unexpectedness and attraction, since success would then be due entirely to minor variations in pilot technique. It is precisely because our knowledge of the air and its habits is still fragmentary that gliding has so much to offer. Any pilot, however impecunious, stands a chance of contributing something new. Because the knowledge of even the most expert pilot is incomplete, a beginner who finds that he possesses a flair for this type of observation and thought can reach the top after only a few years of flying.

Soaring is primarily a craft, or rather two crafts: those of piloting the aircraft, and making use of upcurrents. The art of teaching people to fly gliders is now well understood and will not be dealt with here. However, the teaching of soaring is still haphazard, mainly due to a shortage of suitable gliders and instructors. In consequence soaring is for most pilots a self-taught skill, and since few are able to do very much flying in a year, progress is apt to be slow. We do not suggest that anyone can learn to soar merely by reading a book; skill can only be obtained by much thought and plenty of practice, but we hope that a study of these chapters will help pilots to clarify their ideas as to what they are trying to do, and by showing what is, and what is not, important, enable them to teach themselves more quickly and thoroughly.

In soaring it is unwise to lay down hard and fast rules for procedure and action in particular circumstances. All that can be done is to suggest the various factors which should be considered, and to mention their relative importance. Decisions can only be taken by the pilot on the spot. However, in order to avoid dealing with too many issues at the same time, we have attemped to simplify the chapters on thermal soaring and cross-country flying by dividing them into elementary and advanced sections.

The high performance glider is awkward on the ground, and unable to take off under its own power, but in the air it is elegant, beautiful, and above all quiet. When piloted by the right brains, over the right terrain, and in the right weather, extraordinary results have been achieved. Gliders have climbed 30,000 ft in free flight, and reached 44,000 ft. They have been flown distances of 1000 miles, and averaged speeds of 100 mile/h solely because the pilots understood the air in which they flew and used its energy. But the main reason that flights such as these have been done, and in fact why any soaring is done at all, is purely and simply for the real pleasure, either from the flight itself, or from the sense of

Plates II and III The Janus two-seater, designed by Klaus Holighaus and built by Schempp-Hirth in glass-fibre. Span: 18.2 m, aspect ratio: 20, empty weight: 370 kg, max. AUW: 620 kg, max. L/D: 39 at 95 km/h (51 knots), min. sink: 0.6 m/s (1.18 knots) at 75 km/h (40 knots)

satisfaction that a successful flight can bring.

One feature of soaring since its inception has been competitions at both National and International levels. There is no doubt that these contests have done much to improve our knowledge of soaring, and this has occurred in two ways. Firstly by pilots attempting to put up good performances in conditions which they consider unsuitable or difficult, and secondly by observing how their competitors fly, and by talking with them. Pilots visiting other countries have found that although the conditions in terms of thermal strengths, heights of cloud base and so on, may be different to those which they are accustomed, the actual technique varies but slightly, and in general local knowledge is of less importance than might be supposed. A clear mind free of preconceived ideas is often more successful.

One good feature of soaring is the friendship between gliding people of different countries. The small badges worn by soaring pilots are similar all over the world, and the wearer can be sure of a welcome wherever he goes. The reason for this is that the sort of people who go in for gliding are similar in all countries. They do it because they like it, there being little or no commercial incentive, and they share a desire to find out more about the air in which they fly, with its varieties of solitude and violence, beauty and challenge.

Chapter 3

Circling in Thermals

Most soaring is carried out using warm air upcurrents called thermals. They are created by the sun and so occur only during the day. This automatically puts a limit to the length of a thermal soaring flight. The whole art of soaring has, as a result, been devoted to developing techniques to enable the maximum to be extracted from the weather in the time available.

Thermals occur as a result of the irregular heating of the earth's surface, and take the form of bubbles or patches of warmed, buoyant air which rise until they have cooled to the temperature of the surrounding air, or have reached a layer of air as warm as or warmer than themselves. As the thermal rises and cools it will become less able to hold its moisture in the invisible vapour state, and will produce cumulus cloud if condensation level is below the level at which the thermal reaches its equilibrium.

The pilot uses thermals by circling to keep in the rising air. When he has gained enough height he flies off in search of more lift. By choosing his route he can fly across country or soar locally around the airfield (Fig. 3.1). Although a vast amount of thermal soaring has been done, there is little quantitative information available about the distribution, size or strength of thermals, or about the structure of the individual thermal. (See Appendix 8.) However, it is well known that the characteristics of thermals can vary from a diameter of a few feet to an area of several square miles. The smallest thermal which can effectively be used by a glider is about 400 ft across, but in general the thermals used are larger than this and 1000 ft may be taken as a typical diameter. Thermals may also be smooth or rough, and circular or otherwise in cross section.

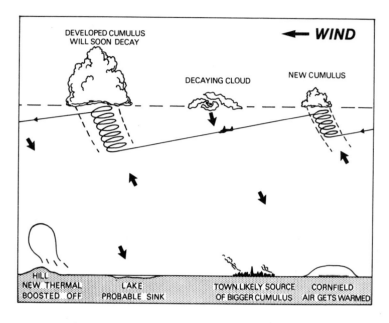

Fig 3.1 Simplified progress of glider flying across country

All these variations demand different techniques, and so to avoid complication this Chapter will deal with what might be called average conditions; a horizontal cross section through a thermal will be taken as circular, with the lift strongest in the middle and decreasing towards the outside.

Let us imagine that the pilot has had an aerotow on a typical European summer day with small cumulus at 4000 ft, and is now gliding straight at about 2000 ft. He is not in lift but the air will not feel entirely steady, and the variometer will show about 2 knots sink. Sooner or later he may fly into a thermal. Just before he does so the air will probably feel rougher and the rate of sink increase. The entry into a good thermal may be marked by a sort of 'woosh' as the airspeed increases and the glider surges upward. After a lag of a second or two the variometer will show climb. The air inside the thermal often has an effervescent feel unlike that outside. As the glider flies through the thermal the rate of climb increases and when the centre is passed starts to decline. Quite suddenly the glider flies out of the lift, and there may be a sort of 'woomp' as the airspeed decreases and the glider sinks. Then after the usual slight lag the variometer will show sink once more. The time taken to fly through the thermal will, of course, depend on its size and on the speed of the glider. For the thermal shown in these diagrams – 1100 ft diameter – the time taken to fly through it at 40 knots will be 16 seconds. If the mean rate of climb in it were 3 knots the glider would gain about 80 ft.

If the straight path is continued another thermal may not be met for a mile or more, by which time the glider will have lost more height than it gained in flying through the thermal.

Introduction to Figs. 3.2-9. The following figures show a highly idealized state of affairs in that the themal is of exactly circular cross section, and has a sharply defined edge. In practice the thermal will probably be of less regular shape and its edge will not be clearly marked. For simplicity the problem has been considered as that of getting into the thermal, but the problem of shifting the circles into the best lift can be tackled in exactly the same way. In each case the figures are on the same scale with a thermal of 1100 ft diameter. The glider is assumed to be an intermediate type with a span of 50 ft and to be flying at a constant speed of 40 knots. When it circles it does so at an angle of bank of 30°. A turn made at this speed and angle of bank will have a radius of 250 ft; the time taken to complete a 360° turn will be 23 seconds. It is assumed that the glider takes 3 seconds to attain 30° of bank from straight flight and the same time to straighten up from the turn. The commencement of the turn from straight flight and the resumption of straight flight from the turn are shown by small squares. The point at which the glider is fully in the turn and the point at which it starts to come out of the turn are shown by small circles. In the diagrams and explanations it is assumed that the glider is fitted with a non-electric variometer having a lag of a few seconds.

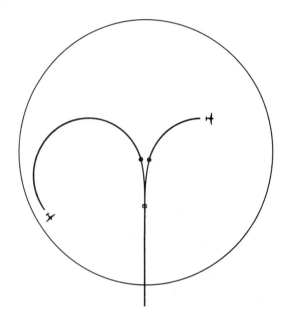

Fig 3.2 Which way to turn? (i) If the thermal is entered with the glider heading towards the centre, it does not matter which way the turn is made

It is, therefore, usually necessary to gain height by circling for some time and then converting this height into distance by gliding straight until another thermal is encountered. The process is then repeated.

Direction of turn. On hitting a thermal the pilot must decide in which direction to start circling. If the glider enters the lift heading towards the centre it obviously does not matter in which direction the turn is made (Fig. 3.2). But if the flight path passes along the edge of the thermal, a circle in one direction will be almost completely outside it, while a circle the other way will be in it (Fig. 3.3). Fortunately it is often possible to tell on which side the stronger lift is to be found, as on entering a thermal the wing nearer the centre may be lifted up first. If this occurs the

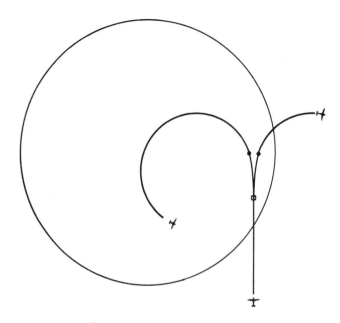

Fig 3.3 Which way to turn? (ii) If the glider flies into the side of a thermal, to turn in one direction will be good; to turn the other way will result in most of the circle coming outside the thermal. Often the fact that the glider has entered the side of the thermal can be discovered as one wing will be pushed up first. In the diagram above the glider will tend to bank to the right on entering the thermal. The pilot should prevent the left wing from lifting and then push it down and turn left

pilot should put it down again, fly straight for a second or so, and then start to turn towards the wing which was lifted up.

If any other gliders are already using the lift there is a convention which requires new arrivals to circle in the same direction as those already there in order to minimise the risk of collision.

Methods of Centring. If the pilot starts to circle as soon as he enters the lift, half the circle will be inside and half out-

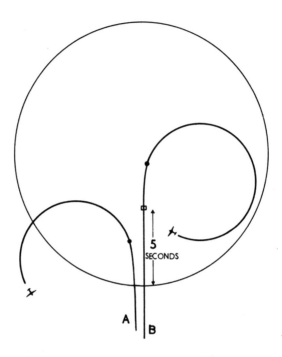

Fig 3.4 How soon to start turning? (i) If the entry is made flying towards the centre of the thermal, and the turn is started immediately, most of the circle will be outside the thermal (path A). Instead, the pilot should fly straight for at least five seconds before starting his turn (path B). Of course, if there is reason to believe that the thermal is large, straight flight should be maintained for a longer time

side the thermal (Fig. 3.4). On the other hand if he waits until he has got to the middle by seeing when the variometer reading starts to decrease, he will probably fly out of the far side as he does his turn. There are a number of different ways of centring; by tightening and loosening the circles, by sideslipping, by reversing the direction of the turn, or by straightening up and then turning again. Each method has its adherents, and they all seem to work, but the simplest is that of

24

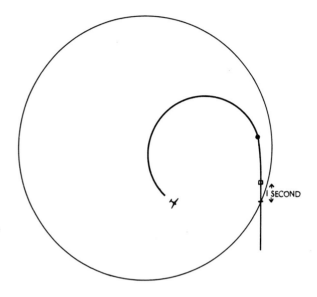

I SECOND

Fig 3.5 How soon to start turning? (ii) If it is suspected that the glider has flown into the side of the thermal, by one wing being pushed up, the turn should be made almost immediately after a pause of only a second or so

straightening up for a short while in the appropriate direction.

The Worst Heading Method. The pilot should notice, by reference to the sun, a cloud, or something prominent on the ground, the direction in which the glider is heading when the variometer shows most sink. Let us say that during a circle the variometer indicates the greatest sink when the glider is facing the sun. This should be checked by doing another circle to see if the same result is obtained. The pilot should then continue turning, but straighten up 60° after passing the sun, fly straight momentarily, and then start circling in the same direction as before. This will have shifted the circle about 200 ft to one side. The reason for turning 60° and not 90°, as might be supposed, is to make allowance for the lag of the ordinary variometer; due to this lag the

25

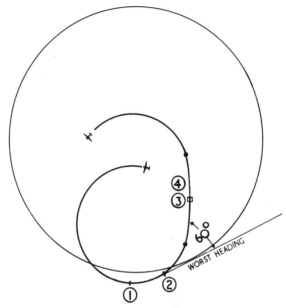

Fig 3.6 Worst Heading method of centring
1 Glider is worst off here
2 Owing to the lag in the variometer it shows that the glider is worst off here. Pilot should observe the aircraft's heading
3 Pilot straightens up 60° later
4 As soon as he is straight he should start to turn again in the same direction
This manoeuvre will have shifted the circle by about 200 ft

instrument will show greatest sink about 2 seconds after the point at which it was actually experienced. If an electric variometer is used the turn should be made through nearly 90°, since the instrument has virtually no lag.

This method may sound mechanical; it is meant to be, because however confused the pilot may become it can be applied easily. All that he has got to do is to decide in which direction he is heading when worst off, turn a further 60°,

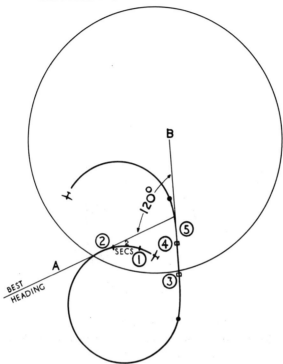

Fig 3.7 Best Heading method of centring.
1 Glider has maximum rate of climb here
2 Owing to the lag of the variometer it shows best rate of climb here. The pilot should observe either (A) the heading or (B) what is under the higher wing tip
3 Pilot continues circling and straightens up 120° short of heading (A) or, what is the same thing, towards (B)
4 Pilot flies straight for two seconds, or if most of the circle has been bad, for a longer time
5 Pilot starts circling again in the same direction as originally

straighten up the glider and forthwith start turning the same way as before (Fig. 3.6).

The Best Heading Method. If most of the circle is in sinking

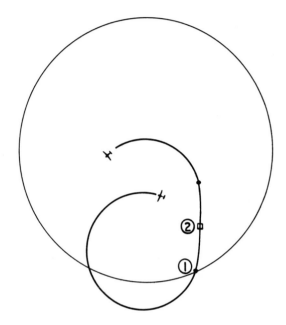

Fig 3.8 Surge method of centring
1 On entering thermal, the glider surges upwards. The pilot should immediately start to straighten up
2 As soon as the aircraft is straight, the turn should be started in the same direction as before

air outside the thermal it is difficult to decide in which direction the glider is heading when it is worst off, because the variometer may show steady sink for a prolonged period. In this case it is easier to decide in which direction the glider is going when it is doing best. The turn should be continued for a little less than 240° from this heading, and then straightened up for one or two seconds before starting to turn again (Fig. 3.7).

It is useless altering the position of the circles unless the pilot is quite certain in which direction they should be shifted, and so to begin with it will be better to do at least two steady circles noticing the distribution of the lift before taking any action. Most people, when learning, alter their circles too frequently, and often lose the thermal in the process.

The Surge Method. Another way of getting into the best lift is to straighten up for a second or two whenever a real surge of lift is felt, or observed on the variometer. This method is often easier to apply than those described above, particularly when the area of lift is sharply defined or the air very turbulent, but it cannot be used with large smooth thermals (Fig. 3.8).

Reversing Direction of Turn. Until some experience in thermal soaring has been gained it is inadvisable to reverse the direction of the turn. If an expert pilot finds himself near the edge of the thermal he may change over and turn the other way at the critical moment (Fig. 3.9), but if a beginner tries this he is very likely to lose the thermal completely. As mentioned earlier there are other ways of adjusting the circles besides those shown in the diagrams and the pilot, as he gains experience will adopt the technique which suits him best.

Circling. Once in the thermal the glider should be kept turning smoothly and steadily at a constant angle of bank for at least two complete circles in order to see what happens. With any luck the variometer will now show climb all the way round, and the glider will go up. A thermal is seldom perfectly smooth inside and so the variometer must not be expected to give an entirely steady reading; in fact even little bits of sink may be indicated. If the glider is climbing, the pilot should not worry about this but instead concentrate on making even circles at a steady airspeed and angle of bank. If, however, the variometer starts to show sink for a fair proportion of the time, the pilot will once more have to alter the position of his circles.

The strongest upcurrents are most often found in the central cores of thermals and so there might appear to be some benefit in keeping in the very middle by making the smallest possible circles. Unfortunately small circles can be achieved only by flying at increased angles of bank; this puts more load on the wing, with the result that the sinking speed is increased. As the rate of climb of the glider is equal to the

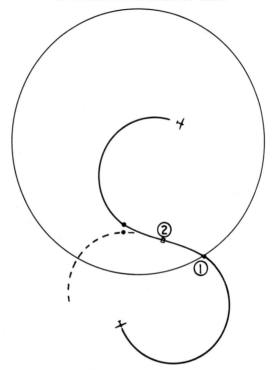

Fig 3.9 Reversing direction of turn. If most of the circle is outside the best lift, the 'surge' method of centring (described in previous figure) will do no good. See dotted line

1 The pilot can shift his path into better lift by straightening up on feeling the surge and then

2 Starting to turn the other way.

This situation can be recognized by the tendency for the bank to increase on entering the thermal and also by the fact that most of the circle has been outside the thermal. The situation should be compared with Fig 3.8 where, if most of the circle is inside the thermal, the effect of the surge will be to reduce the angle of bank

If the reversal of the turn is left until too late, the result may be worse than before. A beginner is not recommended to reverse his direction of turn. He will find it simpler to use the 'Best heading' technique

vertical speed of the thermal less the sinking speed of the glider, it will not pay to reduce the radius of the turn too much, or else the increase in the sinking speed will be greater than the improved strength of the upcurrent at the centre of the thermal. Turns of about 30° are a good compromise to start with, although the skilled pilot may circle at both steeper and flatter angles of bank than this. At 30° of bank a glider flown at 40 knots will take 23 seconds to make a complete 360° turn, the diameter of the circle being 500 ft. Looked at another way, the time taken to fly across the diameter of a circle of this size would be $23/\pi$ seconds—7 seconds. Later on this matter of angles of bank will be dealt with more fully (Chapter 16).

It is important, when circling, that the glider is flown smoothly and accurately. The angle of bank and the airspeed must be kept as steady as possible and there should be no slip or skid. Skill in doing this can only be obtained by practice; accurate turns are most easily made by watching the nose move around the horizon, and not by looking downwards. It is very easy to get into the bad habit of looking at the airspeed indicator every few seconds. This makes flying tiring, and in any case the speed can be kept steadier by reference to the attitude of the glider and the noise it is making.

Variation of Bank due to Location in Thermal. An addition clue for the location of the glider in relation to the core of the thermal is often given by the tendency for the angle of bank to vary. If one wing is in a part of the thermal which is going up more rapidly than the air in which the other wing lies, then the first wing will tend to rise. When circling concentrically to the thermal, the effect of this is negligible since there is only a constant slight moment trying to reduce the angle of bank. However, when circling eccentrically the continual changes may be noticeable. There are two common situations. In the first, where the glider's circle is only slightly eccentric to the thermal, there will be two points where there is no tendency for the angle of bank to be changed and for the remainder of the circle there will be a tendency for the angle of bank to be reduced. The second situation is when the core of the thermal lies completely outside the glider's circle. When the glider is furthest from the core there will be the same tendency for the angle of bank to be reduced, but when it is closest there will be a marked tendency for the angle of bank to be increased. This effect is often noticed when circling in rough air, the sequence as the pilot flies round being: surge up, angle of bank increases, surge down. When this is noticed there is unmistakable evidence that the centre of the thermal lies outside the circle. The solution is to continue round the circle, straighten up when the surge is felt, fly straight for 3–4 seconds, and then circle the same way as before.

SPEED VARIATIONS

If a glider is flown in perfectly calm air and the stick is pulled back, the speed will decrease and the glider go up, or not continue down as rapidly as before. The alterations in height due to quite small alterations in speed are surprising. For example, if the speed is reduced from 45 to 40 knots the glider will be 18 ft higher than it would have been had it continued at 45 knots. This means that if the reduction in speed was spread over 5 seconds a perfect variometer would show an alteration in sink of 2 knots for that period. In practice the variometer has some lag and the alterations in its readings will not be so great, but they are still appreciable. The converse is also true, if the speed is increased the variometer will show a greater rate of descent while the alteration in speed is taking place.

This is a matter of some importance when thermal soaring because if the airspeed is allowed to vary considerably the pilot can easily mistake a 'stick thermal' for the real thing. The best solution is to fit a total energy variometer (Chapter 18), which, in any case, is quite essential for serious soaring. Without it the pilot should try to keep the speed as steady as possible and to ignore minor variations in the variometer readings caused by movements of the elevator control. This 'stick thermal' effect is another reason for the beginner to avoid altering the position of his circles until he has done two complete ones with consistent results, and is quite sure in which direction he wants to move.

The ability to centre accurately and quickly in thermals is essential to getting the best out of the existing weather and making successful cross-country flights. Every opportunity to practice should be taken while soaring locally, even to the extent of leaving thermals before reaching the top so as to search out and centre in the largest number of thermals possible in a given period of time.

THERMAL STRUCTURE
AND FURTHER CIRCLING TECHNIQUE

Although the precise structure of thermals is not fully understood, it is now clear that on many occasions a thermal bubble is in the form of a vortex ring, or doughnut shape, with the air in the bubble circulating as shown in Fig. 3.10, like a smoke-ring. The air in the middle of the ring will move upwards more rapidly than the ring itself, whilst the air in the outer part will descend relative to the bubble, although still ascending relative to the ground.

The circulation within the thermal has two noticeable effects on the circling glider. In the top part of the bubble the glider is in a region where the air is going upwards and outwards; consequently, unless it is centred perfectly, it will tend to be pushed off to one side. Conscious effort will be needed on the part of the pilot to keep centred. On the other hand, a glider in the lower part of the bubble is in a zone where the airflow is upwards and inwards; centring here is almost automatic.

This concept of the vortex ring shape explains many features which have puzzled pilots for a long time. The sudden increase of airspeed often experienced on entering a thermal is easily explained by the outward airflow near the top. It also explains the way in which comparatively small differences in height between gliders can lead to a large difference in the achieved rates of climb. The glider in position 1 of Fig. 3.10 where the rate of rise of the air is equal to the sinking speed of the glider, will just hold its own. But as the thermal bubble rises the glider will gradually lose

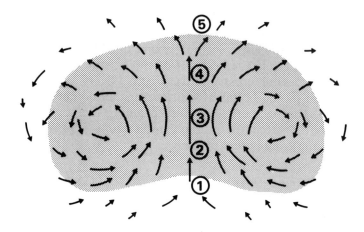

Fig 3.10 Section through vortex ring thermal. As the whole thermal bubble, shown shaded, goes upwards the air contained in it circulates. Notice that the air at the top is flowing upwards and outwards, and at the bottom upwards and inwards

height in the weakly rising wake. A glider slightly higher, in position 2, will climb gently and then, as it rises up into the middle of the ring, more and more rapidly. It will achieve the maximum rate of climb in position 3, and then hold a position which will be constant in relation to the thermal bubble itself (position 4).

A glider first meeting the bubble in position 5 will experience weak lift which will gradually increase and then become steady; the glider will settle close to position 4.

This picture shows the weakness of looking on thermals as being good or bad as a whole. The quality of the thermal, to the pilot, will depend on the part of it that he encountered; striking it lucky just above the bottom he will go romping up, whereas another glider hitting the same thermal at the same time 1000 ft higher may achieve only half the rate of climb.

Normally the larger thermals are found higher up, and this is particularly noticeable in the first few hundred feet above the ground where most of the lift is in small patches. A horizontal cross section through a thermal is usually taken as circular and this is probably not far from the mark, although with a strong wind the cross section may be oval, with the major axis stretching up and down wind. When two thermal bubbles go up side by side, at low altitude, the lift will be found in two circular areas, but they may gradually join and the area of lift take the form of a figure of eight. Finally when the thermals have merged the cross section will once again be of roughly circular shape.

The edges of the upcurrent may or may not be sharply marked. If a thermal is encountered when it is single, the edge can be felt quite clearly and it will be found that the lift increases progressively towards the centre. At a later stage in development a cross section may consist of a larger area of weak lift, with a smaller region of stronger lift caused by another thermal travelling up in the wake of the first. The outside edge of the wake may be less well defined, but the boundary of the smaller will probably be clearly felt. This situation is often encountered; the pilot on flying into the wake notices the turbulence and weak lift, and on penetrating further feels a real surge as he enters the better lift of the following thermal.

There is no reason why the second bubble should travel up in the centre of the wake, nor why, if the wake is large, two or more bubbles should not go up side by side. In these circumstances the concept of 'centring' in the thermal is apt to be misleading. If a pilot circling in what he imagines to be the centre of the thermal notices that another glider circling nearby is gaining on him, he can decide to shift his circles in that direction. But on doing so he may find that the lift does not improve until he has reached the other glider. What has happened is that both gliders were circling in separate zones which were travelling up in the large wake of an earlier thermal.

Sometimes when thermals are large, and this more often occurs later in the day, the edge of the thermal is ill defined and the entry into the best lift very gradual. Since thermals of this type are found only on occasions when their life is longer than usual their smoothness is presumably due to their having had time to settle down; the core area having become larger and less disturbed.

When the area of lift is large and uniform the pilot can fly around at small angles of bank, exploring quietly for anything better. In order to obtain the maximum rate of climb he will naturally wish to sink down through the air as slowly as possible, and should threfore fly at a speed corresponding to minimum sink.

When the thermal is small, or there is only a small area of good lift inside a large thermal, it will be desirable to make steeper turns. The question of the precise airspeed and angle of bank at which the glider should be flown is complicated as it depends on the characteristics of both the glider and the thermal; it is here that our knowledge of thermal structure is somewhat inadequate. Precise information regarding the size of thermals and the distribution of lift across them would not only enable us to improve circling technique with existing gliders, but would also enable us to design new aircraft better tailored to the air in which they fly.

The strength of a thermal can vary widely. In some parts of the world rates of climb in clear air of well over 10 knots (1000 ft/min) are usual, but in Britain an average rate of climb of more than 4 knots (400 ft/min) is good.

DOWN CURRENTS

In thermal weather, unless the air close to the ground is to become very thin, it is inevitable that air must move in to take the place of that which goes up. This can happen by horizontal movement, such as is manifest in sea breezes, and in the wind which blows in towards the centre of a group of mountains during the day. However, a simple sum will show that if this were the only method a howling gale would occur round the coast every time there was a day with a few thermals. This is not the case, because there are downcurrents to help balance the upcurrents. Apart from large scale subsidence associated with anticyclones, downcurrents take two distinct forms; the gradual downward movements which take place over large areas which are unfavourable for thermals, such as a large lake in the middle of a land mass, and the sink found between individual thermals. Surprisingly enough, downcurrents do not often spread themselves uniformly over the area which is not occupied by thermals, but tend to be more concentrated. They are often found close to the thermals and also underneath and in decaying clouds. Downcurrents are not usually as strong as the thermals, and therefore they must cover a larger area. As experience is gained the pilot will devote considerable effort to avoid them.

SEARCHING FOR THERMALS

The technique of making use of thermal lift is not particularly difficult, but the problem of finding thermals, and particularly of finding good ones, is a matter in which no one in the world is a complete master.

Thermals themselves are invisible, but there are occasions, unfortunately few, when the effect of them is directly apparent.

Smoke. If a large mass of smoke is seen rising to appreciable heights, more rapidly than seems usual, this indicates a thermal. Large factory chimneys, bonfires, burning stubble, and heath fires often act as pointers in this way.

Dust. Thermals starting from dry, bare ground may carry a quantity of dust with them which can be seen in the same way as smoke. If the thermal is very strong it may start a dust devil.

Birds. A surprisingly large number of birds indulge in thermal soaring. In England kestrels, buzzards, gulls and rooks can be found soaring at any height up to cloud base. All these birds are far better soaring pilots than humans can ever hope to be; not only have they far more experience, but although their sinking speed is not greatly different from that of a glider, their manoeuvrability is so magnificent that they can use small areas of lift useless to us. Birds seldom practise turns for fun, so if a bird is seen circling, it is almost certainly soaring. Some birds soar in thermals when making cross-country flights (e.g., seagulls). Others, whose primary interest is watching the ground for their prey, (e.g., hawks) like to stay over roughly the same area at a constant height, low enough to see small animals. Consequently, once at this height, they may choose to operate in lift which will just maintain them there; this is not likely to be the best thermal.

Various other birds, such as swallows and swifts, are often seen in lift. They are not making use of the thermal itself but merely chasing the insects which have been carried up in it. They are useful as indicators, but unfortunately seldom carry their chase very high.

Other Indications of Thermals. Occasionally various odd things like pieces of paper, plastic bags, and butterflies get carried up in strong thermals. Once they have gone up, these things have to come down again, so unless a mass of them is seen together, they do not necessarily show the presence of a thermal. Gliders near home are to some extent unreliable, as their pilots may only be circling for practice; along competition task routes, however, thermals will be marked by them.

FINDING THERMALS BY LOOKING AT THE GROUND

Thermals tend to form in a roughly cellular pattern with downdraughts between them. If the country is uniform the pattern will exist fairly evenly and this cellular distribution will also occur over broken country when the wind is strong, or the air wildly unstable. However, on the majority of soaring days any pattern will be considerably modified by the type of country below.

In general, surfaces which are dry or dark, and those which heat up quickly, are the most likely thermal sources, although they will be affected by such things as the amount of shelter from the wind, the aspect of the slope in relation to the sun, and their contrast to the surroundings.

To be of any value to a glider pilot, the thermal must be several hundred yards across, and such a thermal can only come from an area even larger than a good-sized field. Normally dry earth fields, corn crops, towns and runway airfields can be regarded as likely sources.

Thermals seldom come off continuously from a particular piece of ground; it is more likely that the air will go up for about 5 minutes, and then there will be nothing for the next 15 minutes or so until the area has been sufficiently re-warmed. The rate of heating will be slow if the surface is in shadow, and for this reason thermals are seldom found over ground which has been in the shade for more than about 10 minutes.

When a thermal rises air has, of course, to flow in to take its place. The wind upwind of the source will increase, downwind it will be less, and on either side blow inwards. Observation of this effect is sometimes useful when trying to catch thermals from wire launches, since by looking at windsocks it may be possible to determine the right moment to be launched. However, when searching for thermals from the air this method cannot often be used owing to the lack of suitable indicators.

If a thermal cannot be discovered by local variations in the wind, and there are no smoke or bird signs, then it is quite impossible to find a definite thermal by looking at the ground. All that can be done is to assess the probability of thermals coming from particular sources. The pilot must study the type of country below him, decide which is the most likely-looking area, bearing in mind the difference in surface, and the cloud shadows, and then try to assess the probable drift of the thermal.

When the thermal rises it will move away downwind, and it is useless looking for lift immediately over a possible source. Since the exact strength of both the upcurrent and the wind are not likely to be known, it follows that neither is the position of the thermal even if the source is obvious. For this reason a pilot stands a much better chance of finding a thermal which he thinks has come off a particular spot if he flies straight up or down wind through the region in which he thinks it is likely to be found. If he flies across wind he may easily miss it.

EFFECT OF CLOUD SHADOWS

If the air is very dry no cumulus will form, but 'dry' thermals may still exist, although invisible in the clear sky. The pilot will have only the variations in surface to help him search, but thermals may be more regularly distributed owing to the absence of cloud shadows. On a day of cumulus cloud the ground and the air covered by shadows will be cooler than the ground and air in the sunlight, and the cooler air will drift downwind with the shadows. It sometimes happens that the cooler air will undercut the warm air and act as the initial boost to the starting of a thermal. It may pay, therefore, to search for lift downwind of a likely looking source which, having been in sunshine for some time, has just become covered by a cloud shadow. It must be remembered that it will take some time for the thermal to come up to the level of the glider. If the glider is at only 1000 ft, the time will be two or more minutes unless the thermal is exceptionally strong.

WIND SHADOW THERMALS

On strong wind days it is often found that the best thermals come off places sheltered from the wind. There seem to be three reasons for this.

1 A wind always produces mixing of the lower layers of the air.
2 If the air is moving it can only be over the thermal source for a short time.
3 The wind, by increasing the evaporation of the surface moisture, will cause a reduction in temperature.

As all these effects are eliminated or reduced over areas sheltered from the wind, it will be better to look for thermals to the lee of large wind breaks, particularly if the area is facing the sun. Downdraughts caused by a slope may, however, prevent the formation of such thermals locally.

FINDING THERMALS BY THE STUDY OF CLOUDS

Broadly speaking, cumulus-type clouds can be divided into simple individual clouds of short duration, and those which once started develop a circulation of their own, drawing in additional air and often growing into large cumulo-nimbus. These may last for several hours.

We will deal first with the small fair weather cumulus.

When the top of the thermal reaches condensation level a cloud starts to form, and this cloud goes on growing while the thermal is active, and possibly to some extent afterwards. When the air ceases to rise above condensation level the cloud will start to decay, and the time taken for decay is roughly the same as that taken for growth. It therefore follows that about half the clouds in the sky are dying and half are developing. Fortunately, clouds look different in their various stages of growth and decay, and while the difference is not very marked, the pilot must learn to distinguish between them if he is ever to be proficient at thermal soaring. The life of a simple cumulus cloud is about 20 minutes or less.

A cumulus starts as a small collection of wisps. After a time these wisps grow in size and amalgamate and the cloud takes definite shape with a flat bottom. The cloud increases in height and size, and the top and edges get firmer in outline and more rounded. As decay starts, the cloud gets less definite in shape and loses its flat bottom. As the process continues, rifts may appear in the body of the cloud, and it breaks up into separate wisps before finally disappearing.

Normally the cloud will start to decay shortly after the bottom of the bubble reaches cloud base. If the glider is appreciably lower there will be little point in heading towards any cloud which has reached its prime, since unless another bubble is travelling up in the same path no lift will be found underneath. The pilot's job is to select clouds in the active stage of growth. He can teach himself this firstly by noting the shape of the active clouds, and secondly by keeping a minute-to-minute watch on particular clouds to see what they do.

This assessment of clouds is a difficult thing to learn, and it needs constant practice to become proficient, but much can be done by watching clouds from the ground and noting their characteristics in differing weather.

From close to, in the air, the problem is much more difficult because the cloud loses so much definition, and it is exceedingly hard to distinguish between the first wisps of a growing cloud and the last fragments of a decaying one. Colour is sometimes a help, as when seen under similar conditions of lighting a growing wisp will appear whiter and brighter than a dying one of the same size. This is not due to the cloud becoming dirtier, but to droplet size; the smallest ones evaporate first.

From near cloud base it is often difficult to judge both the size and quality of other clouds, but much can be learnt by looking at their shadows. Cumulus clouds are seldom very active when large areas of the ground are covered in shadow, so if the pilot sees signs of this ahead of him, it will probably be wise to make a detour to keep over sunlit ground.

If the clouds are bigger it often happens that a large proportion of the cumulus in the sky is active in one part or another. This may be due, especially in light or no wind conditions, to one thermal following up closely behind another from the same source, or a thermal rising into an area already occupied by an existing cloud. Days may even exist when every cloud is active, but they are rare.

The thermal feeding the cloud will slope up towards it and, as mentioned earlier, it is easiest to locate this lift by flying straight up or down wind. The strongest lift is frequently obtained under the darkest, and therefore thickest, part of the cloud, but the position underneath the cloud in which the best lift, or in fact any lift, is to be found is not necessarily either on the upwind side or under the middle. It is modified by any wind shear at or near cloud base. Such shear will bend the thermal as it goes up and the lift may be found towards one or other of the crosswind sides of the cloud, depending on whether the wind veers or backs with height. Once the position is found for a particular cloud, for instance, on the sunny side, this is likely to hold good for other clouds during a considerable period.

If cumulus are growing upward very rapidly and the sky is developing a thundery appearance, lift may be so strong that the pilot finds himself being sucked rapidly into the cloud. The airbrakes should be opened immediately and the glider flown straight and fast away from the lift, or the darkest part of the cloud. On such days the inexperienced soaring pilot should break off circling at least 500 ft below cloud base, or more if the variometer starts to show more than a normal rate of climb.

CLOUD STREET FLYING

If the wind is strong the clouds will often be seen in lines stretching up and down wind, the distance between the clouds varying from a half to several miles. The clouds are usually separate entities ranged along these lines, but on some occasions may form in continuous streets when it is possible for the glider pilot to maintain or gain height by flying straight along underneath. Usually, however, the good lift is confined to isolated areas underneath some of the clouds, but it is frequently found that there is very little sink when flying between clouds in the same line. On the other hand, very strong sink is often encountered under the blue sky between the lines. On this sort of day the pilot should not attempt to cross from one line to the other unless he is near cloud base, and even then should go square across and not diagonally in his desired direction.

It often happens that a whole line of cloud, having been active for some time, dies. This would appear to be due to the thermal sources of one line becoming covered by the shadows of another line. The pilot must be prepared for this to happen, and if he finds that the lift under his own cloud is dying, and that the clouds both up and down wind look ineffective, he must be prepared to try to go cross wind to another street rather than continue a futile search along his own.

If clouds are visible the fact that the lift is arranged in streets will be shown by the orderly lines of cloud. On cloudless days, or in the late evening, when almost all cloud has faded away, thermals may still lie in rows stretching up and down wind. If this is suspected, the best chance of finding the next thermal will occur if the glider is flown precisely up or down wind, the direction of which should have been determined by observing the way the glider drifts when circling. When trying to stretch a glide, as for example at the end of a distance flight, flying precisely down the line of thermals may make a difference of 15 miles or more, because even if there is no usable lift, there may be streets of weak upcurrents persisting until quite late in the evening. It is best to avoid flying at a gentle angle to the line of the wind, because the glider will have to travel a long way on its diagonal path before it again comes across a street which may contain some lift; if the intended track is diagonal to the wind, then it is better to fly up or down wind using lift, and then across wind more or less at right angles to it towards the next street.

LOCAL SOARING

Before anyone can safely go across country, he must acquire skill in using thermals by putting in some hours of local soaring. Initially, the effort will be just to stay up, but later, as skill is obtained, the emphasis can change to concentrating on finding thermals quickly, making the best use of them and getting orientated in the air.

Initially, the pilot will be briefed to keep within easy reach of the airfield so that should he fail to find lift, or encounter large areas of sink, he will still be able to return to base with sufficient height to make a comfortable landing. If there is no wind, the old empirical rule of 4 miles for every 1000 ft with nothing for the last 1000 is just all right for most club gliders, although it does not leave much in hand for large areas of sink. If there is an appreciable wind the pilot should not let himself go so far downwind of the airfield that he will be unable to get back. This most common mistake on early soaring flights occurs when the pilot drifts in lift away from the airfield, decides that he is getting too far and flies upwind again. He then runs into weak lift, and circles in it without gaining much height; without realizing it, as far as getting back to the airfield is concerned, he is worsening his position. To avoid this, an effort should always be made to keep well on the upwind side of the airfield, and after climbing up, and inevitably drifting downwind, the search for the next thermal should be made more or less upwind.

Once skill in staying up has been acquired, some pilots tend just to drift vaguely around without much effort to improve their technique; the fact that they find they can stay up without much difficulty is sufficiently satisfying. Instead the pilot should try to improve by learning how to climb more quickly. Having reached cloud base, or the top of the lift he should fly off some distance and see how quickly he can find another thermal and climb up again.

During his first few thermal flights the pilot will find that to keep in lift requires a great deal of concentration, but he must remember that he is not alone in the sky. A continuous lookout for other aircraft is essential. If he can work his way upwind of the airfield and find lift there he will find everything much easier. Worries about getting back to the field are eliminated, there is greater freedom of search, and more time to look around.

To begin with, each thermal climb is an event in itself, with its own moments of doubt and exhilaration. But as the pilot gains experience he will see each climb as merely one step in the whole flight, and will find that less concentration is required when going up. Instead of just sitting back and admiring the view, he should teach himself to consider what he is going to do when he reaches the top of his thermal, so that when he does arrive he can fly straight off in the intended direction.

It is impossible to lay down hard and fast rules to be followed when searching for lift. In general the pilot should concentrate on the clouds if he is near cloud base, assessing the shape of individual cumulus and their distribution. If, however, he is low down, the clouds will tell him little except —and this is important — whether the area as a whole is active or not. Unless there is any direct indication of a thermal, all that can be done is to consider the country underneath, and decide which area within easy reach looks the most likely. Bearing in mind the height available for the search, he should then fly over and downwind of this area what he can find.

Chapter 4
Landing in Fields

Cross-country flights are more often than not intended to finish with an arrival back at base or at a declared goal airfield, but sometimes the glider has to be landed in a field. If farmers and landowners were uncooperative soaring would be severely curtailed, so the first essential after any field landing is to find the owner, explain the situation, and be as little trouble to him as possible. Most farmers are friendly and helpful, but it needs only a few selfish or careless pilots to alter the whole situation. Leaving a gate open, frightening a valuable animal, allowing spectators to trample crops, or transferring foot-and-mouth disease to another farm causes financial loss, or at the very least extra work and worry. It will also encourage insurance companies to increase premiums. The glider pilot should remember that he is an uninvited guest and behave accordingly.

The ability to select fields from the air, and to land in them without damage, is one of the most difficult things that the glider pilot has to learn. It can be taken as an axiom that a safe landing in a field should always be possible, and so the glider should never be flown over unsuitable areas unless it has sufficient height to reach a landing place should no further lift be found.

There is no such thing as bad luck when landing in fields. If the glider is damaged by running downhill into a hedge, it was not bad luck that the field was sloping, but an error of the pilot in failing to notice the slope when selecting the field. This may appear a hard philosophy, but it is none the less true.

Compared to the aeroplane pilot, the glider pilot is at disadvantage in that, unless a motor glider is available, he is unable to practise making dummy landings into fields he has chosen; on the other hand, owing to the slower speed of the glider, its better view and the convenience of air brakes, the approach is easier. The choice of field is also greater owing to the shorter landing run, and the variety of surfaces on which a glider can be landed safely.

As a rough guide, the sort of glider used for early cross-country flights will fly four miles for every 1000 ft loss of height. As, however, the approach will waste considerable height until the pilot is experienced, the empirical rule should be regarded as four miles per 1000 ft, with nothing for the last 1000 ft. Thus from 2000 above the ground the pilot has a circle of four miles radius in which to land. If, as is usually the case, there is some wind this circle of choice will be shifted downwind, because for the same 1000 ft loss of height the glider will be able to go much further down- than upwind. In England apart from large built-up areas, forests, or parts of the country which are very hilly, it is possible to find at least one good landing ground every five or six miles. So when flying at more than 2000 ft it is not normally necessary to worry about keeping within reach of an individual field. When down to this height, however, the possibility of having to land within the next ten minutes should be borne in mind, and the flight should not be continued over unsuitable country.

By the time the glider has sunk to 1500 ft above the ground a definite field should be selected and the glider should not be allowed to drift away from it until another suitable one has been chosen. The pilot can then go on drifting across country in weak lift, or no sink, provided he keeps within easy reach of definite fields until he either finds better lift and climbs up, or is down to 1000 ft when he should forget all about soaring and decide to land. In making the decision to land it is the terrain clearance that matters and not the reading on the altimeter.

The heights for selecting the area (2000 ft above ground), for choosing the field (1500 ft) and for deciding to land (1000 ft) may sound very high but the inexperienced pilot should stick to them, although the really experienced pilot can and will work to much finer limits. The decision to concentrate on the landing is difficult to make, but it must be made and the sooner the better. By catching a thermal at

500 ft the flight may be prolonged, but only at the price of a greater risk to the aircraft. This risk is not worth taking until the pilot has enough experience to assess it accurately.

The choice of field must be dictated solely by considerations of the safety of the glider. Such things as the convenience of getting a trailer into the field, or the closeness of a telephone or pub, should not enter into the question. The retrieve crew can carry the glider a long way in a few hours, but as anyone who has ever mended a glider knows only too well, even a small repair may take several days.

The actual selection of a field depends on the following factors, all of which have to be considered:

1 Wind direction and strength;
2 Type of surface;
3 Size of the field;
4 Slope;
5 Approaches and obstructions;
6 Stock (cattle, etc.).

1. *Wind.* Before starting to select a field it is necessary to know which way the wind is blowing. From the air the only reliable indications are smoke, the drift of the glider when circling, wind-socks and flags, and cloud shadows; although this last will only give wind direction at cloud height, which may be different from that on the ground.

It is easy to get confused about wind direction, but this can be avoided by remembering the wind direction in relation to the sun, rather than in terms of the compass. Having observed the wind direction the pilot can remember it by saying to himself, for example, 'When I am facing into the wind, the sun is ahead of me on the right'.

Other points which should be borne in mind are:

That the surface wind near hills or the sea may be quite different from the general wind over the rest of the country.

That the wind at the bottom of a valley usually blows only up it or down it.

That on days of light winds the strength and direction may vary considerably.

That if a front, line of big cloud, or a storm passes over, the wind direction may shift through a large angle.

Having decided upon the wind direction, preferably from smoke, it should be remembered that if at all possible the landing should be made into wind or within 30° of it.

2. *Type of surface.* From the pilot's point of view, the requirements of a landing ground are that it shall be smooth and big enough and that the crop shall not be so tall as to damage the glider. The farmer looks on it in a different light: he dislikes any damage to his crops, fences or gates, whether caused by the glider itself, the retrieve crew, or spectators. Appearances can be deceptive, since some short, innocuous-looking crops can be valuable and easily damaged. Pilots should make a real effort to learn to identify different crops from the air.

The best fields are, in order:

a. Stubble. This is good because the field must have been tilled less than a year ago and so should be smooth. The farmer will not object to a landing as the field will soon be ploughed again. Recently burnt stubble fields are equally smooth although dusty.

b. Grass. This may vary from smooth new or temporary pasture to an old field full of molehills, ditches and hummocks. In general any grass field which looks uniform in colour should be fairly smooth. An exception to this exists where the farmer has strewn fodder for his stock the previous winter. The grass or crop growing over this apparently inconsequential track will be darker in colour and more luxuriant.

If the grass ripples in the wind it is long.

c. Fallow and harrowed fields. These are good particularly if the field has recently been cultivated.

d. Short crops, e.g. corn fields in the spring. These are all right, but unfortunately there are not many of them at the time of the year when most cross-country flying is done. The farmer may not be very pleased, but if the crop is short little damage will be done if spectators can be kept away.

Fields to be avoided are those recently ploughed, particularly in dry or frosty weather. In an emergency a landing should be made along the furrows. Other fields to avoid are those with tall crops and those containing such things as potatoes, kale and beet, since besides being likely to cause damage to the glider a landing will almost certainly damage the crop.

The ground where bracken and heather grows has probably not been cultivated for years, and may be a jumble of ditches, old tree stumps and hillocks. Sometimes fields on heavy land are cultivated with a series of long pitched ridge and furrow between 15 and 30 ft crest to crest. Landings should be made along a ridge, but if any crop is growing this will be difficult to see.

3. The *size of field* required for landing will depend on:

Wind strength;
Type of glider;
The approaches to the field;
The slope;
The surface;
The skill of the pilot.

A good pilot should be able to guarantee to clear a low hedge and finish his run within 150 yd if there is no wind and the field is flat, but he must be pretty good to do this every time. A 250-yd field should be taken as the normal minimum and it will have to be larger than this if the approach is over trees or telephone wires.

It is very difficult to judge sizes from the air, particularly in a district where all the fields are small, when there is a tendency to think of one larger than the rest as a large field. Judgement of size is a matter of experience, but a guide which is sometimes useful is to remember that telephone poles are about 60-80 yd apart. The field should, therefore, be at least 4 telephone pole spacings long.

4. *Slope*. This is the most important aspect of a field. Quite a gentle slope will double the length of the landing run, while a slight to moderate downward slope will prevent the glider being landed at all.

Landing uphill is perfectly feasible provided that the slope is not so steep that the glider will run backwards after landing. Landings across a moderate slope can be made, but if this is steep it is difficult to avoid either hitting the uphill wing, or else running away downhill.

If faced with the alternative of landing uphill and downwind, or downhill and upwind, it is better to pick another field where an into-wind landing on the level or uphill is possible. If there is no other choice, never attempt to land downhill; any slope which can be observed from the air is bound to be quite steep.

It is difficult to learn to detect slope from the air, but the effort must be made. It will be helpful to fly all round the field and consider the lie of the land, rather than just study the field itself, and some points to bear in mind are that:

a. A stream can be taken as level, and will always be at the lowest local line (not so a canal).

b. A pond or marshy bit of land will also be at the lowest point. This does not apply to reservoirs or dew ponds, but these can be distinguished by their embankments or neat circular shape.

c. A railway track usually can be taken as level, and the slope of fields near it can be assessed by the cuttings or embankments.

5. *Approaches and obstructions.* The ideal field has no obstructions on its downwind side, but often there will be a hedge, fence, or row of trees. Having to pass over these will make a great deal of difference to the amount of room needed for landing.

Even with airbrakes open a glider has a gliding angle of about one in eight, so if the obstruction is 30 ft high the first 80 yd of the field will be useless. In practice this will tend to be more owing to the difficulty of judging height accurately when passing over high obstructions.

Telephone and power wires are almost invisible from the air, particularly if their poles are planted along a hedge. If the intended approach path is over a road, it must be assumed that there are telephone wires even if none can be seen.

Power wires are more difficult to spot, as their pylons or poles are even futher apart than those of the telephone, and they frequently wander across country without following any road. For this reason the conscious thought 'Are there any power wires?' should be made when selecting a field, and the surrounding country studied for pylons. If any are seen, the line of the wires should be worked out before deciding on a field. It does not matter if the wires run across the far end of the field, but it is obviously inadvisable to come in over them, and certainly dangerous to try to dive under them owing to the small gap available, and the difficulty of judging how much they sag.

Wire fences are difficult to see, and electric fences often impossible, but their presence can usually be deduced as the surface on either side of them is seldom of exactly the same colour. The confinement of animals to part of a field can also give a clue.

6. *Stock.* Cattle in a field are a nuisance, for not only are they obstructions, and mobile ones at that, but it may be impossible to prevent them damaging the glider after landing. However, it is better to land in a large field with a few cows than in a small clear one. Horses are the worst animals as, if excited, they gallop furiously about. Cows usually stay still during the landing but come clustering round curiously afterwards. Sheep are the most sensible; if frightened they go into a huddle, and after landing they are not likely to do much damage.

THE APPROACH

The approach obviously wants to be done in the easiest possible way, and as straight final approaches should have always been done at base, the same sort of approach should be made into the field. If possible it should start from the same position as it would if the glider had been launched out of the field. This will enable the pilot to get a really good look at the land, and plan his approach in the way that he usually does.

There is a tendency during the first few away landings to start the final approach much too close to the field. This is due to the pilot unconsciously getting into the habit of taking the length of the gliding site as his unit of length, and positioning himself a proportion of this distance downwind of it when on his final crosswind leg. Obviously if the field is 300 yd long instead of the 1000-yd airfield this tendency to get too close to the field will be very marked .

Unlike most gliding sites, the approach into the field will often be bad, and because of obstructions the final part will probably have to be steep. The sort of approach which is often seen on airfields—a good deal of airbraking early on followed by a long flat glide—is useless for getting into small fields. The final part of the approach must be steep, and the speed must be right. It may be acceptable in a slow glider with powerful airbrakes to come in with plenty of extra speed and then use the high airbrake drag to get rid of both unwanted height and speed at a late stage of the approach. In a slippery glass glider with airbrakes of only moderate power, it will be easy to come in either too high or too fast.

The following technique avoids the common trouble of getting too close. When still high, pick a turn-in point some way downwind of the proposed touch-down place. The distance will depend on the wind strength and will range from 800 yd in no wind to 200 yd in a strong wind. A point on the ground should be chosen—a haystack, or the middle of a field—and the circuit planned so that on the final crosswind (base) leg, the glider is headed towards this chosen point. It is made to arrive there at approximately the right height by using the airbrakes. Ideally, the correct height is that which gives the maximum latitude for error; it will be roughly half-way between the height at which the glider could just get in without using any brakes, and the greatest height from which a straight path could be made with full brake. Having got to the proposed turning point at approximately the right height a turn is made and the glider lined up to land at the proposed spot.

It often happens that despite the best intentions the glider is positioned too close in, or too high up to get into the field even with full airbrakes. The ability to sideslip, and particularly to do slipping turns with the brakes full out, is of great value, and so they should be practised. But the temptation to do low turns must be resisted, as they only lead to trouble.

A tail parachute can be most effective when landing in a

small field provided that the pilot has plenty of experience in its use and understand its limitations. It must be appreciated that a tail parachute cannot be made completely reliable. It follows from this that the aircraft should never be put in such a position that the failure of the parachute to open will inevitably result in disaster. For example, if, when making an approach towards the only possible landing field the parachute is deployed when the glider is at 100 ft or so, with the intention of making a steep final glide and a quick round-out, the result will usually be most satisfactory—unless the parachute fails to open properly. The pilot is now faced with an impossible situation. He is too high to land straight ahead and too low to go round again for another approach.

It is better to plan the approach so that the parachute is opened when more than 200 ft up; should it fail there is enough height for another circuit or an approach to another place. Alternatively the parachute can be safely deployed when really close to the ground, to shorten the round-out and ground run.

It is essential that the approach be made at sufficient speed If the pilot has been flying for some hours and is tired, he may tend to fly too slowly, especially if he has been trying to hang on to weak lift. As soon as the decision to land has been made the speed should be adjusted to at least 10 knots above the stall, while if the wind is strong or rough to considerably more than this. If the landing is to be made uphill, the speed should be increased still further.

THE LANDING

As the field may be rough the actual touchdown should be made at the slowest possible speed. If there are tall crops it is important that the glider should be kept level laterally during and after landing, otherwise a wing tip may touch and cause the glider to swing round violently and cause even more damage to be done; the airbrakes should be closed just before landing to further reduce this tendency. A low tailplane is vulnerable and is liable to be damaged when landing in standing corn.

If the field is very small or the approach misjudged, it may be best to put the glider on the ground while it is still flying fairly fast in order to reduce the risk of running into the far hedge. If the glider is fitted with a nose skid, it can be stopped most quickly by gradually pushing the stick hard forward, but this should only be done when really necessary. When landing a glider with a retractable undercarriage, the possibility of stopping more quickly by retracting it should be considered. In an extreme case, when the glider is running towards a hard obstruction, putting one wing on to the ground and doing a ground loop can be attempted. It must be realized that this is the last resort as it is quite likely to break the wing tip or fuselage.

The problem of landing in a strong wind is not so much that of finding a field—the choice is much greater as the landing run will be short—but of the pilot making sure that the landing is exactly into wind, that he does not undershoot, and that the glider is not blown over after landing.

If a field with obstructions on the windward side is picked it will mean that the glider can be taken into shelter after landing, but unless the field is very large the approach and landing will be made in the rough air to the lee of these obstructions, and on balance it may be better to avoid a field sheltered in this way. If a field can be found with an isolated windbreak on one side, but with a clear path for the air on the other, so much the better: the glider can be landed in the steady air, and then pushed behind the windbreak.

In a gale the approach must, of course, be made at a greater speed than usual to allow for a severe wind gradient: about 25 knots above the stall would not be excessive. Little airbrake should be used for the final part of the approach, and the glider should not be held right off but put on the ground at a fairly slow speed at a moment when there is no drift. Immediately after touching down the airbrakes should be opened fully, the glider kept straight, and the wings balanced until help comes.

Skill in choosing the best available field lies in the ability to appreciate the advantages and disadvantages of several fields, and to pick the one which on balance appears best. This is difficult to do. Some people tend to decide on the first field they notice even if there is an airfield near by, while others go on considering the pros and cons of all the fields they can see until they arrive on the ground.

Perhaps an illustration of the mental processes involved in choosing a field will be useful. Imagine a glider pilot flying on an early cross-country. He has been soaring for a couple of hours, and it is now 4 o'clock. He has just climbed up to 4000 ft in a weak thermal, and has set course towards the only clouds remaining in the sky. He has a fair idea where he is, but is not quite sure. He is trying to fly East, with the sun behind him on his right-hand side. He gets to the best-looking cloud at 3000 ft, fumbles for a while underneath it but can find no lift, so for want of anything better to do, presses on again towards the East.

At 2500 ft he suddenly has the thought that perhaps he will not find any more lift and will have to land fairly soon. There is no airfield in sight so it will have to be a field. His thoughts might be something like this:

'I would like to get a little farther if I can, as it would be good to reach my goal airfield. What is the country like ahead? It looks hopeless, but away on the left beyond that big wood it seems all right, with large fields. I'm at 2500 ft now and they are about 3 miles away, so I'll get there easily. Now which way am I going to land? I suppose I am still going roughly downwind, but I'm not sure; can I see any smoke anywhere? No, nothing. Well, we really are coming down now. Surely there must be some smoke from that village. Oh. It is coming straight from my left; that's funny, the wind must have shifted, but then I did a turn after that last useless cloud, so it hasn't really shifted much. I am now going down sun, so I must land with the sun on my left.

'Still no lift, only this horrible sink. Well, which field is it going to be? They all seem to run across wind. Shall I land across wind? No, I think it will be too strong. Surely there is a field going the right way? Oh. Yes, that big grass one over there. It is quite long into wind and I'll come in over that hedge. No cattle. What else was I told to think about? Oh, yes, power wires—that's all right, I can't see any of those—I reckon that will be my field. Good heavens, I've forgotten about slope. Does it? Yes, it really does, down to that mucky-looking pond in the corner of the next field. Well, that's a washout. Still, I've got plenty of time, we are still at 1500 ft. Oh! No! This is horrible. I set that wretched altimeter at sea level so I can't be more than 1200 ft above the ground. Quickly, which field? What about that one the other side of stream which runs out of that pond? It slopes up, it is grass, it is very narrow, but quite long and has power wires, but they are across the far corner. It looks miles from anywhere, but I was told not to worry about that, so I will definitely go in there.'

As the pilot gains experience by landing in fields, he will develop an 'eye for country', and will be able to continue trying to find lift until he is lower down. He can assist this process by making all his home landings on a predetermined spot, and by examining fields around his base from the air. For example, he can say to himself: 'That field is useless. It is about 150 yd long, slopes steeply to the south, is covered with half-grown corn and has telephone wires along the approach', or 'That field looks all right, about 300 yd long into today's wind, fairly flat, short but uncut grass, and a 6-ft hedge on the approach.' After landing he should visit the fields on foot and see how far out his observations were. In this way he will develop considerable experience in learning what usable fields look like from the air. Most field landings take place in good weather, and the problem of actually seeing the field does not arise, but if it is necessary to land in thick haze, rain, or with the cockpit cover still iced up, it may not be possible to see enough to make a safe landing. In such circumstances a sensible clear vision panel is highly desirable. In an extreme case it may be better to jettison the cockpit cover and wreck it, rather than damage the whole aircraft.

There may be occasions, particularly in such countries as Sweden, where a lake is the only large clear space available, when a landing has to be made on water. The landing should be made close to the downwind shore—if necessary being made downwind so that the landing run will end up on or near the lee shore. The glider should not be stalled on to the water, but flown on as lightly as possible with the wings level, and directly downwind. It should be remembered that the touchdown speed will be fairly high, although the glider will not run very far after contact. If the lee shore is flat with rushes growing out into the water, the glider can be run into them reasonably fast, but if it is rocky the glider should be landed farther out, and allowed to be drifted in by the wind. It should not be assumed that a glass fibre or metal glider will remain afloat.

THE RETRIEVE

On arriving within sight of the glider the car and trailer should be parked by the road and one crew should cross the field on foot to meet the pilot. He should walk between the lines if the crop is young, or round the edge of the field to the nearest point to the glider if the crop is long. If there are foot and mouth prohibitions in the area he must not go into the field at all. Usually, of course, the pilot will be by the gate waiting impatiently for his crew, but it may be that he has gone to the farm and left a note in the glider.

If the pilot is not visible the crew should find the farm and enquire, and should not take the trailer into the field, or derig the glider if it is in standing crops, until permission from the owner has been obtained. Before leaving every effort should be made to ensure that gates are left *as they were found*.

Some pilots carry pictures of their glider or vouchers for a flight in the club two-seater to give to farmers in whose field they have landed. Alternatively a note of thanks should be sent.

Chapter 5

Navigation

Navigation is a rather highbrow word to describe finding the way in a glider, since the process is remarkably simple and involves fewer complications than beset the aeroplane pilot. In addition the glider pilot has much longer to think about the problem.

The navigation of a glider is nothing more than competent map reading, plus a few mental calculations and simple use of a compass.

MAPS

The most suitable maps are those designed for use by aeroplane pilots, although in some circumstances it may be better to use a road or touring map on a larger scale. The choice of scale is important. Small scale maps of 1-million are much easier to handle in the cockpit, better for route planning, and can be used without difficulty when flying in good visibility over clearly defined terrain. However, in poor weather accurate map reading is only feasible with larger scale maps.

For most purposes maps of $\frac{1}{2}$-million scale are probably the most convenient, although when trying to find precise pin-points in confused country it may be preferable to use $\frac{1}{4}$-million (about 4 miles to the inch) or, as for example in mountainous Switzerland, even the larger scale maps of 1:100,000.

Any pilot who intends to fly across country should obtain his own maps covering the whole area over which he may get the opportunity to fly. He should keep his maps together in a briefcase or plastic bag, with any pencils or rulers that he wants, and have it always ready.

It is useful to draw circles on the maps with the home site as centre; they are best marked at even intervals of miles or kilometres—every 10 or 20. A simple beam compass can be made from a slat of wood with a nail at one end and a series of holes at 10 or 20 unit intervals to take a ball point pen. If, as always seems to be the case, the home site comes near the edge of a sheet, it is a good thing to stick two maps together before drawing the circles. Control zones and airways should be marked on the map, as well as gliding sites, Gold distances and some suitable triangular or out-and-return courses. When the chance to attempt a really big flight occurs there is usually so much to do at the last minute that a hurried estimate of distances may be disastrously inaccurate.

TRACK AND COURSE

Before actually going on a cross-country flight a line should be drawn on the map showing the intended track. Sometimes this will have to be curved to avoid bad thermal areas, or airspace restrictions but for short distances it will usually be straight. The bearing of this trackline should be worked out; ideally a protractor should be used but with practice the result can be obtained within 5° by study of the map. If there is no wind or if the wind is blowing exactly along this line, the glider will have to be flown between thermals in this direction to attain its goal. But, if there is some crosswind, it will be necessary to cruise between thermals at some angle to the track line.

When flying an aeroplane this angle can easily be found by the triangle of velocities, provided that the cruising speed and wind strength are known. In a glider this cannot be done accurately as it is not known in advance what proportion of the total time the glider will be circled or flown straight.

Despite this, it is worthwhile knowing how to work out this triangle of velocities and thus obtain the theoretical course to steer and the ground speed. It is not suggested that this need be done for every flight, but if real precision is required, as for example in competition flying, then it should be done properly. The method is shown in Figs. 5.1 and 5.2, which introduce some terms which need defining. *Track* in the air navigational sense means the line on the ground which one is trying to follow. If this line is not followed then the path actually taken is called *track made good. Course* is the heading on which the aircraft is steered through the air. Track and course are expressed in the $0-360°$ notation. It is easiest to work with zero as the true, as distinct from the magnetic north, since the track can be obtained with a protractor directly from the map, and also because the wind direction is always given as a true bearing. One source of confusion is the method of expressing wind direction; track is always expressed as the direction one wishes to go, and course as the direction one has to steer, but wind direction is always expressed as the direction from which the wind has come.

The basic triangle of velocities, as used by an aeroplane flying at a steady speed, is shown in Fig. 5.1. Knowing the desired track, the estimated wind speed, the estimated wind direction and the proposed cruising speed, it is possible to work out the course to steer and the ground speed. The light aeroplane pilot can solve this triangle by using a plotter, by drawing the triangle to scale, or by assessing it mentally. With practice it is possible to make reasonably accurate mental calculations, by using several approximations. The wind can be resolved into two components (a) helping or hindering and (b) transverse. (a) is added or subtracted from the cruising speed to give the ground speed and the transverse component is used to asses the *drift*—the angle between the track and the course. This drift can be found by remembering that an angle of one degree is roughly equal to a gradient of one is sixty. Thus if a light aeroplane has a cruising speed of 120 knots and is flying with a beam wind of 20 knots it will be drifting at (60 x 20)/120 degrees, that is $10°$.

With a glider the triangle of velocities can be worked out in the same way, but first it is necessary to estimate what speed will be made good through the air. The relationship between this speed, the cruising speed between thermals and the thermal strength is explained in Chapter 16. A triangle of velocities for a typical glider speed of 35 knots is shown in Fig. 5.2, and it will be noticed that the wind has a much greater effect than it has on an aeroplane. When cruising between thermals the glider should be steered in the direction shown by the course arrow. It may seem surprising, but the course to steer when going from one thermal to the next is not affected by

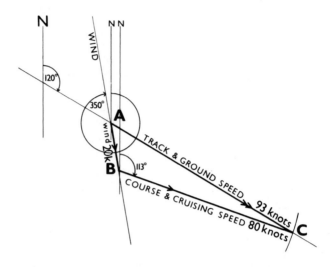

Fig 5.1 Triangle of velocities (i)

PROBLEM: *A pilot wishes to fly on a track of 120°, cruising at 80 knots with a forecast wind of 20 knots from 350°. In what direction should he steer and what ground speed will he achieve?*

1 Draw a track line at the appropriate direction in relation to North, in this case 120°

2 At any point on this line, say point A, draw in the wind direction and continue it downwind. Choose a suitable scale, say 20 knots to the inch—and mark in the wind speed (in this case 20 knots) at point B.

3 From B draw an arc with a radius corresponding to the cruising speed—80 knots—which will be 4 in. on the scale chosen. Let this arc cut the track at C.

4 Triangle ABC is the triangle of velocities.
   AB is the wind speed and direction
   BC is the cruising speed and course to steer
   AC is the ground speed and track

5 Measure direction of line BC *this gives course to steer—113°*

6 Measure length of line AC *this gives ground speed 4.65 in—93 knots*

the cruising speed used; it is determined only by the average speed made good through the air.

The proof of this can be seen in the following example.

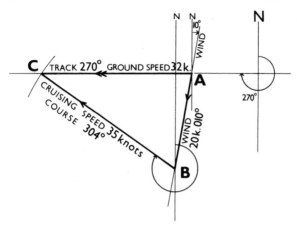

Fig 5.2 Triangle of velocities (ii)

PROBLEM: *A pilot wishes to fly a glider on a cross country to a point due west. He estimates that he will average 35 knots through the air. The wind is 20 knots from 010°. What course should he steer? What will be his ground speed?*

1 Draw a track line due West, that is, 270° from North

2 From any point, A, draw wind direction line; continue downwind for a distance corresponding to 20 knots, point B

3 From B draw an arc with radius corresponding to cruising speed of 35 knots, to cut the track line at C

4 BC is the course; measure its angle from North, in this case 304°

5 AC is the track and ground speed line. Measure its length to determine the ground speed, in this case 32 knots

Consider two gliders, of widely different characteristics: one flies very slowly, hardly circles at all, and goes 30 miles through the air in one hour; the other rushes off very fast but spends so much of its time circling that it also goes 30 miles in the hour. If they both started at the same point in the air, and steered on the same heading when they were cruising, they would both arrive at the same new place in the air one hour later, regardless of whether they had been flying crosswind, upwind, or downwind. Where they finish up in relation to the ground can be most easily visualized by thinking of them flying from their starting point in the appropriate direction through still air for one hour, and then by imagining that the whole mass of air containing them is moved instantly downwind by the distance which the wind actually blows in one hour.

When setting off from one thermal to the next, the appropriate course should be steered; as can be seen in Fig. 5.2 this will be at a considerable angle to the track if there is an appreciable crosswind. The pilot can ensure that he is setting off in the right direction by using three different methods:

 1 By aiming the nose in relation to some known landmark on track. (If there is a crosswind the nose should be aimed upwind of the landmark by the appropriate drift angle.)
 2 By setting course in relation to the sun.
 3 By using the compass.

Most cross-country flights can be done by using the first two methods and it may not be necessary to use the compass at all except when cloud flying.

The sun is (in Britain) due South at midday, Greenwich Mean Time. Its angular movement depends on both the latitude and the season of the year; in March and September the sun moves roughly 15° per hour and is due West at 1800 hrs; in June it moves at roughly 20° per hour and is due West at about 1700 hrs. However, the old rule that it is due South at midday and moves at 15° per hour is easy to remember and sufficiently accurate for most purposes. With this in mind and knowing the time, it is not difficult to set course to within 20° of the right direction by reference to the sun.

THE COMPASS

The compass is a more complicated method of finding direction. First it does not point due North, but to one side or other of the North Pole by an amount known as variation. The exact variation is given on the map (at present in England it is 8° West of the North Pole), so to steer a course of 110° from the North Pole (called 110 true) it will be necessary to steer 118° on the compass (called 118 magnetic). In addition to this variation, the compass, when installed, may have an error due to the presence of steel, iron or electrical circuits. With the maddening similarity which seems inevitable in navigational nomenclature this error is known as deviation. It is possible to correct this error to a large extent by placing small magnets near the compass, or by similarly using a corrector box. While this practice, known as 'swinging the compass', is mandatory on aeroplanes, it is seldom employed in gliders. It should be, since it is not difficult to do and an uncorrected compass may have an error of 20° or even 30°. A method of compass swinging is described in Appendix 10.

When flying a straight course, the compass will stay fairly steady and it is possible to see what course is being flown, but when turning, and particularly when turning rapidly, the compass develops certain errors. The reason need not be gone into here, and all that need be mentioned is that when turning through North the compass is sluggish and will show less than the amount of turn, when turning through South the compass will be lively and exaggerate the amount of turn. Because of this turning error, by far the simplest way of altering course is to estimate the change of angle, note some landmark in the proposed direction, turn on to it, let the compass settle down, and then check.

In addition to turning errors, a compass has what is known as acceleration errors when the aircraft is being flown on easterly or westerly headings. If the glider is accelerated or decelerated the compass will show a turn although the flight path is straight.

CHECK-POINT NAVIGATION

When flying across country the pilot should know generally where he is without map reading at all, by working on a basis of time, direction and distance. It will not often be likely that he will manage to average more than 40 knots through the air: it is far more likely to be about 30 knots and this average air speed combined with wind speed will give the average ground speed.

Most early cross-country flights are done more or less downwind, and so the ground speed will vary between 30 knots in no wind and 70 knots in a strong wind at flying levels. If the time of leaving the site is noted, as it should be, the pilot should have quite a good idea of his position at the end of, say, an hour's flying. Before even looking at the map he should know that he is about 30 miles from his starting point in the appropriate direction.

The basic idea to remember is that one need not know exactly what is immediately under the glider all the time. If a visible landmark, as far ahead as can be properly identified, is selected before the pilot gets out of sight of his last check-point he should never get lost when the visibility is good. It is essential that the landmark ahead (town, hill, television mast, etc.) must be identified with certainty by several different details before it can be safely considered to be the next check-point. On arrival at this point the time should be noted again and the next prominent landmark selected from the map, a very rough mental calculation being made of the time needed to get there.

The idea of this check-point navigation takes a little getting used to, but it is perfectly satisfactory, and takes up very little of the pilot's time. If the pilot allows himself to fall into the easy habit of trying to keep continuous check of minor details, he will not only have to devote a great deal of his energy to doing this, but may even get lost because he fails to check any particular point accurately. There are very few landmarks which can be recognized by themselves alone; it is possible in such cases as the Eiffel Tower, the Rock of Gibraltar or the Forth Bridges, but usually a place can be only identified by its position in relation to other things on the ground, towns by their railways, road, rivers, etc.

Even if the country is featureless, there is usually no need to press off into the blue from one landmark to the next, as it will normally be possible, by looking back, to keep the last one in sight until the next is seen. Water, and particularly coastlines, can be seen from a long way off.

The best time for map-reading is when setting course towards the next chosen area of lift. The next check-point will be in view and there will be time to decide what should be the best landmark beyond it. If the check-point itself is still several miles ahead and it is difficult to see with any clarity beyond it, the time can usefully be spent in observing the general nature of the country and features such as railway lines and the angle at which they converge or diverge from the track line. If the country is particularly featureless, positioning may have to be done entirely by assessing angles between lines of roads or railways and the glider's course.

Sooner or later everyone gets lost, either as a result of faulty map-reading or because flight conditions require the entire attention of the pilot. The problem should be tackled calmly. If it is known that a certain landmark was passed 20 minutes previously and the next has not turned up, or has disappeared, it should be checked that the flight direction has not radically altered. If this does not sort the matter out the pilot should not merely pick a landmark underneath the glider and try to find this on the map, instead he should first of all admit that he is lost, and then:

Note the time, and say (for example):

'One hour ago I was at "X".

'The wind is N.W. 20 knots.

'I have spent most of the time circling and the rest flying more or less downwind.

'Therefore I am between 25 and 35 miles S.E. of "X".'

He should look right round the horizon and see what prominent landmarks he can make out, e.g. coast, river, hills, big towns, etc. He should pick one of these and note the position of some secondary landmark in relation to it.

He should then look at the map and try to find, at the right distance from 'X', something which agrees with what he has noticed on the ground. While doing this he finds on the map a place 'Y', and makes a hypothesis saying, 'If it is "Y" then there should be a bypass road to the South of the town and a river running through the western side.'

He should look at the ground to see if these features exist. If they do he should make additional checks to make sure that the place really is 'Y'. If he finds that it is not he must go back to the map again, and make another hypothesis.

If, when unsure of his position the pilot believes that there is any possibility that he is infringing prohibited airspace he must land at once.

It is natural to be over-optimistic in estimating position, hence the importance of noting the time and having some idea of the ground speed. In working out the position on the map distances can be judged by using the (20 km) circles drawn on it. When using the map many people find it easier to have it correctly orientated, so that the northern edge of the map is towards the North, even though this makes it more difficult to read the place names.

Distance judging from the air needs plenty of practice, but it helps to remember that a large airfield is about a mile across, and judgement of distance between two objects on the ground can be made easier by visualizing how many airfields could be fitted between them.

In Europe there are wartime airfields which are not now marked on aviation maps, and conversely some airfields shown are no longer recognizable. This is particularly so in East Anglia. Service airfields have two large white identification letters near the signals square, which may or may not resemble the name. For example, LC is Leconfield.

Under certain conditions of light and weather, ground features may be difficult to distinguish. On days when there are cumulus clouds their shadows can easily be confused with the woods, and towns may merge completely with the greyness. Sometimes in the early evening thin streamers of mist look like water. An elementary knowledge of geology is a help in map reading, and knowledge of types of soil and where they exist may often provide a clue. The black soil of the fen country is quite distinctive, and chalk pits are easily seen from the air. Vegetation, too, varies to an appreciable extent on different soils, and the sandy heath covered with heather and bracken sharply contrasts with open chalk downland, or the red farmland of Devon.

Practical navigation for glider pilots is not a matter which can be learnt from books; only by constantly seeing the country from above in conditions of good and bad visibility, cloud shadow and clear sky, can the pilot teach himself to recognize its features quickly and with certainty.

The expert seems to be able to orientate himself, and know his whereabouts almost without conscious thought, and a quick map check will show him that his presumptions are invariably correct. Such ability is not inborn, but the result of much careful observation and mental calculation, added to familiarity with the view of the land, and its features, when seen from the air.

Chapter 6

Cross–Country Soaring

Undoubtedly the most delightful part of gliding is soaring cross-country. The attractions of local flying are insignificant compared to the joys of travelling far from home, and the combination of exhilaration, despair, fear and hard work make each cross-country flight a unique adventure. But to do it successfully is not easy. It can be taught to some extent by reading and by ground instruction, and also by flying dual, but it is largely an art which is self taught. The principles are fairly obvious—find good thermals, use them well, stay up, and fly in the right direction at the right speed, but the real difficulty when starting is to be able to concentrate on a number of equally important things at the same time. It is easy to devote attention to staying up—and forget navigation. It is satisfying to succeed in working a thermal low down, but not at the price of failing to keep a properly selected landing field within reach.

It is because such a wide variety of skills is required in cross-country flying that it is sensible to have done quite a number of hours local soaring before first setting off—and to have used these hours to the best advantage. The pilot should feel confident of his ability to use a thermal having found one, and to be practised in relating ground features to the map without muddling himself. Several sorties upwind will give him a good idea of the basics of cross-country flying without actually being out of reach of base, and a few flights in a motor glider or light aeroplane selecting fields and map reading can only be helpful in reducing the work load on THE day.

For the first flight or so the pilot will probably go more or less downwind, aiming for a goal nominated by his instructor, since this greatly increases the chance of success.

In Britain, particularly, where the weather is so variable, a Silver distance flight can be made in quite weak conditions as long as the wind is helping the glider on its way.

Before starting the flight the pilot will be able to assess the wind speed and direction visually, and with a downwind flight the type of weather is likely to be similar to that which has drifted past in the previous hour or so.

It is always advisable to aim for a goal. If it is reached the pilot has a measure of his skill; if the glider is landed short, or directions has to be altered in the light of events during the flight the pilot has a yardstick from which to think over his decisions.

For the first cross-country the goal should be about 50 miles away, enough to cover the Silver badge qualification. Although the required distance for this is 50 km (32 statute miles), there is also a rule that requires that the difference in height from the point of release to landing shall not exceed 1% of the distance covered, so a flight of 50 km would not be enough if the launch was to more than 500 metres (1650 ft) above the height of the subsequent landing place.

The chance of a cross-country flight may often occur unexpectedly, so the pilot keen on going should not allow himself to be caught unawares. He should have his own maps, with possible routes already drawn on, and have with him suitable clothes, sun hat, dark glasses, and whatever other equipment he is likely to need.

If there is any wind blowing, a flight of 50 miles is unlikely to take more than two or three hours. There is, therefore, absolutely no need for the pilot to be in a hurry, or to rush ahead without thought. His main object is to remain airborne, and if necessary let himself drift with the wind towards his goal. For the same reason he should stay near home until he has worked one or two thermals within reach of the landing field, while taking stock of the conditions, and finding out how high he is able to get.

It is undesirable to try to lay down rules for the height at which the departure should be irrevocably made, but less than 3000 ft gives little height or time to search for further lift if the original thermal is lost or fades out unexpectedly. The pilot should get as high as he can while still keeping in reach of the airfield. If the wind is light this implies that he should almost reach cloud base, although if the wind is strong he may have to 'burn his boats' at a lower height. A departure below 2000 ft greatly reduces the chance of success, as the time available for further search is so short, and thermals are usually more difficult to work low down.

The pilot must decide what he is going to do before committing himself to leaving the thermal he is in. He should first of all check his future direction by noting a suitable landmark some miles away towards his goal, and then study the sky in this general direction. If the cumulus look poor he should postpone going until they have improved.

If there are good clouds downwind, one of the nearest should be selected, with, if possible an alternative in case the first does not come up to expectations. The chosen cloud should preferably lie in the intended direction, but since the first essential is to stay airborne, it is better to go a mile or two off track to better clouds rather than accept second best just because they are directly on the route. The selection of the next cloud should be made before the glider is up near cloud base when it will be impossible to see any of them properly. If there are only blue thermals, and no cloud, the pilot should set off directly on course, unless he has other indications of the presence of lift such as circling gliders or birds, or rising smoke. The landmark noted ahead on track should be verified and its angle to the heading of the glider assessed and compared to that on the map.

The time of departure should be noted for navigational purposes. The first glide in search of lift is exciting, as the pilot knows that if he discovers nothing he will shortly have to find a new and strange landing place. If, however, his choice has been well made and timed, he will soon be able to start climbing again. Since he is in no hurry, he should get as high as possible without entering cloud, and while circling confirm the direction towards his goal by reference to his landmarks. It is helpful to use the sun as a general guide, in between more exact navigational checks. The next source of lift in more or less the right direction should now be chosen.

If the selected cloud is found to be lifeless and decaying, or now appears to be less suitable than one growing near it, the plan should be altered. No time should be wasted dithering about looking for lift under an unsuitable cloud merely because of a decision taken a few minutes earlier, or because it happens to be near by. It is only as the pilot gains more experience that he will become better at quickly dismissing useless clouds, selecting those more suitable, and also judging accurately the amount of height he will lose in reaching them. To begin with it is easy to misjudge distance from cumulus, and then fail to arrive with enough height to use the thermal underneath because they turned out to be further away than was thought.

It is helpful to observe the shadows of the clouds on the ground and to judge their distance by a check on surface features. Wherever possible long glides to distant clouds should be avoided, when by a little deviation others can be used as stepping stones on the way.

If conditions ahead look unfavourable owing to absence of cloud, continuous cloud, storms or unsuitable terrain, or if after gliding on to the next expected source of lift none is found, the pilot has three choices.

1 To go on to the next likely place in more or less the intended direction.
2 To glide straight on, converting height into distance without wasting it searching for lift, or
3 To decide what is the best means of remaining airborne regardless of direction.

The choice is often very difficult; obviously if the pilot can be sure of reaching his goal he should just fly straight on, but if this seems unlikely, he should concentrate on staying up even if this means flying back on his tracks, and he must resist the natural urge to blunder hopefully on in the right direction. Any lift found, however weak, should be worked to the limit while the glider is carried along by the wind, and the pilot considers what best to do. It may be advisable to make quite a large detour around the problem, or it may be possible to cross a bad patch by getting sufficiently high before entering it, or it may be best just to hang about for a while. The weather is not necessarily stationary either in relation to the ground or the air. A good patch may become useless in the space of fifteen minutes due to the cloud growing rapidly and then flattening out, and the converse is also true. But the pilot should not embark on complicated schemes involving going miles away from the direction planned unless there is absolutely no alternative. He should develop the habit of watching the weather ahead, and if necessary hang about in the remains of his last thermal, merely maintaining height until the sky ahead again looks more promising.

If the flight is going well the pilot, in his desire to get to his goal, may be so pleased whenever he is going up in a thermal that he does not concentrate fully in extracting the utmost from it. But only by doing so in every thermal he uses will the pilot achieve the skill necessary to stay airborne when lesser people fall to earth. Assuming the pilot can work out as he circles when he is doing well and when badly from his instruments or senses, there still remains the problem of altering his flight path to increase the proportion of it in good lift. In some thermals this is not difficult as the lift in the circle has a maximum on one side and a minimum on the other, and the direction can be shifted in the ways the pilot has already learnt. Unfortunately in practice the distribution of lift is seldom uniform and the pilot may find the better lift coming in patches whose position is frequently shifting, and that in order to climb rapidly the position of the circles have to be altered continually. Often the direction in which they should be shifted seems quite random, probably due to strong little cells in the main mass of the thermal.

However, there are two sorts of thermal which do demand a systematic shift. The first is when the upcurrent leaves the ground as more of a column, usually from a slope or hill. If such a thermal is encountered and circled in, it may eventually seem to have faded out, but the disappearance of the lift is due to the glider sinking through its lower side. By continually shifting his position into wind, the pilot can remain in the lift. The second occurs when the zone of lift associated with a large cloud travels faster than the wind speed. This is common in 'April shower' clouds, and is partly because the cloud itself is growing only on one side, and partly because the wind is stronger higher up. It is usually necessary to keep moving downwind to avoid getting caught in the sink and rain at the back of the stormy cloud.

Since thermals can vary so widely in their behaviour the pilot should avoid developing preconceived ideas about the sort of lift in which he finds himself. Some people think, for example, that it is always necessary to circle in a thermal and to fly up and down a ridge, but it often happens that a series of S turns or a combination of straight flight and circling may prove the most effective. One of the reasons for the slow discovery of wave soaring was that pilots thought that waves could only appear on days without thermals; hence on thermal days any lift was circled in, and if it was wave was promptly lost.

When near cloud base the best lift will be found by searching out the part of the cloud which is growing, often made visible by swirling wisps which are forming just underneath and being sucked up into it. Once the strongest lift has been discovered—and it is not intended to enter cloud— the pilot should enlarge his circles to find the limit of the lift or wander off on an exploratory search, knowing that should even better lift not be found he can return to the previous source because he has learnt its position in relation to the cloud as a whole.

If clouds are lying in lines up- and downwind, and if the goal is exactly downwind, the flight can be made simply by flying down the line and climbing up in any good lift. However, it often happens that the track lies at an oblique angle to the line of cloud. In these circumstances it is best to work two or three clouds in one line, and then fly square across to the nearest likely cloud in the next line. Two or three clouds are then worked in this line before going square across to another one. The reason for doing this is that it is difficult to judge the distance between the lines of clouds, combined with the fact that there will almost certainly be sink in this region. Excessive loss of height may result if the crossing is made diagonally.

It is inadvisable to leave one source of lift before deciding where the next is likely to be found, but once the decision to leave has been made, it should be carried out in the way which will lose the minimum amount of height consistent with getting there rapidly.

As experience is gained it will be appreciated that the best cruising speed from one thermal to another is not a constant, and that there is an optimum for any given thermal strength. This is described in Chapter 7. On early downwind cross-country flights however, it is enough to fly at the most suitable slow speed while circling and a little faster in between thermals. For example, there are often down currents on the lee side of thermals or clouds, and it is therefore preferable to increase speed to fly through them, rather than fly on into the downdraught before putting the nose down to gain speed. On the journey to the next source of lift, downcurrents should be avoided. This may sound a counsel of perfection, but if the direct path leads under an obviously decaying cloud, the temptation to go on and have a look in case there is some lift should be resisted. Course should be altered and the vicinity of the cloud avoided.

RUNNING OUT OF LIFT

Should the glider start to get low the pilot should use any scrap of lift that he can find, and at the same time check his actual height over the ground from the map and relate it to the altimeter reading—assuming that he set the altimeter at airfield height. Otherwise, should he have to start looking for a field he may find that his real height above the ground is less than he thought.

At lower heights the search for lift will be dictated more by the terrain than by the clouds, but as well as considering the ground in this respect, he must study it in terms of its landability, and the glider be kept in reach of suitable areas, even if continuing to drift along in no sink.

The heights at which the pilot should select his landing field, and at which he should abandon the flight and decide to land are discussed in Chapter 4 but the excitement of the moment and the urge to prolong the flight must not be allowed to persuade the pilot to try to work to finer limits until he has considerable experience and is sure of his skill.

FLYING IN COMPANY

Someone learning to soar will tend to fly well away from other gliders. However, the moment will come when the pilot has to find out how to fly with them in the same thermal. The direction of circling is determined by the international convention that subsequent pilots joining the first in a thermal must circle in the direction already established. In order that the two gliders shall go round more or less concentrically the joining pilot should aim to one side of the circle which the other pilot is making; in fact he should aim for that part of the circle in which he sees the tail view of the other glider. As he approaches, he can decide whether he can continue on his course and start to turn so that the other glider is on the opposite side of the circle to him, or whether he should edge out to delay joining and then slide in at a more suitable moment to follow around behind the first glider. A really good lookout is essential. This does not mean a casual glance on each circle, but a good look every four or five seconds not only at the gliders which are known to be already in the thermal, but for any others coming to join it. The mental tally is made easier if the gliders are of different colours or have distinguishing marks. The advantage of an audio variometer is that the pilot can use the thermal more efficiently without the need for looking inside the cockpit.

It is inadvisable to fly a glider closely behind another, since not only is it unfair to the leading pilot by making him worry about the invisible companion on his tail, but also it is a hazard because if he should turn rapidly it may be difficult to avoid a collision. If the two gliders' circles become eccentric they will meet each other head on once in every revolution even though they are both turning in the same direction. In these circumstances one pilot should alter his circle to coincide more closely to that of the other; if the thermal is large he should move out and circle well away from the other. Alternatively, he can go and look for another thermal. There is a tendency to concentrate on other gliders at the same level, but attention must also be given to those below who may be climbing more rapidly, and to those above who are not climbing so fast. If there are any other gliders in the same thermal it is essential not to manoeuvre rapidly by reversing a turn, altering bank suddenly or diving away. If, as sometimes happens, there is a feeling that there is a glider invisible nearby, the best thing is to straighten up gently and fly steadily away.

Beginners tend to confine too much of their attention to the cockpit, studying the variometer and airspeed indicator. Not only is this hazardous to other gliders but it prevents the pilot from observing fully what is going on outside.

There have been collisions between gliders circling in the same thermal. They have usually taken place not, as one might expect, when there are many gliders, but when there are only two or three. In most cases one or both pilots were unaware that there was another glider near them.

LANDING

Although the pilot has to be mentally prepared to deal with a landing in a strange place at any stage of the flight, it is surprisingly easy to be unprepared for a landing at the goal. The feeling of elation because the goal airfield has been reached, combined with a feeling of anticlimax because the flight is finishing tends to take the edge off the pilot's awareness that he still has to get down.

If the goal is an airfield — and it usually is — the pilot should have informed himself of any procedures for landing there. He should now enter the circuit pattern in the proper manner and at the correct height. If he is too low to do this it may be more sensible to pick a good field well outside the airfield area rather than attempted to cut in ahead of landing aeroplanes or gliders. If the landing has, for any reason, to be in a field the pilot must accept that this time his goal is not going to be attainable, forget about trying to scrape in, and devote all his concentration on making a safe and competent outlanding.

Chapter 7

Further Cross–Country Soaring

After a few successful cross-country flights the pilot may begin to feel that he knows how to do it and become complacent. He can become set in his ways and his flying will not improve, because he does not know how low his standard is. The state of affairs is most likely to occur if there is not the stimulus of flying alongside more experienced pilots, of observing how they fly, and of talking with them afterwards. Some people have no urge to become involved in serious competition flying, although they would not have taken up soaring if they did not wish to compete against the weather. But even for the keenly competitive pilot it is as yet too early to enter contests other than Club Task Weeks. Instead, he should arrange to make some flights in company with one or two other pilots, to obtain a measure of his own competence. The mere fact of operating with others will enable him to analyse his flying and teach himself to improve in a way that no amount of wandering around the sky alone will do.

CRUISING SPEEDS–PROLONGING THE GLIDE

During the first few cross-country flights the objective is to go somewhere gently and surely, and there is little or no need for speed. When going from one source of lift to another, the aircraft can be flown slowly at the speed corresponding to the best angle of glide. If an area of sink is encountered, less height will be lost in flying through it if the speed is increased. For example, if the downcurrent is two miles across and the air is sinking uniformly at 2 knots, flying at the speed corresponding to the best angle of glide (51 knots– 1:35) will result in a loss of height of 812 ft. If however the speed is increased to 65 knots (glide ratio 1 : 31)

80

the height lost will be 750 ft.

The pilot can increase his speed intuitively or make use of a simple device called a 'speed to fly' or 'MacCready' ring. This is a rotating ring mounted on the face of the vario-meter and calibrated in the same speed units as the air-speed indicator (knots or km/h). For the straightforward case which we are considering here, of prolonging the glide, the setting mark on the ring is set opposite the 0 on the variometer scale and the aircraft is flown so that the air-speed indicator reading is the same as the speed shown oppo-site the variometer needle (Fig. 7.1). When sink is encoun-tered the variometer will show an increased rate of descent and the aircraft should then be flown faster, the speed being adjusted until it becomes the same as the new speed shown opposite the new position of the variometer needle. Con-versely if the glider flies through an area of lift the speed should be reduced accordingly, but naturally the glider

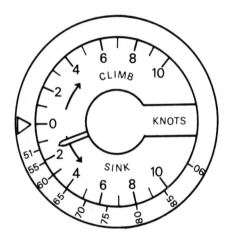

Fig. 7.1 MacCready ring. Shown here set for prolonging the glide. The outer rotating ring is manually set so that the arrow comes opposite the 0 on the inner scale. The pilot adjusts his speed so that the airspeed indicator reading is the same as the speed shown opposite the variometer reading. (Calibrated for a Standard Libelle weighing 695 lb.)

should not be flown slower than the speed corresponding to the minimum rate of sink.

IMPROVING CROSS-COUNTRY SPEEDS

To improve his performance the pilot has to teach himself to fly fast. On any day there are only so many hours in which soaring is possible. These may be between 1000 and 1900 hrs on a textbook day, but in Britain the time available is more likely to consist of a good spell of only two to three hours. The pilot who can put the largest number of miles into each of the hours will obviously fly the furthest, and this is particularly the case when flying into wind. An average of 30 knots through the air will be only 10 knots over the ground against a 20-knot headwind, but if the pilot could increase his speed by 33%, that is to 40 knots, he would double his ground speed. To do this he has to use thermals efficiently, avoid downcurrents, and fly at the optimum speed for the conditions prevailing.

AVERAGE CROSS-COUNTRY SPEED

The theoretical analysis of glider performance is given in Chapter 16, the classical case consisting of a series of climbs made by circling the glider, followed by a series of straight glides. This concept is oversimplified in terms of real life since it is assumed that the glider is flying straight through steady air without up or down currents, and that no time is wasted in circling while trying to locate lift. However, on days when the areas of lift are isolated it does give reasonably accurate results. The analysis shows that in order to achieve the highest average speed there is an optimum cruising speed in straight flight for the particular rate of climb achieved when circling. The following table gives the figures for a Libelle flown at a weight of 695 lb.

With a high performance glider, the choice of cruising speed is not particularly critical. For example, in the case of the Libelle given above, the optimum cruising speed for a day giving rates of climb of 2 knots is 67 knots giving an average speed of 33 knots. But an off-optimum cruising speed of either 55 knots or 80 knots at this rate of climb would still

Average rate of climb when circling, knots	Optimum cruising speed between thermals, knots	Resulting average speed, knots
0	51	0
1	59	19
2	67	33
4	73	40
6	86	52
8	96	60
10	99	63

Table 7.1 Optimum cruising speeds at different rates of climb

give average speeds of 30 knots.

In practice it will always be best to fly somewhat more slowly than the theoretical optimum, since this brings two significant advantages at the price of a very small reduction in average speed. Firstly the time spent in circling is reduced, with consequent saving in pilot effort and a reduction in the number of thermals which must be located and used. Secondly it increases the chance of being successful in finding the next thermal.

The speed to fly between thermals can be obtained by reference to a table, or more simply by reference to the Mac-Cready ring. Instead of setting the mark on the ring opposite the zero of the variometer, it is set opposite the reading corresponding to the average rate of climb (Fig. 16.16; Plate IV).

When cruising between thermals the airspeed should be held at the value given on the ring opposite the variometer needle. If the glider is flown through areas of sink or climb, the variometer reading will increase or decrease and the speed should be adjusted accordingly. Getting the speed right to deal with areas of sink or climb, is of greater importance than starting off at the theoretically correct cruising speed. A correctly adjusted total-energy variometer is essential for good results.

In practice the pilot will want to calculate the average speed he will need to maintain in order to decide what length of flight is possible for the day. If the flight is for more than the few hours covering the strongest part of the day when

Plate IV A PZL variometer fitted with a MacCready ring. The inner ends of the diagonal lines on the ring represent the optimum gliding speeds (50, 60, etc., knots) at sea-level whilst the outer ends correspond to a height of 10,000 ft. (See also Chapter 18)

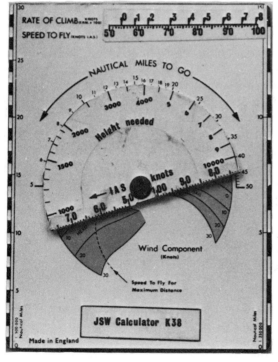

Plate V The JWS calculator. A small calculator ($4\frac{1}{2} \times 3\frac{1}{2}''$) used to solve angle of glide and final glide problems. This example is for use with a Standard Libelle

1 On top fixed scale against 'Rate of Climb' of, say, 3 kt read 'Speed to Fly'–70 knots
2 Move semi-circular scale so that 70 knots on bottom scale comes opposite appropriate wind speed line–say, 10 knots headwind.
3 Read 'Height Needed' against 'Nautical Miles to Go'. e.g. 20 miles and 5000 ft

conditions are expected to be fairly uniform, he will need to attempt to calculate what average speed he will be able to achieve during each of the weaker hours early and late in the day.

OPERATIONAL HEIGHTS

On a day with isolated thermals the average speed which can be obtained depends on the average rate of climb in the lift and the speed at which the cruise between thermals is made. The choice of cruising speed coupled with skill in avoiding strong downcurrents is important, but much more so is the ability to obtain a high average rate of climb. On any particular day it seldom happens that the thermals are of uniform strength, or that each one is of constant strength all the way up. It therefore follows that if the pilot wishes to obtain the highest possible rate of climb he must not only select the range of height over which to operate, but also the best thermals. Unfortunately the pursuit of these requirements decreases the chances of remaining airborne, because the pilot out for speed must discard thermals if they do not come up to what he considers adequate strength for the time and place, and as a result he will tend to fly lower down than the pilot whose only object is to stay in the air. The more closely he specifies his operational height range, and the more ruthless he is at discarding all but the best thermals, the greater his chances of coming unstuck. The pilot must learn to strike the right compromise between obtaining a high average speed and a certain degree of success. It is better to fly for four hours at an average speed of 30 knots and get back, than for two hours at 40 knots and land out.

The key to the successful completion of whatever cross-country flight has been attempted is competent and continual decision-making. Each thermal has to be assessed on its merits, used if good enough, and discarded at the right moment, and each downcurrent has to be flown through at the most efficient speed.

SELECTION OF THERMALS

The time spent in the initial assessment of a thermal can be greatly reduced if a total-energy variometer is used, as with this instrument it is possible while still slowing down from the higher speed of the straight glide to measure the thermal strength.

However, the decision whether to make use of the thermal or not can be difficult. The pilot may say something like this: 'When I am above 5000 ft I will only use thermals which will give me more than 5 knots, above 4000 ft, 3 knots; 3000 ft; 2 knots; and below 2000 ft, anything I can find'. It is not easy for him to choose either numerical values, or actually to measure the rate of climb that he is obtaining. Furthermore, if he works too much on a numerical basis, he may, in disregarding a series of weak thermals, find himself down to his lower limit before appreciating that the average thermal strength of the country over which he is now flying is less than it was.

It is, as stated earlier, in the ability to climb rapidly that the greatest progress is made, and one only has to watch a number of pilots flying in the same thermal to realize quite how much difference this can make. The pilot has three variables to contend with: his angle of bank, his airspeed, and where he flies. The first two are largely interdependent. In large thermals the pilot should fly slowly at a gentle angle of bank, and in small ones, somewhat faster and steeper.

However, both these conditions are insignificant compared to the importance of flying in the right part of the sky. Having found a thermal, the maximum rate of climb will not be obtained merely by getting somewhere inside it, locking the glider in a circle, and just going round and round. It is necessary to observe the behaviour of the glider all the time, work out which way the circle should be shifted, and practically drive the aircraft into the best lift. If this is not done the rate of climb will soon deteriorate since the thermal may tend to push the glider farther out. Amongst good pilots it is surprising how much their circling technique differs even in the same thermal at the same time. Some pilots continually alter the angle of bank, and almost fight into what they consider to be the best part of the thermal. Others fly in more gently banked turns in what appears to be a lazy and effortless way.

It is remarkable that these widely different techniques all seem to be equally effective in the hands of their exponents, no one consistently outclimbing the other. What they have in common, and what distinguishes them from the less competent, is not only skill in shifting their circles to keep in the strongest lift, but, and this is probably more important, their ability to go on doing this after having flown and concentrated for several hours. It is very easy for the pilot to allow his concentration to slacken and, particularly when high in a good thermal, to sit back in bovine content. The maximum rate of climb can only be obtained by continual hard work, and the pilot should go on asking himself whether he is still concentrating as hard as he would have been at 500 ft.

Another feature characteristic of the expert pilot is his habit when circling of exploring the air in and around the thermal. If he thinks that better lift may be obtained a few hundred yards away he goes and has a look, and because he is accustomed to orientate himself in the air, he can successfully return should he fail to find anything better.

Pilots vary widely in the degree to which they make use of the instruments and their feelings and one cannot say that there is a right or wrong way of assessing the lift. It is probable that the majority of good pilots use their variometer to tell them the average rate at which they are climbing, and their senses to tell them increases and decreases in this value. A variometer which was absolutely without lag would make the problem easier, as it would remove the period of doubt between the perception and the recorded information.

It is possible to manoeuvre into the best lift entirely by reference to the variometer, or solely by feel without making use of instruments. This may seem difficult for an aeroplane pilot to believe, but the trained glider pilot can feel the vertical accelerations and hear the increase in air speed, as he encounters a patch of more rapidly rising air; conversely he feels the sink and hears the reduced noise when he flies into weaker lift or downcurrent. However, if the areas of lift are large and uniform it is sometimes impossible to distinguish lift from steady or sinking air, although it can be done sometimes from the different feel of the turbulence.

DOLPHINING

This is a technique which is increasingly practicable as glider performance improves. With fast clean gliders there are many occasions when the pilot can fly more or less straight at slow speeds through lift, at higher speeds through steady air, and at still higher speeds through downcurrents with little or no loss of height. The path followed may deviate from side to side in order to pass through the largest proportion of up-currents and the smallest proportion of downcurrents. The glider is pulled up when entering the lift, and the nose is put down and the glider flown fast through the down, preferably before actually leaving the thermal. In this way any strong down around the periphery of the thermal is traversed as fast as possible.

For many years this technique has been used flying under cloud streets, where it is easy to see where the lift and sink might be occurring.

However, with the use of a really good total-energy variometer and a fast high-performance glider the vertical undulations can be very pronounced. Consider the case of a glider cruising at 100 knots. If on entering a thermal the speed is reduced gradually a very considerable distance will be covered while decelerating, and the average speed of the passage through the area of lift will be high. If, on the other hand, immediately on entry the glider is pulled up into a steep climb, the speed will drop off quickly and the time spent flying through the lift will be longer, with a consequent increase in the height contributed by the area of lift. The difference in kinetic energy between a cruising speed of say 100 knots and a slow 50 knots amounts to a potential increase in height of about 200 ft. This height will be gained when pulling up in the climb, but although the same height will have to be lost when picking up speed again, the gains and losses will occur in favourable air.

THE FINAL GLIDE

To the competition pilot the consideration of the final glide is of great importance since it will markedly affect the average speed of the whole flight. On a 500-km triangle the final glide may occupy 10% of the total distance, but on a 100-km flight it may be as much as 30%. The objective is to judge this phase of the flight so as to reach the goal without excessive height at the highest average speed. The non-competition pilot may not be quite so interested in achieving high speed over the last part of the journey, but he certainly is interested in finding out in advance when to stop soaring and go on to his goal. To judge the final glide correctly needs considerable skill, but fortunately it is an aspect of flying which is comparatively easy to practise. In competitions the aim is to arrive a few feet over the finishing line at the optimum speed; starting too low or flying too fast will result in an ignominious landing a mile or so outside the goal. When practising, therefore, it is best to allow a margin for error and initially aim to arrive at an exact height over the airfield boundary — say, 1000 ft. Practice final glides can be done this way from distances of 10 miles and upwards. The pilot will need a calculator and can learn to use it in the proper way on practice glides except for the extra margin of 1000 ft. With increasing experience he will be able to reduce the margin.

Normally the pilot will start thinking about the final glide well before the time that he could actually start it, but by this stage of the flight he should have a good knowledge of the conditions. The pilot should assess what his probable maximum height will be — let us say 6000 ft. Then, knowing the wind component — say, plus 10 knots — he can by means of his calculator work out how far he could glide from this 6000 ft. For the Libelle this would be 45 miles at the best-angle-of-glide speed. He then knows that once he gets about this distance from his goal he must start thinking about the final glide. He does not want to start it yet because he would prefer to fly in faster than the best L/D speed. The wind component should be assessed as accurately as possible, and decisions taken on how much allowance ought to be made for possible large areas of sink, sea breeze effects, and changes in wind strength or direction. Rather than add extra height as insurance it is more logical to plan the final glide at a steeper angle than the theoretical minimum, and then if it is found that too much height is being lost, speed can be reduced.

The speed at which the final glide should be made is determined by the rate of climb at the moment of leaving the final thermal and not, as is commonly supposed, by the average rate of climb achieved in that thermal. Consider the case of a glider circling up in a thermal; it has just reached the position from which it can make a straight glide to its goal when flying at the best angle of glide. What has happened up to that moment is history and is outside the control of the pilot; he can, however, decide to glide off straight away at a slow speed, or spend time climbing up higher in order to be able to fly off faster, and still just get to his goal.

The standard technique for working out the cruising speed between thermals, based on the MacCready ring, gives a cruising speed appropriate to each rate of climb (see Chapter 17). The theory for the final glide will not be proved here, but it can be shown that once the glider is in a position from which it can reach the goal it should continue climbing as long as the rate of climb is greater than that appropriate to the cruising speed which could be used from its present height. However, once the rate of climb falls away, even momentarily, to that appropriate for the cruising speed, then it is best to set course right away.

USE OF THE CALCULATOR

The best moment to start the final glide is difficult to determine mentally; it needs the use of a graph, or tables of some sort, or a calculator. Whatever method of calculation is used the basic principle is to use inputs of 'distance to go' (obtained by map reading), and 'height above goal' (from the altimeter with allowance for height of goal above sea level) to give the glide ratio over the ground that will be needed. The next step is to feed in the 'wind speed component' (pilot's estimate of the equivalent head or tail wind) and the 'glider's performance' (built into the tables or calculator) and determine the appropriate gliding speed. Finally the rate of climb for which this airspeed would be the optimum can be obtained from a table or from the MacCready ring.

Whatever means of solving the problem is used, it must also provide the pilot with the value of the theoretical glide ratio over the ground at which the final glide was started, and some simple way of checking as he flies along whether he is above or below the planned glide path. Knowing this he can then make corrections by flying faster or slower. There are many different types of graphs, table or calculators which can be used to solve the problem. Graphs are often difficult to read in the air, and although tables can be better, having to find the answer in a block of figures can be confusing. It is for these reasons that most pilots prefer calculators, usually of the simple circular slide rule type. In the smaller models the 'distance to goal' has to be determined from the pilot's map, which can be done either by measurement with a scale or by reference to circles or marks previously drawn on the map. This distance must then be transferred to the calculator. The widely-used JWS calculator is of this type (Plate V).

Other calculators, of which the Australian WAC is a good example, incorporate a section of map (Plates VI and VII). In this case there is no need to actually determine the distance; the calculator is set up by bringing the appropriate height mark on a transparent disc above the position marked on the map. The choice is largely a matter of pilot preference. However, when deciding which type to use it is as well to choose something which is really simple to understand, easy to read, and capable of being operated by one hand.

During the final glide, the speed should not be kept constant, but increased or decreased as sink is met using the MacCready ring in the usual way. Periodically the distance to go and the height available should be checked with the calculator. Rather than think in terms of so many feet above or

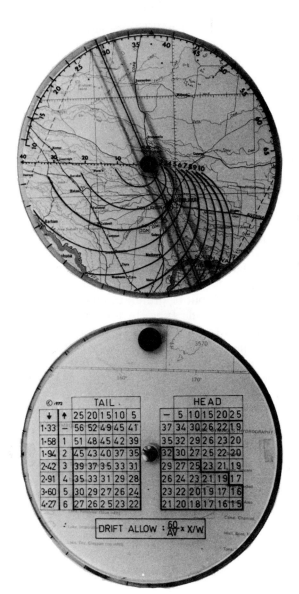

Plate VI and VII The Australian WAC calculator. Diameter 6 in. For solving final glide problems the tables on the reverse side (Plate VII) are used. 1: Knowing the rate of climb and the head, or tail wind the appropriate glide ratio and the height/distance relationship is shown by the curved height lines in respect to the ground features on the map, which can be rotated to line up with the cursor.

below the chosen glide path, it is probably easier to appreciate the situation by considering the angles of glide over the ground. If, for example, the glide was started from 25 miles out at 6000 ft, at a glide ratio of 1:25 and at 17 miles out the height is 3700 ft, it can be easily worked out from the calculator that the glide ratio necessary to reach the goal has flattened to 1:27. The speed must therefore be reduced. If the situation continues to worsen the pilot will have to find and use some extra lift to get home.

The direction of the final glide is important; if the air is absolutely stable then it should naturally be in a straight line. If, however, lift and sink are still present, it will pay to deviate. A thermal may be marked by a circling glider, or a dead-looking area can be avoided. If visibility is bad larger margins should be applied to the calculation, as it may be best to edge off to one side to converge on a road or river as a lead-in to the goal.

The whole process of planning a final glide can be completely upset by large areas of sink, or by an unexpectedly strong wind. In particular, an approach into a different air mass (e.g., near the coast) or into a blue zone surrounded by large clouds should be viewed with suspicion and an extra allowance made. In addition, the wind speed and direction should be checked by cloud shadows or smoke, before the pilot commits himself. Approaching downwind, the glide angle may be less than 2°. At this angle, it may be very difficult to identify the goal airfield positively. A plan to reduce the difficulty should have been made in advance.

Because the final glide is one of the few aspects of soaring which is amenable to analysis in flight, it has received an undue importance. The theoretical rate of climb at which the last thermal should be discarded is not really very critical. It is usually better to go a little higher and thus reduce the risk of having to slow right down, or even break off the glide to gain some more height. If the assessment of distance, wind component, areas of sink etc, are inaccurate or unfavourable, or if the pilot has failed to obtain the height of the goal above sea level, some extra allowance of height must be made.

FLAPS

Flaps on high-performance gliders give some increase in performance; by lowering the flaps, the minimum rate of sink and the speed at which this occurs have both been reduced, with considerable gain in the rate of climb when circling. By raising the flaps, gliding angles at moderate and high speeds have been improved. (For a more detailed explanation, see Chapter 17).

From the pilot's point of view flaps are a complication since he has to remember to adjust them every time he makes a significant alteration in speed. Normally the manufacturer of the aircraft will provide a table showing the best flap setting for use when circling slowly and when flying straight at various speeds. It is as well for the pilot to check that these recommendations are based on proper flight tests and that on his particular aircraft the adjustment of the flap mechanism is correct so that the flaps really are set at the angles indicated by the cockpit lever. The best flap setting for a particular speed will depend on the weight at which the aircraft is being flown, or to put this in a more logical way the speed appropriate for a particular flap setting will be increased when ballast is carried, since the objective is to fly at a certain angle of attack at each flap setting. For example, if a particular flap setting is correct for a speed of 100 knots when the aircraft is flown without ballast, this same setting will be correct for 110 knots if 20% ballast is carried.

Quite apart from the performance aspect there are a number of factors affecting the handling of an aircraft fitted with flaps. For example, there may well be a speed limitation when the flaps are lowered more than a certain amount. Overspeeding in this configuration can lead to structural failure. Also the flight attitude, at the same speed, will alter with the flap setting – with flaps down, the nose is further down. This may significantly improve the forward view when being aerotowed.

Normally on flapped aircraft the ailerons are connected to the flap mechanism so that both ailerons are drooped as the flaps are lowered. This sometimes has the effect of reducing the aileron power and thus making it more difficult to avoid dropping a wing on take-off. It may therefore be better to start the take-off run with the flaps up in order to obtain the best aileron control, and only lower them shortly before take-off speed is reached. The objections to this practice are obvious — forgetfulness can lead to a prolonged and possibly hazardous take-off. But then flapped aircraft should not be flown by forgetful people. Another trap is to fail to lower the flaps before landing after making a spectacular high-speed crossing of the finishing line; the increased stalling speed with flaps up can lead to an equally spectacular arrival on the ground.

FIELD LANDINGS

The technique of selecting fields and of landing in them has been covered in chapter 4, where the emphasis was placed on picking the field in plenty of time, and of choosing the best field from the landing point of view regardless of other factors. These considerations must be paramount for the first few field landings but as experience is gained the restraints can be reduced — the selection can be left until later and an inferior field can be accepted. However, it is easy to become over-confident and to assume that a safe landing can always be pulled off from a low height however bad the country underneath. This is not so. Continual practice and observation is needed if lower margins are not going to bring greater risks.

The pilot must not allow himself to get into the habit of just going back to his airfield and landing wherever convenient. He must practise by picking his spot and approach on to it at the right speed and at the appropriately steep angle. Above all he must really teach himself all about the countryside over which he is flying (or going to fly) — the types of crops, and what they look like from the air, the methods of farming, the characteristics of any uncultivated surface cover such as heather or scrub, and the lie of the land in general.

TURNING-POINT PHOTOGRAPHY

Taking a satisfactory turning-point photograph without wasting time is not nearly so easy as it might seem. In theory the requirements are simple — the photograph must show the turning point, be taken from the correct quadrant (normally the quadrant whose centre line is opposite the centre line of the approach and departure lines), to be taken just, but only just, beyond the turning point, and be taken quickly with the minimum loss of height.

Since turning-point photographs will be needed in competitions and for badge and record flights, this photography is something which should be practised a great deal before it has to be used in earnest. This can be easily done when soaring locally.

The regulations concerning the procedure for taking turning point photographs in World Championships are laid down clearly in the FAI Sporting Code, copies of which can be bought from the National Gliding Associations. These same regulations are normally used in national and regional competitions, with simpler procedures permissible for records and badges.

In competitions it is specified that a particular type of camera and film be used in order to facilitate the development and interpretation of large batches of film at the end of each contest day. At present the camera type specified covers any of the basic Instamatics using film approximately 35 mm wide in standard cassettes. Although these cameras are extremely reliable it is laid down that there shall be two cameras, and that these must be rigidly mounted in the aircraft, aligned so as to bring the left wing-tip into the picture.

The procedure to be used in competitions is also laid down; before take-off the cameras are mounted and used to photograph a declaration board held by an Official Observer, in flight the various turning-points are taken, and after landing the cameras are removed from their fixings and used to photograph the identifying number on the fin of the glider. The films are then handed to the Organisers for developing as a negative strip and for interpretation.

It might be supposed that by having the camera pointing at the wingtip all that was necessary to photograph the turning point was to do a steep turn around it and press the button at the appropriate moment. Unfortunately this is not so, as a look at the geometry will show. Fig 7.2 gives the sit-

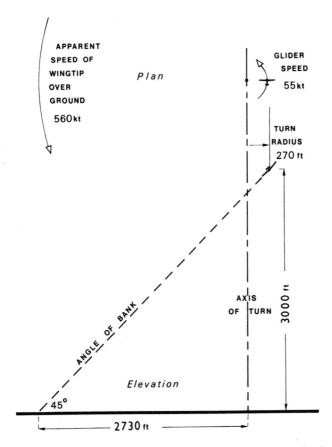

APPARENT
SPEED OF
WINGTIP   *Plan*
OVER
GROUND

560 kt

GLIDER
SPEED
55 kt

TURN
RADIUS
270 ft

ANGLE OF BANK

AXIS
OF TURN

3000 ft

Elevation

45°

2730 ft

Fig. 7.2 Turning-point photography. Apparent speed of movement of wingtip when turning. Height 3000 ft; angle of bank 45°; speed 55 knots

uation when the camera is aligned at the wingtip, the aircraft is at 3000 ft and its airspeed is 55 knots in a 45° turn; the corresponding radius of turn works out at 270 ft. It shows that the centre of the picture will be 3000 ft (940 m) to the left of the glider. Even if the angle of bank is increased to 60° the horizontal distance will still be 1730 ft (530 m). Quite apart from these large offsets, which imply flying considerable distances beyond the turning point, there is a real problem in aligning the wingtip at the turning point.

When circling an aircraft low down or at high speed, the wingtip appears to move forward over the ground around the point about which the aircraft is circling and it is easy to keep a point on the ground in clear view. However, when circling at greater heights or at a slow speed the wingtip appears to move backwards at a surprisingly high speed. For the mathematically minded it is easy to show that the apparent speed of movement of the wingtip over the ground is independent of the angle of bank and depends only on the height and airspeed. This apparent backwards speed equals (Hg/V)–V, where H is the height above the ground, V is the aircraft speed and g is the gravitational constant. If H is 3000 ft and V is 55 knots, the speed turns out to be 560 knots! (Fig. 7.2).

The whole problem of aligning a camera on to the turning point is made much easier if it is mounted so as to point well below the wingtip level: 30°-40° is probably the best, but this is not practicable if the requirement of having the wingtip come out in the photograph is to be satisfied. Making allowances for the actual wing dihedral in circling flight, the location of the camera, and for inaccuracies in its lining up, it is clear that the camera must be fixed so that the top of the picture is about 10° above the horizontal in level flight. Since the Instamatic, which takes a square picture, has a field of view of 48° this means that the bottom of the picture will be 38° and the centre of the picture 14° below the horizon when the glider is level. Consequently to point the centre line of the camera straight downwards requires an angle of bank of 90 – 14 = 76°, and to have the bottom of the picture on the vertical requires an angle of bank of 76-14 = 52°. Rather than point the camera straight out sideways it is best to angle it about 20° forwards, as this gives more time for the pilot to pick up the turning point as it appears from underneath the wing.

In practice therefore the cameras should be mounted so that the left wingtip just comes into the top left-hand corner of the picture. When lining up the cameras on the ground, allowance should be made for the amount the wingtip will bend upwards when flying in a steep turn, typically about 2 feet, and this point should be checked by taking a test photograph in the air. It is important that the pilot knows the field of view of the camera as it is when sitting in the cockpit, and while a proper viewfinder fixed as appropriate to the canopy or cockpit side is an unnecessary complication, it may be useful to mark the perspex so that when he holds his head in a set position he will know that the top of the picture will be level with the wingtip, the bottom, say, level with the clear vision panel, and the left and right will be in line with two marks on the perspex. Fig. 7.3 shows the photographic angles of a camera installed in a glider banked in a 60° turn, and also the area of ground photographed from 3000 ft.

If we now consider the best position for the glider in relation to the turning point, it is clear that it should be positioned so that the turning point lies somewhere between V and T in Fig. 7.4. If an attempt is made to take the photograph when too close to the turning point there is a risk of being inside it. If, however, the photograph is taken so that the turning point appears at T, then time will be wasted in the extra flying involved. It is also necessary that the picture is taken from the correct quadrant and for this reason alone some overflying of the turning point is essential.

Taking the simple case of a turning point involving an alteration of track of 60° to the left, and assuming the conditions given in Fig. 7.4, the ideal position could be achieved by running in a few hundred feet to the right of the turning point, and then when slightly past it taking the photograph whilst doing a quick steep turn to the left before straightening up on the new heading.

In practice this degree of precision is difficult to achieve owing to the comparatively poor downward view both sideways and forwards from most gliders. The cutoff angles may be 60° below the horizon sideways and 15° forwards. This means that when flying level at 3000 ft and looking out to one side and downwards, nothing can be seen on the ground within 1500 ft of the point immediately beneath.

It is usually necessary to make small rolls or yaws to ensure that the glider is being flown in on the right track to the

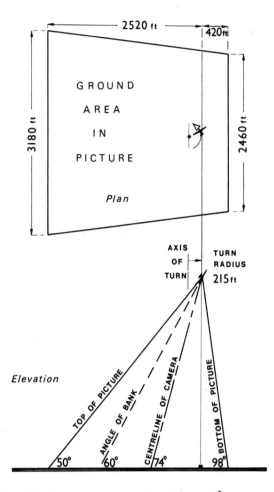

Fig 7.3 Camera angles. Angles of bank 60°; camera field of view 48° up and down and 48° sideways. Camera aligned 14° down and 20° forwards. Glider speed 65 knots; height 3000 ft

turning-point. Once the turning-point has been identified, it is often possible to pick a sighting point well beyond it to maintain the heading, and to pick another point level with the turning-point, but well off to the left, which can still be seen from the cockpit when the turning-point itself is obscured.

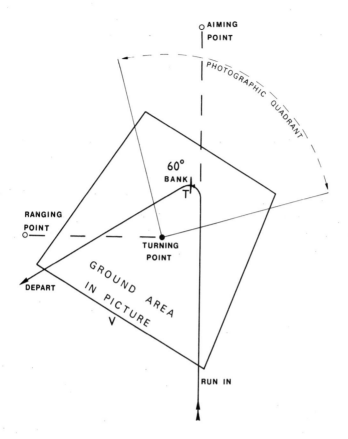

Fig 7.4 Idealised photography of turning point. Conditions as in Fig 7.3. Aiming point and ranging point are selected when some way off. Run in is made towards aiming point, and turn is started after glider comes level with ranging point. Photograph is taken in 60° turn

The turn can then be started once past this ranging point. If all has gone well and the glider is found to be in the correct quadrant the photograph can then be taken immediately; if not the glider must be flown off to a new position, before starting a left-handed turn again, ready for another photograph.

Since photographs are always taken to the left, photographing a turning-point requires an alteration of course to

101

the right will inevitably involve the turn being started in the direction away from the turning-point and the turn made through 270° or so. In some lucky cases a thermal may be found near the turning-point and the photograph can be taken when circling up.

Even when the problems are understood there is no substitute for practice if the pilot wishes to get his turning-point photographs with 100% accuracy and minimum time waste. With this practice he will undoubtedly devise a technique which suits his own way of flying and which always works for him.

Chapter 8

Hills and Mountains

Soaring first started when it was found that the wind blowing on to a hill had a sufficiently large vertical component to support the glider, and slope soaring is practicable on hills more than 200 or 300 ft high. Because the technique is well understood and easily learnt it will not be dealt with here. However, considerable skill and knowledge are needed to make the best use of the lift; pilots who have never slope-soared before, or those who are not familiar with the particular site should obtain local briefing. Once a pilot has gained experience of slope soaring on a particular hill he may find that his interest in this form of flying will flag, unless he uses the slope lift as a means of reaching waves or thermals.

For this purpose the slope lift should be used primarily as a jumping-off place for extensive explorations of the air and the surrounding hills, and not, as is so often the case, an excuse for merely tramping back and forth along the home beat somewhere near the top of the hill lift. The object should not be to get as high as possible and stay there, but to sally forth on experimental tours, even if this means frequent returns to the slope at hill top level.

Perhaps the most interesting aspect of hill soaring is flying from and exploring unknown hilly regions. Expeditions to new places with a glider and a bungey (a rubber catapult) can be tremendous fun. Unfortunately, many gliders are unsuitable for bungey launching owing to their high wing-loading and small angle of incidence, but there are still gliders such as the Ka8, Olympia and Skylarks which can be used. Alternatively, winch launching or aerotowing may be the simplest way to get the glider into the slope lift.

The leader of the expedition must have sufficient knowledge to be able to assess the suitability of possible launching and landing sites in the prevailing weather. Today there are few people with experience of doing this, and as a result such expeditions have become rare owing to the lack of someone to take charge.

Most hill soaring is done from club sites where the conditions are known and the best operating techniques are understood. When flying from strange hills, and particularly when making use of an unknown slope on a cross-country, such knowledge is not available; care should be taken to avoid flying into areas where turbulence or downdraughts are likely. When soaring high above a sharp-edged cliff, for example, the lift may be beautifully smooth and steady. However, there will probably be a curl-over close to the edge of the cliff so that an approach to land low over the top may be through violent turbulence. If there is any possibility of this, it is advisable to select a landing place some hundreds of yards back from the edge, and avoid flying low down over the cliff.

MOUNTAIN SOARING

While hill soaring at its worst can be dreary and monotonous, mountain soaring at its best is flying in the supreme form. Not only are mountains beautiful or magnificent in themselves, but by giving depth to the scene, make the pilot feel part of it, instead of merely a fly above an infinite flatness. When close to the mountain face he has an immense sensation of speed, sometimes akin to a fantastic form of ski-ing, and, unlike any other sort of flying, there is the unexpected charm of, literally, being able to go round a corner and discover what lies beyond.

The art of soaring amongst mountains, as distinct from wave soaring over them, has been highly developed in Europe particularly in the Alps. Mountain soaring makes use of a mixture of slope and thermal lift; in addition, lift from waves (see Chapter 9) can often be exploited.

Initially, bungey-launching sites were used, as for example at the Gaisberg in Austria. Later, with the development of winch-launching, it was found more convenient to use sites in the valleys. Now aero-towing is very largely used as it makes the initial climb much easier, and means that a particular site can be used in a wider range of wind directions.

As the wind usually blows straight up or down the valley, it is impractical to slope soar along the side, and it is necessary to use a spur or low slope of a lateral, or subsidiary, valley. From the winch launch the pilot flies to this face, and tries to work his way up to the top, but if the lift is inadequate he will have to retreat hurriedly to regain his landing field. The lift on these low slopes is usually confined to a narrow band very close to the side of the hill, and if the pilot flies along more than about 2 or 3 wingspans from the face, he will probably fail to stay up. If height is gained the beat can be extended, and it is sometimes possible to fly a considerable distance up the side valley, while working up towards the crests of the foothills. From above this hill the pilot can either go off to another higher ridge in the hope of obtaining further slope lift, or alternatively climb in thermals.

In reality the situation is not as simple as implied, partticularly to someone brought up in flat country who is used to thinking of wind as wind, and thermals as thermals, and who in addition, has the idea that the wind blows from a definite direction. When he starts soaring in the mountains such a pilot may be rudely awakened, since the wind and the thermals are inextricably mixed up; the wind direction in the valleys bearing little resemblance to what might be expected from a study of the weather chart.

Under favourable soaring conditions, once thermal activity has started, a wind will blow along the main valleys towards the centre of the mountain mass, and these winds will persist until thermal activity dies away; they are, in fact, very similar in behaviour to sea breezes. It is exceedingly difficult to assess the direction in which the wind is blowing on a given slope, but the matter is also made more complicated by the behaviour of the thermals themselves. They will seldom go up in the middle of a narrow valley, but instead will be found close to the mountain sides. Sometimes thermals will be found on both sides of a valley, but mainly they occur on the slopes facing the sun. The thermals on such a slope may go up continuously, and be sufficient to determine the wind direction on the mountain face, so that the thermal and slope lift may be often combined. The technique is to beat along the slope keeping close to it in the ordinary hill soaring manner until a thermal is encountered. Its lift may be surprisingly strong, of the order of 1000 ft per minute or so, and the pilot has the magnificent feeling of rushing along past the rock, going up at an angle of about 1 in 4.

Thermal lift is often not in the form of a circular bubble, but a narrow strip close to the side of the mountain, several hundred yards long. The pilot can make short beats in this good lift, turning outwards from the hill on each occasion, but if the length of the beat is too short he will have to circle. The first few times he does this will probably fill him with

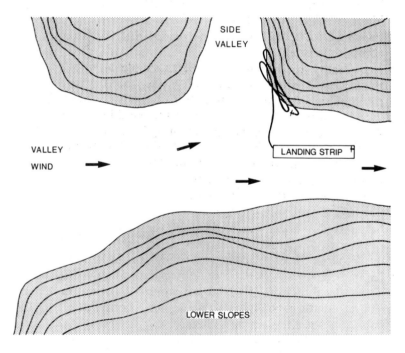

SIDE
VALLEY

VALLEY

WIND

LANDING STRIP

LOWER SLOPES

Fig 8.1 Slope soaring in mountain valleys. Wind blows along the main valley and produces slope lift on the corner of the side valley

alarm, but with practice it is possible to circle surprisingly close to the slope, if the wind is not strong, although the pilot will need to take care that he neither runs into the mountain horizontally, nor sinks on to it vertically. Using the combination of slope and thermal lift the pilot can reach the crest of the hill on which he is soaring, and then if no further lift is found, continue slope soaring above it. The surprising thing to anyone used to soaring on low hills is the small height which can be achieved above the crest of a mountain several thousand feet high. It may be only 200 or 300 ft. If the pilot wishes to go higher and is unable to find thermals he will have to work his way along the crest towards higher mountains or fly off to another face and once again work his way to the top.

If he decides on the first course he will usually find that the top of the crest is irregular in both height and direction, and that he has some awkward decisions to make. Should he scrape over the top of a knob sticking out from the ridge, or should he go round it? The lift above the crest of a side valley may be due to a wind which is striking the mountain only a few hundred feet below the top, and if much height is lost it may be impossible to regain it. The author (L.W.) has vivid memories of flying along a ridge which led into the Bernina group of mountains. The lift was reasonable and the glider was worked right up into the head of a valley, with a glacier at the bottom. On turning a corner in the valley all lift disappeared, and, when after having gone a few hundred yards further very strong sink was encountered, it was decided to return. On flying back along the same ridge that provided lift on the way out, but only 200 ft lower down, severe sink was met for a mile or more, and in desperation the glider was flown diagonally across the valley, but there was sink in the middle and on the far side. The main valley was finally reached with a height of only a few hundred feet; a total of 6000 ft having been lost in covering 8 miles. When selecting new slopes it is difficult to discover whether or not the wind is blowing on to them. The suitability of the slope will be influenced by its aspect and its surface. A dry rocky slope facing the sun will be more likely to produce lift than any other, although even this is not certain, and the foreigner in his bewilderment may be reduced to flying all round a mountain looking for lift.

While it is not particularly hard for the pilot to force himself to keep close to his 'home' mountain, it is much more difficult to go close to a strange face which has been reached after a long glide. However, it must be done if valuable height is not to be lost.

If a thermal can be found and used to take the glider up well above the peaks, the soaring is similar to that over flatter country, apart from the fantastic view. The distribution of thermals and clouds will be influenced by the ground underneath to a marked extent, there usually being least lift over the wider valleys. If the pilot can keep really high above the level of the summits, he can fly across country in a direct line, although he will naturally select his route to visit the best clouds, but if he is unable to do this he will be forced to work within reach of a valley to avoid the risk of finding himself low down over an inhospitable plateau.

Flights in among the mountains are much more difficult than those made high up, and considerable cunning and courage is needed to do such things as creeping over a pass from one valley to the next. One of the finest mountain flights was made by F. Legler in 1947 who, on a trip lasting no less than $10\frac{1}{2}$ hr, soared among mountains for a distance of over 300 km across Switzerland without ever once getting above the level of the peaks. On several occasions he was right down among the foothills, and forced to spend long periods in weak lift scraping up enough height to get to the next possible slope.

It is no use pretending that mountain soaring is inherently as safe as ordinary thermalling, but by knowing and respecting the hazards the risk is quite acceptable. The problems that the pilot has to contend with are: 1. Hitting the mountain due to a moment's inattention: 2. Clouds stuffed with mountains: 3. Invisible cables: and 4. Poor landing fields.

1 This point is self-evident. It is surprising how very few people have hit a mountain hard, although several have returned with branch marks or scrapes on their wingtips.

2 It is most unwise to go into cloud unless the base is above the level of all the mountain peaks for some considerable distance around. The reason for this is that cloud can build up and vary its base exceedingly rapidly. If a pilot enters a small cloud just above some medium height mountains, and the cloud then develops and spreads out horizontally, he may be unable to come out unless he flies a considerable distance, in which case there is a risk of flying into a mountain which was previously in clear air. A pilot from flat country is apt to think of cumulus as having a definite base at a definite height, but among mountains this simply is not true. The air in neighbouring valleys may be different, and produces clouds with their base at different heights, but in addition large masses of cloud can form suddenly well below the level of the ordinary cloud. The speed with which a slope can become covered, or a valley filled with this orographic cloud is staggering to the visitor. It is an axiom that mountains, clouds and aircraft should not be mixed.

3 There are two sorts of cables strung up in mountains, electrical and transport. The spans used for the former can be much greater than in flat country, and be a considerable height above the valley bottom; as the pylons are inconspicuous the cables will be unnoticeable, unless, as is sometimes the case, they are adorned with yellow spheres.

Transport cables cannot be so marked, as pulleys have to run on the cables, and they range in size from nearly 2 in. in diameter, used to support cable cars holding 100 passengers, to $\frac{1}{4}$ in. in diameter slung up to shift bundles of wood and fodder, there are also the more elaborate cable ways of foresters for the transport of logs to the sawmills. The end attachments of all these cables are usually insignificant, and since the wires themselves are invisible they are a real hazard; although sometimes their presence can be deduced by felling on the mountainside, or a sawmill at the bottom.

4 The problem of landing is not great, but is made a little more complicated by the small size, by the slope of the fields, and by the difficulty of discovering the wind direction.

It is to be hoped that more mountain soaring sites will be developed other than in the Alps, as it is without question a most exhilarating form of flying. In case it might be supposed that it is only practicable where the valleys are cultivated, it should be realized that the landing places can be quite widely separated, as although the glider is working close to the mountain side, it is well above the bottom of the valley, and able to fly some distance before having to land. Any lowland pilot of Silver Standard who has the opportunity to get up into the mountains with a glider should take it, for there is little doubt that he will enjoy himself immensely.

One of the most interesting developments in soaring so far has been the combination of mountain, wave, and thermal soaring in the same flight. A number of flights have started by slope soaring, working this up to wave lift, exploiting the system, and then flying away from the wave area to continue the flight on thermals.

A reverse technique of concluding a thermal flight by using waves in the evening is more difficult to apply, firstly because the thermals may be weak on the edge of the wave zone, and secondly because the pilot will probably be trying to slope soar and locate waves over country with which he is not familiar. This technique was, however, used to great effect from St Yan, France, in 1956 by using a northerly wind over the mountains to the east of the Lower Rhone.

Chapter 9

Waves

When the variations of wind speed and air temperature with height are suitable, ground features can produce large disturbances in the airflow above and to the lee of them. A ridge may produce useful lift extending to many times its own height, and the streamlines may lie in a series of waves downwind of the ridge. The amplitude of the waves and the strength of the lift may increase with height instead of dying away like ordinary hill lift. In general, favourable conditions involve a stable airstream and an increase of wind speed with height. Even the relatively small mountains in Wales and Scotland produce useful waves up to 20,000 ft or so; 30,000 ft has been attained in the Alps and in the lee of the Massif Central of France; and the World Height Record of 46,267 ft was achieved in the lee of the Sierra Nevada in the U.S.A. The usual object of flying in waves is simply to go high, often in the pursuit of a height Diamond, but they have been exploited for cross-country purposes, notably in New Zealand. The theory of cross-country soaring in waves is explained in Chapter 17.

PREPARATIONS

Wave flying often involves exposing the pilot and the glider to low air pressures and temperatures for long periods, sometimes coupled with difficult navigation and periods of severe turbulence. The physiological considerations of Chapter 14 become very important and suitable preparation is essential for safe operation.

It goes without saying that the glider should be really serviceable and since it is likely to be exposed to extreme conditions, certain additional precautions and modifications are desirable. Control cables should not be very tight on the ground, since they will become appreciably tighter at low

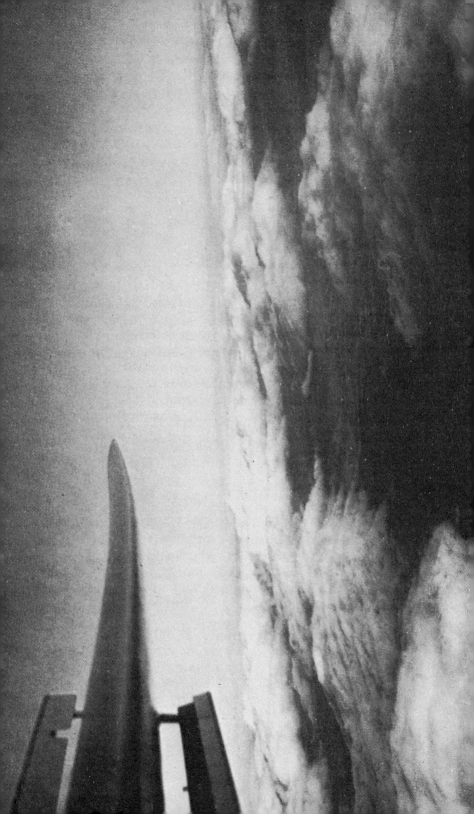

temperatures, possibly to the extent of making the controls quite stiff. Control mechanisms should be lubricated with silicone grease or an anti-freeze grease such as DTD 577, and on gliders with retracting undercarriages it will be advisable to apply liberal quantities of grease to bearings and locking mechanisms to prevent their becoming jammed with frozen mud.

Great care should be taken to prevent draughts within the cockpit: a cool breeze around the feet in normal soaring may be pleasant, but when its temperature is $-25°C$, it rapidly becomes intolerable. Common sources of draughts are badly fitting canopies, leaks around the towing hook, and from the rear fuselage or wing roots, drain holes, badly-fitting clear vision panels and so on. Most draughts can be prevented by the judicious use of foam plastic strip or masking tape, but care must be taken not to interfere with the proper working of the release control or cockpit canopy, and the normal ventilator should function when required.

The elimination of draughts in the small volume of the cockpit immediately introduces another severe problem: that of internal misting or icing. Since the pilot is likely to be using oxygen for much of a serious flight, the best solution is to pipe the mask exhaust to the outside world instead of allowing it to increase the humidity inside the cockpit. The diameter of the pipe should be large, ideally 2 in or so, to avoid restriction from internal icing. Such measures should only be undertaken with advice from the manufacturer of the mask: for example, it would be very dangerous to fit a long pipe to the outlet from many types of mask used with continuous-flow oxygen systems. The 'outlet' is also an inlet, and the pilot might well find himself inhaling used air with a dangerously high carbon-dioxide content.

Internal cockpit icing can be at least disconcerting and

Plate VIII Wave clouds near Portmoak, Scotland. The clouds are at about 6000 ft and the photograph was taken at about 13,000 ft whilst descending from 15,000 ft. The wind is blowing from the right to the left of the picture

possibly dangerous. Once it starts, it becomes quite impossible to rub it off the inside of the canopy fast enough, and most ventilator/demisters are unlikely to be sufficiently effective. In clear air, the pilot finds himself switching on the gyro instruments only to discover that their faces are rapidly icing-up too. The expensive solution, given enough battery capacity, is to fit an electrically-heated windscreen but this is something of a counsel of perfection. Alternatively, the inside of the canopy and the faces of the instruments may be wiped over with a suitable anti-icing fluid such as glycerine, or even potato. A cloth moistened with the de-icing fluid should also be carried. Aerosols of the type used to clear ice from the outside of car windscreens must not be used: they emit strong vapours and may damage perspex.

Oxygen systems are described in Chapter 19, so it will suffice here to say that the quantity of oxygen carried must be adequate (the little 230-litre bottles are not big enough) and the mask and tubing must be suitable for use at low temperatures. It is worth remembering that a climb can be quite rapid, and the pilot should not be trying to fit the mask when concentrating on flying. The mask should be carefully adjusted beforehand and should either be worn properly from take-off, or should be hanging round the pilot's neck or attached to his helmet ready for use.

Really warm clothing is essential, to an extent which surprises even those accustomed to bleak airfields. The pilot is indulging in very little physical activity in a very cold environment and easily becomes chilled, particularly at the extremities. Apart from the obvious provisions mentioned in Chapter 14, particular care should be taken at the ankles and wrists. For example, ski-trousers which fit into ankle-boots are greatly preferable to ordinary trousers, which permit draughts to play upon the ankles and lower legs. A track or polar suit, or even pyjamas, can be worn underneath. Dry socks are essential, and a lined flying-suit completes the ensemble. Thus clad, the pilot is satisfactorily insulated against stratospheric temperatures at the cost of being rather a tight fit in the cockpit. Gloves are also essential, and most pilots will have their favourite type which are warm enough, without interfering with the delicate use of the controls. As with ankles, the wrists should be well covered. Choice of headgear may well be conditioned by the need to listen to a radio loudspeaker, but whatever type of hat is worn, it should protect the ears.

Many established wave soaring sites insist on radio. It can be a useful source of information on wind strength, extent of cloud cover and ground turbulence, thus contributing to the safety of the operation. The ability to compare notes with other pilots in the vicinity will also be helpful. It is worth remembering that the effective capacity of lead/ acid batteries is reduced at low temperatures, and the characteristics of transistors may alter sufficiently to cause considerable distortion over the radio.

PRE-FLIGHT PRECAUTIONS

Many pilots make special journeys to unfamiliar sites for wave flying. In such circumstances the surrounding terrain should be studied so that the flying, which may be quite difficult in itself, is not carried out against a background of worry about navigation and landing fields.

In addition to having good maps of the locality, it is useful to be shown the countryside from a light aeroplane: it may well be covered with snow, and difficult to recognize from the map. Prominent landmarks such as a large town, a river, an airfield, and an oddly-shaped wood — all clearly visible from a great height — should be noted, as should potential sources of confusion, such as a parallel valley downwind of one's home valley and ridge, and potential bolt-holes if one runs out of lift or visibility. The local pilots are usually all too willing to provide endless advice of variable reliability on the probable location of good lift, and the likelihood or otherwise of the gaps in the wave cloud closing-up or layer cloud developing below.

In addition to the obvious pre-flight routines and the various elaborations mentioned above, it is worth stressing once again that one can encounter very great turbulence, both during the launch and in free flight. The cockpit may be more cluttered than usual and the pilot's movements may be somewhat restricted by extra clothing and connections to the oxygen mask. It is therefore vital to ensure that all the gear including cameras is properly stowed, and that the pilot can operate all the controls fully and easily, and is tightly strapped in.

FLYING

The launch may consist of a short winch launch into hill lift or a long aero-tow to several thousand feet, miles away from the flying field, or anything in between. One may be launched in entirely smooth conditions, although the ground-wind may be strong, or one may have to traverse very turbulent regions, such as the rotor beneath a wave cloud. In the case of a tow through turbulent conditions, it is not uncommon to find air so rough that the pilot's ability to maintain his position relative to the tug is taxed to the utmost. There may well be a real risk of having to abandon the tow, and any sensible tug pilot will arrange his route so that the glider can return to the site.

When flying in hill lift, there may be a problem in contacting the wave, even when it is known to exist. If the pilot encounters smooth lift, even if very weak, it pays to assume that it is wave. He should attempt to remain more or less over the same place on the ground, gently exploring the vicinity. Needless to say, the behaviour of nearby gliders is often a good guide to the location of lift.

Genuine wave lift is usually very smooth indeed, to an almost uncanny extent. Having trimmed the glider accurately, one can sometimes sit for minutes on end, with only the lightest of touches to the controls. The machine seems poised in space, the only visible motion being the gentle rotation of the altimeter pointer. The problem, of course, is to stay in the best lift. Since the regions of lift consist of bands running crosswind and more or less stationary with respect to the ground, the situation is rather similar to hill soaring. If near a lenticular wave cloud, it is often possible to make a series of beats a little ahead of the cloud exactly as would be done along a hill. But in the absence of cloud, or if the pilot is at some greatly different height from the lenticulars, it may be quite difficult not to drift up or down wind. One would like to fly at the speed for minimum rate of sink, and the calmness of wave tends to encourage one to fly slowly. If the local wind speed is less than the glider's airspeed, it will be necessary to head somewhat crosswind, and perform a series of beats along the wave. It can easily happen that the wind speed at appreciable heights is greater than the speed for minimum rate of sink. The glider must then be flown faster than this ideal speed to remain stationary over the ground whilst facing straight into wind.

When flying at a considerable height, it may be quite difficult to judge when the glider is stationary over a point on the ground, and since the band of lift may be only a few hundred feet wide, it can be quite easy to drift out of it without being sure whether it lies ahead or behind. Apart from the decreased variometer reading, flying out of the lift is often accompanied by mild 'cobblestone' turbulence. In such circumstances, it pays to assume that the glider has drifted downwind out of the lift: speed should be increased, and the glider be moved upwind. Only if the lift is not regained should the opposite correction be tried. The point is that making headway over the ground in, say a 50-knot wind is not easy. If the downwind correction is tried first, and turns out to be unsuccessful, it is then necessary to make good an appreciable amount of lost ground whilst flying at a high speed with a correspondingly great rate of sink through air which is itself sinking. If, on the other hand, the upwind correction is unsuccessful, it is easy to move downwind.

As with any other sort of lift, the strength of waves is very variable from day to day and in different places on the same day. One can drift slowly upwards at 1 knot, or be exposed to the heady experience of this astonishingly smooth lift with the variometer needles hard on the stops. The pilot may also wish to explore different parts of the wave, moving from one band of lift to another. Going downwind presents no problem, since he will arrive quickly at the next wave with little loss of height. Penetrating upwind to the next wave is a different story. Suppose the strengths of the maximum up and down components of the wind velocity are about the same. The glider is climbing at 4 knots and the wind speed is 50 knots. At this speed, the glider's rate of sink will be about $1\frac{1}{2}$ knots, so the vertical velocity of the air will total $5\frac{1}{2}$ knots. To advance to the upwind wave, the pilot flies at, say, 75 knots, when his rate of sink is now 3 knots. The maximum total rate of sink he is likely to encounter becomes $5\frac{1}{2} + 3$, i.e., $8\frac{1}{2}$ knots. Clearly, he can lose a great deal of height in such circumstances.

POTENTIAL HAZARDS

The main sources of potential danger peculiar to wave flying are:

1 Running out of oxygen;
2 Closing-in of cloud below or around the glider;
3 Nightfall.

As the pilot wanders around the area of lift looking for that little extra height, time and oxygen can be consumed quickly. The pilot must keep an eye on the pressure gauge, and descend to a safe level before the supply is exhausted. Obviously, a knowledge of one's own tolerance to heights is useful, but the effects of anoxia are so insidious that it is unwise to press on until little oxygen is left, on the assumption that a rapid descent is always available by using the airbrakes. Although anoxia is unlikely to occur in a quick descent from 20,000 ft or so, the only satisfactory procedure is to keep enough oxygen for the descent plus a margin.

There are plenty of wave soaring sites where the pilot simply must not lose sight of the ground, usually because the terrain away from the airfield is mountainous or otherwise unsuitable for landing. At others, no great harm would result provided that any continuous layer of cloud is at a reasonable height above the ground. The pilot must exercise his own judgement, having regard to his knowledge of the locality and perhaps helped by information over the radio from the ground, and remembering that he can fly a very long way down wind from a great height in a strong wind. He should also bear in mind the possibility that confident statements from local pilots to the effect that 'the gap in front of the second wave never closes in' may not be entirely accurate, and that once a hole starts to cloud over, it may fill in completely with startling rapidity.

Waves often improve towards the end of a day, and there may be a temptation to go on flying just a little longer, particularly if the pilot is just a few hundred feet short of Diamond height. This tendency can be accentuated by the feeling that one can always open the airbrakes and descend very quickly, and by the fact that the glider may still be bathed in the rays of the setting sun although the ground is almost dark. It is as well to remember that, even using the airbrakes, a descent can be quite prolonged: even at a rate of sink of 20 knots, it takes 10 minutes to descend 20,000 ft, and 10 minutes can easily represent the difference between slightly marginal twilight and almost complete darkness. Of course, given terminal velocity brakes, much higher rates of descent can be achieved, but more often the possibility of running into strong turbulence will discourage very high speeds.

Wave flying is often a singularly beautiful, quiet and enjoyable form of aviation. One tends to view the distant earth with a sort of Olympian detachment. But, as is usual in flying, such peace of mind has to be earned by making sensible preparation in advance and by keeping a constant lookout for changing weather.

Chapter 10

Instrument Flying

A rising thermal will form cloud when it is cooled below the temperature at which it can hold all its moisture in the invisible vapour state.

As the moisture condenses heat is developed, with the result that a mass of clear air which has a lapse rate of 3°C per thousand feet possesses a lower lapse rate of 1.5°C when it becomes cloud. If the lapse rate of the air away from the cloud is fairly constant it follows that a mass of rising air will find itself more buoyant after the cloud has condensed. It is for this reason that upcurrents inside cloud are frequently stronger than those below. A thermal will form a cloud only of cumulus type, the size ranging from the very small fair-weather cumulus to vast cumulo-nimbus towering to over 40,000 ft, and the shape varying from the classical small cauliflower to the thunderhead with its anvil. The size and shape is dependent on that of the original thermal, the lapse rate of the air, and the humidity.

There are three reasons for making use of the upcurrents found inside cumulus:

1 It is interesting to fly high.
2 A glide from a great height may enable the pilot to go across poor areas or water, or on occasion to get to other clouds where lift can be found.
3 The lift in cloud is usually stronger than underneath, and this helps in achieving higher average speeds.

The actual flying of the glider inside cloud is more difficult than in clear air, since it is necessary to use instruments. How this is done will be considered later. For the moment we will deal with the technique of using clouds as distinct from the handling of the glider.

THE USE OF CLOUDS

The strategy of when, and when not, to use clouds is probably best understood by considerations of the tactics involved, and to illustrate this we will consider a flight made on a day with fairly large cumulus, base 4000 ft, and tops 10,000 ft.

A pilot circling in a thermal will find himself climbing up towards one of these cumulus clouds. If the thermal is newly formed, the cloud will not appear until he is quite close to condensation level. It will then take the form of a few wisps of white vapour. As he climbs the vague wisps will grow in size, become more solid, and frequently give the impression of whirling about. After a minute or so the wisps will coalesce and form into a little solid cloud, which if seen from the side will seem to have a flat bottom, and to the pilot seeing it from underneath will be roughly circular in shape. As the pilot climbs on up the cloud will grow bigger, and as he approaches the bottom it will be seen to be less definite in outline. If the bubble persists and he goes on flying in the best lift he will find himself circling up into cloud. It is sometimes, but not always, noticeable in bigger cumulus, that the horizon is obscured by cloud while the glider is still in clear air, thus showing that the cloud has a slightly concave bottom.

If the pilot goes on circling, first the horizon and then the ground underneath will disappear and he will be flying in a pale grey world. The feel of the glider will be just the same, although it often seems as if it is making a more muffled sound After a while the pilot may find that the rate of climb has increased over that which he was getting in clear air. Despite this the lift will often stay perfectly smooth, and the pilot can go on circling at what he hopes is a constant angle of bank. However, if he is unlucky or unskilful he may find that only part of his circle is in lift and that he is not climbing in the other part, and that because of this the air is rougher. If he has no method of determining his heading he will find it difficult to shift his circles into the area of better lift. He can do it only by feel, either by straightening up a little while after he has experienced the worst sink, and then flying straight for a few seconds before continuing his turn in the same direction, or, and this is usually more profitable, straightening up immedi-

ately he feels a real surge of lift, flying straight for a few seconds and then turning as before. Either procedure is difficult
and until the pilot has gained experience, which can of course
be increased by visualizing the problem while circling in clear
air, he will often find that his efforts at centring make matters
worse, and that he either flies into continuous sink, or comes
rushing out of the side of the cloud. In this latter case he
should get clear of the cloud, have a look to see where the main
mass lies, and then fly in again on a compass course. With any
luck he will strike the main upcurrent and can circle once
more.

Since a glider is always sinking down in relation to the air
in which it is flying, it is obviously quite impossible for it to
come right out of the top of a domed cumulus, as this would
imply a clear air upcurrent blowing out through the top of the
cloud. If the pilot can keep in the lift he will find that as he
approaches the top this decreases and the air becomes more
turbulent. This is usually quite marked, the turbulence being
of a characteristic nature. If the pilot continues circling he will
find that his rate of climb gradually gets less and less until he
is no longer climbing. The cloud will appear glaringly white,
and he may be able to see the form of the sun through it.
Sooner or later he will emerge from the side and find himself
a few hundred feet below the top of the main massif of the
cloud, or one of its cells. The contrast between the uniform
greyness inside the cloud and the brightness of the blue sky,
whiteness of the clouds and distance of the earth below is
magnificent, and fully justifies any queasy feeling which may
be felt on the way up inside.

If the pilot flies around keeping an eye on the cloud in
which he has climbed, he may see that a buttress on one side
grows rapidly both in height and size until it becomes even
bigger than the original main mass. He will notice that when
decay starts the cloud loses its sharp outline, and develops rifts
so that it can be seen through. Sometimes decay will start at
the base while the top goes on growing, while at other times a
pillar will fade away while the main mass remains active and
pushes up another pillar in a different place. In the first example the bottom decays because it is no longer fed by a thermal

bubble; in the second, another bubble comes up and enters the cloud at the bottom, thrusts through and forms another buttress. It often happens that the new buttress grows on the upwind side of the cloud.

As the cloud grows it may enter heights at which the wind is blowing at a different speed from its base, and there will be a tendency for deflection from the vertical form which it should be expected to take, the cloud being seen to lean. Usually the wind speed gets stronger with height so that the clouds lean down wind, the lift being found on the windward side with a tendency for downcurrents to form on the lee side. Sometimes the wind changes direction with height and will cause the clouds to slope accordingly. Wind shear is unlikely to alter much in the course of a flight, and therefore once the side of the cloud on which the lift lies has been found, this will usually hold good for the rest of the day.

Entry into cloud is not always easy. The pilot may climb up to within a few hundred feet of cloud base, and then the lift appears to fade out. By wandering around underneath the cloud it is often possible to find a small patch of lift which will take the glider up and into it. This patch, probably only a small proportion of the total area of the cloud, is sometimes located near the centre, and other times very close to the edge. In clouds of this type the lift may be good once the pilot has succeeded in getting well inside.

If the cumulus is very small or shallow, it will be almost impossible to enter as the upcurrents at the base will be weak. But large clouds which may seem shallow can be deceptive. There are days when cumulus form rapidly, and on reaching an inversion, or stable layer of air, spread out horizontally and persist for some time as strato-cumulus. Sometimes they will gradually fade away and new cumulus will form, but occasionally thermals coming up from the ground may succeed in penetrating the stable layer and going up through it to form quite high clouds, with a ruff of the old cloud girdled round them. From underneath it is easy to dismiss such clouds as useless, but if lift into them can be found, it is sometimes possible to climb quite high, and come out of a pillar projecting above the lower layer of old cloud.

Turbulence. Cumulo-nimbus clouds are always large, and extend to heights which bring in problems of icing, and oxygen for the pilot. If turbulence is met it may be severe, and any pilot who willingly enters such clouds should be competent at instrument flying, and possess a glider with speed-limiting brakes. Climbing in cumulo-nimbus can be immensely exciting, in a similar manner to climbing high peaks in the Himalayas.

The glider is designed to withstand flying at certain airspeeds, and being subjected to gusts of a certain severity. The two are interconnected since on entering a violent gust when flying at low speeds, the wings will stall and limit the loads imposed on the machine. When entering a strong updraught at high speeds the wings will not stall, but instead develop a large amount of lift and impose heavy accelerations on the aircraft. Most gliders can, in theory, withstand gusts of any strength at speeds up to about $2\frac{1}{4}$ times the stalling speed. When flying in cloud which is liable to be rough it is advisable to fly at slow speeds, which will normally be the operational requirement also. High speeds will only be attained unwillingly, and they should be avoided by the pilot opening his brakes if he finds his speed rising above about 60–70 knots.

ICING

Apart from gust effects there are other phenomena which may affect the safety of a glider flying in cloud. These are hail, ice and lightning. Hail, because in large sizes it will literally batter the aircraft, breaking any fabric covering and possibly the cockpit cover. Ice can be a nuisance in two ways; by jamming the controls and brakes, and by the effect of its shape and weight on performance. The avoidance of jamming is largely a matter of design and the pilot has little control over it, but the fault is most apparent with the dive brakes. It was at one time thought that it was advisable to open the brakes every 500–1000 ft of climb in order to break up any small bits of ice which may have joined the brakes to the wing. It is now found that this practice does more harm than good as it allows in more water under the brakes, which then freezes.

Ice normally forms on the wing in a rather peculiar manner. It builds up along the front of the leading edge in a series of small lumps, looking like a large rubber scrubbing brush. Ice will form also on the front of the cockpit cover, pitot tube etc. In exceptional circumstances the ice can build up very rapidly and spread right back over almost the entire surface of the aircraft, but on a climb through freezing level in an ordinary large cumulus the amount of ice collected is quite small, 3 in. by $\frac{1}{2}$ in on the wings, and about $\frac{1}{2}$ in thick on the front of the cockpit cover. Ice obviously affects the performance to an unknown extent, and takes a long time to melt and fall off even in bright sunlight. The first sign of this happening is often when a lump from the wings or canopy hits the tail with a frightening bang. The glider is not usually clear of ice until it is 2000 or 3000 ft below freezing level.

LIGHTNING

Lightning is a real hazard, it can be present inside cumulonimbus clouds, beneath them, and occasionally in clear air between two clouds. It is dangerous for two reasons: the pilot can be shocked or electrocuted, and the glider can be damaged. It is unwise to enter into areas where it is known that severe lightning is likely to be present; few people would do this anyway. The difficulty arises in assessing the risk of flying in or near cloud on days when there is only a chance of lightning occurring.

The risk to the pilot is reduced if the aircraft is properly bonded, by ensuring that the large metallic parts are connected together, and if these are connected to discharge points on the wing tips and tail. The connections between the various parts are usually made with flat strips of copper instead of wire, since, for the same weight, they can carry a larger high-voltage current.

The safety of the pilot can be further increased by placing him in a *Faraday Cage*; this may involve additional conductors around the front of the fuselage and possibly across the cockpit canopy.

A lightning strike on an aircraft is always very alarming, but on landing there may be nothing to show for it except some

torn fabric or possibly a few pin holes in the wing surface.
Despite this, the aircraft must be inspected with extreme care.
All control cables must be removed and examined since there
have been cases where they have been found to be fused although there was nothing visible from the outside. On a
wooden aircraft, a lightning strke on to a wing may be marked
by only a tiny pinhole; the spar boom inside, however, may
be reduced to the consistency of dry pith.

TACTICS OF CLOUD–FLYING

On a cross-country flight the decision to use or not use
cloud will depend on whether the extra height gained is
worthwhile. If the clouds are small and entry difficult it will
be seldom profitable to go into them unless the air ahead
looks dud, and it is necessary to gain every inch of height
regardless of time wasted. If the clouds are larger, entry will
be easier and the height gained greater. Although the lift inside is usually stronger than underneath, it should be realized
that it is more difficult to find it, and unless the pilot is very
good at getting quickly on to a compass course he can waste
a great deal of time, and height, blundering around inside the
cloud when he should be on his way to the next objective.

With medium-sized clouds where it is possible to gain three
thousand or so feet, cloud flying is usually worth while. Each
climb will take the glider 10-15 miles, and as clouds of this
size will seldom be as far apart as this, the pilot can pick and
choose the best ones to use. After climbing up in one cloud,
coming out and gliding on, it is very tempting to charge
through any cloud which may be encountered on the way.
This may be inevitable if there are large masses about, but if
the cumulus are isolated it is often inadvisable to do so; finding the part of the cloud which produces lift is often difficult when attacking a shapeless heap of unknown age from
the side. It may be preferable to choose a cloud which can
be reached at its base, and enter through the bottom. On such
days with medium-sized clouds it is inadvisable to make rules
about using or not using clouds. If the thermal takes the glider
easily up into cloud, it is as well to use it until the lift starts
weakening. On the other hand should entry prove difficult

the flight can be continued without wasting further time. Perhaps the next cloud will prove easier of access.

CUMULO–NIMBUS

The term 'cumulo-nimbus' can describe clouds of widely differing size and ferocity. There are some which are merely overgrown cumulus, and others which are storms of such violence that they may wreck any aircraft. On days when cloud development is such that storms are likely to grow the pilot should realize that the little cumulus which he enters without a care in the world may grow to huge proportions and become quite violent during the time in which he is circling up inside it.

The glider pilot can divide cumulo-nimbus clouds into two types, the heat thunderstorm, and the frontal storm. The first type will usually occur on days without strong winds, and the cloud will grow as the result of powerful convection starting originally from ground heating. Under certain conditions, once the cloud has built up, it may be self-stoking. The simplest cloud of this type is similar to an overgrown cumulus. The growth is the same to start with, but the cloud extends much higher and may develop an anvil top composed of ice crystals. Hail will fall when the cloud has reached maximum size.

Larger summer thunderstorm clouds may consist of a vast mass composed of several cells, each of which may be at a different stage of development. For example, hail or heavy rain may be falling from one part, while in another strong upcurrents may be found. When flying inside the cloud from one cell to another extreme turbulence may be found. Alternatively a flight in a thunderhead cumulo-nimbus may be perfectly straightforward, smooth steady lift being found over a large area, and despite the alarming size of the cloud no great turbulence may be encountered. Some turbulence will always exist in any cloud towards the extreme top since a current of air which is slowing down assumes an irregular motion. The main upcurrent itself is usually smooth, and when climbing in it turbulence is encountered only at the edge. It follows therefore that if the pilot is lucky enough to go up in the central core of the cell, everything may be perfectly smooth until he decides to leave it, when flying into the dead or descending air in or around the upcurrent it may become very rough.

Before going into any cloud it is always prudent to decide on what heading to fly should conditions become unpleasant, and in thunderstorms it is probably wise to come out on the same side as entering. Clouds of this type seldom develop before the afternoon, although they often continue into the night.

The frontal type of cumulo-nimbus can consist of the classical line of cloud associated with cold fronts or secondary cold fronts, or an isolated mass. The cold air is undercutting the warmer air ahead of it and forcing it up. Such clouds, which may have a roll cloud in front of them, sometimes stretch for hundreds of miles along the line of the front. Strong upcurrents are found immediately on the downwind side of the cloud, and it is possible to gain height in this without entering cloud. The roll cloud in front is usually exceedingly turbulent.

Strong upcurrents also exist in the main part of the cloud mass, while downcurrents will be found in the rain or hail at the back, and also in the area of blue sky still further behind. Such textbook cold fronts are seldom found in England, but are more common over continental land masses. In England the main front is usually much less clearly defined although secondary fronts do occasionally approximate to pattern. Cold fronts are usually seen as a hard line of cloud with a considerably lower and darker base than that of any indeterminate cloud ahead.

Smaller clouds of very similar characteristics occur in 'April shower' weather, and such clouds may be only a mile or so in extent, although they are often larger. The storm itself does not depend on convection from one particular piece of ground. The rear side of the cloud is usually clearly defined, and will produce rain, hail, or snow, and may have a very low base in the area from which precipitation is coming.

To a pilot flying in front of the cloud it will appear to move downwind towards him, and when flying underneath he will find that if he circles in the lift on the downwind side he will soon find himself in sink and rain on the upwind side of the cloud. This is because the cloud is, as it were, travelling downwind through the air; it does this by building up on the downwind side and fading away on the upwind. When involved in clouds of this type it is most important to keep on going downwind.

In strong precipitation the cloud base may be several thousand feet lower than that elsewhere. On this sort of day it is obviously hazardous to go into cloud, particularly if there is any possibility of high land or hills being in cloud, or very heavy rain.

NAVIGATION IN CLOUD

As it is improbable that the glider will be equipped with any radio-navigational aids or be able to obtain astro sights or radar plots from the ground, it follows that when out of sight of the ground the pilot must rely entirely on dead reckoning for his position. This theory of plotting by dead reckoning is explained at interminable length in treatises on aircraft navigation. In our case we are not likely to be in cloud for any great length of time, nor do we wish to know our position with great accuracy, so very simplified methods can be used. The important things to know are wind speed and direction, and the time of entry into cloud. On a simple climb in a large cloud the whole procedure can be done mentally provided that one or two notes are made. For example:

1 12.40   Entered cloud Taunton.
2 12.58   Still in cloud, set course 090°.
3 13.07   Came out of cloud. Position?

The wind is supposed to be 25 knots from the SW. About one third of an hour was spent circling so that the glider moved 8 miles NE from the point of entry. It then flew with the wind on its quarter for 9 minutes which is roughly one sixth of an hour. Ground speed will be 50 knots (flying speed) plus something a bit less than 25, say 18. So ground speed equals 68 knots. Distance covered in one sixth hour is therefore about 11 miles. The actual track will be a little North of

East so from the point of entry the glider will have gone 8 miles NE and then 11 miles E of NE. It will be therefore roughly 18 miles ENE of Taunton. With a little practice mental calculations of this nature can be done without much difficulty and with an accuracy of ± 20%. There is no object in trying to calculate more accurately than this since the wind speed and direction will never be known with precision, and it is most improbable that the pilot will in practice manage to fly a straight course. However, it is well worth while making this type of approximate calculation. As soon as the pilot emerges from cloud his position is known within a few miles, and this usually enables an accurate pin-point check to be made, even if only a small area of ground is visible through the clouds. Such calculations are particularly necessary when flying near the coast in order to avoid being drifted out to sea.

It often happens that the time in cloud is so short, or the view on emergence so extensive that there is no navigational problem, and no calculations are necessary. However, occasionally horizontal layers of cloud may build up rapidly and flight in cloud continue for an hour or more. It is at times like these that one gets worried about flying out over the sea, into airways, or other inhospitable areas. Such worries can be limited by the dead reckoning plot, provided, and only provided, that the pilot took his time and position on entering cloud, and has some idea of the time he spent circling and flying straight.

In two-seater flying all this work can be done by the second pilot who, if at all competent, should always know the position of the glider within a few miles. Quite apart from the fact that he can if necessary use a slide rule and draw vector diagrams, he can also work back, and by knowing when and where the glider went into cloud, the time spent circling, the courses flown, and the position and time of exit, discover the strength of the wind.

INSTRUMENT FLYING

In order to be able to fly a glider in cloud it is necessary to know three things:

1 Whether the aircraft is turning or flying straight.
2 Its speed, or attitude and
3 Whether the aircraft is slipping or skidding.

An experienced glider pilot can obtain information concerning the last two points without any instruments – the speed by the noise, and the slip or skid by whether he is sitting upright in his seat or leaning one way or the other. No one, however, regardless of his experience can find out if he is flying straight or turning gently or rapidly unless he has either some external reference point, or instruments. The reason for this is that the balance mechanism in the human head, while capable of detecting fairly small variations in rates of turn cannot distinguish between a steady turn and movement in a straight line. Most misleading impressions can arise. For example, if after circling continuously the pilot straightens up, he gets a strong feeling that he is starting to turn in the opposite direction. It must be strongly emphasized that all turning perceptions are thoroughly unreliable for the purpose of flying an aircraft blind. Knowledge of the amount or rate of turn can only be obtained from instruments, and the pilot's senses must be disregarded. Considerable self-discipline and training will be required before the pilot can fly blind with any degree of reliability.

As was mentioned earlier a skilled pilot can obtain indications of speed and slip or skid from his senses, although in general it is easier to use instruments. Most blind flying instruction, however, overemphasizes the unreliability of the pilot's senses, which at any rate for gliding, seems to be a mistake. Merely because the turning senses are useless is no reason for insisting that pilots should refrain from using their hearing, or the feel on their bottoms. There is little doubt that the pilot who flies to some extent by feel in keeping his speed steady and avoiding slip and skid will obtain a smoother ride than the one who relies entirely on instruments.

The minimum instruments required for blind flying are a turn-and-slip indicator, altimeter, ASI and compass. A rate of climb indicator is also necessary if any useful soaring is to be done.

The entry into cloud from a glider will normally be made from underneath while in circling flight. The turn-and-slip indicator should be switched on a few minutes before entering, and the position which the turn needle takes up noted while doing a suitably banked turn, say $20-30°$. The glider should be trimmed so that it circles hands off at a slightly greater speed than normal. The rate of turn is kept constant by keeping the turn needle steady. If the needle shows an increased rate of turn this is reduced by taking off bank with the ailerons and a little rudder at the same time. The speed is adjusted with the elevators, and slip or skid as in ordinary flight. It is very difficult to keep a constant rate of turn, and the usual tendency is for the rate of turn to increase. This must be watched for, and as soon as an increase is noted the bank must be reduced. On a stable glider the control of speed is usually simple, once the pilot has learnt not to over-correct. The technique is to make very small movements with the stick and to check these movements as soon as the speed starts to increase or decrease, as the case may be. If the movement is not checked until the speed has reached the desired value, a further correction inevitably will be required. Corrections for slip and skid are easily made and are in any case of much less importance.

If the rate of turn increases appreciably it will signify that the aircraft is in a steeply banked turn. If the speed should then increase, as it probably will, and the pilot attempt to reduce it by pulling the stick back, he will find that this movement, instead of producing the desired effect, will result in a large increase in the rate of turn, and the feeling of considerable 'g'. What has happened is that by pulling back on the stick the pilot has tightened up the turn and started the aircraft going in a fast spiral dive. To recover, it is necessary first of all to reduce the rate of turn, and then, when the glider is flying straight or in only a gentle turn, the speed can be carefully reduced. The dive brakes should be opened gently if twice stalling speed is reached. These high speed spirals can be avoided by paying particular attention to the turn indicator, and by ensuring that only the correct rate of turn exists before attempting to alter the speed.

Straight flight is obtained by applying opposite bank and rudder and bringing the needle back to the centre, the pilot getting a strong sensation that he is turning the other way. Since a straight path is unique, and a large variety of curves will produce more or less the same effect, it is much more difficult to fly straight than to circle. It may be found easier to keep the turn needle wandering a little from one side to the other rather than rigidly in the middle. If a gentle inadvertent turn is made this should be corrected and the needle brought slightly beyond centre before once again trying to keep it in the middle.

Most gliders are equipped with aircraft dashboard type compasses which, in them, are singularly ineffective. Normally when making circles small enough to stay inside a cloud the compass is likely to surge violently, but a turn in which the compass shows the glider's heading reliably will be of too big radius for flying in ordinary cumulus.

The pilot wishing to come out of cloud in a particular direction has two alternatives. He can reduce his rate of turn considerably, and then start to straighten up when the compass suggests that he is pointing in the right direction, or he can straighten up at once from his turn, let the compass settle, see in which direction he is pointing, make a correction turn one way or the other and get straight again. Of these two methods the second probably wastes less time despite Newton's fifth law (of cussedness) which ensures that the initial recovery is almost invariably made in the wrong direction. If this method is employed, the turn from the initial to the desired heading can be made by counting seconds when turning at a known rate of turn. The technique is to work out through what angle, and in which direction, it is desired to turn, start a normal turn and continue it for the appropriate number of seconds, bearing in mind that the glider will turn about 90° in 6 seconds. The glider is then straightened up and held straight while the compass settles down again.

The installation of a directional gyro would solve the problem of leaving clouds in the desired direction, but it is doubtful if the weight or expense would be justified. However, the Cook compass (described in Chapter 19) is much better than the normal type for giving indications of directions when turning. If the Cook compass is mounted rigidly in the glider it does not work well; but if it is mounted in a gimbal, the pilot can, when circling, set the compass so that the shaft on which the magnet is mounted is roughly in the true vertical. The compass then moves smoothly when circling, which makes it easier for the pilot to determine his heading, and to decide when to start straightening up in order to come out in the right direction. As he comes out of the turn and resumes straight flight, he twists the compass so that it is now upright with respect to the glider.

STALLING IN CLOUD

Since the glider will normally be flown in cloud some 10 knots above the stall, and the air inside may be quite rough, it follows that however good the pilot the glider will occasionally be momentarily, and inadvertently, stalled. The pilot will, of course, observe this from his ASI and the marked quietness around him. If he does nothing the glider will normally unstall itself and carry on, but the process can obviously be accelerated by taking normal recovery action, i.e. moving the stick forward and preventing the nose from swinging by use of the rudder. The desired flying speed and rate of turn can then be resumed.

A gust may sometimes put the glider's nose down instead of stalling it, causing it to gain speed rapidly. If this happens and the glider is going more or less straight, the pilot should ease gently back on the stick, and as soon as the speed starts to decrease, make a slight forward movement. This prevents him from pulling the nose right above the horizon.

DIVEBRAKES

The development of divebrakes has done a great deal to make blind flying safe and simple, since by their use the pilot can prevent his aircraft from exceeding its placard speeds. When flying in cloud it is wise for the pilot to keep his hand on the brake lever, and ease the brakes gently open whenever the speed reaches twice stalling speed. Once the speed has been reduced the brakes can be gently closed again. Divebrakes should be used in this way as a matter of course, and not as a last resort.

SPINNING

Most gliders are singularly reluctant to spin, and even if well and truly stalled in a steep turn will normally only do an incipient spin before recovering themselves. However, a full spin may develop and no pilot should go into cloud until he can recover from a spin by the use of instruments alone. When the aircraft is spinning the turn needle will be fully over to one side, but the position of the slip indicator will depend on the spin characteristics of the machine; on most gliders it will show a skid outwards. The airspeed reading will also vary from type to type, and with the position of the pitot head, but will normally show about $1\frac{1}{4}$ times stalling speed and stay at this value. The recovery is made in exactly the same way as in clear air, as follows:—Full opposite rudder, slight pause, and stick steadily forward until the spinning stops. The cessation of the spin will be shown by the turn indicator swinging violently across to the other side. The pilot should try to keep it central, or at any rate swinging an approximately equal amount either way. The dive brakes should in general be opened the moment it has been realized that a spin has started, although there are some gliders in which spin recovery is more difficult with the brakes open; in such cases the brakes should be opened as soon as the glider stops spinning.

It is quite easy to get the glider out of a spin, but to get it cleanly out of the resultant dive is much more difficult, particularly on clean glass gliders. Most people pull back too much, and get the nose well up in the air without realizing it and the result may be a stall or in an extreme case an undesirable tailslide. To emphasize yet once again, as soon as the speed starts to decrease move the stick forward, and then try to reduce speed very gradually.

Before the invention of dive brakes it was an accepted idea that if a pilot got into difficulties in cloud, he should spin the glider out of it, thereby keeping the speeds, and loads on the glider comparatively low. It is doubtful if this technique was ever practised to any extent, and certainly is not likely to be very practical with the modern glider, as most of them are reluctant to spin steadily, and entry into the spin is difficult. If the glider has good divebrakes the question of doing a voluntary spin out of cloud will not arise, but even if the brakes have frozen up it is probably wise to avoid this manoeuvre if at all possible.

Half the art of blind flying well is the ability to sit in a relaxed state, to observe the instruments calmly, and to make smooth and gentle corrections with the controls. The beginner is inclined to keep his eyes glued on the turn indicator needle and sit rigidly. It is much easier if the instruments are observed regularly and in order — turn indicator, airspeed, slip indicator, with occasional glances at the variometer and altimeter, and also as something different such as the ice on the wings, so as to avoid the lack of perception which comes with over-concentration.

THE ARTIFICIAL HORIZON

Although blind flying is perfectly practical on a turn-and-slip indicator, it is made easier if the glider is equipped with an artificial horizon, since instead of having to visualize his attitude from the rate of turn and airspeed, the pilot gets a direct picture of his angle of bank and the relation of the nose to the horizon.

The reason why gliders are not always equipped with this aid is that it is both heavy and expensive. There are a few artificial horizons which cannot be toppled however the glider is manoeuvred but the usual type is upset when the aircraft gets much over the vertical in a bank, or near it in a climb or dive. If this happens the horizon bar wobbles rapidly and the instrument takes some minutes to settle down again. While it is most unlikely that a glider will get into these extreme attitudes, it may happen, and if the only gyroscopic instrument is an artificial horizon, it will prove embarrassing to the pilot. To avoid this eventually it is wise to carry a turn-and-slip indicator as well.

Using a horizon is simplicity itself. The position of the 'little aeroplane' in relation to the horizon bar is noted when the glider is in normal circling flight. The pilot has then merely to keep this relationship in exactly the same way as he does with the nose of his aircraft and the horizon in clear air. Venturi-driven instruments – turn-and-slip, and artificial horizon – are no longer fitted to gliders because venturis ice up when most needed. However, their replacements – electrically driven – need properly maintained batteries to be of value, and it is these which give most trouble.

FAILURE OF INSTRUMENTS

Although an essential part of blind flying training is that of instilling into the pilot the belief that his instruments are right, and his senses wrong, it is no use pretending that instruments are infallible, and it is therefore as well to list the faults which may arise, and give some idea how these faults can be identified.

The most common fault is a failure of the electrical supply – a flat battery or a loose connection. To eliminate the chance of both turn-and-slip and artificial horizon failing together, each should have its own electrical supply from separate batteries.

As most electrical instruments require the connections to be made with the correct polarity, irreversible plugs and sockets should be used and the battery terminals should be clearly marked + and −. Further, if the batteries are changed, or if any work is done on the electrical system, a proper check should be carried out on the ground to ensure that the instruments work in the correct sense. For the turn-and-slip this is merely a matter of moving the tail a few feet to one side and observing that the instrument shows the correct directions of turn. The horizon can be checked as described in Chapter 19.

Turn-and-Slip Indicator. If the battery runs down or becomes disconnected the needle will gradually become less sensitive and eventually finish up in the middle position regardless of whether the glider is turning or not. If quick movements of the rudder do not produce corresponding movements of the needle this fault has occurred.

Artificial Horizon. Battery failure will produce a gradual wander of the horizon bar which may not be obvious, as the instrument will behave normally for small changes of pitch and bank, but the discrepancy between the true horizon and the horizon bar will gradually widen. This failure can be noticed by getting the aircraft flying correctly on the ASI and the turn-and-slip indicator, and then seeing if it looks right on the artificial horizon.

The Air Speed Indicator. Ice building up in the pitot head or in extreme cases on the nose pitot will cause trouble. Sometimes the ice itself blocks the pitot tube, and on other occasions the instrument may work satisfactorily during the climb when the ice is building up, but fail on the descent when the tube gets filled with melting ice.

The exact behaviour of the instrument will depend on the existence of leaks in the system. Usually the instrument gets more and more sluggish, finally settling back to an impossibly slow figure. The pilot's first realization of this fault usually occurs when he wakes up with a start to the fact that the glider is making a screaming noise although the ASI is showing only 30 knots. If the ASI does go wrong the pilot will have to rely on his artificial horizon, if fitted, or on the noise and feel of the glider, and unless hail or heavy rain is encountered he should not have much difficulty.

The Variometer. A variometer of any type will be rendered unserviceable if ice or water obstructs the static or venturi connections. When this happens the instrument will either read zero or give an erratic indication. It is sometimes possible to prevent this trouble by having a cock installed at the lowest part of the circuit and using this to vent the system and let out any water.

If the vario is connected to a total-energy diaphragm, icing of the pitot merely eliminates the total-energy effect. The instrument continues to work. However, should the diaphragm fail or leak, then the instrument becomes useless, indicating fully down.

Altimeter. If the altimeter is open to the cockpit the chance of failure is very small indeed. But, as described in Chapter 19, p. 313 this arrangement can introduce errors, which can only be overcome by connecting the instrument to the static. It then becomes susceptible to a blockage due to ice or water. If there are no leaks the instrument will continue to indicate the height at which the blockage occurred.

BLIND FLYING INSTRUCTION

There is no doubt that the best way to learn to fly blind is in a two-seater glider, either under the hood or in cloud, with an instructor in the other seat. As well as practising circling, flying straight and turning on to courses, experience should be gained in stalling, spinning, and recovery from unusual attitudes.

If such instruction is not available, it is possible for a good and patient pilot to teach himself by practising on instruments in clear air to a considerable extent before venturing into cloud. Numerous pilots have done this and it says much for their courage and skill that they have been successful, but the path can be made much easier by having a few lessons in a light aeroplane, or a ground trainer. Full advantage of these methods will be obtained if the instructor is familiar with the problems of flying gliders blind, and gives instruction in circling and recovering from unusual attitudes, and does not waste time flying pretty patterns on compass courses.

It is no use pretending that blind flying is easy. To do it competently demands hard work when learning and then plenty of practice. However, the advantages to be gained by the possession of blind flying skill are considerable. Not only is the pilot more likely to make a success of his cross-country flying, but he will no longer be tied to the world below cloud base.

Chapter 11

Using Soaring Weather

Cross-country flights may be made in lee waves at great heights above the mountains, in the slope lift along hills and ridges, and by using the incredibly powerful lift inside thunderstorms; but most are made in thermals. These, and the cumulus clouds that ride their crests, need warmth and unstable air for their creation, and they will develop to a greater or lesser extent in a wide variety of weather. The problem is to know in advance when conditions are going to be good, and then to get the best possible flight from whatever weather actually turns up.

Unfortunately, in many countries including Britain, super weather is the exception, and most soaring flights will be done in conditions that are far from ideal. If this were not so the pilot would get an unsatisfactorily small amount of flying. However, waiting to see what the day brings forth and then hastily dreaming up a flight that hopefully fits the weather does not really work; either it will be too small and make insufficiently good use of the available thermals, or it will be too large, or go in the wrong direction, and a field landing will be inevitable. It is better to work out well in advance a selection of flights that would be possible in different sorts of weather, taking into consideration pilot experience, performance of the aircraft, and the time at which a launch could be obtained. If the pilot has not much cross-country flying to his credit he should include some quite short tasks to attempt in difficult weather, as well as the beautiful big flights that he dreams about.

Planning to use the weather should start by the pilot plotting on his map flights which others at the club have flown and finding out from them what sort of weather was used on each occasion, and how long the flight took. Information about the weather on flights that did not succeed can be just as useful, such as that in a SW wind cool sea air penetrated right up the Avon river valley much earlier than seemed possible. With such preplanning done the pilot will be able to select a small number of alternative tasks for himself on the previous evening forecast. On the morning of the great day, with the latest weather information available, he should quickly be able to narrow the choice and go for the task that will enable him to use the day fully with a good chance of success. Becoming a better soaring pilot means being able to use the weather that exists to the best advantage, and not waiting for the easy day.

The always hoped-for Very Good Day is easily visualised. It is warm and sunny with small cumulus clouds dotted evenly over the sky, with their bases not below 4000 ft. The air is not too moist, so that cloud will not overdevelop and spread all over the sky, cutting off the sun. There are no large patches of cirrus and no high cloud creeping up the sky ahead of an approaching depression. The air must be sufficiently unstable for thermals to start early in the morning and continue until early evening, but not so unstable that the cumulus will run away into thunderheads. The wind is light to moderate. On such a day the pilot, even with modest experience and a medium performance glider, should be able to romp around a 300-km triangle, or even achieve a 500 provided that he can launch at the right time. Unfortunately, it is likely that most days will produce at least one unwanted weather characteristic. There will be good thermals, for example, but the wind is far too strong; or the wind is light, but the air is wildly unstable. By early afternoon the sky will be filled with masses of unorganised cloud up to 20,000 ft, and flinging out bursts of heavy rain. There will be days which stray even further from the ideal; not only is the wind on the strong side and thermals a bit weak, but the day will die early because of the effect of a slowly approaching depression. On less than ideal days the pilot has to decide not only what is the most that can be extracted from the weather, but what he himself wants to do — what is the flight supposed to achieve? On some days soaring would be possible in the weak conditions for 7 hours, provided that the pilot is prepared to go downwind. But his 7 hours experience has to be related to a 300-mile car retrieve, with its expense and complications. The pilot will not have learnt very much either, except that he can stay airborne in weak conditions, and he probably knows that already. It would be far more profitable to select a shorter flight for these conditions, either a triangle or out-and-return, to plan it carefully, and try to do it in a given time. Such a flight, successfully completed, will not go on any records list, but it will have given the pilot the best possible value from the day. He will have learnt how good, or otherwise, his planning was, quite a lot about how not to waste time when flying against the wind, how to make the most of dying lift, and on the last few miles home, probably quite a lot about the need to be able to select a good field and to get that right too.

WHAT SORT OF WEATHER?

Since good soaring weather means different things in different parts of the world, this chapter will concern itself with some of the typical situations that can give good summer soaring in Britian.

High-pressure weather, when the country is under the influence of an anticyclone, is the most reliable for flying triangles. The high-pressure centre does not have to be over the country, in fact it is better that it is not, because of the calm and hazy air it collects there. The haze may be very thick owing to the strength, and often lowness, of the temperature inversion caused by the subsiding anticyclonic air. If the inversion is low, down to perhaps 2000 ft, thermals will be unable to penetrate above this height, and it is unlikely that cumulus will develop to mark them. The haze will be particularly dense downwind of industrial towns. At the other extreme, around the periphery of a High the wind may be far from calm, blowing too hard for any effective into-wind flying. Somewhere between the centre and the periphery will be best, and if possible this should be over the middle of the task area (Fig. 11.1).

Good soaring weather, although quite often accompanied by fresh winds, can also occur following the passing of a cold front. The wind will be around W to NW, and the air

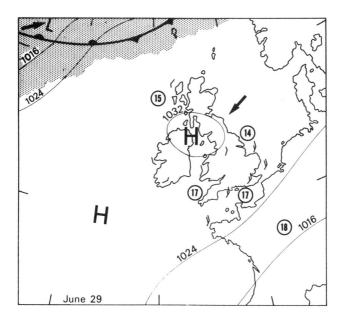

Fig 11.1 High over Britain. The high is giving very light winds flowing in a clockwise direction around the centre. Away from the centre winds are stronger, particularly where aligned with the length of the English Channel.

The absence of isobars shows a slack pressure gradient over a wide area and a settled situation. Being June the weather in such conditions can be hot and fine, though probably hazy

Numbers in circles are degrees centigrade, wind arrows indicate direction: half feather 5 knots; full feather 10 knots. The pressure is in millibars. Shaded areas are cloud cover of considerable thickness and extent with some rain

clean with good visibility. The important check to be made on this sort of day is the degree of instability present. Such quantities of cool moist air which have come a long way over the sea, create an unstable situation when they flow over the sun-heated land. Instead of cumulus that stay small and well separated, the cloud grows fat and tall, and may well coalesce

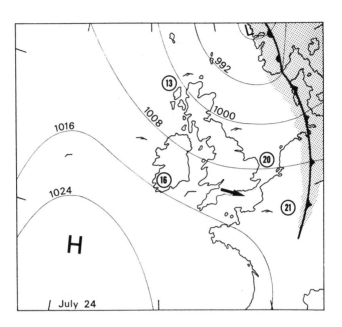

Fig 11.2 Ridge. The extensive cloud associated with the warm front (hemispheres on the front line) and cold front (spikes) has moved across Britain from the Atlantic bringing in its wake W to WNW winds in a probably showery airstream. The ridge of high pressure following from the west typically brings a fine and sunny day. As the ridge moves across the country the pressure rises and the wind veers and slackens. When the peak passes the wind will start to back and probably increase, though maybe slowly. Pressure will start to go down and the cloud amount increase as a following depression develops and moves in from the Atlantic

into large masses with extensive areas of sinking air between them. Usually the air stabilises more as the distance behind the front increases. If the front passed through during the night, the next day would be more likely to produce better-organised cumulus than if it came through after breakfast. In this case it would probably, but not necessarily, pay to plan a flight to start in the afternoon.

144

Sometimes Britain finds herself squeezed between an anti-cyclone on one side and a depression on the other. This gives a unified but often strong flow of wind over the length of the country. When the high is in the Atlantic, and the Low over Holland or Germany the flow will be from the North, and although the air may feel cool, the thermals will probably be very good. Whether the wind is strong or light will depend on the extent of the squeeze between the two systems. Another situation to watch for is a ridge out in the Atlantic, that will move over Britain during the next 24-36 hours. (Fig. 11.2) It can give a single really good day sandwiched between wet and windy weather. It will be seen from all this that learning more about the weather will be a profitable project for the long winter evenings.

FINDING OUT ABOUT THE WEATHER

The pilot can help himself by reading books, but even more by studying the daily newspaper or TV weather maps, relating them to the official forecasts, and then watching the sky to see how things turn out. If it does not appear to be working as expected, he should try to assess what is actually happening. Some pilots take a sudden interest in the weather for a few days when the start of the soaring season seems imminent, and then forget all about it. Learning about the weather is a continuous process, and the weather is always there to be observed. Even if it is not practicable to cut out daily news-paper maps and study them as a series, it is certainly worth making a special effort to do so for several days prior to any opportunity for cross-country flying. By comparing successive days' charts, a pattern of movement emerges and this extra knowledge is valuable in assessing the worth of forecasts for and on the day itself. When other pilots make good flights the weather map for that day should be studied to see why the day was so good, and to serve as a reminder for future opportunities.

Obviously, it is most useful to have a talk with a meteorologist about any forthcoming flight, or even about a recent flight that did not come off. If the met man is a glider pilot or understands what is needed, so much the better, though this is not always possible. If he is not, then the pilot, in addition to listening to what he has to say generally, needs to ask specific questions when getting a forecast. These should include: what maximum height are thermals likely to reach, will cumulus develop and what height can cloud base be expected, how big are the clouds likely to grow and, if there is an inversion, at what height will it be – and is it weakening or not? Further questions include: what surface temperature is needed before convection can start, how strong are thermals likely to be, and over what period of the day will they be usable? As more knowledge of meteorology is gained the pilot will, of course, be able to ask specifically for the precise information that he needs. The big problem on the day itself is to decide in the early morning whether or not the forecast looks like being right. This is the first big chance to make a mistake; if take-off is delayed too long it will be impossible to make up that time lost dithering through indecision. Unless the forecast is so wildly wrong that, for example, the warm front forecast to arrive in the evening has already come in with its drizzling rain, the pilot should get up and go to the airfield without delay, with or without the courage of his convictions. He should prepare everything for the flight assuming that the forecast will be correct, and go on watching the sky to see how the actual weather develops.

THE WEATHER ON THE DAY

The early morning of a promising day may be windless and without a cloud to be seen. This is the first good omen, because a wind at night or early in the morning more often than not indicates that the air on a big scale is on the move and that the weather is somewhat unsettled. After a while, but sometimes as early as 0900, little rags of cloud may start appearing at perhaps 1000 – 1500 ft. There may still be little or no wind, or a gentle and variable breeze may have developed. The little clouds will each live only a minute or so, appearing and disappearing in an apparently random fashion. After a while they may even disappear entirely, leaving a clear sky. They were the first indications of future thermals, and the sky should now be watched for the appearance of more genuine-looking cumulus at a greater height – perhaps 2000 ft or more.

Suppose that the pilot has decided that this could be THE day to try his first 300-km triangle. He has everything ready, but he has never made such a long flight before, is hopeful rather than certain about his navigation over so much strange country, and he has no idea how long it is going to take him – if he does not land on the way.

The first essential is that he should not start too late. He is not in a speed contest determined to race only in the best part of the day; his concern is to get around the triangle with all the margins that he can give himself. If there are other gliders already flying, he should watch for any signs of their staying up. If there are no others he should take a launch himself at the earliest time it seems sensible, and not be worried if he is too early and has to land back. If the air during this first flight felt at all bubbly, he should launch again after about 20 minutes. Airborne, and now staying up, he should fly locally for a while to get a feel of the day, get himself sorted out in the cockpit with maps ready, and plan how and when he will leave. He will not need a start line since he is not racing, so he can depart as soon as the thermals reach a useful height, say 3000 ft, and there are signs of further cumulus appearing along his intended course. Before leaving, he should check the direction of the surface wind from the airfield windsock, the direction at cloud level from the movement of their shadows over the ground, note the strength of the thermal, or thermals, that he has already used, the height of cloud base if reached, and check the time. When ready he should go.

If the forecast was for good thermals up to 4500 ft, moderate cumulus development, and NE wind of 5 – 10 knots, the pilot has now to concern himself as to whether all this is happening or not. On a normal day of good convection thermals will increase in strength, cloud base in height, and cumulus in size until about the middle of the afternoon. After this thermals will start to weaken although they may stay large, and cumulus will start to flatten although cloud base will stay high.

If the pilot departed from his home airfield at 1030 and

thermals are expected to last until 1800, he has a total of $7\frac{1}{2}$ hours soaring available, with maximum thermal strength occurring around 1500 hrs. He therefore has, or hopes to have, about $4\frac{1}{2}$ hours flying during which thermals are getting stronger and cloud base higher. Since this is almost as much time as is needed to fly all of a 300-km triangle he is in no hurry; it is much more important to avoid making mistakes and taking wrong decisions. As cumulus develops he should watch to see whether cloud base is rising as fast or more slowly than expected, or if the clouds are looking flatter and spreading out. If this is happening, there soon seems to be far too much cloud everywhere and the ground is in shadow for miles in every direction. This is the time to pussyfoot, keep as high as possible using any lift that turns up, and wait. In due course, the existing cloud will decay, and where it does so the sun's heat will be let through and patches of sunlight appear on the ground. As soon as the surface has had a chance to warm up again thermals will restart and progress can once more be made.

If the air is more unstable than expected and cumulus are growing tall and large, the pilot has a different problem. There will be lift all right under the clouds, but as they grow bigger he will find them generally further apart, and so will have to modify his tactics to make sure that he will be able to reach the next along his course. Here, again, he should use any available lift provided that it is taking him generally in the right direction or allows him to hang about in a suitable place to wait for the sky to improve.

Apart from his concern with thermal strengths and the whereabouts of the next good cumulus, the pilot should keep watch on any high-level cloud. If a front is forecast for later he will probably have been watching anyway for signs of cirrus near the horizon, but he may miss seeing unexpected patches of cirrus, sometimes quite dense, which have developed and which will affect his future thermals. He should appreciate that *a*) such patches of cirrus will reduce thermal strength and perhaps frequency, *b*) that they will almost certainly not be moving in the same direction as the cloud at cumulus level, and *c*) that they may be increasing. If possible the cirrus cloud shadow should be located on the ground and watched for its directional movement, to see how it will affect the course yet to be flown. A dense shadow over a turning-point, for example, with the next leg into wind can lead easily to a premature landing. Quite a lot of height will probably be lost in turning the point and the pilot is then faced with starting a leg which is not only going to be slow, but without much height and with little or no lift until he can break out into sunshine. If the cloud shadow is moving away the glider should be kept circling around locally until there is a chance of good lift for the next into-wind leg. If the pilot feels that he has already been so slow that he risks running out of time, he should equate an almost certain landing near the turning point, say 60 miles from home, with not quite making it later, say 15 miles short. It is important at this stage that he makes the right decisions, even if he does not complete the flight. Possible changes of wind direction and strength also have to be watched for during cross country flight. If they are not noticed in time they can not only contribute to a premature field landing, but may result in the arrival itself being a dis-aster because the pilot landed down wind.

SEA BREEZES

The most likely cause of a substantial change in wind strength and direction on a good soaring day, apart from any local effect around thunderstorms, is a sea breeze. This wind from the sea towards the land is pulled in to replace air which is rising over the land due to strong convection; the stronger the thermals, the further inland the sea breeze is likely to penetrate. In Britain sea breezes have been found 30 miles in from the coast. The interface between the sea breeze and the land air may produce a line of cumulus if the two winds are convergent, or may be indistinguishable if the sea and land winds are from the same direction. There is often strong lift under the line of convergence cloud, but on its sea side there will be little or none. When the two winds are in the same direction, and both blowing in off the sea, there may be little thermal lift for quite a long way inland, which only gradually improves as the distance from the sea increases (Fig. 11.3). In this air there will be little or no cumulus, and what there is may have a much lower cloud base than that well inland. Cloud base along the line of convergence cumulus will also be lower than the inland cumulus. Occasionally a convergence zone exists without any cloud, and the interface may be discerned by a difference in clarity or haziness of the air on each side of the line. Lift is often found along it.

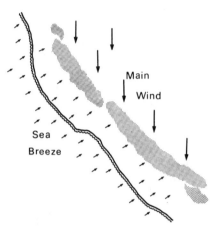

Fig 11.3 Sea breeze. When the sea breeze blows in towards the main mass of the land and meets a converging prevailing wind a line of lift producing cumulus often develops along the convergent line. If the prevailing wind is from the sea a sea breeze will simply augment the general flow, covering the land for some miles inland with cool air. Little lift is likely to be found in this region

In a small country like Britain sea breezes should be expected on any good soaring day within 30 miles of the coast, which means that they should be taken into account on any big flight planning. If a turning-point has to be relatively near the coast the flight should be so arranged that the glider is there early in the day before the sea breeze has had time to

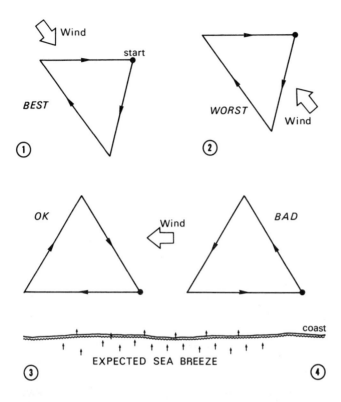

Fig. 11.4. Best way around triangles in sea-breeze conditions

penetrate. Sometimes sea breezes can be used by having one leg of a triangle along its expected position, but this is not an easily predictable situation. The risk near the end of a big flight is that thermals start to weaken and die earlier than expected. If no high cloud cover can be seen to be responsible the cause is most likely due to the air becoming more stable. This will happen when pressure rises, perhaps due to the influence of a nearby anticyclone or merely because the pressure all over the region has taken a gentle upward turn. Such activity leaves its mark, and should cumulus not grow as large as expected during the afternoon, or become flatter and more widely spaced, or should the air become hazier, there is a good chance of thermals dying earlier and the pilot having to land out.

PLANNING A FLIGHT

What has been said here is only very little of what the pilot can teach himself by noticing changes in the pattern of clouds and interpreting their meaning to his advantage. The more he knows the better he will be able to make plans that will turn out successful.

Let us now assume that the pilot knows that on Saturday it will be his turn on the club Pilatus. He completed his Silver Distance last autumn, and this year scrambled successfully but slowly around a 100-km triangle, and flew an out-and-return which left him 5 miles short of the airfield on the way back when the thermals stopped.

The weather during the week has been unsettled and westerly, but pressure is beginning to rise SW of Britain. The forecast gives the wind as WNW 15 knots moderating, weather bright and sunny with some cumulus development, visibility 5 miles, hazy. Cloud base is not expected to rise above 3500 ft. He can add for himself that the ground is damp after recent rain so some of the sun's warmth will be consumed in a drying-off process. However, it should be a moderately good day, although nothing special. So how can it best be used?

The first consideration in deciding what to do is to check whether the wind strength is going to make an into-wind leg of any length impracticable. The forecast gives 15 knots moderating which is not too bad. Thermals are expected to be reasonably good, but cloud base is not all that high, so it will be a day for care and cunning, and not too much ambition. It would be nice to go for a 200-km triangle, but how would this work out?

On the assumption that the middle of the flight should approximately coincide with the middle part of the day when the lift is strongest, the pilot can start to work out how his triangle should be arranged. Very simply, he should have increasingly vigorous thermals on his first leg, the best of the day on the second leg, and weakening conditions on the last leg home. Relating this to the wind, it is obviously sensible to do the into-wind leg in the middle in the strongest lift, and ideally do the last leg downwind so that if lift becomes very weak he has just to stay airborne and the wind will drift him back. But usually the solution is not so simple, because controlled airspace and the location of suitable turning-points often prevent weather considerations being paramount. The diagrams show a few of the possibilities. If there is a small choice of turning-points it will be better to have the windward leg *directly* into wind if there is any chance at all of cloud or thermal streets developing, as once the street lines have been located the glider can be flown straight along them and not have to be worked diagonally through the intervening sink. This also applies to the last leg; if this can be directly downwind, so much the better. Obviously terrain has to be considered, for example, to avoid drifting home over a large town at a marginal height.

After the flight the pilot will see how his plan worked out, and whether or not the weather came up to expectations. The sort of weather information that is needed for soaring is not always easily available; sometimes not available at all. So the soaring pilot has to build up his own knowledge, taking when he needs from published forecasts, comparing notes with other pilots about to fly, and observing and analysing what he needs from published forecasts, comparing notes really good by cultivating a feel, an instinct, for the behaviour of the air.

Chapter 12

Championship Flying

Gliding makes for really good competitions. As well as the direct element of flying against, and hopefully beating, other contestants, the techniques and decisions necessary to achieve success are highly individual. As a result competition flying is to most pilots an obvious and interesting step towards the 'compleat' pilot. But it is not very profitable accepting the many disciplines imposed by contests unless they are taken seriously. Gliding championships are both stimulating and a lot of fun, with plenty of friendly rivalry and few squabbles, but they do demand considerable intellectual effort and physical stamina. A pilot just entering for a bit of flying and without any real interest in trying to do well is likely to find the exercise irksome, not to say expensive.

CHAMPIONSHIP CLASSES

There are a small number of different classes in championships, to cater for differences in aircraft performance – and costs – and to enable all the pilots in a class to be launched as rapidly as possible into the same bit of weather. The maximum number found to be acceptable for each class is about 40. At present there are two classes in World Championships: Open and Standard. Open is what it says it is, without restriction; although there is a World Cup within the Class for the best-placed glider not exceeding a maximum span of 19 m. In 1978 there are to be three classes; Open, 15-m Unrestricted (the only restriction being a maximum span of 15m) and the Restricted Class, being a modification of the present Standard Class.

There are also international 'Club Class' competitions based on performance limitation, to provide for the many pilots wanting either a middle-level competition or means of working up to World Championships. Although most competitions follow the international pattern, clubs can run any other sort of contest to fulfil local demand.

Over the years the form of competitions has changed. Initially, in the early twenties it was for duration flights, then came distance and altitude. Now speed is the main task, usually over triangular or out-and-return courses of considerable dimensions. Although a 700-km triangle has been successfully given in World Championships, speed tasks are more usually of 300 or 500 km in length, sometimes being achieved by several pilots within seconds of each other's times. In marginal and weak weather, triangle tasks as small as 100 km may be set for national and local competitions, although this distance is no longer regarded as suitable for a good contest day at World level.

Instead of speed, competitors may be given a task scored only on distance flown, if this is most suited to the weather. The old task of free distance is no longer practicable, since competitors are likely to go so far that they will be unable to return in time to fly the following day. Instead, distance freely selected around a number of turn points, known usually as Cats Cradle, is used. Considerable distances can be flown this way without the pilot ending up unreasonably far from base. Distance flying demands somewhat different skills to speed flying, notably those of decision taking in a meteorological and navigational sense. This is often reflected in the daily scores, with those other than the usually fastest pilots doing well.

World Championships extend over 16 days and must have a minimum of four contest days; national and regional championships usually last 7 – 9 days.

PREPARING FOR CHAMPIONSHIPS

No one stands much chance in championships unless he, his crew, glider, and equipment are fit for the job, and to attain this state needs considerable preparation and practice. A contest is not the time to try out new aircraft or unknown personalities; the important thing is to have the necessary minimum of equipment all in a thoroughly serviceable and proven state. Since the pilot's time is usually limited in the months before a championship, he will have to choose between doing training flights, and improving his glider, car, and trailer. The right balance needs to be struck. Once some people start fiddling they never know when to stop, and waste the best part of a soaring day messing about with their equipment. Championships can be lost just as easily by an unserviceable trailer as by a defect in the glider. The quality to be aimed at above all else in ground equipment is reliability, and if it is of new design it should be properly tested before being subjected to the rigours of a competition. For example, weaknesses in the towing attachments of the two vehicles are a quite common cause of trouble. The trailer itself should not only be in good condition, but the fittings into which the glider components rest should be permanent and secure, any temporary lash-up being ruthlessly replaced. Almost the most stupid way to lose a competition is through a wing coming adrift in the trailer during a retrieve. A check list on the inside of the rear door will help ensure that nothing is forgotten, especially de-rigging aids or tools left behind in the field. The crew is most important. A cheerful, willing crew who are also competent at looking after the glider, car, radio, and finances, contribute largely to the success of their pilot. The work is made easier if each member has a clearly defined job, and if the pilot refrains from interfering with the way they do it. One may be responsible for serviceability of the ground equipment and the aircraft, while the other looks after money, food, navigation, and task information, etc. Then all that is left is for the pilot to concentrate on his flying.

One job that can be done well in advance and at home is sorting out maps. It is a great advantage if these can be obtained in advance for foreign competitions, so that the pilot can become familiar with the information presentation, and acquire some knowledge of the characteristics of the country. It may be helpful to stick two sheets together so as to avoid having to change maps at awkward times, and to draw concentric circles at, say 50 or 100 km distance from the starting site. It is also useful to have a small-scale map covering the entire area over which flying may take place, so that it may be seen in its entirety when planning flights.

When flying abroad some difficulties may arise over measurements, so the pilot can profitably practice a little thinking in both metric units and knots. Heights in feet are used internationally, so the only problem may be over distances in kilometres and rates of climb in metres per second. The pilot used to knots for speed and vertical rates should certainly not attempt to change and thus confuse himself, but it is helpful to carry a small conversion table to make discussions with other pilots more meaningful. Knots have the advantage that 1 knot is for all practical purposes 100 ft/min.

The most useful preparation is flying at the actual championship site in order to find out about:

The local weather and climate, including the hours of the day in which thermals can be expected.

The strength and size of thermals.

The landability of the country, including learning what suitable landing places look like from the air.

The feel of flying in the particular region, and the physical effects of local food and climate.

RULES AND TASKS

Championships are not necessarily won by the best pilot, but by the one who accumulates the maximum points under a particular set of rules. To succeed, therefore, it it necessary to understand the regulations fully so that the most advantageous tactics can be employed.

Scoring is usually based on the winner being awarded the maximum points for the day—usually 1000—with other competitors scored in proportion. Once he knows the task for the day the pilot must assess the weather and consider how he can best carry it out. It is unwise to place too much reliance on the forecast unless the ability of the meteorologist is known, as there are some who do not give the probability of the various parts of their forecast being correct. In dealing with strange met men, particularly if they do not themselves fly, it should be appreciated that their assessment of a good thermal day may be widely different from that of the pilot. It is worth talking to the met man each day, not only to clarify detail, but to get a feel for his optimism or pessimism.

PLANNING AND STRATEGY

Whether or not the pilot is successful depends on the quality of his brain power on that day and throughout the flight. Few people work at their best if the take-off is made in a panic.

Apart from the job of rigging, inspecting, and taking the glider to the launch point, which is largely done by the crew, decisions may be required as to whether weight should be increased by filling the water ballast tanks, or reduced by dispensing with the oxygen bottle or artificial horizon batteries. Since the reduction in weight is only a few percent, and the theoretical improvement in slow speed performance is even less, the advantage is marginal; subsequent worries about having made the wrong decision makes such small weight reductions barely worth while.

Increasing weight with water ballast can be much more profitable (see pages 268 – 269 for the theoretical aspects). It is well known that, provided conditions are good enough, very substantial increases of speed can be obtained by flying aircraft with some hundreds of pounds of extra weight on board. Comparing a fully-ballasted glider with one flown empty, the break-even point is probably around 300 – 400 ft/min average rate of climb for the same cross country performance. Since the water can always be jettisoned, it will usually be best to take off with ballast and then decide whether or not to retain it. Even if the average rate of climb is good and at a value which fully justifies the use of ballast, it should be jettisoned if the pilot is unlucky enough to risk having to land.

Significant amounts of ballast, e.g., up to 100 kg, have a marked effect on the performance characteristics of the aircraft. If, for example, the weight of the glider is increased 20% by ballast the stall speed, the speed for minimum sink, the rate of sink, and the speed for the best angle of glide will all be increased by about 10%. The actual best angle of glide will remain unchanged. This extra weight will put greater loads on the aircraft and accordingly ballast should be jettisoned in extreme turbulence and before landing.

For simplicity it may be easiest to consider the performance of the glider with either maximum ballast or none at all, but

Plate IX *Refitting a tail parachute after use.*

there may be occasions when partial ballast serves the best purpose. On some aircraft the ballast takes an appreciable time to drain and the drain cocks should therefore be opened early on the approach.

Flying with large amounts of ballast does not make a marked difference in the aircraft handling, although on some gliders a reduction in the acceleration in roll may be noticeable. Take-off will be longer and the rate of climb on tow worse, but provided the circling speed is increased by the appropriate amount the behaviour when circling will not seem to be significantly different. The glide to the next thermal should be made at a higher airspeed than with an unballasted aircraft, and ideally this will call for a different MacCready ring. The fact that a different calibration of the ring is needed (not just a different setting) is stated in Chapter 7. For example, the speed to fly for the best L/D — MacCready ring setting of 0 rate of climb — is 49 knots for a Libelle at a weight of 633 lb and 54 knots for the same aircraft with ballast at a weight of 772 lb. In each case the angle of glide will be the same at 1:35.

Flying with ballast is only an advantage if really good rates of climb can be achieved. If lift is not particularly good it will be better to jettison, since not only will the rate of sink be reduced but the circling speed will also be less, making it easier to climb in small or broken thermals. If the decision to jettison ballast is taken when circling in a weak thermal, showering it on another glider will be most unpopular because water droplets on a wing spoil the laminar flow and take a long time to evaporate.

For normal cross-country flying the risk of water ballast freezing is negligible, but if the flight is likely to be above freezing level for several hours, the use of some anti-freeze additive should be considered.

BRIEFING

Assuming that his crew can deal with the aircraft, the pilot can concentrate on his own plans. At briefing he should ensure that he really has got all the details of the task. Usually this is made straightforward by a printed briefing form which acts

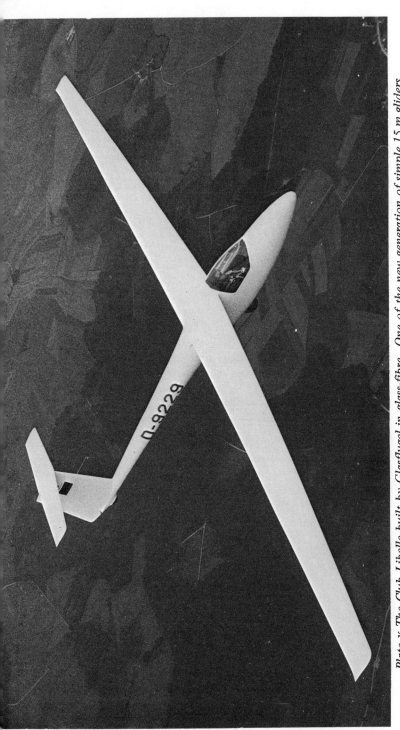

Plate x The Club Libelle built by Glasflugel in glass-fibre. One of the new generation of simple 15 m gliders with very effective airbrakes. Span: 15 m, aspect ratio: 23, empty weight: 225 kg, max. AUW: 350 kg, max. L/D: 35 at 97 km/h (52 knots), min. sink: 0.59 m/s (1.15 knots) at 70 km/h (38 knots)

as a check list. Included should be the time of take-off, position of start line and any opening time for the line, position of finish line, times of last take-off, and closing of the finish line, precise details of turning-points including their height above sea level, and information on controlled airspace or other hazards. All this, and the met information, should be written clearly so that it can be easily referred to in flight. In big competitions the weather information is usually presented to each pilot in diagrammatic form, but in any case the pilot may want to add extra data which perhaps has come out as a result of questions at briefing.

Armed with all the information the pilot should sit in a quiet place – not always possible – and plan his flight. From the estimate of thermal strength, he can assess his probable cross-country speed in still air. Knowing the track and the forecast wind speed at the likely operational heights he can now work out the ground speed, elapsed time, and course to steer on each leg. This will give him an idea of the total time the task will take and he will then be able to work out the best time to cross the start line and go. It may be thought that such calculations are a waste of time since the met information on which it is all based is unlikely to be accurate: this may be but it is easier to shift a start time or reduce an expected average speed than to have to do all the necessary calculations when airborne.

Having worked out the general flight plan, the route should be studied in detail. In the absence of any reliable local information it is normally best to fly exactly on track; however, there may be a notorious bad patch on the route and by going slightly to one side it will be possible to keep over better country. This kind of decision is difficult, but a surprisingly large deviation from the route can, in fact, be made for only a comparatively small increase in the distance flown (Table, page 168). It may, therefore, be worthwile considering such a detour from the beginning.

If the course and turn points are not familiar, all the possible data should be collected. Odd bits of information often come in handy – there is a reservoir here which is not marked on the map, or that airfield has now been ploughed up; this town is made of stone which merges with the background, or that new motorway really stands out. The map should be studied in detail, the track drawn, distances from the turning-points and finish line marked, and then maps folded so that they can be easily read in flight.

When all this has been done it is time to go out to the glider and discuss the plan with the crew, and to arrange whether the trailer should stay on the airfield or go off, and if so where to and on which roads. To avoid the last-minute hassles which can have such a devastating effect on the pilot's temper and tensions, to say nothing of his flying, arrangements should be made to use a check list — one for the car and trailer and one for the glider — such as the following:

CHECK LIST

Daily inspection of aircraft
Water ballast
Pickets
First aid kit
Ground handling rope
Water bottle
Food
Money
Artificial horizon, turn-and-slip, variometer batteries
Radio batteries and radio working
Barograph wound, sealed, installed and ON
Altimeter set
Tape on wing/fuselage joint
Canopy cleaned
Towing wheel fitted
Oxygen mask and oxygen ON
(To be checked before take-off)
Maps
Knee-pad and flight plan, pencils, calculator
Landing certificate
Official documents, passport
Turning-point camera, ground photo taken
Towing wheel removed

SETTING THE ALTIMETER

There are some differences of opinion concerning the best altimeter setting to use when cross-country flying, since there are three possibilities.

(*a*) To set the height of the take-off point above sea level. By this method the altimeter reads the height of the glider above sea level; to determine the height above any other place, for example, a turning-point, it is necessary to subtract the height above sea level of that place from the altimeter reading.

(*b*) To set the altimeter at zero on take-off. The instrument will now read the height above the take-off point. In order to find the height above any other place, an additional calculation is necessary, and it is easy to get muddled and do the wrong sum. However, the altimeter will give a lower reading than method (a) all the time and this reading may be closer to the actual ground clearance.

(*c*) To set the altimeter at 1013 mb on the millibar scale. This is the international standard sea level pressure and is the setting to which all flight levels are referred, as for example bases of airways.

Since few, if any, references to flight levels are made during a soaring flight, whereas the pilot frequently wishes to determine his ground clearance, method (c) is unnecessarily complicated. In practice the choice lies between setting the altimeter at zero or at take-off height. If the flight is to be made into a mountainous region, where frequent references to height may be needed, or if it is to be a cross-country to a landing place at a different height, there is no doubt that method (a), setting the altimeter at sea level, is best.

For out-and-return or triangles over reasonably flat country it does not really matter which method is used; many pilots set their altimeter to zero. They must, however, remember which method they are using or an extra source of confusion can be introduced. For these reasons, it is suggested that the simplest and best method is always to set the altimeter at take-off height. If there is any chance of flying near controlled airspace, the altimeter reading appropriate to the flight level of the base of the airspace should be worked out before take-off.

SPEED TASKS

The Start. Normally, when the task is for speed the gliders are arranged on a grid and launched as quickly as possible one after the other at a time determined by the Organisers. Consequently the pilot has no choice over his time of take-off.

The start of a speed task is taken from the moment of crossing a starting line above the airfield, with a limit of 1000 m (3280 ft) for the maximum height of crossing. In order to gain full advantage of the start, the crossing should be made at nearly the maximum permissible height, and as fast as is reasonable and safe in order to be able to convert the speed into extra height. It is inadvisable to go too fast and follow the example of one competitor who twisted a wing off and had to make a spectacular descent by parachute. A speed somewhat less than the placard never-exceed speed should be regarded as the maximum, but if the air is really turbulent the maximum rough-air speed should not be exceeded (Chapter 20).

The pilot can choose his own moment for crossing the starting line. If he thinks that a task has been set which will be impossible to complete in the time available, he should start as soon as he can. If, however, he reckons that the task can be done easily, then he must decide what later time will be best. This will largely be determined on strategical considerations in order to make the best use of the peak of the day, but the immediate tactics of starting are also important, since it will obviously pay to cross the line at the best height and speed and go straight to a proven source of lift. Proof that the lift is working can be provided by a preliminary sortie, or more usually by the presence of other gliders circling ahead along the route. If, after going a few miles, it is realised that progress has been slower than expected it may be best to return and make another start.

Recognition Time Interval. If the task is a small triangle, the Organisers have to be satisfied that a competitor cannot visit and photograph the first turn point between take off and officially crossing the starting line. This is done by their declaring a Recognition Time Interval at briefing which requires the pilot to make his aircraft visible to ground observers for a check on his position, usually by making a pass over the starting line within the interval given. If, for example, the RTI is 30 minutes and the pilot does not want to start for $1\frac{1}{2}$ hours he must pass over the line at intervals not longer than 30 minutes during this period. If he is unable to do so he has to land, re-photograph the Start Board, and have another launch.

ON COURSE – ON THE WAY

Inevitably the first few thermals will be filled with other gliders. Not only are the thermals made visible, but so are the best areas of lift and in addition each pilot can see how well or badly he is doing compared with the others. However, the disadvantages are real. The necessity of avoiding other aircraft may force a pilot to alter his circles in a way which he does not desire, and consideration for others may prevent him from flying as he would like – for instance, it is obviously hazardous to straighten up suddenly or alter the direction of the turn. In addition there is the numbing effect of the herd instinct; each pilot tends to think that because the others are there, he must be all right, and the whole lot can go on circling round in weak lift for quite a while before someone has the courage to press off on his own in an attempt to find something better. The mentality of the pilot, too, is involved. Some loathe gaggling and find that they get much better results on their own, whilst others find the cut-and-thrust stimulating.

Whichever policy the pilot adopts, he wants to be his own master. He should decide for himself in which height band to operate. Obviously he cannot be too dogmatic; if the first few thermals start getting weak at 3000 ft but the next one is still going strong at this height, he should stay with it until he decides that it is beginning to weaken.

The thing that matters is going up quickly, and not wasting the precious height gained. When pressing off from one thermal to the next, the nose should be put down and the glider set on its way before the edge of the thermal is reached. When a new thermal is encountered and it looks as if it is reasonable, the nose should be pulled up and a quick turn made. If the findings are disappointing and there is still plenty of height, it is usually best to go straight on rather than waste time in a search.

Some attention must be paid to navigation even when circling with other gliders as the herd instinct can take charge, and everyone may drift unnecessarily off track.

If there is a crosswind, it is wise to keep upwind of the track while the going is good, and then if conditions deteriorate there will be less of a struggle to keep on the line. It is best to arrive at the turning point high when going more or less downwind. If, however, the wind will be a help on the next leg, then in theory it would be best to arrive at the turning point as low as prudence would allow. In real life this technique is often difficult to apply, since the act of dealing with the turning point breaks up the rhythm of the flight and frequently leads to delays in locating the next source of lift, particularly on weak days.

When cruising between thermals the correct speed is best maintained by reference to the MacCready ring, which should be set to the appropriate rate of climb (see Chapter 7 page 83). Ideally, the cruising speed should be determined by the rate of climb averaged over all the future thermals and not the preceding one, but this is a counsel of perfection. Flying at the theoretical speed brings one to earth in a much shorter distance than when flying at the speed for best angle of glide; as a result, the chance of finding lift is reduced. It would be ludicrous to continue at the theoretical cruise speed until the ground came up; the pilot must therefore set himself a height at which he swallows his pride, slows down, and continues in more or less the right direction looking for lift. Lower still, when all is almost lost, he must be prepared to go off in any direction in a last effort to stay up. Each low point results either in failure, or an appalling waste of time, and this situation usually occurs because the pilot fails to appreciate that conditions are deteriorating, and continues discarding weak thermals before realising that all the thermals are now weak. Such general deterioration may be associated with the type of ground, the over-development of cumulus or increase of high cloud, the presence of haze to the lee of an industrial area, a change in the airmass, the proximity of the sea, or simply the time of day. Sometimes in the late afternoon the thermal strength may quite suddenly lessen, although feeble thermals may persist for a further few hours. A failure to realise that the time has come to hang on to every scrap of lift has brought many gliders early to earth.

It is seldom that a flight can be made absolutely straight, a zig-zag course from thermal to thermal being necessary. The problem is to decide what deviation is acceptable from the straight course. Is it better to go off sideways 30° for 2 miles to an obviously good source of lift, or only 10° for 4 miles to a slightly less good cloud? In the second case the chance of finding good lift is reduced, but the distance is shorter. If the zig-zag does not exceed 20° it does not matter much, as the following table shows:

Angle of zig-zag from direct course (°)	Distance
0	100
10	102
20	106
30	115
40	130
50	156

Table 12.1   Effect of deviation from course on distance travelled.

Beyond 20° the distance increases rapidly. The important point is to be sure that the zig-zag is not biased one way or the other. The pilot who has a properly corrected compass, has worked out his course for the forecast wind, and who has sufficient skill to steer accurately is less likely to waste time getting unnecessarily miles off course.

LOW LOSS FLYING

Throughout the entire flight the pilot is trying to save seconds. Since in world champtionships the difference in time between top pilots on a course more than 500 km in length is often less than one minute, it will be seen that this sort of time can be saved if the pilot can avoid doing no more than 3 redundant circles. In a four-hour flight using perhaps 20 thermals a total of 3 is not much—except that it may make the difference between winning or not. A detailed analysis of low loss flying has been written by champion George Moffat describing the many ways in which seconds can be saved. When practising for a champtionships a thorough post-examination of each flight should be carried out, and the findings used to try to save those irreplaceable seconds.

NAVIGATION

Good navigation is an essential part of competition flying and it needs more of the pilot's attention in Britain than in most countries. There is a superfluity of landmarks and visibility is not always of the best, particularly in anticyclonic weather. There may often be soaring conditions combined with really thick haze. The whole country may be covered but it will always be worse to the lee of large industrial areas. Navigating in this haze, while trying to fly as fast as possible and find turning-points without any delay can be exceedingly difficult. It helps to keep an accurate log of times and to use all possible forethought. Sometimes the target may lie on a prominent road, railway or river or even line of hills running across the track line. Rather than aim straight at the target and then be uncertain whether it is to the left or right when the prominent line is met, it may be better to aim off a little to one side and then turn along the prominent line to the target.

DISTANCE FLYING

The theory is simple—to start early and fly as long as possible. The difficulty lies in deciding how soon to leave without too great a risk of having to land within the first few miles. Apart from Silver badge flights and attempts on world records, very little pure distance flying is now done, primarily because of the cost in both time and money of the retrieve. In championships, however, there may be days on which the weather is more suited to a task in which the pilot has freedom to select his route in flight. For example, on a day of slow-moving isolated thunderstorms a task around a triangular course could fail if one of the turning-points was totally obscured by heavy rain for perhaps half the competitors. It is for such days that Distance around a Prescribed Area, or Cats Cradle, of 4 – 7 turning points which may be turned in any order (Appendix 9) is useful; the cunning pilot is able to keep himself airborne in the best weather.

A typical Cats Cradle course will cover an area of perhaps 150 by 100 miles and, depending on the location of the competition site in relation to controlled airspace, may be substantially up or downwind of it. It is preferable that it should be generally upwind so that pilots can use the last weak thermals of the day to drift with the wind towards home, but the organisers of the contest may have no choice. The pilot, however, will need to employ quite differenct tactics. His intention is always to use the strongest part of the day to pack in the miles which, on a Cats Cradle upwind, would mean using this time to work to windward to a position which will allow him to make the best use of later, weaker lift. Careful planning and flying may even permit the pilot to reach base on a final glide after thermals have died away completely. If the Cats Cradle is substantially downwind, the pilot will have little chance of avoiding a retrieve, so should use the best lift for maximum distance regardless of direction, and position himself to utilise as much as possible of the weak evening lift. Whether or not he uses the period of strongest thermals to fly substantially into wind or across wind will depend to a large extent on thermal distribution. If, for example, clouds are in streets the route chosen should have little or no crosswind flying, with few turning points, so that streets can be used to cover the miles. If, however, the cumulus are large, tending to shower, and are surrounded by quite big areas of sink, it will be better to keep in a good corner of the task area, even if this demands breaking off several times from good lift to

photograph a turn point. Before take-off, an overall plan
for the flight should be made based on the forecast, and likely
average speeds calculated for the thermal strength expected
to prevail during the whole flight period. To a pilot used only
to exploiting the strongest part of the day on speed flights it
may be difficult to work out how best to use the weaker early
and late hours during which it is possible to stay airborne,
but not very easy to go anywhere except downwind. It is on
good overall strategy that Cats Cradle days are won. Such
days may also need concentration for much longer periods
than for many speed flights. After 8 – 10 hours airborne, endless skill and patience is necessary to extract all possible energy
from the last feeble thermal of the day, and then be able to
make a neat and accurate landing in a difficult field.

CLOUD FLYING

Even if cloud flying is permitted in the rules it is impracticable to make any previous decisions as to whether or not cloud
should be entered; if it is easy and an appreciable height is
needed and can be gained it may be worthwhile. But if, however, getting into cloud is difficult, and climbs of only a few
hundred feet are likely, then it is almost certainly a waste of
time. In these circumstances it is better to climb up to near
cloud base or until the lift weakens, and then go off at high
speed keeping clear of cloud, but steering a course under those
parts of the cumulus which look as though they might give
lift. By cunning use of this method it may be possible to go
quite a long way without having to circle at all.

RADIO

Radio between glider and retrieve car, and between competitors and Organiser is essential in serious competitions. It
reduces the retrieve problems and enables control at the start
line to be accurate; without radio it is easy for a small number
of gliders to be missed if the air is hazy, or if several aircraft
cross the line within seconds of each other. Radios used in
gliders carry anything from the minimum of the two exclusive
glider frequencies (in the UK 130.1 and 130.4 MHz) up to
360 channels. The air-to-ground range is normally able to cope

easily with a 500-km triangle, but the ground-to-ground is much less, perhaps 10 miles in flat open country, but less than a mile in mountainous regions.

Unfortunately, the two glider channels are so often filled with chatter that it is difficult to get a message across, for which to a large extent gliding people have only themselves to blame. Obviously, if there are only a few people on the air, long conversations do not matter; but during a contest with, say, 40 gliders on the same frequency, each glider has only one-and-a-half minutes per hour as its share of radio time. It is thus essential that messages are both short and necessary. There is seldom any need for the ground crew to call up a pilot, nor for him to give them instructions. It is necessary only for the pilot to tell his crew his location and height, and if there is any change of plan, what he proposes doing.

It is best not to use place names when reporting positions since they are often misunderstood. It is much quicker and clearer just to give the distance along the track line, and if the glider is far off track, to give the distance sideways, e.g., '40 miles out,' or '40 miles out, 10 miles right.' As has already been explained, the crew will have a much better appreciation of the glider's future course if they know its height, but there is no need for this to be given precisely. A complete position report, therefore, need be nothing more than 'Three six, 48 miles, 4500 over.' To which the crew replies 'Three six from three six mobile out.'

If the message is not heard clearly, the crew should call 'Three six from three six mobile, say again.' The pilot should then repeat his original message, using the same words. This point is frequently not appreciated and people try to rephrase their messages in order to make them more easily understood. This is wrong since if communication is bad, a message repeated several times can often be heard correctly, whereas continual alterations merely confuse still further.

PAIR FLYING

Pair flying—of two gliders flying together—is used to a considerable extent in competition flying. There is nothing in the rules to prevent it, provided that both gliders are competing and flying the task set for their class; receiving assistance from non-competing gliders or aeroplanes is not allowed. The advantage of pair flying lies in the increased chance which two aircraft flying generally alongside each other have of finding lift compared to a single aircraft. If either of the pair locates a good source of lift his partner can join him. Obviously radio is a help both in attracting attention and passing information; and a few simple codewords can be used to avoid telling the rest of the competitors what is going on. The two gliders use the same thermal and then set course to again fly side-by-side a few hundred yards apart. Alternatively, a leap frogging technique can be used.

The values of pair flying are obvious, but there are problems which can easily lead to impaired performances by both pilots. If one gets low, for example, should his partner wait for him and lose time or go on his way alone? If one pilot becomes the leader the presence of his partner will not help him much while the latter, by assuming the role of follower may lose his initiative and fail to see possibilities which exist. Some competition pilots, perhaps most of them, treat their flying in a highly individualistic way and do not take kindly to the idea of cooperating with a partner. But there are others, who without losing their drive can pair-fly to the benefit of both. To achieve best results much practice is needed.

TRAILERING

On speed tasks the trailer crew, after seeing their glider launched and well established on the climb, should concentrate on ensuring that the pilot is officially observed to cross the starting line. This is normally done by radio.

The crew should now prepare to leave the field at a moment's notice should the pilot land out prematurely, but if all is going well the crew should follow the plan made with the pilot prior to take-off. In poor conditions this may involve taking the trailer some way out along the course in order to get the pilot back quickly for a fresh start (provided that this is permitted in the rules), but in really good weather there may be no need for the crew to leave the field at all. On big triangles it may be useful to take the trailer to a high point somewhere in the middle, preferably on a hill and away from power and telephone lines. From here the crew can listen to their pilot as he flies around the course, and if all is well can return to base so as to arrive back at the airfield at the same time as the glider. A log should be kept of the pilot's position reports together with his height, so that should he fail to call up, the crew have an approximate idea of where he might be.

Should the task be distance or speed to a distant goal the crew should set off as soon as they feel certain that the glider will probably stay airborne. The plan should be based on the possibility of quickly getting the glider back for another start (if permitted) or at least being able to return at a civilised time in the evening so the pilot can have a proper meal and night's sleep. If conditions are poor the crew should be careful not to get ahead of the pilot, since if they then lose contact on the radio, they will not know whether to look for him ahead or behind, and a lot of time will probably be wasted.

Should the radio fail to function, or contact with the pilot is otherwise lost, the crew should get themselves to a suitable telephone and try to regain contact via the competition retrieve controller. Sometimes another pilot will call the crew and offer to transmit messages to the pilot, but the crew should not bother other pilots with their problems unless they genuinely believe that an emergency situation has developed. The pilot and crew should always have a contingency plan in case of radio failure, and the simplest one is to know the times at which the other will telephone Control. If, say, the pilot tries to phone on the hour and the crew at quarter past, there will be less chance of the pilot just missing a crew call.

The most likely time for radio contact to be lost is, of course, when it is needed most, when the pilot is getting low and may have to land. The wise pilot, knowing the problem, will give extra position reports while he still has height in hand, and the crew should study place names in the area on the map, so that if later messages are less intelligible they will have more chance of recognising the half-heard words. It is also useful, particularly on a weak day when the pilot may often be low, to use the words, landing-landing-landing, so that the crew will know that this is not just another low point from which the pilot will emerge over the radio in twenty minutes' time.

Finally, the crew should remember that it is the pilot who is expected to have all the excitement, not them. Competitions are not won by a crew that gets bogged down, lost, or arrested. The pilot should be able to fly believing that his crew will arrive without delay, without problems, and without having consumed the last of the refreshments on board!

Chapter 13

Parachutes and other Survival Matters

It is a convention, and a good one, that parachutes are worn in gliders for aerotowing, aerobatics, and cloud flying. Since the pilot never knows when the opportunity for soaring will arise, the parachute should be part of the glider's standard equipment, and if carried it is only logical that it should be put on properly each time, even if the flight is intended to be short.

There is no point in having a parachute which is not reliable, and so it must be properly looked after. The daily inspection should ensure that the straps, buckles and pack cover are in good condition, that the ripcord pin is not bent, and that its red thread is unbroken. It is important to keep the parachute dry, and to avoid getting oil, grease or battery acid on it. When not in use it should be kept in a dry place, and the parachute should be repacked about every three months; a job for a professional packer. Each parachute should have a bag of its own and this should be carried in the glider, so that the bagged parachute can be used as a wingtip weight when the glider is landed after a cross-country flight.

If it is worth putting on a parachute at all, it should be reasonably well adjusted.

Aeroplane pilots having engine failure over bad country may on occasions decide that it is preferable to bale out rather than to attempt a landing. When flying gliders and faced with the same decision it will usually be preferable to land, because the landing speed is so much slower, and in any case if the country is unsuitable for landing a glider it may be equally bad for parachuting. Because of this, and because the risk of fire in a glider is remote, it appears that the only occasion when it may be necessary to bale out is when the glider is out of control. The loss of control may be due to structural failure, or failure of the control system caused by faults in the aircraft itself, or by collision. If the glider is out of control it will probably be doing the most peculiar evolutions and losing height rapidly. It may therefore be a matter of extreme difficulty to get out at all, apart from the fact that there may be little time to do this.

Once the pilot has decided to bale out, he must put his decision into practice immediately; getting rid of the cockpit canopy, undoing the harness, and then getting out. A legend has sprung up that it is better to get out on the inside of a turn or spin. While this was undoubtedly the best technique with certain types of biplane aeroplane, there is little evidence to suggest that it is necessarily better with gliders. There are two separate considerations: the actual exit from the cockpit, and getting clear of the aircraft without being hit by it. Since both these may be influenced greatly by whether the glider is slipping and skidding, and its behaviour generally, it is probably best not to have any fixed ideas, but to get out on the side which seems easiest.

The parachute should be ripped as soon as the pilot is really well clear of the aircraft. When the glider is relieved of the pilot's weight it may change its antics, and there have been two cases of the glider doing a quick loop and coming round into the opening parachute, and so if there is height to spare, the parachute should not be opened while the glider is still close. If for some reason the pilot falls for a considerable time before opening the parachute, the attitude of his body may become stabilized. He may be unaware of this if falling through cloud, or in heavy rain which may be hitting his eyes at a relative speed of up to 70 knots. The danger is that if he stabilizes on his back he may start spinning with his limbs spread out by centrifugal force. Unless he can upset the geometrical symmetry the rotational speed will increase, making it even more difficult to get at the ripcord. It is possible that the rotational speed will get so high that the pilot may be incapacitated or killed by this alone. If, for any reason, it seems necessary to delay before pulling the ripcord, the pilot should attempt to achieve the sport parachutist's basic spread position – face down.

If the pilot leaves his glider in cloud, at a great height, he must try to assess which is the greater risk – that of opening the parachute and being carried higher in strong upcurrents, which may involve frostbite or anoxia, or that of being unable to open it. On balance it is probably better to open the parachute without undue delay, particularly if the altitude is less than 20,000 ft.

Difficulty is sometimes experienced in finding the ripcord ring. Ideally the pilot should leave the glider with his hand on it, but if this is impossible he should put his head down and look for it rather than grope wildly around. Having pulled the ripcord, and it needs quite a pull, there will be a ghastly pause when nothing seems to happen, followed by a sudden jerk. The pilot will then find himself hanging by straps from each shoulder. The parachute may oscillate considerably, and while an experienced parachutist can stop this swinging, it is too much to expect anyone to learn this on his first drop.

A lot of nonsense has been talked about steering a glider parachute on the way down; an experienced man can do this to a limited extent, but it is again out of the question the first time.

By looking down between his feet the parachutist can see which way he is drifting over the ground. It is an advantage to land facing more or less downwind. The easiest way to do this is to reach up and grasp the opposite straps with each hand; by pulling the hands slightly together the body will be rotated. During the last few hundred feet the ground seems to rush up at a great rate; the parachutist should try to stay as limp as possible, keep his feet together with his knees slightly bent, and then as his feet touch the ground, pull up on his arms. After landing he should get his parachute off as quickly as possible to avoid being dragged about.

If the descent is made into water, the knob of the quick release box should be twisted while still in the air and one hand held ready to hit it as soon as the feet actually **touch** the water. The other hand should be used to pinch the nostrils together and prevent water going up the nose. Getting rid of the parachute in this way should ensure that the pilot does not come up under the canopy and get entangled with it. However, if the wind is strong and blowing towards the shore, it may be better not to detach the parachute as it will probably act as a sail and drag the pilot towards land.

It is quite impossible to lay down any hard and fast rules of the minimum height at which it is practicable to bale out of a glider; so much depends on the circumstances. However, it can be said that if the pilot can get out and clear at more than 500 ft above the ground he should have every chance of survival.

If a parachute is ever needed, it will be wanted suddenly, and this is not the time to start remembering instructions and thinking out means of exit. The pilot should try to visualize the scene and have all his actions clear in his mind. When putting on a parachute he should make a habit of feeling for the ripcord handle so that he knows exactly where it is. When getting out of a glider on the ground the pilot should often do so wearing his parachute, and then if he ever has to use it in the air, he will have had some practice in getting out of the cockpit with it on. To emphasize the importance of this mental approach it is worth mentioning that several aircrew, when baling out, have operated their parachute harness quick release instead of pulling the ripcord.

HOSTILE ENVIRONMENTS

When ambling around a 100-km triangle on a warm English summer day the idea of survival equipment and suchlike matters seems remote. But not all gliding is done in a mild climate. In some countries, and in some circumstances in the British Isles, such as soaring the Scottish mountains in winter, survival considerations are important. It is the pilot who has not thought about them, or who does not believe that anything needs to be done, who usually finds out the hard way.

Survival in a hostile environment is not only a matter of having sensible equipment and knowing how to use it, but of understanding the circumstances that exist at the time and being sensible about those, too. People vary enormously in their ability to deal with unusual situations. One person, hav-

ing got himself into a predicament, such as inadvertently landing on a snow covered mountain at dusk, will subsequently
do everything right. Another pilot will land miles from anywhere in dry desert scrub, and promptly set it on fire lighting
a cigarette.

Glider pilots will go long distances to find good soaring,
but some of the best areas in the world can be rugged. If the
day temperature rises over the 90's (35°C), and there is little
or no shade and no people, it is essential that a really adequate
amount of drinking water – at least 2 litres – is carried in the
glider, and that the pilot has a brimmed hat and tough boots
or shoes. Glider pilots have landed in Southern USA,
Argentina, Australia and South Africa more, sometimes much
more, than 10 miles from the nearest house. If the radio has
died, or someone lost the message, or the retrieve car broke
down the pilot could be stuck for up to two days before
being located.

There is, of course, a great temptation to walk out and return to blissful civilization, but this should not be attempted
unless the route is known – precisely. That flat sandy desert
viewed from 8000 ft may not be in the least flat seen from a
height of 5ft 10 in, and wandering around trying to find ends
to ravines is a good way to get lost. If it is positively known
that, for example, there is a track to a river 6 miles away, and
that the river has flat open banks and leads to a telephone,
then it may be reasonable to trek off. The glider should be
properly secured and a note left visibly in the cockpit saying
what the pilot intends and the time of departure. If an air
search is mounted this is most likely to take place at first light
and a glider is far more visible than a dust covered human. If
in any doubt at all, stay with the glider.

The other need for survival sense can occur when soaring
in mountains, at any time of the year. The temperature drops
about 3°C with every thousand feet of height, so a night valley
floor temperature of 10°C will change to below freezing at
around 4000 ft. higher. Arriving inadvertently up in the Alps
or the Cairngorms may be due to a variety of causes. Control
of the glider or of the situation may have been lost due to
severe turbulence or heavy sink, orographic cloud may have

developed suddenly and enveloped the glider, or snow glare may have resulted in disorientation. Whatever the reason the chances are that the arrival will be less than a neat landing. Even if the pilot is not hurt he may be faced with a number of different problems if there is no one around and no one knows where he is. These include, first of all, checking if the glider is in a precarious situation; it is after all the only useful asset the pilot has. Is there any risk that it will slide off the slope, or if in snow that this will slide taking the glider with it? If the afternoon sun is on the slope and it is at all steep, the pilot should get off it and not return until the temperature has dropped with sunset. Avalanches give little warning and even a small snow slide can do damage.

The next problem is to attract attention. Unlike the pilot 10 miles from anywhere in a sun-drenched desert, the pilot on the mountain may in fact be visible to a number of people if he can attract their attention. Anything that will make a patch of colour, such as spreading an orange anorak next to a red wingtip, or treading out a large x (unable to proceed) or □ (aircraft seriously damaged) in the snow will help. Such signs should be made in the middle of a clean patch of snow, and advantage should be taken of the angle of sun to make any shadows contribute to the contrast of the sign. If there are any flares in the glider the pilot should fire two at an interval of about 2 minutes, but before doing so should work out the location of possible observers in the valley, and fire the flares across their line of vision with some dark mountain as a background. Bright sunshine reduces the effectiveness of flares.

If it is apparent that the night may have to be spent on the mountain and there is no shelter, the glider should be made as habitable as possible before dark. Snow banked up or timber or brush of any sort should be used to make a windbreak, remembering that the wind may change direction to flow down the valley during the night. More snow, or again anything suitable such as heather, should be banked up against the side of the cockpit to improve the insulation, and if anything can be done to improve the 'roof' insulation so much the better. It will probably become extremely cold, so all spare clothes — and there ought be some — should be put on before the temperature starts to drop. While making his habitat the pilot should avoid getting either hot and sweaty or exhausted. Any drink carried should be rationed as snow is extremely uneconomical in terms of heat energy consumed per quantity of liquid obtained. High mountain streams, if any, are usually safe to drink. At no time should there be any hesitation in opening the parachute and using it as a signal panel, clothing or bedding. Again, the pilot should stay with or near the glider – it is even less profitable trying to walk out in strange mountains than it is in a scrubby desert.

FIRST AID

It is a rule in some countries that the glider must carry a first aid pack. In hot countries this should include suitable snakebit serum, mosquito repellent, and sunburn cream. Also when flying in mountains the kit should include sunburn cream, which will additionally slightly reduce the heat loss from the skin in a wind; and glucose, as well as the usual contents.

SECURING THE AIRCRAFT

Although the glider can usually be replaced and is therefore less important than the pilot, it should be properly picketed or otherwise secured at the first opportunity. Quite apart from the waste, an aircraft blown over after landing is much less useful as a shelter.

CRASH PROTECTION

Pilots are often unnecessarily injured in quite minor accidents because they have not organised sensible seat cushions for themselves, or because they have allowed switches, knobs, and even the instruments to become a near relative to the bed of nails. Care about crash protection is particularly important where a landing may be made far from people; even very slight injuries can be serious because the pilot may need all of his physical stamina and undivided attention to extricate himself from an unwelcome situation.

COMMUNICATION

Rescuers have a big problem when they do not know even where to start looking. A pilot soaring on his own has a responsibility to at least tell some friends where he is going and about what time he expects to get back or to telephone. Radio is obviously valuable to give position reports and to indicate any changes of plan. Calls about possible landings should be made while the glider is still high. If left too late the message may never be heard; this is particularly true in mountains as the glider may be screened by an intervening peak.

Immediately on landing an attempt should be made to establish contact, and the set then switched off; every bit of urge in the battery may be needed to guide searchers later.

Survival is best achieved by use of the imagination *before* starting to fly in possible problem areas, and by making proper provision for likely emergencies; an essential small pocket flashlight is of little use when left at home.

Chapter 14

Physiological Considerations

As every pilot discovers in the course of his flying career, the human body is not ideally adapted to flight. This often becomes apparent when enthusiasm to get into the air overcomes the need to avoid flying with a cold; the resultant pain and deafness usually clear up quite quickly, but are tedious while they last.

When flying locally, in good health and clear air, there are few problems which affect the soaring pilot other than catarrh, over-indulgence, and moderate amounts of *g* when doing aerobatics. More ambitious flying offers a variety of hazards and it is prudent to understand how the body is affected by the conditions and situations in which the pilot may find himself. Such knowledge will at least add to the interest of flying, and it could be the only means of saving his life.

Broadly, the efficiency of a pilot is determined by the manner in which his body reacts to its environment. The unaided human body cannot cope with all the conditions likely to be encountered, and suitable equipment must be provided to enable it to continue functioning satisfactorily. An understanding of how the body is assisted by such aids is required, together with a technical knowledge of the equipment so that it can be correctly used.

COLD

Cold is the most usual of the bodily discomforts which detracts from the pleasure of flying and the efficiency of the pilot. In cool countries, most pilots have some experience of being cold. Pupils spend their early days at the launch point with wet feet, and often progress to their first unexpectedly long flight shivering in shirt sleeves. On such occasions as these, cold is little more than a temporary inconvenience; but on high altitude flights it can be serious.

The temperature of the air decreases with height at a fairly steady rate – about 2 to 3°C per 1000 ft – up to about 36,000 ft, the tropopause, where it becomes more or less constant at around – 56°C. On a summer soaring day with a temperature on the airfield of 20°C, we can estimate how cold it is likely to be higher up. If the pilot has an aerotow to 2000 ft, the temperature at release height will have dropped to about 15°C. At Gold 'C' height (about 10,000 ft plus 2000 ft) the air will have cooled to about – 10°C. If the pilot presses on to get his Diamond (about 16,500 ft plus 2000 ft), the temperature at this height will be down to about – 30°C, or colder than it is ever likely to get on a winter's night in Britain. However, the temperature inside a well-fitting canopy will not get as low as outside, particularly if the glider is in the sun, and the flight short.

The extent to which the pilot is cooled by low temperature will depend (1) how damp he was at the beginning of the flight through being hot and sweaty, (2) the length of time he remains in the low temperature, and (3) the rate at which he is losing his body heat through his clothing.

As the pilot begins to get cold, his skin will initially produce goose-pimples, which are caused by the tiny muscles at the base of the hairs. Since man lost his fur coat long ago, he soon starts shivering, which is an effort made by the muscles to increase the circulation of the blood. If the body is further cooled, it has no more natural remedies and a progressive slowing down of the circulation will commence; with the more sluggish blood-flow the pilot's face, lips, nails, and eventually his limbs and body will become bluish. This will be followed by numbness and then pain in the hands and feet. It is now less likely that he will take positive steps to alleviate his situation, since his reflexes and thought processes will have slowed down with his general circulation. At this point there is a real risk of frostbite or congestion of the lungs, first felt as a constrictive pain in the chest and probably followed by hiccoughs and the risk of becoming unconscious.

If we consider how such a situation can come about it, it will be easier to avoid. Whatever precautions the pilot has taken in order to keep warm, there will almost certainly come a time on any altitude flight when he notices that he is feeling cold. If he observes the outside temperature at this moment he may think that he is coping with it very well, particularly if the climb has been rapid. This is because it takes a surprisingly long time for the glider itself to cool down, especially if it has a well-sealed cockpit, and the sun is providing some warmth on the pilot's head and the top part of his body. It is easy to forget that the glider still has to be brought down, and that the temperature lag will affect it while descending, so that it will then be cooler than the surrounding air. It may have slipped the pilot's memory that it often takes longer than expected to descend, and that cut-off of the sun, either because it is setting or because it is obscured by cloud or mountain, will markedly reduce any warmth that the pilot may still possess. Even if the actual temperature is now low – say around freezing point – prolonging the flight will continue to chill the pilot although the cockpit temperature does not get less. This is because there is a continuous loss of heat from the body which is not being replaced. A flight can be greatly prolonged if the pilot, not unreasonably cold, tries to work weak lift at altitude in an attempt to gain a few more feet. His concentration on the flying obscures perception of his situation, and if he is short of oxygen, he will get cold even quicker.

In the absence of an external source of heat, the pilot must rely on his clothes for warmth. The body of the normal adult tries to maintain a temperature of 37°C, using the skin to do so. If the pilot gets hot, as he frequently does when pulling his glider to the launch point, or even just by sitting in it on a sunny day waiting to start, his blood-flow to the skin increases. This causes the surplus heat to escape by sweating and evaporation and much of this dampness ends up in the clothes, especially his socks. If the pilot is now steadily cooled by climbing high, he will discover that his damp clothing has lost some of its normal insulating properties, and that his feet may be starting to freeze. Every effort should be made to start a flight wearing dry clothes. If necessary, the pilot should change into warm dry socks just before take-off, not forgetting to dry his feet thoroughly first. He should then avoid getting hot even if this means resorting to such prima-donna tactics as carrying a sunshade and persuading others to push the glider into position.

Most people only make the mistake of wearing inadequate clothing once. Thereafter, if there is any chance of going high, they take special precautions; they soon learn that a number of thin layers, which trap air between them, are better than one thick sweater which is too hot at the beginning and of little protection later. It is obvious that clothing should cover all the body including the head, and there should be no gaps. Since the feet are most susceptible to cold, adequate protection at the ankles is necessary. It is not enough to pull a pair of thin socks over the trouser ends – it is better to have two pairs of loose wool socks under flying boots. Tight shoes are undesirable. If gloves are not used at the start of the flight, they should be put on before the hands cool. For those who dislike flying in thick gloves, a pair of silk or cotton ones may be enough for much of the flight, with a pair of thick mitts kept ready for when it gets really cold. If the pilot has not previously flown in big boots or thick gloves he should make sure that he can operate all controls and switches before take-off.

The opportunity to go high may turn up unexpectedly when no suitable clothing is available. As a last resort, newspaper wrapped round the body and legs is a good insulator, although it may lead to ribald comments. To some extent, the effects of cold can be combated by frequently exercising the toes and fingers.

Apart from cold, there are several other ways in which flying affects the human body. It is sensitive to changes in air pressure, accelerations and rotational movements. The normal working of the various mechanisms that cope with these effects depend to some extent on the health of the pilot – the most usual deterioration being due to the common cold. This affects the free passage of air in the bone cavities of the head and ear, the hearing, and sometimes the balance sense.

BALANCE

Each ear consists of the external part, the middle ear which carries the ear drum, the little bones called ossicles which transmit sound vibrations to the brain, and the upper end of the eustachian tube connecting the ear to the throat. The inner ear is the space on the inside of the middle ear, which includes the organs of balance — the semicircular canals — together with the cochlea, which converts the movements of the drum, transmitted by the ossicles, into impulses which can be appreciated by the brain as hearing.

There are three semicircular canals in each ear, which take the form of loops nearly at right angles to each other. These tubes, which end in a common sac, are filled with a thick liquid. Each tube has hairs growing on the inside of its walls. The tubes are positioned in relation to each other so that they provide the brain with the information that the body is rolling, pitching or turning. When the pilot's body starts to rotate in any of these directions, the inertia of the liquid causes it to lag behind his motion. This lag causes the hairs to be deflected, thus conveying an indication of rotation to the brain. If the rotation continues, friction between the fluid and the semicircular canals eventually causes the fluid to rotate at the same speed as the body. No indication of rotation is then conveyed to the brain. If at this stage, the rotation of the body is stopped, the inertia of the fluids causes it to continue rotating. This deflects the hairs the other way, producing a signal as if the body were starting to rotate in the opposite direction.

Another effect of the signals from the semicircular canals is that the eyes are automatically caused to turn in the head so that they remain looking in a steady direction in space. If the body turns through a large angle, the time will come when the eyes, trying to point in a set direction, will have turned as far as they can. When this happens, they immediately flick fully the other way and continue pointing in the new set direction. When the fluid in the semicircular canals has caught up with the movement of the head, the turning signal will cease and consequently this flicking motion of the eyes will stop. It is at this moment that the rider on a merry-go-round finds that the outside world becomes a blur. When the rotation ceases, the signals from the semicircular canals are reversed and the eyes tend to flick in the opposite sense. These motions of the eyes are quite involuntary; however, a person with suitable training such as a ballet dancer can learn to allow for them.

When performing normal turns in clear air the experienced pilot has little difficulty in reconciling the signals from his semicircular canals with the visual information received from his eyes, but sometimes confusion can occur. This may be due to illness, the use of some drugs, or by the semicircular canals being overloaded by false stimuli – the Coriolis effect. This can happen if the occupant of the circling glider suddenly rotates his head about an axis different from the axis of rotation of the glider. The feeling of disorientation can sometimes be noticed when photographing turning-points, suddenly coming out of cloud, or after seeing the horizon in an unexpected position and making an instinctive correction. The experienced pilot will usually wait for a few seconds for things to settle down before trying to do anything else, and has, of course, long since learnt how to look at things in the air and on the ground without confusing himself. It is the inexperienced pilot, not knowing about his condition, who finds it frightening. Pupil pilots, who are not yet used to moving in several directions at the same time, can be completely disorientated by aerobatics, or by dropping a wing off an *unexpected* stall in rough air, or even by doing as little as the last 50 ft of a winch launch in cloud. At low heights, spatial disorientation frequently results in the glider hitting the ground before control is regained. The pupil becomes irretrievably muddled, dizzy or so frightened by the feeling of tumbling, falling, or detachment that he may well let go of the stick and hang on to the cockpit itself for support; if he stays with the controls, he may dive into the ground in a panic desire to get back to the ground, because it is the only familiar thing left. Even experienced pilots may notice temporary sensations of disorientation when indulging in manoeuvres such as recovery from a long spin.

When cloud flying, external visual reference is absent, and the only sensations of turning are those conveyed by the semicircular canals. Due to effects of the inertia of the fluid, these sensations of turning may be very misleading as explained above. The answer is, of course, to have serviceable blind-flying instruments and the training to believe in them and use them well.

PRESSURE CHANGES ON THE EAR

When the pressure of the air outside the ear changes, the ear drum is deflected inward if the exterior pressure is increasing, and outwards if it is decreasing. When climbing into reducing pressure, equalization is fairly automatic since air expanding in the middle ear can escape down the eustachian tube into the throat. The ear will be felt to click as this happens. When the pilot descends, however, the pressure on the outside of the drum increases, and to keep pace with this, air has to be forced up the eustachian tube. Sometimes it may be necessary only to swallow, yawn or work the lower jaw with the mouth open to obtain equalization and relief in the ears, but if any pain is felt the nose should be held closed with the fingers, and a firm breath forced into it with the mouth shut. Since it may not be possible to climb the glider up again to relieve pressure on the drum, every effort should be made to keep the ears clear, if necessary by pinching the nose and blowing at frequent intervals, even if the discomfort is only very slight. Temporary deafness is a common result of failure to clear the ears properly. If attempts are made to fly at all high with a cold, the pilot may be unable to clear the blocked eustachian tube, and will be lucky if he does not burst an ear drum, quite apart from the pain and deafness that he will have. He should also remember that it is usually more difficult to equalize pressure on the descent.

The ear is not the only part of the head to contain air spaces. The sinuses in the bones of the forehead and cheeks are also connected with the nose, and if blocked or swollen by infection, will be prevented from pressure adjustment.

If, at the start of a descent from a considerable height such as 25,000 ft there seems to be no difficulty, it should not be assumed that there will be no trouble later. As the ground is approached, in a steady descent, pressure increases rapidly, and it requires greater efforts to maintain equalization. The ears should be continually cleared by swallowing or other means. If, after landing, the ears are still blocked, advice from a doctor should be obtained.

Pressure changes will affect any part of the body where there is compressible, or expandable, air. It pays not to eat a heavy indigestible meal, or have gassy drinks, before flying.

OXYGEN

For the pilot who aims to go really high, obtaining enough oxygen to breathe becomes important. The atmospheric pressure is about 14.7 lb/sq in. at sea level and steadily decreases with height. At 18,000 ft it is only half the surface value.

The composition of the air is approximately 78% nitrogen, 21% oxygen, and 1% other gases, including carbon dioxide. The air that is breathed out differs in that it is less dry — there is always water vapour and carbon dioxide present in the lungs. The following simple description of how the body makes use of the air is taken from *Gliding Kiwi*.

The human body is comparable to an internal combustion engine. It takes in fuel and oxygen, and converts this or burns it to form energy and waste gas — carbon dioxide.

The mechanism of breathing is provided to convey oxygen into the blood and carbon dioxide out. Also it assists in controlling body temperature and acidity.

We normally breathe about 12–16 times a minute, taking in 400 ml (a pint) of air with each breath, or about 7 litres a minute. This can be accelerated to about 70 litres a minute under stress of exercise. Muscular effort is required for breathing in, when the chest wall moves out and the diaphragm moves down. This creates a negative pressure in the chest cavity causing the lungs to expand and take in air.

The lungs are like great sponges consisting of tiny air passages ending in minute air sacs called alveoli. The access is via the nose and throat and air flows down through the bronchial tubes to the alveoli having been moistened, warmed and filtered on the way. The alveoli are lined by very thin walls of membrane containing thousands of small blood vessels. With air pressure, oxygen from the air passes through the walls into the blood while simultaneously carbon dioxide passes out.

It will be seen from this that respiration and circulation of the blood are closely linked. Both are affected more quickly by an increase in the carbon dioxide level in the blood, than by a reduction in oxygen pressure. Any increase in the carbon dioxide speeds up both the heart and the respiration and circulation rates, resulting in the pilot needing to take in more air. With increasing altitude there may not be sufficient oxygen available to him since its partial pressure, which is about $\frac{1}{5}$ of the local atmospheric pressure, may be too low. Eventually, this partial pressure becomes insufficient for the blood to absorb enough oxygen to maintain the normal bodily functions. This results in a condition called anoxia, or hypoxia. Breathing more rapidly cannot avert this situation; it merely disturbs the CO_2 balance in the body, which results in the condition of hyperventilation described later.

Most people know of the symptoms of anoxia, or have seen them simulated in flying films. There is usually a mixture of faintness or dizziness, oddly combined with a feeling of well-being and confidence. Since the pilot may have, at the same time, a headache, blurred vision, blue finger nails, and be continually yawning, it will be seen that he may not be coping well with his flying. If he continues to climb without increasing his oxygen supply he may become unconscious.

Even at the fairly low level of about 10,000 ft, long periods without oxygen may induce symptoms of anoxia. Once these are present, the pilot is less likely to look after himself by putting on his mask, or turning on the supply. Since he is working quite hard with his brain while flying, the glider pilot needs his full quota of oxygen to fly efficiently. It is therefore sensible to start using it at 10,000 ft or even lower when feeling tired.

Up to a height of about 20,000 ft most healthy pilots will have several minutes' latitude to rectify failures of the oxygen supply before losing consciousness, but as further height is gained the available time becomes rapidly less. The table on p. 193 shows how soon loss of consciousness occurs if the oxygen supply is cut off.

Above 30,000 ft there will be very little warning of oxygen loss and, for all practical purposes, negligible time to restore the supply. Recovery from anoxia at any height, provided that the pilot is still alive, is rapid if he can obtain plenty of oxygen.

Height in feet	Time to lose consciousness
22,000	8–10 minutes
25,000	2–3 minutes
28,000	1–1$\frac{1}{2}$ minutes
30,000	$\frac{3}{4}$–1 minute
35,000	30–45 seconds
40,000	15–30 seconds

Table 14.1   Loss of consciousness with height

PRESSURE BREATHING

Up to 10,000 ft, ordinary air at the local pressure is adequate to provide the pilot with enough oxygen. By 28,000 ft he will need neat oxygen, this will enable a really fit man to go up to 40,000 ft. Above this height the oxygen pressure will be insufficient to force enough into his blood, and a pressure mask system becomes necessary. This raises complications, since oxygen provided at above atmospheric pressure will overdistend the chest, with resultant overbreathing, unless this is prevented by special clothing. Such techniques require training in a decompression chamber. The world absolute altitude record of 46,500 ft is now unlikely to be broken except by someone wearing a complete pressure suit, or using a pressure cabin.

DECOMPRESSION SICKNESS

Occasionally high flying causes decompression sickness, more usually known as the bends. This seldom occurs below 25,000 ft unless the pilot is old, overweight, or has gone up very fast and then spends a long time at altitude. The bends are caused by an excess of nitrogen in the blood.

As the air pressure lowers, the surplus nitrogen in the blood forms bubbles which get lodged in the small blood vessels, usually at the joints. The symptoms are pain in the joints, itching of the skin, faulty vision and some paralysis and confusion. In severe cases there may be coughing, choking or unconsciousness. Occasionally decompression sickness does not occur until some time after the flight. If the bends are suspected, the pilot should see his doctor without delay, and even if the symptoms disappear fairly soon, he should not do any flying at all for at least 24 hours. If further high flying is attempted a worse attack may result. A sensible time interval should be allowed between high flying and scuba diving.

HYPERVENTILATION

This is the condition of overbreathing which can be set off by anoxia, but can also be stimulated by fear of suspense. The symptoms are a feeling of being unable to get any air, some pain in the chest, and faintness. The breathing is fast and shallow and the heart may thump. If the condition is severe, consciousness may be lost. The cause of the trouble is the breathing out of too much carbon dioxide which disturbs the oxygen/CO_2 balance. This body attempts to return things to normal, and this can be assisted by the pilot deliberately slowing down his breathing, or holding his breath.

At above 10,000 ft the onset of hyperventilation may simply be due to anoxia. If oxygen is already being used, the supply should be checked; if not, it should be turned on. At the same time, breathing should be consciously slow and gentle until everything is normal again. It should be realized that hyperventilation is not a rare condition, and that if it occurs it can be dealt with.

THE EFFECT OF *G*

Anything which is moving will continue to travel in a straight line at a steady speed unless a force is applied to it. For example, when starting a loop, the glider wants to continue in its original direction and an upwards force has to be applied to it in order to curve its flight path upwards. This produces an acceleration of the aircraft which is usually expressed in *g* units. If a body is allowed to fall freely, the force acting upon it is its weight, and this produces an acceleration of 32.2 ft/sec^2 (about 19 knots/sec). This acceleration is known as 1 *g*.

If a loop is said to be carried out at 3 *g*, the pilot is subjected to an upwards force of three times his own weight by the seat of the glider. In straight and level flight the force applied to him by the seat is equal to his weight; the additional force of twice his weight is due to the upward acceleration. The effect, so far as his body is concerned, is as if the weight had been trebled. The amount of g which a person can take varies with the individual, the length of time to which he is exposed to the g, and the orientation of his body to the acceleration. Astronauts lie flat during blast off because in this position they are least affected by vertical acceleration; the supine seating of many gliders gives similar resistance to g, but also less warning of high g forces. This should be remembered when doing aerobatics or any manoeuvre which puts large loads on to the glider, because they can withstand little more than their pilots. Since g forces increase the apparent weight of the pilot, it becomes difficult to eject from an aircraft, or even raise the arms. The pull on the body causes it to sag, and thus may affect breathing. When the body is upright, positive g pulls the blood towards the feet, and negative g moves it towards the head. When the blood is pulled downward, its circulation in the head is reduced – or ceases. The effect on the eyes is that vision is first restricted, then followed by loss of colour sensitivity with the result that everything appears grey; if g is increased still further nothing can be seen. Five seconds at 5 g will produce a blackout in the average pilot, but hangovers and hunger reduce resistance. Higher g produces unconsciousness, but is not usually encountered in gliders.

The human body is less resistant to negative g about $-3 g$ being enough for most pilots and more than enough for their gliders.

The application of sudden accelerations, particularly in the negative sense, can be rather alarming. An inexperienced pilot may be very sensitive to negative g and its unfamiliar feeling. For example, when the nose of the glider is put down suddenly after a cable break on a winch launch, it may be so disconcerting that he will not appreciate what has happened and just hang on to the controls.

As mentioned above, the amount of g a pilot can withstand depends on the length of time he is subjected to it. Provided that it is applied for only a very short time, surprisingly high values can be tolerated. This is useful in the event of a crash, when a man may be subjected up to 50 *g* and survive – provided that he is well strapped in, the structure in front does not telescope right back, and he is not hit on the head by a missile such as a barograph or camera.

A medical consideration not generally well known is the possible effect of flying with a full bladder – as well as being uncomfortable, this can be hazardous in the event of a crash.

FATIGUE

Health and fatigue are linked in that a pilot who normally lives a sedentary life, eating and drinking too much, will be more quickly tired by the activity of gliding than one who is really fit. Tiredness is obviously increased by lack of sleep, insufficient food, hangover, or the result of hard physical or mental effort; but boredom, apprehension, monotony and frustration due to not flying, excessive flying, or eyestrain can also cause fatigue. It is natural that a tired pilot will not fly as efficiently as one who is fresh; his reactions will be slower, his appreciation of the situation incomplete, and there is a risk that he will make incorrect decisions. Pilots with heavy responsibilities and tiring jobs in their daily lives, who use gliding as a relaxation, may tend to relax far too much when they are flying and fail to appreciate the degree of alertness and concentration which is needed for safety.

ILL HEALTH

There will always be those who decide to fly knowing that they are unfit. The risks in doing so are mainly (1) aggravating the trouble, as in earache, (2) not knowing the side-effects of any drugs that have been taken, and (3) most serious of all, flying with any condition which causes giddiness, fits or fainting.

If a pilot is taking anti-histamines, antibiotics, any form of sedatives or tranquillizers, or cough or cold mixtures, he should not fly without clearance from a doctor. Such drugs may make a person sleepy, cause feeling of depression, affect balance, co-ordination or vision, or require oxygen to be used at a lower height than usual. No pilot should ever fly on a mixture of tranquillizers or sedatives and alcohol.

If a person has ever suffered from any heart condition, or has had dizzy or fainting fits, a doctor's examination and clearance is essential; this information should not be concealed. Some people who have been free of attacks for years convince themselves that they are now all right. What they may not realize is that moments of fear, mental stress, or even intense concentration, can stimulate the recurrence of such illness. From time to time, accidents take place which seem quite inexplicable until enquiry discloses a complaint which the pilot had chosen to keep secret. It is always possible that some innocent person may also be involved.

DRINK

Drinking and flying should be kept quite separate. Even a person who is apparently unaffected by 'normal' amounts of alcohol should not fly within 4–5 hours of a single beer or glass of wine. The period should be appreciably longer if the quantity of alcohol is greater, to the extent that a pilot is unwise to fly if he has a hangover from drinking on the previous evening. The problem with alcohol is that although the handling of the glider may not be directly impaired, the pilot's ability to take decisions, and his judgement, deteriorate. Insufficient information is received from the senses for the situation to be fully comprehended, which results in the aircraft being flown with a confidence that is not justified.

AIRSICKNESS

Airsickness is not uncommon in passengers, or inexperienced pilots when subjected to continuous circling, particularly if the air is at all rough. This is because their balance mechanism becomes confused and upset. They become somewhat disorientated and in an effort to reassure themselves look fixedly at some part of the solid aircraft while the horizon moves past seemingly at random. Airsickness can be brought about by the person assuming in advance that he will probably be sick. Heat, lack of ventilation, cold, rough air, unfamiliar smells or an upset stomach can all be contributory factors.

If a passenger complains of feeling ill, or looks pale and uninterested, it is obviously sensible to land as soon as possible. If this cannot be done, the pilot should try to get the passenger to look in the direction that the glider is turning, so as to anticipate its progress with his eyes; the purpose of this is to try to stop the passenger fixing his eyes on something while the sky or ground are moving past it.

If airsickness is found to occur frequently, it is possible that one of the motion-sickness drugs will help overcome what may be a temporary disability; but no solo flying should be done whilst taking them.

Finally, as with all aspects of flying there is no substitute for overall competence combined with thorough preparation for the flight, and an acknowledgement by the pilot of his own personal physical and mental limitations. If the pilot is ambitious, particularly in the direction of height records, a knowledge of how his body is affected by flying is just as much part of his stock-in-trade as navigation or the ability to fly by instruments.

Chapter 15

Glider Design and Assessment

This chapter is written from the point of view of the soaring pilot who is concerned with flying a satisfactory glider, either as a private owner or a member of a club. It does not deal with one-off specialized designs although these obviously have a valuable function in stimulating progress and training designers. Nor will structural design be specifically mentioned, except when it is involved in other considerations. It is hoped that a theme will emerge from this chapter; that whilst performance is important, since it is the *raison d'être* of the glider, it is not all-important. Good aerodynamic performance is only one of the attributes of a satisfactory glider, since the overall performance may be regarded as a synthesis in which the qualities of the glider and the skill of the pilot are combined. The nature of soaring flight is such that the skill of the pilot is still, and doubtless always will be, of prime importance and it follows that a 'good' glider is one which enables him to apply his skill to the best advantage. Safety, comfort, simplicity, pleasant flying characteristics, ease of ground handling and maintenance all contribute to this and are just as essential as a good performance. All too often does one encounter designs to which immense care and ingenuity have been applied to minimize the aerodynamic losses, but which fall short of being practical soaring machines due to a neglect of this principle.

Whilst good aerodynamic design can hardly be said to be easy, it is essentially a fairly straightforward technical problem, but translating it into good engineering is quite difficult. This difficulty is not peculiar to glider design, of course, but applies to almost any useful man-made object from pots and pans to motorcars and airliners and much has been written on both the practical and philosophical aspects of the matter. It will suffice to observe here that apart from being a competent engineer, the glider designer must be able to visualize the various circumstances in which his machine will be used, he must be able to scan previous experience with a discerning eye, rejecting what was found to be bad, and he should ideally have at his disposal some of that ill-defined attribute called inspiration. Then he may be able to produce a machine in which the pilot will instinctively feel happy at first acquaintance and which he will rapidly come to regard subconsciously as an extension of himself.

Although the best aerodynamic layout may be somewhat varied to suit local conditions, the qualities of a glider which lead to this happy result do not differ from one country to another so much as is commonly supposed, since glider pilots are of much the same physical and mental characteristics the world over. This chapter is therefore devoted to examining some of those features of glider design which directly affect the pilot and to presenting some opinions of the authors, who are strongly inclined to the view that refined aerodynamics, good handling, comfort and mechanical reliability are not mutually incompatible. There are also some notes on the assessment of the flying qualities of a glider.

COCKPIT LAYOUT

Since the pilot hopes to spend many hours at a time sitting in the cockpit, its comfort and convenience are obviously vital. Unfortunately, the human frame does not conform to a standard specification, so that the cockpit must be large enough for a big man without losing sight of those of slighter build — in both the literal and figurative senses. Ideally, the rudder pedals would be adjustable and the seat position would be variable, both horizontally and vertically. In practice, cost dictates a simpler arrangement and the pilot usually has to adjust the seat by means of cushions. It is well worth having a specially tailored seat cushion giving proper support under the thighs, since few things are more trying than paralysis due to excessive bearing pressure on the seat during a long flight. Various seating positions have been tried, from the prone pilot looking downwards, through the bolt-upright to a psychiatrist's-couch reclining posture, the more extreme positions being unhappy compromises between comfort, view and small frontal area. In the recent past, some designers reduced the frontal area of the fuselage to a minimum by placing the pilot in a near-horizontal supine attitude. This position can be made very comfortable but it does involve problems in providing adequate pilot restraint and forward view. If the pilot's line of sight makes a very small angle with the perspex he will have little view straight ahead. When circling in a thermal, lack of forward view is of less consequence than might be thought, since one is usually looking somewhat sideways. But good forward view is important during final glides and when on tow. More recent designs recognize the importance of the pilot's view and are less extreme. Even so, the conventional 4-strap harness is not entirely satisfactory since a supine pilot can slide forwards through it, but a safe and comfortable substitute has yet to be provided. Contouring of the seat is often a weak point of cockpit design. Various diagrams of the 'average man' are available showing the hinge points of the conventional body (and – gruesome thought – the centres of gravity and weights of its various members), but they should be regarded as giving only the roughest guide. The only real test of cockpit comfort is made by causing pilots of different shapes and sizes to sit in it.

The width of the cockpit is frequently inadequate, since it seems to assume that a lightly-clad slender figure is prepared to sit precisely on the centre line for long periods. Another two or three inches of width may increase the drag by some small amount but will prevent the sense of frustration due to an inaccessible packet of sandwiches. These may seem small matters, perhaps expressed rather facetiously, but the effect on one's peace of mind and body during a long flight is very real.

It goes without saying that the primary controls should come readily to hand and foot and should be movable through their full travels without any sensation of discomfort or strain. Similar requirements apply to the secondary controls, and in this respect cockpit layouts are often unsatisfactory. The airbrake lever, for example, frequently causes discomfort to the left leg and it may even lead to a restriction of the stick travel in this sense. An airbrake lever which folds towards the cockpit side can be very satisfactory. Another important control is the tow-release knob, painted yellow according to the airworthiness requirements and located near the left-hand corner of the instrument panel. Since failure to release may lead to great danger, it is quite apparent that this control must be plainly visible, easily reached, and of such size and shape that it can be grasped by a gloved hand so as to apply a large pull-force. If there is more than one tow hook, the same knob must operate both simultaneously.

The pilot must be able to reach the adjustment knob of the altimeter and operate switches. In some modern designs it is not particularly easy to reach the instrument panel, and it may be necessary to locate such controls elsewhere. In a perfect world, the de-misting arrangements for the inside of the canopy would be so good that the pilot would never need to wipe it. Unfortunately, they often fall short of this standard, so it must be possible for the pilot to reach enough of the canopy for him to maintain a good view, even if the extreme front mists up.

To prevent the entry of water and cold draughts the cockpit must be properly sealed with the canopy closed, and ventilation should be deliberate rather than fortuitous. In the small space of a cockpit, really good ventilation and de-misting is difficult to achieve, and can account for enough drag to be just significant. In order to avoid spoiling the flow over the front fuselage, a projecting pitot-type intake at the nose is undesirable. Presumably, a flush hole with rounded edges is less inclined to produce adverse effects but an even better arrangement consists of a flush NACA-type intake further aft, where the boundary layer has become turbulent. A suitable position would be just aft of the cockpit. The air must then be carefully ducted to suitable points in the cockpit, and should be exhausted in an orderly fashion. At least one clear-vision panel must be installed in such a position that the pilot has sufficient view to land the machine even if the rest of the canopy is covered with water or ice.

Sufficient space should be provided to stow all the miscellaneous property carried by the pilot, such as maps, computers, food and drink. It also follows that the cockpit floor should be continuous so that such articles cannot fall into the control mechanism. The bottom of the stick should also be faired to the floor and seat by means of a suitable flexible gaiter.

A completely detachable cockpit canopy, as opposed to one which is hinged, has considerable nuisance value and is liable to be easily damaged. The method of securing the canopy must be positive and arranged so that it cannot be inadvertently undone, but on the other hand it should be possible to jettison the whole canopy in emergency and, if need be, a handle fixed to the fuselage should be provided above the instrument panel to assist the pilot in baling-out. All projections which might cause injury to the pilot in the event of an accident must be adequately padded.

PRACTICAL DETAILS

One of the more familiar sights at a gliding club is a group of members pushing a glider to the launching point. Whilst such exercise is doubtless very salutary, it is often rendered unnecessarily difficult by the failure of the designer to provide proper handling points. Glider pilots are long-suffering, and have become hardened to being confronted by a tailplane bearing the legend 'NO HANDLING', but without any constructive suggestion. Sometimes one finds a small hole in the rear fuselage, apparently designed to do violence to the human hand and wrist. The only satisfactory arrangement is a proper lifting bar: for club purposes, its drag is a small price for the convenience, whilst the purist can always take it out and stow it in the luggage locker. However, neither holes nor lifting bars are acceptable on high-performance gliders. Their ground-handling can be greatly improved by providing either a separate swivelling tailwheel, temporarily attached by a clamp around the rear fuselage, or by a towing trolley attached to the skid or tailwheel, enabling the aircraft to be towed backwards behind a car.

In addition to Mr Stout's famous dictum 'Simplicate and add more lightness', there is another which seems to be particularly relevant to glider design: 'You cannot make control cable pulleys too big.' One still finds pulleys about one inch

in diameter, usually in dark corners where it is difficult to in-
spect the cable. They are far too small. Furthermore, it is a
fallacy to suppose that the pulley size can be reduced if it
only deflects the cable through a small angle. It is strongly
suggested that a pulley taking 10 cwt cable should not be less
than $2\frac{1}{2}$ in. diameter. By far the best solution is to avoid the
use of cables and pulleys by using push-pull rods wherever
possible. They are heavier, but far more reliable and convenient.

It should also go without saying that turnbuckles should
be readily accessible for adjustment and that main rigging pins
should have handles. Unless they are taper-pins, rigging and
de-rigging with a mallet is undesirable. Experience shows that
control circuits containing levers working at short centres are
unsatisfactory, since the loads tend to be high, the rate of
wear of pivots correspondingly great and the effect of backlash much more noticeable.

FLYING QUALITIES. LONGITUDINAL   STABILITY
AND CONTROL

One of the major improvements in sailplane design in recent
years has been in the provision of greatly improved stability
and control; indeed one marvels at the courage of those early
pilots who flew in turbulent clouds in gliders whose flying
characteristics would now be quite unacceptable, with inadequate instruments and no airbrakes.

Longitudinal stability and control was placed on a sound
practical basis largely by the work of Gates and Lyon in this
country. Plenty of data is available, and there is no difficulty
in obtaining satisfactory longitudinal characteristics. As explained in Chapter 20, a conventional glider may be just
acceptable with zero stick-fixed stability, provided that the
stick-free stability is still positive, and for a glider whose stick-
free neutral point is aft of the stick-fixed neutral point this
condition may well determine the aftmost position of the
centre of gravity. Once a glider has been built, the stick-fixed
neutral point position cannot be easily modified but the stick-
free neutral point can be readily altered (see Chapter 20 for
an explanation of these terms). The stick-free neutral point

can be moved aft and hence the stick-free stability increased for a given c.g. position by incorporating a weight or spring in the elevator circuit tending to pull the elevator down, by fitting a geared tab working in the same direction as the elevator, by means of horn balances and to a lesser extent by other means. The effect of a weight in the elevator circuit, usually due to the weight of the elevator itself, is frequently encountered as a result of deliberate or fortuitous lack of mass-balance. If the elevator weight moment is small this effect is generally useful, but a weighty elevator may produce unpleasant characteristics, since inertia forces will be fed back to the stick and an appreciable change of longitudinal trim occurs when a turn is initiated.

A weight in the elevator circuit also affects the 'stick force per g' as well as the stick-free stability. If one considers a pilot pulling-out of a dive, the elevator having no balance weight, the force applied to the stick not only depends on the airloads on the elevator but is further increased by the effect of the increased normal acceleration which tends to pull the elevator down. Since springs are not influenced by acceleration, they do not affect the stick force per g. This quantity is a measure of the manoeuvrability of the glider as explained in Chapter 20.

In the past various gliders, (e.g., Rhonadler) have been fitted with all-moving tailplanes and in the absence of a geared tab this arrangement leads to zero stick-free stability under all conditions, which is undesirable. The addition of a geared tab moving in the same direction as the main surface (i.e. in the anti-balance sense) does provide stick-free stability as on the Dart (see Fig. 15.1). If two otherwise identical machines have horizontal tails of the same size and plan-form, one being of the conventional fixed-tailplane-moving-elevator type and the other of the all-moving tail and geared tab variety, the latter can be arranged to give a stick-free neutral point which is further aft than for the former by suitably arranging the hinge point, tab size and gear ratio, although the stick-fixed neutral point will be the same in both cases. Conversely, for a given stick-free stability, the all-moving tail can be made smaller but it is doubtful whether this process can be taken very far

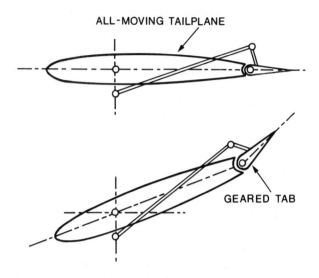

Fig 15.1 All-moving tailplane with geared tab to give stick-free static longitudinal stability

ALL-MOVING TAILPLANE

GEARED TAB

due to the reduction in stick-fixed stability.

Another method of providing some stick force with an untabbed all-moving tail is to provide a centring spring in the elevator circuit. Trimming is then accomplished by shifting the spring datum so as to give zero stick force at the desired speed. This system is not entirely satisfactory: if the spring stiffness is sufficient to give a reasonable feel at low speeds, the elevator tends to get very light and twitchy at high speeds. An alternative arrangement involves the use of a tailplane with positive camber. The aerodynamic moment about the pivot point which then occurs is balanced by a spring force which, again, can be varied for trimming purposes. This system can give a very satisfactory degree of stick-free stability, in terms of stick force to change speed from one steady value to another. On the other hand, only the spring stiffness contributes to the stick force per g, which may be quite small; so releasing the stick in an out-of-trim condition may produce an unexpectedly brisk response.

Tails come in various configurations: 'conventional', and

the T-tail (Standard Cirrus and Kestrel). After a period of popularity, the V-tail is no longer to be found on new designs. It looks as if its drag should be less for a given effectiveness but, on grounds of induced drag, this is not necessarily so. It gives better ground clearance and simpler assembly, usually at the cost of some complexity in the control system. There is some evidence that trouble can occur if it becomes encompassed by the wake of a stalled wing. The T-tail has the advantages of good ground-clearance, a favourable 'end-plate' effect on the fin and rudder and simplicity of rigging and in the control system. It tends to be heavy, since the fin must take the asymmetric bending loads, and it is difficult to achieve a really clean junction with the fin.

RATE OF ROLL

There is no doubt that a good rate of roll combined with small lateral stick forces is a great asset in a glider. Not only is the glider more readily controlled in rough conditions without undue pilot fatigue, but locating and staying in the best part of a thermal is made easier. In recent designs, the attainment of a good rate of roll has been facilitated by the use of wings with great torsional stiffness. The previous generation of gliders with the classical 'D'-nose torsion box suffered from a low aileron reversal speed and the rate of roll fell off appreciably at high speeds. Calculation shows that for a given stick force, a better rate of roll is obtained by making the aileron span large and the chord correspondingly small. The optimum span of each aileron is usually found to be about 60%−70% of the wing semi-span.

LATERAL AND DIRECTIONAL STABILITY

A surprising number of types of glider have been built with inadequate weathercock stability and inadequate rudder power: one can only suppose that the designer sketched out an aesthetically satisfying fin and rudder and hoped for the best. Inadequate weathercock stability renders accurate flying very tiring, particularly in rough thermals. In the past there was also a tendency to provide excessively light rudder forces, so that the controls were lacking in harmony.

However, weathercock stability is an over-simplified concept and, in practice, one has to take into account motions which simultaneously involve yaw, sideslip and roll, such as the 'spiral mode'. Imagine a glider performing a turn with a small amount of slip. The outer wing has, on the average, a higher airspeed than the inner wing so it produces more lift, which tends to roll the glider in the direction of the turn. On the other hand, the outer wing also produces more drag, leading to a yawing moment tending to oppose the turn. The sideslip produces a sideways lift on the vertical tail tending to yaw the glider in the direction of the turn but, if the wing has dihedral, the sideslip will also produce a rolling moment tending to diminish the bank angle. There are therefore four effects present, two tending to tighten the turn and two having the opposite effect. If the turn tends to tighten, the glider is said to be spirally unstable. This is a fairly common situation but the rate at which the turn tightens is usually so slow that the pilot hardly notices the instability. As the previous discussion suggests, the spiral stability can be improved by reducing the vertical tail size or increasing the dihedral and roughly neutral stability would seem to be desirable. With some aeroplane configurations, achieving stability in the spiral mode can lead to instability in another lateral mode (the 'Dutch roll') but this mode is not normally a consideration in gliders. The final conclusion is that one would like a large vertical tail for adequate weathercock stability in straight flight, and good rudder power for prompt spin recovery and cross-wind take-offs and landings; other things being equal, pleasant circling characteristics and general drag reduction imply not too large a vertical tail. In practice, pilots can deal with a very large spread of characteristics and a comparison of tail sizes suggests that designers have widely differing ideas on the most desirable compromise. The general tendency seems to be in the direction of fairly large vertical tails (see Figure 1.3).

AIRBRAKES

For cloud flying airbrakes which would limit the terminal velocity in a vertical dive to about the placarded never-exceed speed were, until recently, thought to be essential. Such brakes also provided a very powerful control of glide angle at approach speeds. More modern requirements in Germany are appreciably less demanding: the brakes need only be powerful enough to limit the speed to V_{NE} in a 45° dive, presumably on the grounds that, in practice, pilots do not achieve more extreme attitudes in upsets when cloud flying and big brakes tend to produce leakage drag even when shut. Brakes which only just meet this requirement tend to be a little marginal for facilitating landings in small fields. Those of the top-surface-only variety (like the upper half of Fig. 15.2 (a)) may fell adequate at some distance from the ground but may permit considerable 'float' before touch-down. This current trend in airbrake design coupled with higher wing loadings has meant that accurate control of speed during the approach is much more important than formerly: in rough conditions, fine judgment may be required to select a speed which gives adequate control and sufficient margin above the stall in the presence of gusts and wind gradient but is not so high as to produce an excessive landing distance.

It should be remembered, however, that brakes have not yet been devised which will not ice-up, and it is still possible to be deprived of their use when most needed, since they may be rendered immovable when shut by water freezing in the mechanism. They are very prone to ice-up when open; but this is not dangerous in itself, although it may involve an unpremeditated and rapid loss of height. The practice of opening the brakes at intervals when in cloud to free them from small amounts of ice is therefore of doubtful value, since it may accelerate icing.

Ideally the pilot should be able to open and close the brakes without undue exertion at any speed and the sucking-out force should not be such that the brakes will come out at launching speeds even if the pilot fails to lock them shut, but they should have a slight tendency to stay open when fully extended. Brakes which require a force to hold them open, increasing with airspeed, are plainly undesirable.

Since the object of fitting airbrakes is to increase the drag as required by the pilot, they should do so without producing other effects such as trim or lift coefficient changes. In general, the type of brakes shown in Fig. 15.2 (a) do not produce any noticeable change of trim, but lead to a loss of lift coefficient at constant incidence. Provided the latter effect is small it is not of great importance, but a large increase in stalling speed would be most undesirable. Brakes which increase the lift coefficient are apt to be disconcerting during the approach, since closing them causes an initial sink and in an extreme case might even lead to stalling. The standard type of DFS airbrake is shown in Fig. 15.2 (a). When mounted in the location shown here, it is difficult to avoid leakage past the edges of the brakes at rather a sensitive point on the upper surface of the wing from the point of view of disturbing the boundary layer. There is therefore a tendency to mount them further aft, but the effectiveness at low speeds is then reduced. However, trailing-edge airbrakes, (shown in Fig. 15.2(b)) can be of large area. Well-designed examples are very effective, progressive in action and have light operating forces.

To avoid disturbances to the flow over the wings, various other forms of airbrake have been devised. The commonest

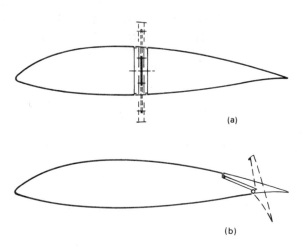

(a)

(b)

Fig 15.2 Typical wing-mounted airbrakes. (a) DFS brakes as developed in the late 1930s. (b) Trailing-edge brakes

types either consist of flaps or simply of a tail parachute. If the flaps are of the plain type, intended also for use as a camber-changing device, it is difficult to provide sufficiently small operating loads and trim changes. It can easily happen that they cannot be extended at high speeds, when they are most likely to be required. Various trailing-edge flaps with aerodynamic balance have also been tried, but it is still difficult to achieve smooth operation and sufficient low-speed effectiveness. Tail parachutes have not been particularly reliable in the past, and tend to be 'all-or-nothing' devices. They provide a large amount of drag and give a very steep approach, so their use requires a special technique and considerable practice, as explained in Chapter 4. Apart from increasing the drag, they effectively increase the longitudinal stability so the round-out requires rather more stick travel than might be expected. At least one well-known type of glider has reverted from a tail-parachute to ordinary brakes. All things considered, the provision of adequate airbrakes consitutes a major difficulty in modern glider design.

In very round figures, the drag coefficient of wing-mounted airbrakes is about 1.3, based on the total area of brakes, gaps and included wing normal to the airflow direction.

LOW–DRAG AEROFOILS

Fig. 15.3 illustrates how fashions in glider aerofoil section have changed during the past forty years or so. Göttingen 652 is typical of the type of section used for machines primarily designed for slope soaring; the camber is considerable, so that the minimum drag coefficient occurs at a high lift coefficient and the maximum lift coefficient is large, with a gentle stall. The Rhonadler is probably the best-known machine to employ this section. Cross-country thermal soaring brought a demand for lower drag coefficients, and since there was less accent on slow-speed flight, aerofoil sections became thinner, less cambered and with the maximum thickness further aft. Göttingen 549 was used on the Meise-Olympia and Weihe, and gives a good performance and pleasant stalling characteristics. In this country, many pre-war Slingsby machines used NACA four-digit series aerofoils, such as 4416 or 4418. Such

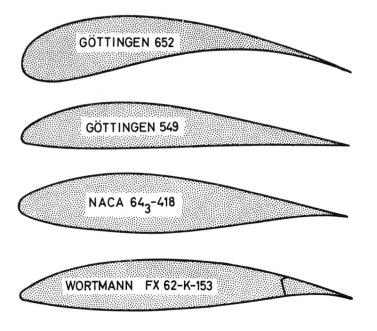

GÖTTINGEN 652

GÖTTINGEN 549

NACA 64_3-418

WORTMANN FX 62-K-153

Fig 15.3 Fashions in wing sections

aerofoil sections were designed by various methods; some were shapes which resulted from a mathematical process enabling the flow about them to be easily calculated whilst others were arbitrary geometrical shapes which ad-hoc experiments had shown to give good aerodynamic qualities.

It was realized that the boundary layer had considerable influence on the characteristics of aerofoils, particularly the drag and maximum lift coefficient, but it was only about 33 years ago that methods began to be developed for designing aerofoils having extensive regions of laminar boundary layer. The boundary layer is the region in the flow near the surface of a body where the velocity is reduced, relative to the local free-stream velocity, by the action of viscosity. Its thickness might be about one inch near the trailing edge of a wing of 4 ft 6 in. chord at 50 knots at sea-level, but towards the leading edge it will be much thinner. Other things being equal, the boundary layer will become thinner as the speed increases.

In general, the boundary layer is the only part of the flow in which viscous effects need be considered, at any rate so far as gliders are concerned; elsewhere, the air may be supposed to correspond to the inviscid fluid of classical hydrodynamics. Boundary layers may be either laminar, when the paths of particles of air are substantially parallel to the surface of the body, or turbulent, when the particles move in a more or less random fashion. It follows that in the latter case, the velocity near the surface will be higher than in the former case, other things being equal, because high-velocity particles can move from the outside of the boundary layer to regions near the surface. Since the velocity just at the surface must be zero, the rate of shear near the surface will be high for a turbulent boundary layer, and the friction drag will also be high. It foilows, therefore, that the skin friction of an aerofoil, or any other body for that matter, will be reduced as the region over which the boundary layer in laminar is increased.

The factors causing transition from a laminar to a turbulent boundary layer include the pressures to which the boundary layer is subjected, as determined by the shape of the aerofoil or body ('shape' being not only the general outline but also local waviness), the roughness of the surface and any turbulence in the free-stream. The phenomenon is not even now fully understood, but certain principles can be applied and there is a large amount of experimental data. The main concern of the designers of a low-drag aerofoil is to obtain a satisfactory distribution of pressures over the surface for a useful range of lift coefficient. Considering the upper surface, the pressures will generally be less than the free-stream atmospheric pressure, at positive lift coefficients. Somewhere near the leading edge, usually a little below it, the air will be brought to rest, giving the total head or pitot pressure at that point. Proceeding along the upper surface, the pressure falls, reaches a minimum and then rises again towards the trailing edge. In the absence of the other effects mentioned above, the transition position will be determined by the location of the minimum pressure point and will often be at roughly the same place. Whilst the pressure is decreasing as one proceeds in the down-stream direction, the local air velocity (just out-

side the boundary layer) is increasing, and this acceleration
may be regarded as counterbalancing the retarding effect of
the viscosity. Once the pressure starts to rise again, the air in
the boundary layer is retarded by the effects of both the rising pressure and the viscosity, the laminar boundary layer
will thicken rapidly, and become unstable in a fashion which
leads to transition. It therefore follows that it pays to ensure
that the minimum pressure point is reasonably far aft of the
leading edge. Low-drag aerofoils therefore tend to have their
maximum thickness further aft than the 'conventional' sections.

By the application of the principles outlined above, various
families of aerofoils have been designed, of which the best
known and most extensively tested is the NACA 6-series. A
typical member of this family is shown in Fig. 15.3, and similar sections but with slightly more camber were used on the
Skylark series of gliders.

Typical of the latest type of section is that designed by
Wortmann in Fig. 15.3 in which the principles explained above
are applied even more carefully, so as to prevent undesirable

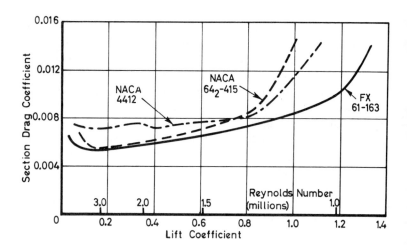

*Fig 15.4 A comparison of the properties of some wing
sections*

separations of the boundary layer and to reduce the drag to a low value even where the boundary layer is turbulent.

Fig. 15.4 compares the properties of various aerofoil sections. The pre-war NACA 4-digit section has a sharply defined minimum drag coefficient (for an explanation of these terms see Chapter 16), with the drag rapidly increasing as the lift coefficient becomes more or less than the optimum. The 6-series section has a fairly wide low-drag 'bucket': it provides a low drag coefficient over a reasonable range of lift coefficient. The Wortmann section takes this process even further and continues to operate at a low drag coefficient up to quite high lift coefficients, thus rendering it more suitable under circling conditions. A considerable drag rise occurs only just before the aerofoil stalls.

When comparing the characteristics of wing sections, it is important to do so at the correct Reynolds number, as indicated in Fig. 15.4.

Mention of Reynolds number is inclined to excite some alarm in gliding circles, and statements which say that it is 'a non-dimensional measure of aerodynamic scale' or 'represents the ratio of the inertia forces to the viscous forces in the fluid' are rarely greeted with a display of enthusiastic comprehension. In reference books it usually either appears as an austere mathematical conception or surrounded by such a haze of verbiage that even more confusion is produced. Not wishing to join the latter category, it is simplest to state a fact: if one wishes to apply the results of a wind tunnel test to, say, the design of a glider wing, the Reynolds number of the tests must be roughly the same as the Reynolds number which will occur in flight. Reynolds numbers are explained in more detail in Appendix 6, from which rapid estimates of actual values can be made. It should be remembered that since the Reynolds number alters with the speed of the glider, a comparison of section characteristics at a single value is not the whole story. The curves should really show values of drag coefficient at the different Reynolds numbers corresponding to the airspeeds appropriate to the wing loading of the glider at each lift coefficient, as has been done in Fig. 15.4.

ASSESSMENT OF FLYING QUALITIES

The ordinary experienced pilot is seldom concerned with carrying out extensive flight tests, but from time to time he is called upon to assess a machine in terms of its suitability for his private or club needs. If it is of an established type, it will have a certificate of airworthiness and, in general, will have been test flown in its country of origin as part of the process of certification. For example, many types of 15-metre Standard-Class glider are available, of undoubted safety and broadly similar performance. Approval of a type by a national airworthiness authority means that certain standards of safety have been satisfied, but approval does not necessarily mean that all aspects of its handling are entirely pleasant. The choice of a machine by an individual will depend on numerous factors such as price, delivery, convenience in rigging, its appearance and, as much as anything else, whether he finds it pleasant to fly.

To an appreciable extent, this is a subjective matter. It is also associated with safety since, certificates of airworthiness notwithstanding, different authorities have varying ideas on what constitutes acceptable behaviour and, inevitably, some gliders are more forgiving than others. Likewise, some gliders have been designed with a specific context in mind, and a machine suited to the flat plains of northern Europe may be something of an embarrassment in a country whose landing fields consist of vineyards and goat pastures. So, in addition to performing a few vague circuits and declaring that it all seems rather nice, the pilot would do well to carry out a more searching assessment to ensure that the machine remains safe and pleasant under less commonplace conditions.

Undesirable behaviour is usually most likely to occur with the centre of gravity of the laden machine at the aft limit, i.e. when the cockpit load is the minimum permitted. This is not always so, but it is a reasonable assumption for conventional machines. It is therefore prudent to make one's preliminary assessment with a cockpit load of rather more than the minimum. A brief test programme would comprise:

1 Behaviour on winch and aerotow launch.
2 General handling.
3 Straight stalls.
4 Stalls off turns.
5 Spinning.
6 Use of airbrakes.
7 Qualitative longitudinal stability.
8 Behaviour at high speeds.

If all of these charateristics are satisfactory with the centre of gravity about half-way along the permitted range, they should be repeated with the minimum permitted load in the cockpit. It goes without saying that caution should be exercised at all times and that care should be taken not to exceed the placarded limits. When carrying out airworthiness tests, all of the above aspects of the machine's behaviour, and many others, are investigated in great detail. For the present purposes it would be unreasonable to consume several high aerotows in spinning the machine and, in any case, a pilot who is not particularly experienced in testing would probably find the recording of detailed observations under such conditions rather too difficult to be useful. In making the present assessment, it will suffice to carry out the manoeuvres in a normal fashion, only exploring in detail any behaviour which seems to be peculiar. After all, it is unlikely that an approved type will display any really dangerous behaviour: it is much more likely to have a few mildly curious or irritating habits. The features which the pilot is trying to observe are detailed below, in most cases in the form of a list of desirable characteristics.

Winch Launching. It should be easy to get the machine balanced on its wheel without fore-and-aft pitching on to its nose and/or tail skid. There should be no difficulty in keeping the wings level, nor in keeping straight in a reasonable crosswind. As the speed increases, it should be possible to ease the glider into the air and gently steepen the climb without any tendency for the machine to pitch nose-up of its own accord. During the climb, a reasonable pull-force on the stick is desirable, but no large deflections of any control should be required. Some gliders develop a tendency to indulge in rapid pitching oscillations towards the top of the launch. These are undesirable, but not necessarily of much consequence if they damp out rapidly on easing the stick forwards. There should be no difficulty in keeping on the desired flight path at all times.

Aerotowing. The desired ground-run and take-off should be as described above. During the tow, the towing aeroplane should be clearly visible, and it should be possible to trim the glider to give zero-stick force. In averagely rough air, it should be possible to keep the glider in its proper position without undue effort, both in straight flight and when turning.

General Handling. This is the most subjective part of the whole process. The pilot is trying to assess whether the controls are well harmonized over the normal speed range. If the machine has extremely heavy ailerons and a very light rudder, or vice-versa, most pilots would object. There is obviously a great range of intermediate characteristics which can be the subject of endless debate.

On entering and leaving turns, the 'aileron drag' should not be excessive. This effect is due to the difference in drag between the up- and down-going ailerons, and causes the machine to yaw in the undesired sense. Excessive aileron drag has to be balanced-out by applying large rudder deflections, which become tiresome.

The rate of roll should be adequate. The formal test consists of finding the time to roll from a 45°-banked turn in one direction to 45° of bank in the other direction, at 1.4 times the stalling speed. The usual requirement is that this time in seconds should not exceed one-tenth of the wingspan in feet. In practice, most pilots would regard this rate of roll as being too low; it is, after all, a minimum figure from the point of view of safety. So far as the present assessment is concerned, it is more useful to see whether the rate of roll feels adequate at a typical circling speed.

The pilot is also trying to assess whether he can trim the glider over an adequate range of speed, whether the elevator is pleasantly light without being 'twitchy', and whether tedious and incessant re-trimming is necessary when altering the radius of turn.

The main object of general handling, apart from observing the detail mentioned above, is for the pilot to see whether he likes flying the machine. If he does, he will be prepared to forgive minor shortcomings, and to regard them as part of the glider's personality.

Stalls. The stalling speed is of prime importance, since it is a good guide to the ability to perform slow turns. It should be observed carefully, approaching the stall slowly until control is lost. Likewise, the effectiveness of the ailerons and rudder should be observed as the stall is approached: they will obviously become rather vague just before the glider stalls, but they should still function in their correct senses.

Wing-dropping at the stall is a considerable source of controversy. Ideally, it should not happen, and the stall should simply involve a straight nose-drop. This situation is unlikely to occur in real life, since a copy-book stall may require an inefficient spanwise distribution of the lift. A certain amount of wing-drop is acceptable provided that it can be corrected reasonably rapidly, and certainly before it turns into a spin, by using the controls in the normal sense. Fortunately, most modern wing sections have gentle stalling characteristics and, whilst wing-dropping is fairly common, it is seldom a significant problem. Similarly, stall warning by way of buffeting or strange aerodynamic noises is theoretically desirable but in practice usually indicates a premature separation of the flow. If such separations are prevented, in the interests of good low-speed performance, there is very little stall warning. Most pilots prefer to have the performance. If flaps are fitted, lowering them will decrease the stalling speed. The stalling characteristics may also be affected, together with other features such as aileron effectiveness, as noted in Chapter 7.

Stalls off Turns. The procedure consists of starting a 30° banked turn at a normal circling speed, and gently reducing speed until the glider stalls. Normally the pilot achieves a large 'holding-off-bank' aileron deflection, a fair rudder deflection in the normal sense, and almost full nose-up elevator. At the stall, the inner wing and the nose drop with more or less vigour. It is undesirable that the wing-drop should be very sudden and steep, and even less desirable that the manoeuvre should turn into a genuine spin before the average pilot can correct it. Such behaviour in a crowded thermal is pretty antisocial. Whilst performing this test, it is useful to note the minimum speed at which a steady turn can be held without excessive control deflections.

Spinning. A noticeable proportion of accidents occur due to inadvertent spins near the ground, and a fair amount of fright can be caused even when they occur well away from it. Some people perform them for fun. In all cases it is useful to know what behaviour to expect and how rapidly the machine recovers. Spins are explained at some length in Chapter 20, but it is necessary to add that the behaviour may be influenced considerably by the position of the ailerons. The five-turn spins of British Civil Airworthiness Requirements are something of a luxury in a rapid assessment, but it is worth remembering that a glider which indulges in a really full-blooded spin may not achieve a steady motion even after five turns.

Recovery should be rapid and straightforward by the 'standard' method (see Chapter 20, page 356). Gliders whose 'pilot's notes' contain elaborate non-standard instructions about spin recovery should be regarded as highly suspect. Before attempting spins in a high-performance glider it is advisable to have a fair amount of experience of the manoeuvre in humbler types. The high-performance machine may be quite disconcerting to the unaccustomed pilot: the spin may be rapid and perhaps oscillatory; the attitude may be very variable, as between one type and another; the glider may want to recover by itself; in most cases, it will be difficult to avoid attaining a high speed in the recovery, so one hand should be poised on the airbrake lever. Inadvertent spins are most likely to occur, on flapped machines, with the flaps at the thermalling or the approach setting. In such configurations, the never exceed speed is probably fairly low, so care should be taken to avoid excessive speeds during recovery from practice spins with flaps deflected.

The net loss of height when spinning, between entry and the top of the zoom after recovery, is usually about 300 ft per turn.

Airbrakes. The desirable qualities of airbrakes are explained earlier in this chapter, so their assessment consists of operating them at a series of increasing speeds up to the maximum permitted, and observing how they conform. It is most imprudent to open them at a high speed without initial experience at lower speeds: they may come open with disconcerting violence and produce a spectacular deceleration. In a brief assessment, it is not usually possible to observe whether they are genuinely speed-limiting, but most pilots have a pretty good idea of the feel of adequate brakes.

Longitudinal Stability. As explained in Chapter 20, it is essential that, when trimmed at a certain speed, a push-force on the stick should be required to go faster and a pull-force to go slower. This situation should be explored at a series of gently increasing trimmed speeds. In many gliders, the stability decreases as the speed increases, and the stick forces may reverse at high speeds. In the case of machines with all moving tails without geared tabs, but with a centralizing spring in the elevator circuit, the effective stability decreases at higher speeds but this tendency is sometimes concealed by limiting the maximum speed at which the machine can be trimmed.

The 'heaviness' of the elevator is again a matter largely of personal preference and custom.

High Speeds. In the course of the previous test, the glider will have been taken up to quite a high speed, and one important aspect of its behaviour will have already been explored. Obviously, such tests should only be carried out under very calm conditions. Further tests consist of flying the glider at a series of increasing speeds up to the never-exceed speed. The ailerons and rudder will naturally become increasingly heavy, but this tendency should not be excessive and they should continue to function properly. Most Design Requirements state that 'there shall be no vibration or snatching of the controls', a somewhat obscure turn of phrase when one considers that such effects may well be the prelude to disastrous flutter.

General Observations. In carrying out such an assessment, the pilot will automatically be able to observe various characteristics other than those listed above. He will carry out several landings, for example. He should also take note of the various practical engineering features, some of which have been mentioned earlier in this chapter. In the UK, great importance is attached to ease of rigging and de-rigging: it is of vital importance to ensure not only that these processes are quick and simple, but also that there is no possibility of incorrect assembly.

To summarize, the pilot should know what constitutes good practice, and should preferably have some knowledge of airworthiness requirements, so that his assessment can be carried out in a discerning and logical fashion.

Chapter 16

Theory of Glider Performance

INTRODUCTION

In order to make the best use of a glider, the pilot wishes to know the actual performance of his machine, expressed as a graph in which its rate of sink in still air is plotted against forward speed, taking due account of appropriate flap settings if necessary. The only performance figures which really matter are those obtained by flight tests of an identical machine. Such tests involve making a number of timed descents at a series of steady speeds, a process which sounds simple enough but which turns out to be remarkably difficult in real life. Apart from the obvious corrections to be applied to take into account instrument errors, non-standard atmospheric temperature, etc, the rates of descent being measured are often very small and significant errors can be introduced by vertical motions of the atmosphere which would normally be regarded as negligible. So the results have to be analysed on a statistical basis to obtain a reliable curve. Even so, measurements conducted by entirely reputable organisations in different places, using substantially identical aircraft, may show discernible differences. Such differences may often be traceable to the tests being conducted with the centre of gravity in different places, or to the mean height of the tests being different. Although test results are normally corrected to give sea-level values, the corrections cannot readily take into account the effect of Reynolds number on the drag and, other things being equal, Reynolds number depends on height (See Appendix 6). For example, Paul Bikle's classical series of tests in 1971, which form the basis of the 'Libelle' figures quoted in this book, were conducted at an average height of about 7000 ft in the USA and may well be pessimistic by 2 to 3% compared with true sea-level figures.

Before embarking on the construction of a new type of glider, the designer must obviously estimate the performance and endeavour to optimise it, usually subject to certain constraints such as wing span or cost. The basis of such calculations is broadly indicated in the theory which follows but it is not possible to pursue all the details in a book such as this. When carefully done, such calculations can be remarkably precise, helped by the fact that modern glass-fibre gliders tend to behave like the accurate models used for obtaining the data in wind tunnels. Even so, brochure curves based on estimates still tend to be somewhat optimistic and the prudent pilot will wish to know the genuine flight-test figures.

Strictly speaking, neither estimated nor measured performance curves correspond to any simple algebraic formula: it would be surprising if they did, when full account is taken of all the complicated effects arising from the airflow, particularly in the boundary layers, and the consequences of structural distortion. From the pilot's point of view, the most important part of this chapter is that relating to cross-country performance and the MacCready best-speed-to-fly construction. This is applicable to any shape of performance curve and all the information required can be obtained by graphical methods.

However, the intention of this chapter is to show that the drag and hence the rate of sink of a glider can be described in fairly simple mathematical terms and formulae can be derived such as equations (16.16) and (16.17) which correspond quite closely to the behaviour of actual gliders over much of the useful speed range. It is easy enough to produce such expressions on the basis of rather crude simplifying assumptions: the surprise is the extent to which they also accommodate the more complicated real effects. Accepting that an analytical curve can be made to fit the real performance curve to a high degree of accuracy, the theory is expanded to show that the performance of a glider can usually be expressed in terms of only two quantities, such as the maximum lift/drag ratio and the speed at which it occurs. This approach enables the graphical methods associated with the MacCready construction to be replaced by simple calculations. It also provides a basis for some general deductions, such as those relating to errors in gliding speeds, which can readily be applied to any gliders as in Appendix 7.

The performance of the Standard Libelle has been used as the basis of the calculations throughout this book because it is in widespread use and represents a straightforward fixed-geometry glider whose performance is well established.

Subject to structural and economic limitations, a glider designer wishes to produce a machine which will make the best use of the available energy of the atmosphere, usually in order to fly at the maximum possible average speeds across country. This is obviously what is required in a speed task but even for straightforward distance flying it is important to make the best use of the available time, as explained in Chapter 7. It will therefore be useful to study performance in some detail, not only because these considerations are essential in the design and development of gliders but also because the pilot will wish to know how to use a given machine to the best effect.

THE DRAG OF A GLIDER

In elementary performance calculations, both for gliders and aeroplanes, it is assumed that the drag has two components. One of these is proportional to the square of the speed, other things being equal, and is loosely termed the *profile drag*. This is essentially due to the viscosity of the air, and may be regarded as the result of the machine dragging with it some of the air through which it is flying. This component of the drag would be expected to increase as the size of the machine and the air density increase. It is interesting to consider why this component of drag should be proportional to the square of the speed, since verbal explanations are not usually given in reference books on aerodynamics. Consider two identical machines, one flying at twice the speed of the other. The faster machine not only influences twice the mass of air in a given time, but drags it along at twice the speed as compared with the slower machine so that the ratio of profile drags is four to one. This is obviously a very crude explanation, but it does indicate the nature of the problem.

The above remarks therefore suggest that the profile drag will depend on $\rho V^2 S$, where ρ is the air density, V is the true airspeed and S is the wing area. It will depend on the shape of the glider, so finally

$$D_p = C_{D_0} \tfrac{1}{2} \rho V^2 S \qquad (16.1)$$

where C_{D_0} is a 'profile drag coefficient', which expresses the effect of the shape. The '$\tfrac{1}{2}$' is inserted because the quantity $\tfrac{1}{2} \rho V^2$, the dynamic head of the air moving relative to the glider, is a useful quantity in its own right.

If D_p is to be in pounds force, then ρ must be in slugs/ft^3. The 'slug' is a curious unit, seldom encountered outside aerodynamics. One slug is 32.17lb mass. V must be in ft/s and S in ft^2.

Whilst the profile drag coefficient depends primarily on the detailed shape of the glider, it also varies to some extent with the attitude at which it is flying through the air, usually expressed in terms of the angle of attack. For wing sections, this is normally taken as the angle between the direction of the undisturbed airflow and the chord-line of the wing section, which for all practical purposes is the line joining the extremities of the section. For a complete aircraft, any convenient datum line may be used instead of the chord-line.

Whilst the profile drag arises because the passage of the machine through the air imparts momentum to some of the air in the direction of motion of the glider, some momentum must also be imparted to the air in a downwards sense, since the glider pushes downwards on the air with a force equal to the lift. Again, the force produced will depend on the air density, the wing area and the square of the speed, so that the lift is

$$L = C_L \tfrac{1}{2} \rho V^2 S \qquad (16.2)$$

C_L is the 'lift coefficient' which again depends on the shape of the machine (primarily on the wing geometry) and on its angle of attack. Fig. 16.1 shows how the lift and profile drag coefficients vary with angle of attack for a typical glider wing sec-

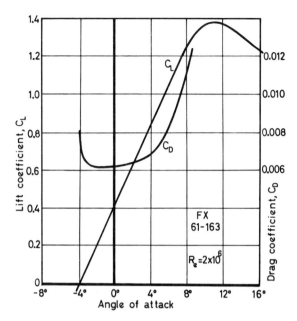

Fig 16.1 Lift and profile drag coefficients of a modern wing section as determined by wind tunnel tests. C_D in this diagram refers to an isolated wing effectively of infinite aspect ratio

tion: the coefficients for a complete glider will be somewhat different.

In order to produce lift, the wing has to impart downwards momentum at a certain rate to the air through which it is flying. The mechanism for imparting the momentum is the system of vortices trailing behind the wing, particularly from the tips. Associated with the downward velocity of the air is a certain amount of wasted kinetic energy which leads to another contribution to the drag, termed the *induced drag*. Because this drag is associated with the wing pushing air downwards, it ultimately appears as pressures on the surfaces of the wing.

A somewhat qualitative way of considering induced drag is as follows:

Suppose, as in Fig. 16.2, the influence of the wing is con-

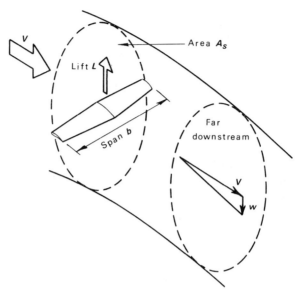

Fig 16.2 Diagram to illustrate the relationship between lift, induced drag and downwash

fined to a stream tube of cross-sectional area A_s. Then, using the previous notation, the rate of mass flow through the stream tube will be $\rho A_s V$. If, far downstream, the wing has imparted a downwards velocity w to all the air passing through the stream tube, the lift will be

$$L = \rho A_s V w, \qquad (16.3)$$

and the rate of dissipation of kinetic energy will be $\tfrac{1}{2}(\rho A_s V)w^2$ This will be equal to the induced drag *power* so we can write

$$D_i V = \tfrac{1}{2}(\rho A_s V)w^2, \qquad (16.4)$$

where D_i is the induced drag. Eliminating w from equations (16.3) and (16.4) finally gives

$$D_i = \tfrac{1}{2}L^2/\rho A_s V^2. \qquad (16.5)$$

Now a separate and much more complicated calculation shows that when the induced drag is a minimum, the spanwise distribution of lift is elliptical and, from the point of view of the above equations, A_s is effectively the area of a circle whose diameter is equal to the wing span. Note that this is *not* the physical reality: the wing does not just influence a circular stream tube into which it fits, but the effect is the same when one integrates the influence of the wing on the whole field of flow. In these circumstances, equation (16.5) becomes

$$D_{i\,\mathrm{min}} = (1/\pi)(1/\tfrac{1}{2}\rho V^2)(L/b)^2, \qquad (16.6)$$

where b is the span in feet.

More generally, the spanwise lift distribution will not be elliptical and the induced drag will be greater than indicated by equation (16.6). It is usually written

$$D_i = (k/\pi)(1/\tfrac{1}{2}\rho V^2)(L/b)^2 \qquad (16.7)$$

where k is a constant, greater than 1.0, which depends primarily on the wing geometry.

A curious feature of the induced drag is, therefore, that it is *inversely* proportional to the air density and the square of the speed and *directly* proportional to the square of the span loading. Note that aspect ratio, as such, does not appear in this expression.

In level flight, the lift is equal to the weight W. When gliding, the weight is strictly equal to the resultant of the lift and drag, but the angle of glide is usually so flat that no significant error is introduced by substituting W for L in equation (16.7). It should be remembered that, when turning, the lift can be appreciably more than the weight, and the induced drag is then increased accordingly.

THE THEORY OF THE POLAR

If these two components of drag are added together, the total drag in straight flight is

$$D = C_{D_0}\tfrac{1}{2}\rho V^2 S + \frac{k}{\pi}\left(\frac{1}{\tfrac{1}{2}\rho V^2}\right)\left(\frac{W}{b}\right)^2. \qquad (16.8)$$

It is often more convenient to deal with the 'equivalent' airspeed rather than the true airspeed, where the equivalent airspeed V_i is defined thus:

$$V_i = V\sqrt{(\rho/\rho_0)}. \qquad (16.9)$$

ρ_0 is the standard sea-level air density, and hence V_i may be loosely considered as the reading of a perfect airspeed indicator in the glider.

Equation (16.8) can therefore be expressed in terms of V_i:

$$D = (C_{D_0}\tfrac{1}{2}\rho_0 S)V_i^2 + \left(\frac{kW^2}{\tfrac{1}{2}\pi\rho_0 b^2}\right)\frac{1}{V_i^2} \qquad (16.10)$$

Now the quantities in brackets are more or less constant for a given glider, so finally, in shorthand form:

$$D = AV_i^2 + B/V_i^2 \qquad (16.11)$$

If the distribution of lift across the wing were always elliptical, then the induced drag would be a minimum and k in the above equations would be 1.0. The constant k takes into account the slightly non-elliptical lift distribution which usually occurs in practice, increasing its value to about 1.05 for a typical glider.

In general, the wing profile drag coefficient is not constant but is a function of lift coefficient and Reynolds number. At a given height and wing loading, both effects may be combined to produce curves such as those shown in Fig. 15.4. Except near the ends of the solid line, the shape of this curve is roughly parabolic so the effect of variations of profile drag coefficient (including parts other than the wing) can be taken into account by supposing C_{D_0} in equation (16.10) to be constant but k to be increased somewhat above the 'vortex' value. Its final value then becomes typically 1.25 to 1.50. This behaviour of the profile drag is not usually satisfied when the lift coefficient is high, when a large drag rise may occur, but equation (16.10) may be assumed to be reasonably accurate for the present purposes.

An alternative way of writing equation (16.7) is to substitute for L from equations (16.2) and (16.9):

$$D_i = \left(\frac{kC_L{}^2}{\pi A}\right) \tfrac{1}{2} \rho_0 V_i{}^2 S \qquad (16.12)$$

where A is the aspect ratio, b^2/S. The quantity $kC_L{}^2/\pi A$ is then the induced drag coefficient, and the total drag coefficient becomes

$$C_D = C_{D_0} + (kC_L{}^2/\pi A) \qquad (16.13)$$

This equation suggests that if all the previous assumptions are correct, then plotting the drag coefficient against the square of the lift coefficient should give a substantially straight line. Fig. 16.3 shows such a curve for the Standard

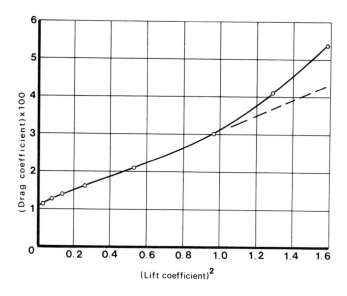

Fig 16.3 C_D plotted against $C_L{}^2$ for the Standard Libelle

Libelle deduced from performance measurements by Paul Bikle (Fig. 16.4). It will be seen that most of the significant part of the curve is indeed roughly linear, corresponding to $k = 1.425$, but there is some additional drag at lift coefficients above about 0.9.

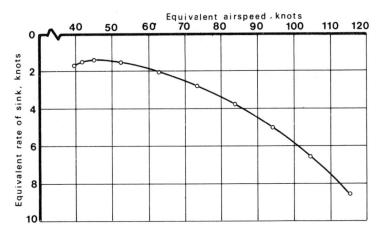

Fig 16.4 Performance curve for the Standard Libelle at
W = 695 lb deduced from flight tests at 633 lb

In steady flight, the rate of dissipation of energy due to the
drag must equal the rate of loss of potential energy and
therefore

$$DV = WV_s \qquad (16.14)$$

where W = weight of glider in pounds and
V_s = true rate of sink in ft/sec.

If both sides of equation (16.14) are multiplied by $\sqrt{(\rho/\rho_0)}$
and $V_s\sqrt{(\rho/\rho_0)}$ is regarded as an equivalent rate of sink, V_{si},
analogous to equivalent airspeed, then

$$DV_i = WV_{si} \qquad (16.15)$$

From equations (16.11) and (16.15):

$$WV_{si} = AV_i^3 + B/V_i, \qquad (16.16)$$

where A and B are constants for a given glider in a fixed configuration at a certain weight. (Note that A in this expression
is not the aspect ratio).

By the application of a little differentiation to this expression, it may be shown that at the minimum rate of sink the
profile drag is one third of the induced drag, and that at the
best gliding angle (i.e. minimum V_s/V) the profile and in-

duced drags are equal. The values of the important speeds and rates of sink corresponding to minimum sinking speed and best gliding angle may easily be deduced and hence the 'polar', or curve of rate of sink against forward speed may be shown to be as in Fig. 16.5. In this figure all speeds are 'equivalent' and w is the wing loading $(W/S, \text{lb/ft}^2)$.

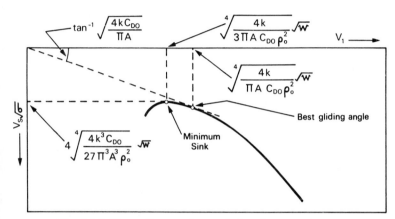

Fig 16.5 *The salient points of the theoretical glider polar curve*

If follows from equation (16.16) that the performance curves of all fixed-geometry gliders are basically of the same shape. This equation may be re-written in dimensionless terms as follows

$$V_{si}/V_{si_0} = \tfrac{1}{2}[(V_i/V_{i_0})^3 + (V_{i_0}/V_i)] \qquad (16.17)$$

where V_{si_0} and V_{i_0} are the equivalent rate of sink and equivalent forward speed, respectively, at the condition for best gliding angle. With the lift substantially equal to the weight it follows from equation (16.14) that the best gliding angle condition also corresponds to the maximum ratio of lift to drag, $(L/D)_{max}$.
So,

$$V_{i_0}/V_{si_0} = (L/D)_{max} \qquad (16.18)$$

(see Appendix 7 for a more detailed explanation)

EFFECT OF DESIGN VARIABLES

If equation (16.17) is substantially accurate, the whole performance of a fixed-geometry glider is determined by $(L/D)_{max}$ and the corresponding value of equivalent airspeed, V_{i_0}. In turn, these quantities depend on:

k, the 'induced drag factor';
C_{D_0}, the drag coefficient at zero lift;
A, the aspect ratio;
w, the wing loading.

Now, arguing generally, a glider is maintained in flight by using energy derived from the atmosphere and hence it is important to take all possible steps to minimize the rate of dissipation of energy by the glider. C_{D_0} and k should therefore be as small as possible. At first sight, it would appear that A should be as large as possible, but other considerations render this simple conclusion invalid. In fact these variables are not entirely independent: for example, an increase in aspect ratio will increase the wing loading and slightly increase the profile drag coefficient. Assuming that the designer intends to achieve the best possible performance under certain weather conditions, the main variables open to his choice are the span, aspect ratio and wing loading. Although span, as such, does not appear as a significant variable in the foregoing considerations, it is of primary importance: the bigger the span, the smaller becomes the fraction of the profile drag attributable to the fuselage and tail, and the lower becomes C_{D_0}. Also, other things being equal – particularly the aspect ratio – bigger machines operate at higher Reynolds numbers, again decreasing C_{D_0}. So, if the span is open to choice, the bigger the better. However, experience suggests that a practical upper limit is around 21 m: this span is an appreciable fraction of a typical radius of turn when thermalling and the effect of rolling moment due to rate of yaw (see page 208) tends to become large: also, the sheer size and weight of the wing makes for awkward ground handling. Nevertheless, gliders with spans as great as 30 m have been built. In the case of Standard Class gliders, the designer's decision is made for him: the span must not exceed 15 m, so he tries to make it

14999 mm. Having settled the span, the shape of the wing in terms of planform, taper ratio and twist is then important. The minimum vortex drag is obtained by designing the wing so that the spanwise distribution of lift is elliptical. To achieve this result at all lift coefficients requires a wing of elliptical planform with zero twist but such a wing is impracticable: the shape is difficult to make and the small tip chords and correspondingly low Reynolds numbers would have adverse effects. For convenience in construction, designers use either a straight taper or, more often, a compound taper (see Fig. 1.3) which more nearly approaches an ellipse. Depending on the amount of taper, some twist may also have to be incorporated from root to tip, so that the angle of attack at the tip is less than at the root. This ensures that the tips are more lightly loaded and will therefore stall after the inner parts of the wing, so as to reduce the danger of an inadvertent spin. As it happens, the straight-tapered high aspect-ratio wing with the minimum induced drag factor k has a taper ratio (defined as tip chord divided by root chord) of about 0.5 to 0.6, and such a wing does not require any twist to achieve acceptable stalling characteristics. Gliders are occasionally fitted with dummy 'tip-tanks', in an attempt to increase the effective aspect ratio. When the aspect ratio is already large, they probably have little effect, and in any case it will be largely cancelled by the increased profile drag.

The choice of aspect ratio, in conjunction with the above features of wing geometry, determines the 'vortex drag' contribution to k. Assuming a high level of competence in the design of the parts other than the wing, and supposing a prudent choice of wing section, the remaining contribution of k (due to the dependence of profile drag coefficient on lift coefficient and Reynolds number) will also be determined, as will C_{D_0}. Finally, the choice of the glider's geometry in conjunction with the design load factors, material, and general structural design technique will determine the *minimum* wing loading. A higher wing loading can always be achieved by the use of ballast, within limits imposed by the structural design.

Given a certain level of competence in aerodynamic design and having chosen a span, it is apparent that aspect ratio is then the really important design variable. For all practical purposes, it determines the performance in the un-ballasted condition and hence the performance with ballast. The choice of a suitable aspect ratio is by no means obvious, since a compromise is involved. In Fig. 16.5, it would be desirable to place the minimum sink point towards the top left-hand corner of the diagram, to permit circling at a low rate of sink and a small radius of turn in thermals. However, for good inter-thermal performance, the right-hand part of the polar should be as far as possible towards the top right-hand corner of the diagram. These two requirements are incompatible: a high aspect ratio will help in fulfilling the latter requirement, since it improves $(L/D)_{max}$ and increases the minimum wing loading but has the undesirable effect of increasing the speed at which minimum sink occurs. A rational choice can only be made by considering a series of gliders with different aspect ratios and examining their cross-country performance in the presence of various types of thermals, as explained later.

It is probably true to say that during the last 15 years or so, the greatest gains in glider performance have resulted from a reduction in profile drag. Fundamentally, this is achieved by obtaining extensive amounts of laminar boundary layer over the external surfaces of the glider and by reducing the wetted area as much as possible. The major contribution to the profile drag comes from the wing, and great effort has been lavished on the design of wing sections of reasonable thickness so as to accommodate the structure, but having a low drag coefficient over a wide range of lift coefficient, as indicated in Fig. 15.4. A good pre-war glider would have a C_{D_0} of 0.016, whereas the corresponding figure for a modern design would be 0.010, or perhaps as low as 0.008. Such a figure can only be attained by very careful attention to small details, since the total effect of wing root interference and early separation, leakage through air-brake slots and control gaps, surface waviness and roughness of wings etc., may be appreciable. The maximum tolerable waviness of wings, which will not affect the chordwise position of transition of the boundary layer from laminar to turbulent, is surprisingly large. Calculations based on theory suggest that the waviness should not exceed 0.018 in. over a 2-in. gauge length, and that the surface roughness should not be greater than that of sandpaper with 0.001-in. grains. However, it now seems that these criteria are not very reliable, and the position of the transition point is not the only parameter which affects the drag. There is evidence that *any* degree of waviness or roughness increases the drag, so the aim is simply perfection. Needless to say, paint lines and fabric lap joints should be carefully avoided, all holes, gaps and slots should be sealed and the wings should always be dusted before flight. Raindrops on a low-drag wing may cause an appreciable decrease in performance.

Whatever the aspect ratio, it should be remembered that the use of very small wing chords is undesirable, since both the maximum lift and profile drag coefficients are then adversely affected. Such considerations have led to the modern wing of high aspect ratio and moderate taper.

MINIMUM SINKING SPEED

The greater the aspect ratio, the greater will be the lift coefficient at the minimum rate of sink. From the previous equations it follows that this lift coefficient is given by

$$C_{L_{ms}} = \sqrt{(3\pi A C_{D_0}/k)} \qquad (16.19)$$

The previous equations take no account of the limitations imposed by the maximum lift coefficient attainable by the glider wing, which is commonly about 1.4 when flaps are not fitted. Assuming typical values of C_{D_0} and k, the theoretical $C_{L_{ms}}$ will be about 1.1 for a 15 m glider with a low aspect ratio and about 1.3 for a large high-aspect-ratio machine. As Fig. 15.4 indicates, the wing profile drag starts to increase rapidly at lift coefficients above about 0.9 for an unflapped wing. The performance at low speeds tends to be worse than the previous theory would imply and, in particular, the minimum rate of sink increases slightly and tends to occur at a higher speed than that appropriate to the theoretical value of $C_{L_{ms}}$. In the case of the Libelle, minimum sink occurs at a lift coefficient just under 1.0, which is the sort of result one might expect from curves such as those of Fig. 16.1. Hence the situation displayed in Fig. 16.5 no longer prevails near minimum sink and, as previously indicated, it is usually unprofitable to attempt to fit an analytical curve to measured performance figures at a speed below that corresponding to $(L/D)_{max}$.

It is apparent that the low-drag regime of a wing section should extend to quite high lift coefficients and it is in this direction that aerodynamicists such as Professor Wortmann have made significant improvements. The even higher lift coefficients required by gliders with very high aspect ratios can, to some extent, be achieved by the use of flapped wing sections (see page 280).

CIRCLING PERFORMANCE

The performance in circling flight can be readily deduced from the straight-flight curve of Fig. 16.4. A point on this polar corresponds to a certain lift coefficient so, if the load factor (see Chapter 20) when circling is n, the forward speed at the same lift coefficient will be increased by $\sqrt{n}$, from equation (16.2). Since the lift/drag ratio at a certain lift coefficient is substantially constant, the drag will be multiplied by n. It then follows from equation (16.14) that the corresponding rate of sink must be multiplied by the factor $n^{3/2}$. From Fig. 20.3, if the angle of bank is ϕ, then $n = \sec \phi$ and the final results are:

$$V_\phi / V_0 = (\sec \phi)^{\frac{1}{2}} \qquad (16.20)$$

$$V_{s_\phi} / V_{s_0} = (\sec \phi)^{3/2} \qquad (16.21)$$

where V_0 and V_{s_0} are the forward speed and rate of sink corresponding to a certain point on the straight-flight polar. V_ϕ and V_{s_ϕ} are the corresponding values at a point on the polar where the lift coefficient is the same but the angle of bank is ϕ.

The curves of Fig. 16.6 show the performance of the Libelle when circling at various angles of bank, deduced in this fashion. The little circles show the minimum sink at each angle of bank.

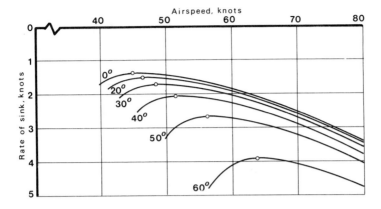

Fig 16.6 The performance of the Standard Libelle at W = 695 lb and various angles of bank

The radius of turn r (in feet) is related to the true speed V_ϕ (ft/s) and the angle of bank ϕ by:

$$r = V_\phi^2 / g\tan\phi, \qquad (16.22)$$

where g is the acceleration due to gravity (32.17 ft/s^2).

Fig. 16.7 can therefore be obtained from the turning-flight polars of Fig. 16.6, and shows the rate of sink plotted against radius of turn for various angles of bank. The numbers on the curves are the airspeeds in knots appropriate to the particular radii and rates of sink and the black spots show the minimum sink conditions. It will be noticed on the one hand how a comparatively small increase in speed results in a large increase in the radius of turn and, on the other hand, how a reduction in speed below the minimum sink condition results in a large increase in the rate of sink for a small reduction in the radius of turn.

The line through the black spots shows the minimum rate of sink which can be achieved at each particular angle of bank. This line corresponds to circling flights at a constant lift coefficient and the speed increases as the angle of bank increases. If an efficient angle of attack meter were available,

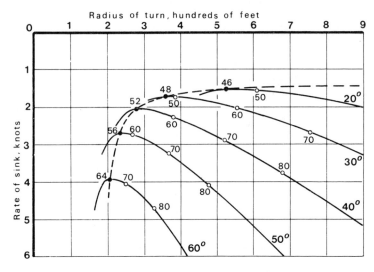

Fig 16.7 Rate of sink plotted against radius of turn for various angles of bank. The figures against the small circles are airspeeds in knots. The dotted line through the black circles represents the minimum rate of sink for each angle of bank. The diagram applies to the Standard Libelle at W = 695 lb

$\phi°$	Speed, knots	Rate of sink, knots	Load factor	Radius of turn, ft	Time for 360°, sec	Height lost in 360°, ft
60	64	3.92	2.0	208	12.1	80
50	56	2.69	1.6	236	15.6	71
45	54	2.34	1.4	255	17.7	70
40	52	2.07	1.3	281	20.3	71
35	50	1.87	1.2	315	23.5	74
30	48	1.72	1.2	361	27.7	81
25	47	1.61	1.1	427	33.5	91
20	47	1.52	1.1	528	42.2	108
15	46	1.46	1.0	698	56.5	140
10	46	1.42	1.0	1040	85.0	204
0	45	1.39	1.0	∞	∞	∞

Table 16.1 Circling performance of the Standard Libelle at an all-up weight of 695 lb near sea-level.

it would be a most useful device, since the pilot could then fly at the same lift coefficient whatever his angle of bank. Table 16.1 is derived from Fig. 16.7 and gives detailed information about the optimum turns of various radii corresponding, in each case, to the minimum rate of sink condition. The forward speeds are rounded-off to the nearest knot.

It will be noted that the minimum loss of height for a complete 360° turn occurs at an angle of bank of 45°, a result which may be shown to be true for any glider.

The line through the black spots in Fig. 16.7 and the figures in the table above therefore describe the best attainable performance, in terms of minimum rate of sink at various angles of bank. As previously indicated, the calculations are based on the assumption that the lift/drag ratio at any particular lift coefficient is constant and hence is unaffected by the curvature of the flight path. In practice, this assumption is unlikely to be realized exactly: in turning flight, the flow past the glider is not quite the same as in straight flight, so that parts of the fuselage remote from the centre of gravity are subjected to slight sideways velocity components and there is a gradation of forward airspeed across the wing span. The latter effect produces a rolling moment (see page 208) which has to be cancelled-out by the pilot applying an aileron deflection ('holding-off bank'). The consequence of all these effects is an increase, relative to straight flight at the same lift coefficient, in both the profile and induced drag coefficients, so the performance actually attained will be slightly worse than that calculated in the fashion explained above. Without making extremely careful tests it is difficult to allow for the effect of the increments in drag in turning flight and, for the present purposes, they have been neglected. In principle, it would be possible to reduce the rate of sink for a given radius of turn by flying at a speed slightly less than that appropriate to minimum sink at a given angle of bank. In practice, the effect of doing so would not be significant and the angle of attack would become uncomfortably close to the stall.

CLIMB PERFORMANCE

To achieve the maximum rate of climb in a given thermal, the glider must be flown at the speed which corresponds to minimum rate of sink at the appropriate angle of bank, as derived above. The pilot therefore has to decide what angle of bank is 'appropriate'. For the present purposes, the thermal may be visualised as an ascending column of air whose vertical velocity is a maximum on its axis and diminishes as one moves radially outwards from the axis. The most appropriate angle of bank will then depend on the thermal strength (i.e., the vertical velocity on the axis) and the way in which the vertical velocity varies with radius. Neither of these features can be readily observed by the pilot, who is likely to be thinking in rather qualitative terms such as 'wide and strong' or 'narrow and weak'. Nevertheless, it is useful to investigate optimum climbs in plausible thermals (a) as a general guide to piloting techniques, (b) for handicapping purposes, and (c) as a guide to the overall optimisation of glider designs.

Appendix 8 describes various plausible thermals and gives equations describing their vertical profiles. The present investigation relates to the simplest profile, the 'parabolic' thermal, where the vertical velocity V_T is assumed to vary with radius r according to the law

$$V_T/V_{T_0} = 1 - (r/R)^2. \qquad (16.23)$$

V_{T_0} is the vertical velocity on the axis, i.e. where $r = 0$, and R is the 'thermal radius' i.e. the value of r at which $V_T = 0$.

As explained in Appendix 8, this thermal looks reasonable provided r is not too large a fraction of R. However, the velocity *gradient* increases as r increases, and the velocity V_T becomes increasingly more negative when r exceeds R and the representation is clearly unrealistic at large values of r. So it seems reasonable to use this parabolic profile only so long as r/R is not too large: in the case considered below, it is 0.36, so we are reasonably well away from the unrealistic regions. This type of thermal was originally proposed by H.C.N. Goodhart who went on to deduce suitable values of V_{T_0} and R for the 'British Standard Thermal' from the angles of bank typically used by pilots and their achieved rates of climb. The main object in deriving a standard thermal was to facilitate the development of a rational system of handicapping gliders for some competition purposes. Nick Goodhart's original figures have been slightly modified in the light of experience of this handicapping system and the figures which are now

(1975) thought to be 'realistic' are V_{T_0} = 4.2 knots and R = 1000 ft.

The vertical velocity of the air at a radius r is then given by

$$V_T = 4.2 \, [1-(r/1000)^2], \qquad (16.24)$$

V_T being in knots and r in feet.

This variation in vertical velocity is shown as the upper curve in Fig. 16.8. Also shown is another curve showing the rate of climb which would be attained by a Libelle circling concentrically with the thermal at different angles of bank.

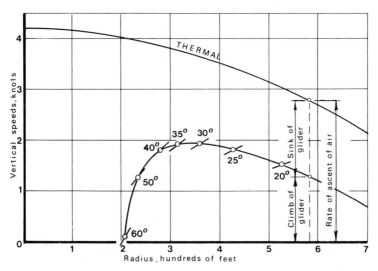

Fig 16.8 Climbing in the 'standard' British thermal. The upper curve shows thermal strength, the lower the circling performance of the Standard Libelle at W = 695 lb when flown at the minimum rate of sink condition at each angle of bank

This latter curve is derived from Fig. 16.7 by taking a point at a particular radius on the thermal curve and subtracting from the vertical velocity of the air the minimum rate of sink of the glider when circling at the same radius.

It will be seen that the maximum rate of climb is 1.94 knots when the angle of bank is 30° and the radius of turn is

360 ft. The angle of bank is not very critical since the rate of climb exceeds 1.90 knots, corresponding to a maximum loss of only 2%, for angles of bank anywhere between 27° and 37°.

This analysis can be made rather more general. The optimum circling performance of a glider is entirely determined by the values of minimum rate of sink $V_{s_{min}}$ and corresponding forward speed V_{ms} in straight flight so, if these two quantities are known, the optimum climbing performance in a given thermal can be determined. The rather tedious graph-plotting, as in Fig. 16.7, can be short-circuited by a little further analysis. It may be shown that the optimum angle of bank ϕ is that which satisfies

$$3 \tan^4 \phi \, \cos^{\frac{1}{2}} \phi = 4 (V_{ms}^2 / gR)^2 (V_{T0} / V_{s\,min}). \qquad (16.25)$$

This value of ϕ is then inserted in the following equation to give the maximum rate of climb:

$$V_c/V_{s_{min}} = (V_{T0}/V_{s_{min}})[1 - (V_{ms}^2/gR)^2 \, \mathrm{cosec}^2 \, \phi]$$
$$-(\sec\phi)^{3/2} \qquad (16.26)$$

It is therefore possible to calculate the maximum rate of climb of any glider in the standard thermal, presenting the results as in Fig. 16.9.

Even more generally, it will be seen that equations (16.25) and (16.26) involve only the dimensionless quantities (V_{ms}^2/gR) and $(V_{T0}/V_{s_{min}})$ as independent variables. (Given these quantities, ϕ and $V_c/V_{s_{min}}$) can be found. Using these equations, it is therefore possible to derive a dimensionless plot showing the optimum climb performance of any glider in any 'parabolic' thermal.

Similar calculations could obviously be carried out for gliders circling in thermals with other types of profiles but, unless the profile can be described by a very simple equation, or unless a computer can be used, the work becomes rather lengthy.

It is clear that such calculations relate to very idealised situations: the velocity profile of the thermal is described by a simple mathematical expression and the piloting technique is

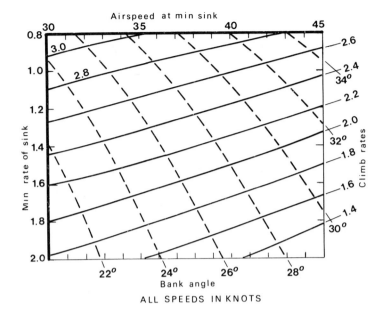

Fig 16.9 'Isoclimbs' for the standard British thermal. Lines of constant rate of climb are shown solid; lines of constant bank angle are dotted

assumed to be perfect. Nevertheless it is a useful investigation, particularly as a guide to piloting techniques.

For example, Fig. 16.10 shows a plot of optimum angle of bank against rate of climb – which is what the pilot observes – for various thermal strengths and radii for the Libelle. Remembering that a few degrees error in bank angle has very little effect on the achieved rate of climb, a rough rule of thumb would be to use a little over 30° of bank in wide thermals and up to 10° more in narrow ones. Only in rather exceptional circumstances would 45° of bank be required assuming, of course, that the velocity profile of the thermal is more or less parabolic.

Throughout this analysis of climbing, all speeds are 'true' so those relating to the performance of the glider only correspond with the 'equivalent' values from the performance curve near sea-level.

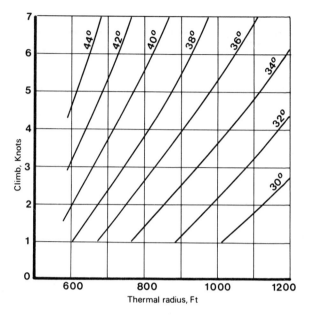

Fig 16.10 Optimum angles for the Standard Libelle at W = 695 lb for varying rate of climb and thermal radius

CROSS–COUNTRY PERFORMANCE

Climbing is merely a means to an end: potential energy is gained in a thermal and is then dissipated in the course of gliding to the next one. The previous section indicates how the best rate of climb is achieved under given conditions whereas now the problem is to discover how the pilot should fly between thermals to achieve the best overall result. The usual criterion of 'best' in this context is that the average speed for the whole flight should be a maximum.

The simplest analysis assumes that the glider makes a series of climbs in thermals, flying from one thermal to the next at a steady speed. Downcurrents between the thermals are, for the present, neglected and no account is taken of the loss of time which can occur in searching for thermals and optimising the climb. Although the situation is an idealized one and might appear to lead to excessively optimistic results, even higher average speeds can be achieved in practice by taking advantage of feeble upcurrents whilst flying between the major thermals. 'You have to follow the energy,' to borrow Hans Werner Grosse's felicitous phrase. However artificial this calculation may be, it is a most important one, for it is the starting-point for all other optimisation calculations.

In order to optimise the whole flight, all the climbs and all the glides are added together. For the moment, any effects due to the reduced air density at altitude are neglected. The flight is then the equivalent of a single climb from A to B (Fig. 16.11) followed by a steady glide from B to C. Before analysing such a flight, the height difference between A and C relative to the height gain from A to B must be known. It is usual to assume that A and C are at the same height for the sake of simplicity. In practice, the height difference could well be about 3000 ft, which is not entirely negligible compared with the height gain of say 40,000 ft required for many a 300-km flight. For the moment, the conventional assumption will be made.

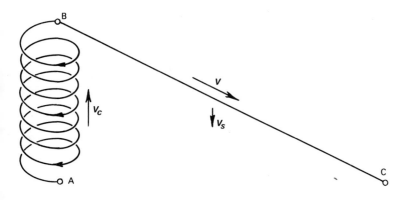

Fig 16.11 Diagram of an idealised cross-country flight

Suppose that the average rate of climb from A to B is V_c and the time spent climbing is t_c. Then the height gained is $V_c t_c$. If the pilot glides from B to C in time t_g at a speed V, the corresponding rate of sink being V_s, then the loss of height will be $t_g V_s$. Equating the gain and loss of height, it follows that

$$t_g = V_c t_c / V_s \tag{16.27}$$

and hence the distance covered is

$$t_g V = V V_c t_c / V_s . \tag{16.28}$$

The total time for the climb and glide will be

$$t_c + t_g = t_c (1 + V_c / V_s). \tag{16.29}$$

So, dividing the total distance by the total time, the average speed is

$$\overline{V} = V V_c / (V_s + V_c). \tag{16.30}$$

The problem is then to choose V so as to make $\overline{V}$ a maximum, V_c being known.

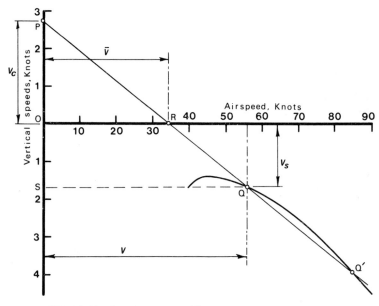

Fig 16.12 Construction to find the average cross-country speed, knowing the achieved rate of climb and the gliding speed between thermals. The polar is that of the Standard Libelle at W = 695 lb

Consider the construction shown in Fig. 16.12. From a point P, such that OP represents V_c to a suitable scale, a line is drawn to a point Q on the polar. Q represents the conditions V and V_s during the glide. Triangles POR and PSQ are similar and hence the relationship between the various speeds shown corresponds to equation (16.30) if $\overline{V}$ is represented by OR. By a similar argument, the same average speed is attained if the glide is carried out at conditions corresponding to Q′.

It is immediately apparent that, other things being equal, $\overline{V}$ is maximised by arranging for PR produced to be tangential to the polar, as in Fig. 16.13. The point T then represents the optimum speed to glide, V_{opt}, and OR represents $\overline{V}_{max}$, the maximum average speed. It is clear that any other gliding speed, represented by points such as Q or Q′ gives a lower value of $\overline{V}$.

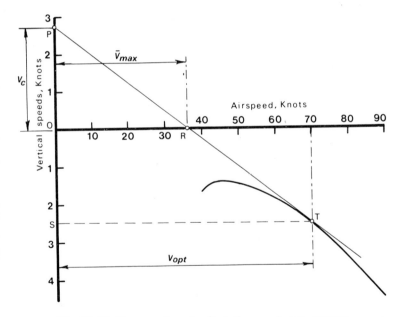

Fig 16.13 *Construction to find the maximum average cross-country speed and the corresponding optimum gliding speed between thermals knowing the achieved rate of climb. The polar is that of the Standard Libelle at W = 695 lb*

The condition corresponding to Fig. 16.13 is that, at the optimum gliding speed, the slope of the polar must have the value PS/PT or, in the symbols of the calculus, at $V = V_{opt}$,

$$dV_s/dV = (V_s + V_c)/V , \qquad (16.31)$$

a result which could also be obtained by differentiating equation (16.30).

This criterion, apparently so simple, has all the force of a great Law of Nature so far as glider pilots are concerned. An excursion into the Calculus of Variations, rather outside the scope of this book, shows that it, or something very like it, is invariably the criterion for optimising any aspect of overall performance. In this present application, V_c has an obvious physical significance; in other circumstances, it simply becomes a parameter defining one of a family of possible flight paths and its physical significance may be much more obscure.

Using the construction of Fig. 16.13, in conjunction with the polar of the Libelle (Fig. 16.4) shows that a rate of climb of 2.7 knots gives an average speed of 37 knots and the glider

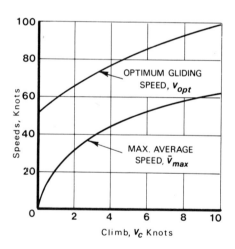

Fig 16.14 Optimum gliding speed between thermals and average cross-country speed plotted against achieved rate of climb, as deduced from Fig. 16.13

should be flown at 70 knots between the thermals. By drawing a whole series of tangents the figures of Table 16.2 and
the curves of Fig. 16.14 can be deduced.

It is important to appreciate that this calculation makes no
assumptions about the details of the thermals or the skill of
the pilot in exploiting them: the final result depends only on
an actual rate of climb figure. But which rate of climb?

V_c knots	V knots between thermals	$\bar{V}$ knots average speed
0	51	0
0.44	55	11.8
1.10	60	22.6
1.84	65	30.4
2.68	70	36.7
3.62	75	42.1
4.67	80	46.9
5.85	85	51.4
7.16	90	55.6
8.62	95	59.6
10.23	100	63.5

*Table 16.2 Speeds to fly between thermals and average speeds
for various rates of climb for the Libelle at W = 695 lb.*

The criterion displayed graphically in Fig. 16.13 and
mathematically in equation (16.31) is applicable to any climb/
glide sequence, or to any series of such sequences, provided
the net height change is negligible compared with the height
gained in the climb or climbs. Hence, it is not normally applicable to a single climb/glide sequence in a real cross-country
flight, since the condition relating to height differences will
not, in general, be satisfied and the pilot has little means of
deciding at the beginning of a glide whether or not it is likely
to be satisfied. And even if equal gains and losses of height
did occur in each climb/glide sequence, it would not pay to
optimise each sequence separately if the rates of climb were
different. A simple calculation for two such sequences shows
that it would be better to take the overall average rate of
climb and perform both glides at the same speed, (that appropriate to this average rate of climb) rather than make the two
glides at different speeds (those appropriate to the individual

rates of climb in the immediately preceding thermals). In other words, optimisation of the whole flight gives a better result than piecewise, thermal-by-thermal, optimisation. In order to apply such theory to an actual flight, the pilot therefore needs to know the rate of climb to be achieved, averaged over all the thermals, and he needs to know it at the beginning of the flight. As explained in Chapter 7, the usual absence of powers of prophecy means that he cannot know an accurate figure and has to make do with something much rougher.

To calculate the overall performance of a given glider for purposes such as handicapping, the rate of climb in an idealised thermal can be found as in the previous section. It is then usual to suppose that the average cross-country speed corresponds to the construction of Fig. 16.13. The implicit assumption is that the effect of any vertical motions in the atmosphere between the thermals can be ignored or, perhaps more realistically, that they cancel out.

In real life, they certainly exist and the principle of continuity suggests that, overall, there will be a slight downwards motion between the thermals since the atmosphere is not disappearing into outer space. The pilot therefore needs to know how to deal with vertical motions of the air between the thermals.

If the previous theory is repeated, but now with the air descending at a velocity V_a between the thermals, then the total rate of descent becomes $(V_s + V_a)$. This quantity therefore replaces V_s in the previous calculations. The average speed therefore becomes

$$\overline{V} = VV_c /(V_s + V_a + V_c) \qquad (16.32)$$

and the criterion for maximising the average speed is now that at $V = V_{opt}$,

$$dV_s/dV = (V_s + V_a + V_c)/V \qquad (16.33)$$

The graphical interpretation of these results is shown in Fig. 16.15.

This particular method of analysis seems to suggest that V_a is a similar sort of quantity to V_c, a sort of long-term average.

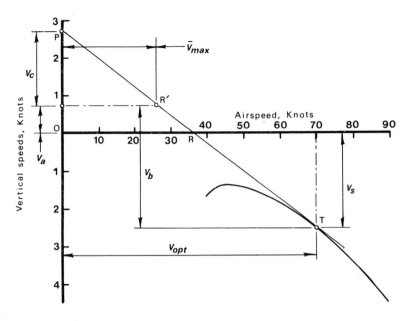

Fig 16.15 The construction of Fig. 16.13 modified to take into account the effect of a downdraught V_a during the glide

Intuitively, this interpretation seems unlikely: it would suggest that the glide should be flown at constant speed whereas, in reality, loitering in regions of strong down-draught is a most unprofitable occupation. A more rigorous analysis shows the pilot's intuition to be correct: V_a in the above expressions is the *instantaneous* downdraught velocity and, as it varies from one instant to the next, the pilot should adjust his forward speed in accordance with equation (**16.33**) and Fig. 16.15. There is, however, a precaution which the rigorous analysis shows to be essential. If the pilot were flying at a constant speed, his variometer would show the total rate of descent ($V_s + V_a$). Since his speed is now varying, the variometer will only show correct readings of ($V_s + V_a$) if it is of the total energy type (see pages 286 and 288).

The pilot must be provided with some simple indication of the instantaneous value of the optimum gliding speed, according to the above criterion, based on information readily available in the cockpit. Comparing Figs. 16.13 and 16.15 it is clear that the values in the first column of Table 16.2 are equally applicable to the situation displayed in the latter diagram provided that they now represent $(V_c + V_a)$. The table may now be modified by adding to the figure in the first column the still-air rates of sink V_s corresponding to the values of V in the second column, thus giving $(V_c + V_a + V_s)$. This last quantity is also equal to $(V_c + V_b)$, where V_b is the variometer reading. Table 16.3 is derived from the values of Table 16.2 in such a fashion. Figures for $\overline{V}$ are no longer shown: they are not very relevant when V_a is varying in some arbitrary fashion, they would have to be separately tabulated for each value of V_c and finally, if one assumes that the overall effect of the varying ups and downs in the atmosphere traversed by the glides is small, the values in Table 16.2 will be as good as any. In this context it is important to appreciate that, although V_a has been treated as a downdraught velocity for the purposes of the above analysis its sign can be either positive (downdraught) or negative (updraught).

$(V_c + V_b)$ knots	V knots between thermals
1.49	51
2.05	55
2.92	60
3.94	65
5.11	70
6.44	75
7.97	80
9.68	85
11.59	90
13.74	95
16.10	100

Table 16.3. Relationships between optimum speed and location on rotatable ring with datum set to zero for the Libelle at W = 695

A series of tables, based on Table 16.3, could then be drawn up, showing the best speed to fly as a function of the instantaneous variometer reading V_b for various constant values of V_c, the long-term average rate of climb. The crudest way of optimising a glide would be for the pilot to choose the particular table corresponding to his best estimate of V_c and to endeavour to match his airspeed and variometer readings in accordance with the tabulated values. A more convenient solution is to construct a best-speed-to-fly indicator, fitted to the variometer so that optimum speeds are directly displayed.

Such a device is the rotatable ring surrounding the variometer dial invented by Dr. P. B. MacCready, Jnr., the use of which was described in Chapter 7 (See Fig. 16.16).

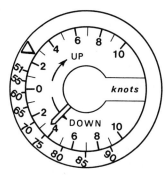

Fig 16.16 The MacCready best-speed-to-fly ring fitted to a variometer. The datum is set to a rate of climb of 2.7 knots in still air, the optimum gliding speed would be 70 knots. As shown here, the glider has encountered slightly sinking air and the speed should be increased. (The ring is calibrated for the Standard Libelle at W = 695 lb)

The scales of most mechanical variometers (e.g., Winter or PZL) and some electrical variometers (e.g., Cambridge) are sufficiently nearly linear to enable this type of indicator to be used.

With a datum mark on the ring set opposite zero on the variometer scale, speeds are marked around the ring opposite rate of sink indications on the variometer scale. The relationship between the speeds and rates of sink is that between V and $(V_c + V_b)$ in Table 16.3. For example, 60 knots on the bezel ring should be opposite a sink value of 2.9 knots on the variometer scale.

For use in flight, the ring is rotated so that the datum is opposite the figure on the rate of climb scale which corresponds to the pilot's estimate of V_c. When the variometer is indicating a total rate of sink V_b when flying between thermals, the displacement of the pointer from the datum mark is $(V_c + V_b)$ and it therefore indicates the best speed to fly on the ring.

As a rule, the use of any of these devices requires a series of successive approximations. From the variometer and best speed indicator, a certain speed-to-fly is read. The speed is adjusted to this figure, whereupon the rate of sink of the glider alters. From the changed variometer reading, a new speed-to-fly will be read, another adjustment to the speed will be required and so on. In practice this is not as difficult as it sounds: in mathematical terms, the process is convergent, so that little readjustment is actually required and with practice it is possible to judge the degree of overshoot required. A MacCready ring applies to a certain glider at a fixed weight. If the weight is increased appreciably by the use of ballast, an appropriately calibrated ring will be required.

However, this successive-approximation process is a nuisance and various devices have been invented to eliminate it. It follows from Fig. 16.15 that, for a given glider, the optimum gliding speed depends only on $(V_c + V_a)$. If the variometer could be persuaded to display V_a, the 'air mass movement', a suitably-calibrated ring with its datum set to V_c as before would give direct indications of optimum speed, even if the speed of the glider at that instant differed from the optimum. Methods of modifying the variometer in this fashion are explained in Chapter 18. In such a case, with the datum on the ring set opposite zero on the variometer scale, the relationship between speeds and rates of sink is that between V and V_c in Table 16.2. For example, 60 knots on the ring would now be opposite 1.1 knots on the variometer scale.

Taking this process one stage further involves arranging the variometer system so that the instrument always shows a constant climb reading when the glider is being flown at its optimum speed (again, see Chapter 18). If the variometer shows more 'climb', the speed is decreased; if it shows less climb, the speed is increased. With such a 'zero-reader', no speed-to-fly scale is required: the pilot simply does what he is told.

These various systems, intended to facilitate flying at the optimum speed, are available as adaptations to both mechanical and electric variometers. There are now various other devices, effectively small on-board computers, which receive electrical inputs corresponding to the airspeed and variometer readings and perform the above calculations electrically once the pilot has set V_c. They can have various advantages compared with the mechanical variometer: the same indicator can function as a total-energy variometer, an air-mass indicator or a zero reader; the correction for the actual flying weight (e.g., with or without ballast) can easily be made, whereas the conventional variometer would require different rings; and readouts appropriate to other situations such as final glides can also be obtained.

Throughout this chapter, it should be understood that glider airspeeds are equivalent airspeeds, and polar curves are usually plotted on this basis. The equivalent airspeed (EAS) differs from (and is usually greater than) the indicated airspeed (IAS) by a quantity known as the pressure error, for reasons explained in Chapter 20. In calculating best-speeds-to-fly for a glider whose polar is given in terms of EAS, all the above calculations should be carried out in terms of EAS and finally converted to IAS for practical use. The position error is quoted either as a curve of EAS plotted against IAS or a curve of position error correction (PEC) against IAS. The EAS is then the algebraic sum of the IAS and the PEC and for gliders the PEC is usually positive.

Finally, it should be noted that a polar must be drawn relative to a true zero for the purposes of this chapter; in order to save space, published polars frequently have a false zero.

Chapter 17

Further Theory of Glider Performance

INTRODUCTION

In the previous chapter, the theory relating to glider performance curves was examined, including an explanation of the MacCready construction for determining the optimum speed to fly between thermals. This chapter considers some special applications of such theory and discusses matters, such as the use of water ballast, which are mainly of interest to pilots trying to achieve the highest performance in advanced gliders.

'DOLPHIN' FLYING

As explained in Chapter 7, it may be possible to fly considerable distances without circling in the thermals. The pilot flies slowly through lift and more rapidly elsewhere so that he progresses in a series of undulations, somewhat reminiscent of the leaping progress of a dolphin.

Such a segment of a flight can be regarded as a glide which traverses considerable regions of up-going air, interspersed with downdraughts. Although the foregoing analysis of optimum glides in the presence of vertical air motions, leading to equation (16.33) is written as if V_a were always a downdraught, there is nothing in the mathematics which prevents V_a being either positive, corresponding to a downdraught, or negative, corresponding to an updraught. So the technique is basically the same as before: the pilot simply regulates his speed according to the indications of the MacCready ring. The difficulty is to decide what datum-setting, V_c, to use.

An analysis of a flight carried out entirely without circling shows that V_c no longer has quite the simple interpretation of the earlier analyses of this chapter. It becomes a parameter which defines the ring setting and its value depends on the strength and distribution of the upcurrents along the flight path, together with some statement about the initial and final conditions, such as no net height change. The value of V_c is therefore indeterminable in advance and the pilot has no choice but to proceed by trial and error. If the flight is long enough, he can initially set the ring datum to some rather conservative value such as zero. If he finds that there is a tendency to gain more height than he desires, the datum can be reset, say to 2 knots climb, and so on.

For a flight which combines circling in thermals with some 'dolphin' flying, somewhat similar considerations apply. The pilot's assessment of a suitable ring setting needs to be modified to take into account the effects of dolphining but, again, he can only resort to trial and error.

For normal cross-country flying, the lowest speed calibration on the MacCready ring is that corresponding to $(L/D)_{max}$ since, from Figure 16.15, this case corresponds to zero rate of climb and zero downdraught. However, when flying under the present circumstances, the point P in Figure 16.15 could fall below the point 0. This would occur when the monetary strength of the upcurrent exceeded the value of the datum setting V_c, since OP represents $V_a + V_c$ and V_a is now negative. Indeed, if V_a were strong enough, the MacCready ring – now extended to lower speeds by drawing tangents from points below O – might even tell the pilot to fly at a speed below the speed for minimum rate of sink. In effect, it would require him to loiter in the regions of greatest available energy. The deterioration of the handling and controllability of the glider at speeds close to the stall often makes such slow flying rather impractical.

The usual analysis of dolphin-flying indicates that when the glider flies from an upcurrent to a downcurrent or viceversa its speed should be re-adjusted to the new optimum as rapidly as possible. The analyses carried out so far, with the exception of some tentative computer studies, do not take into account the effect of changing load factor on the induced drag. Qualitatively, it would seem that if the changes of load factor are reasonably modest, the increments in induced drag in pull-ups will be roughly cancelled out by the decreases in push-overs from the point of view of overall energy loss. This consideration is something of a disincentive to fierce pull-ups since, other things being equal, the induced drag depends on the square of the load factor.

As mentioned previously, when considering the glide in the presence of down-draughts, it is quite essential that the variometer should be of the total-energy type.

THE PHILOSOPHY OF THE MacCREADY RING SETTING

In optimising any cross-country flight, the MacCready ring datum setting, corresponding to V_c in the analysis, is of prime importance. For conventional flights consisting of climbs made by circling in thermals followed by glides, V_c can be regarded as the mean achieved rate of climb averaged over all the thermals. In other circumstances, its significance is similar but less simply related to observable physical quantities. It is unfortunately an elusive quantity, since it *always* depends on what is going to happen in the future. The previous analysis shows that piece-wise optimization of a flight (i.e., by considering separately each climb/glide sequence) does not give the best result. Ideally, one should consider the flight as a whole. However, at any particular point in a flight, a certain distance has been covered in a certain time: whatever the pilot does next has no influence on what has already happened, so he is only concerned with optimising his performance during the remainder of the flight. He can only assess the value of V_c to be used for the remainder of the flight by extrapolating from the current situation into the future, taking into account any information he can glean on future weather prospects. Whilst the average cross-country speed actually achieved is remarkably insensitive to errors in gliding speed or MacCready ring setting, compounding such errors can lead to a loss in average speed which begins to become significant in competitions, where the best results are often very close. So, whilst great accuracy is neither essential not attainable, a pilot striving for maximum performance will try to up-date his assessment of V_c from time to time. It is also apparent that, whilst he is really interested in a fairly long-term average, he must be prepared to change rapidly to a 'survival' setting (usually $V_c = 0$) should conditions deteriorate. If errors in speed are inevitable, it pays to err on the slow side. The reason is that flying too slowly flattens the glide angle, increases the chance of finding the next thermal and reduces the total height to be gained in a flight over a given distance. In a typical case, a loss of only 0.6% in average speed would reduce the time spent climbing in thermals by about 12%, saving about 5000 ft of height gain in the course of a 300-km flight. Flying too fast has the converse effect: it reduces the average speed but increases the pilot's workload.

EFFECTS OF ALTITUDE

The analyses leading to the criteria of equations (16.31) and (16.33) are written in terms of true speeds. However, the performance curve of the glider applies at all altitudes provided that both the forward speed and rate of sink are 'equivalent' speeds (see p. 232) and minor Reynolds number effects are ignored. The MacCready construction and the above criteria will also be correct at all altitudes provided that all the speeds involved, both vertically and along the flight path, are 'equivalent'. Unfortunately, the pilot is presented with data from two sources: the airspeed indicator, which displays something close to equivalent airspeed, and the variometer. If the latter is of the mechanical type, it displays something very close to true vertical speed at all heights, whilst an electric variometer displays something like

$$\text{(true vertical speed)} \times \sigma^n, \qquad (17.1)$$

where σ is the local atmospheric relative density and n, which may depend on the details of the variometer design, might well be about 1.0. So, if the variometer is calibrated for sea-level conditions, the MacCready ring will only be correct at sea-level, where true and equivalent speeds are the same.

At any appreciable altitude, using a mechanical variometer, the use of a 'sea-level' MacCready ring leads to excessive inter-thermal speeds as a consequence of two additive effects:

(*i*)   The pilot may set the ring datum to too high a value
since his estimate of $V_{c'}$ will be based on true rates of
climb as opposed to equivalent values. This error
causes the airspeed figure opposite a given sink indication of the variometer to be too high.

(*ii*) When gliding between thermals, the variometer indicates true rate of sink and, since this is greater than
the corresponding equivalent value, there is an additional increment to the optimum gliding speed displayed opposite the pointer.

When operating a Standard Class sailplane at a mean height
of 10,000 ft with a mean equivalent rate of climb of 5 knots,
the gliding speed will be about 6 knots too fast. The corresponding loss in average speed is only about 0.6% but, the time
spent climbing in thermals is increased from 39% of the total
flight time to 44%.

In the case of electric variometers, the converse situation
prevails. If n in equation (17.1) were 0.5, the variometer
would read equivalent vertical speeds. With $n\sim1$, it reads less
than the equivalent value. If the MacCready ring is calibrated
for sea-level, the pilot will tend to fly too slowly, between
thermals. Again, there is a small loss in average speed, but the
cockpit workload is reduced.

All these problems would disappear if the variometer could
be caused to display equivalent vertical speeds. Mechanically,
it could be done only at considerable expense. The electric
variometer seems to offer better possibilities and some progress has been made in the direction of applying a density correction to its output by sensing the air temperature and applying a correction based on the Standard Atmosphere density/
temperature relationship. In principle, it would not be difficult to devise a proper system which sensed both temperature
and pressure.

A simpler alternative is to provide different MacCready
rings for different mean heights, by expanding the scale, relative to the datum mark by a factor $1/\sqrt{\sigma}$, where σ is the atmospheric relative density at the appropriate height. A simple
method of achieving this result is shown in Plate IV, where the
inner edge of the MacCready Ring is calibrated for sea-level

and the outer edge for 10,000 ft. Since great accuracy is not required, the pilot can readily interpolate or extrapolate for other heights. Similarly, an approximate correction could be applied to an electric variometer by using the same MacCready ring at all heights but modifying the sensitivity of the indicator by a suitable potentiometer. Likewise, if electronic computing devices are to be fitted to the variometer, their value is reduced if some form of altitude compensation is not included.

EFFECT OF WIND: CROSS–COUNTRY FLIGHTS
USING LEE WAVES

It is implicit in all the above theory that the wind has no effect on the optimum speed for gliding between thermals since the climbs and glides are all taking place in an air mass moving bodily over the countryside. This situation is broadly true but the wind affects the break-off height from the last thermal in a goal race and will obviously affect average speeds attained over the ground.

Whereas thermals are assumed to move with the wind, some sources of lift remain more or less stationary with respect to the ground. In lee waves, or simple hill lift, the pattern of streamlines in the atmosphere may remain stationary with the wind blowing through it.

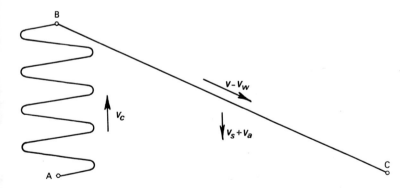

Fig 17.1 Diagram of an idealised cross-country flight using wave lift

Imagine a cross-country flight conducted by climbing in a wave, gliding against the wind to the next wave, and so on. To a stationary observer, the diagram representing the flight looks like Figure 16.11, except that the speed over the ground during the glide is $(V - V_w)$ (see Figure 17.1).

The theory is substantially the same as on page 248, except that V is replaced by $(V - V_w)$, and hence the average speed is

$$\bar{V} = V_c (V - V_w)/(V_s + V_a + V_c) \qquad (17.2)$$

and the construction giving speed to fly which maximises $\bar{V}$ is that of Figure 17.2

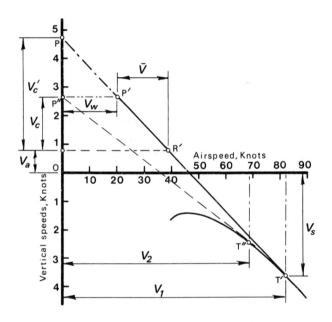

Fig 17.2 Construction to find the optimum gliding speed to give the maximum average cross-country speed when using wave lift. The tangent P'T' is drawn from P', located as shown and corresponding to a MacCready ring setting V_c'. Setting the ring to the actual rate of climb V_c would correspond to the tangent P"T", giving too low a gliding speed

It is clear that, if the MacCready ring is set to V_c, it will display an optimum gliding speed V_2, which is too low. The correct speed is V_1, corresponding to a scaled-up ring setting V_c'; Assuming that the pilot has reasonable estimates of V_c and V_w, he wishes to know the appropriate ring setting. Unfortunately, there is no solution to this problem which can be applied to simple instrumentation, although one could doubtless devise a computer which would display the correct V_1, after the pilot had fed in values for V_w and V_c.

Alternatively, if the pilot sets V_c on the MacCready ring and observes V_2, can he then derive the correct speed V_1 if he knows V_w? Again, if one assumes the performance curve to be of the form of equation (16.17), the calculation is quite straightforward but gives a result of some obscurity from the pilot's viewpoint. Fortunately, it can be used to provide a rule-of-thumb as follows:

(a) For low wind speeds (about one-quarter of the speed for $(L/D)_{max}$) increase V_2 by half the wind speed.

(b) For high wind speeds (about the same as the speed for $(L/D)_{max}$) increase V_2 by three-quarters of the wind speed.

OPTIMUM GLIDE ANGLES

If the pilot is concerned with the best gliding angle through the air in the presence of downdraughts, as may be the case when he is trying to reach a distant cumulus cloud, then the best speed to fly will correspond with the point L in Figure 17.3, such that DL is a tangent to the performance curve.

If L were located anywhere else on the curve, the slope of DL would still represent the glide angle but would obviously be less than the optimum. From the pilot's point of view and by analogy with Figure 16.15, this condition can be attained by setting the MacCready ring datum to zero and then by following the indications of the variometer in the usual fashion.

Circumstances may also arise in which the pilot wishes to achieve the best gliding angle over the ground in the presence of a head-or tailwind and downcurrents. In such a case, points M and N respectively in Figure 17.3 represent the best speeds. Here, the situation is analogous to that in Figure 17.2 and, if

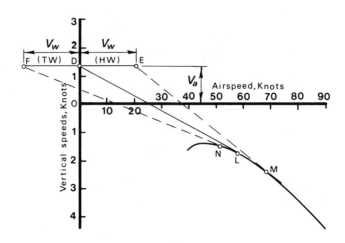

Fig 17.3 Construction to find the gliding speed to give the best angle of glide over the ground in the presence of a downdraught and with a headwind or tailwind

the MacCready ring is to be used, it should theoretically be set to some datum other than zero, with the rather awkward proviso that the datum setting will depend on the instantaneous downdraught. Again, the rules proposed in the previous section will apply reasonably accurately, with the ring datum set to zero.

OPTIMUM WING LOADING

Since the wing loading of a given glider can be increased by means of ballast weights, it is interesting to consider the influence of wing loading on average speed. If polar 1 in Fig. 17.4 relates to a glider whose wing loading is w_1, then polar 2, relating to the same machine at a higher wing loading w_2, is obtained by multiplying corresponding co-ordinates of polar 1 by $\sqrt{(w_2/w_1)}$. Suppose now that the construction of Fig. 16.13 is carried out for 'strong' and 'weak' thermals. (The tangents intersect the vertical axis at different points in Fig. 17.4(a) because an increase in wing loading will decrease the rate of climb in a thermal of constant strength: similarly for Fig. 17.4(b).)

If the thermals are strong, in the case illustrated, $\overline{V}_2$ will exceed $\overline{V}_1$ and hence an increase in wing loading is beneficial. If, on the other hand, the thermals are weak, $\overline{V}_2$ is less than $\overline{V}_1$ and then an increase in wing loading has an adverse effect. It therefore follows that, other things being equal, there is an optimum wing loading corresponding to each thermal strength.

In some gliders, provision has been made for the carriage of water ballast, so that a high speed may be attained whilst the thermals are strong. Towards the evening, as the thermals grow weaker, water is jettisoned. Installation of the water

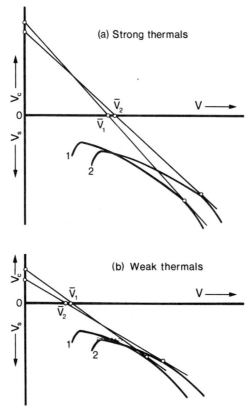

Fig 17.4 Diagrams to illustrate the effect of wing loading on average speed in strong and weak thermals

tanks in the fuselage is undesirable, since the added water greatly increases the wing-root bending moment. An alternative method is to use ballast distributed across the wingspan.

USE OF BALLAST

In gliders where provision is made for the carriage of water ballast, the pilot wishes to know when he should retain it or jettison it. The previous section has been written in terms of 'strong' or 'weak' thermals but this is something of an oversimplification. As Figure 17.4 indicates, jettisoning ballast is worthwhile if the effect of the improvement in the climb outweighs the effect of the lower cruising speeds. When ballast is jettisoned, the rate of climb is improved because the optimum radius of turn in a given thermal diminishes and the rate of sink also becomes less. So, the improvement in rate of climb depends not only on the weight change but also on both the effective radius and strength of the thermal, as visualized in the analysis of page 244. In general, therefore, the pilot cannot simply observe a single quantity such as the variometer reading and use it as a guide to the desirability of retaining or jettisoning water ballast. He requires some other additional guide which, in the unlikely circumstance that all conditions correspond with optimum climbing conditions in an idealised thermal, would be his angle of bank.

Figure 17.5 has been calculated for the Libelle using parabolic thermals of various radii and core strengths. It shows the advantage to be gained, in terms of average cross-country speed, by dropping ballast so as to reduce the weight from 772 lb to 633 lb plotted against rate of climb obtained at the higher weight. If the thermals are very narrow, requiring angles of bank of about 45°, it pays to fly at the lower weight. (The optimum angles of bank shown on the diagram correspond to the higher weight, but alter very little if the weight is reduced). If the optimum angle of bank is about 35°, it pays to fly at the higher weight if the rate of climb exceeds about 3.2 knots. This figure increases to about 3.6 knots if the optimum bank angle is 40°.

In practical terms, it is difficult to devise a simple, unambiguous rule. It seems that in average circumstances it will

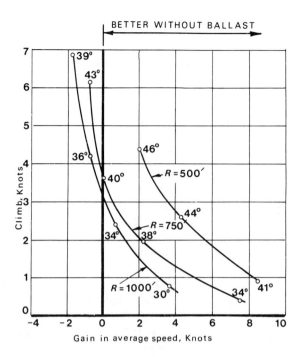

Fig 17.5 The gain in average cross-country speed when ballast is jettisoned for various rates of climb with ballast and different thermal radii. The angles of bank shown against the little circles correspond to the ballasted condition. The diagram applies to the Standard Libelle at W = 695 lb in parabolic thermals

rarely pay to retain the ballast if the rate of climb is less than 3 knots. If the rate of climb is more than 4 knots it will usually pay to retain it. Although there is a region between these rates of climb where the best course of action is rather indeterminate, it need not worry the pilot, since the effect of weight changes is likely to be negligible. In very narrow thermals, it almost pays to fly at the lower weight.

HEIGHT TO LEAVE THE LAST THERMAL

It might be inferred from the analysis of optimum gliding speed on page 249 and the remarks about V_c on page 251 that there is nothing particularly special about the final glide which just takes the pilot to his goal. If V_c has been well-chosen, it will apply to the final glide just as it applies to the earlier glides.

However, as indicated on page 260, the pilot is always concerned to optimize the part of the flight yet to come. So, when he is climbing in the final thermal the previous part of the flight is history: nothing can be done to alter the time taken so far. The best he can do is to minimize the time for the final climb/glide sequence. Assuming zero wind for the moment, he will eventually achieve a height in the last thermal from which he can just reach the goal. He cannot leave the thermal any earlier but, if the thermal is strong, it may pay to stay in it and climb to some greater height since he will then be able to fly faster on the final glide, thus saving more time than he spends on the additional climb. The chances of arriving at the goal are also improved since there is now scope for flattening the glide angle if necessary. The portion of the flight for which he wishes to minimize the time therefore starts from the point in the thermal from which he can just reach the goal by gliding at $(L/D)_{max}$ and extends up to his arrival at the goal. In Fig. 17.6 he wishes to minimize the total time for the climb AB and the glide BC. This situa-

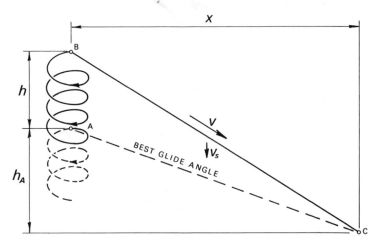

Fig 17.6 Leaving the last thermal of a cross-country flight

tion can be analysed in the usual fashion, remembering that the distance X is now fixed but the height h is open to choice. If it is assumed that the vertical motions of the air during the glide cancel out, the criterion which fixes the optimum gliding speed is that of equation (16.31), viz:

$$dV_s/dV = (V_c + V_s)/V,$$

$$\text{at } V = V_{\text{opt}}.$$

Also, since the glide angle must be such that the goal is reached,

$$(h + h_A)/X = V_s/V_{\text{opt}}. \qquad (17.3)$$

In a sense, the situation is simpler than at earlier times in the flight since the pilot need only think about the thermal in which he is climbing. The usual considerations apply to the relationship between rate of climb and best gliding speed but with the added complexity that the flight should finish at the goal.

So, choosing a certain value of V_c, the optimum gliding speed V_{opt} and the corresponding value of V_s can be found from the usual construction (Figure 16.13). Knowing the distance X, the total height $(h + h_A)$ can be found from equation (17.3). The lowest height at which the thermal can be left corresponds to gliding at $(L/D)_{\text{max}}$ and implicity corresponds to $V_c = 0$. Also, there is now enough information to calculate t_c, the time to climb from h_A to $(h + h_A)$ and t_g, the time for the final glide. The above considerations enable $(t_c + t_g)$ to be minimized. By choosing a series of values of V_c, curves such as those of Figure 17.7 can be drawn. On the right is a single curve of gliding time against height whilst the series of lines on the left show times to various heights for constant values of the rate of climb. If the total time is to be minimized the required height is that which makes the distance least between the single curve on the right and the line on the left corresponding to the rate of climb. This will occur when the slope of the 'glide' line equals the slope of the 'climb' line, a condition expressed mathematically by the above equations.

So far, it is implied that the rate of climb is constant. If it

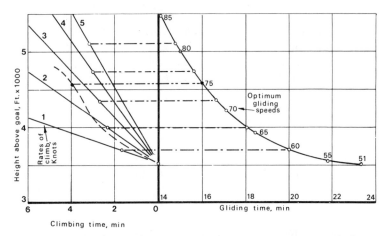

Fig 17.7 Optimum break-off heights for various rates of climb. The horizontal dotted lines give the heights corresponding to rates of climb of 1, 2, 3 . . . . . knots. The diagram corresponds to the Standard Libelle at W = 695 lb in zero wind. The curved dotted line on the left represents the varying rate of climb achieved in a real thermal. Note that the instantaneous rate of climb is shown by the local slope of this line. The distance to go is 20 nautical miles.

varies, as indicated by the dotted line, the pilot should continue to climb so long as the climb and glide lines are converging. As soon as they diverge, he should leave the thermal and start to glide. Putting it another way, he continues to climb until the rate of climb no longer exceeds that appropriate to the speed at which the glider could be flown to the goal at that instant, the relationship between climb rate and speed being that of the simple MacCready construction. So, in the example shown, if the height is 4300 ft and the rate of climb is 4 knots, the pilot goes on climbing but if the rate of climb falls off to about 3.5 knots at 4600 ft, he stops climbing, sets the MacCready ring datum to 3.5 knots and departs for his goal. An interesting feature of this situation is that, just for once, the pilot is primarily interested in the instantaneous rate of climb. If he correctly assesses the break-off height, his instantaneous rate of climb will be the same as the average rate of climb from h_A to $(h + h_A)$.

In the presence of a headwind, the details become rather more complicated. Equation (16.31) still relates the optimum gliding speed to the rate of climb and the wind does not appear in this part of the calculation – a result which involves about a page of mathematics to display formally. Again, there is a height h_A from which the pilot can just reach a goal at a distance X, but the best gliding speed is now given by the construction of Fig. 17.8. Extrapolating the tangent to the left to intersect the vertical axis implies that, on the MacCready basis, this situation corresponds to a certain rate of climb, that which causes the glider to climb whilst drifting downwind, always just able to reach the goal.

At greater rates of climb, it again pays to stay with the

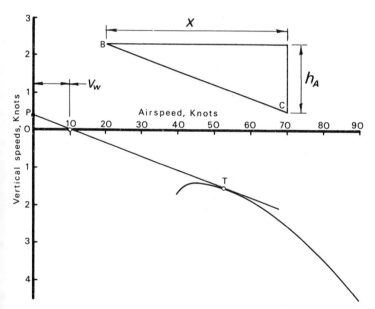

Fig 17.8 Determination of the minimum height to leave the last thermal in the presence of a headwind. The line BC *is parallel to the tangent* PT *(allowing for the different vertical and horizontal scales). Knowing V_w and X, h_A is determined. The intercept* OP *represents the thermal strength which just keeps the goal within reach as the glider drifts downwind in the thermal*

thermal to some height greater than h_A. The expression corresponding to (17.3) is now

$$(h + h_A)/(X + hV_w/V_c) = V_s/(V_{opt} - V_w) \qquad (17.4)$$

This relation takes into account the fact that, if the glider is at distance X from the goal when at height h_A, it will drift back a distance hV_w/V_c whilst climbing to $(h + h_A)$.

For a given X, it is again possible to calculate values of h corresponding to various rates of climb V_c. A diagram similar to Figure 17.7 could again be drawn, except that the 'glide' line would be further to the right. The optimum height to leave the thermal when its strength varies with height is determined by exactly the same consideration as in the zero-wind case. Tailwinds can be considered in a similar fashion, simply by reversing the sign of V_w above.

Table 17.1 displays the appropriate figures for a Libelle at a weight of 695 lb. It should be remembered that X (20 nautical miles in this case) is the distance to go from the minimum break-off height. For greater break-off heights, the distance will be increased or decreased in the presence of head- or tailwind components respectively.

For practical use, the pilot can either carry tables similar to these or he can make use of a calculator, as explained in Chapter 7. In practice, of course, he would wish to arrive at the goal with some margin of height in hand.

Wind (knots)		10 head	0	10 tail
Min. height ft		4350	3530	2940
	1	4500	3700	3130
Rates of	2	4800	4000	3400
Climb	3	5150	4340	3720
(knots)	4	5570	4720	4080
	5	6020	5140	4450
	6	6500	5560	4850

Table 17.1 Optimum heights in feet to leave the last thermal for the Libelle at W = 695 lb. The distance to the goal when the glider is at the minimum break-off height is 20 nautical miles. For other distances, the heights should be factored accordingly. A safety margin should also be added.

WIND COMPONENTS

In the analyses which involve the effect of wind, V_w has been regarded as a headwind component or, with a sign change, as a tailwind component. Under most circumstances, the wind will be directed at some angle to the desired track and, if its strength and direction are known, pilots and task-setters will wish to assess its effect.

It is immediately apparent from Fig. 17.9 that the effective wind component, from the point of view of speed made good along the track, is not simply the projection of the wind vector on to the track line, $V_w \cos \gamma$.

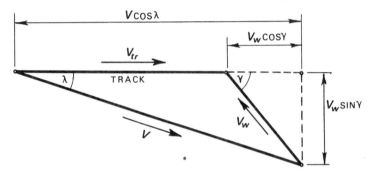

Fig 17.9 Triangle of velocities when flying in the presence of a wind

Suppose that V is the true airspeed of the glider. If a long task is under consideration, V will be the average cross-country speed; if a single glide is to be analysed, it will simply be the speed during that glide.

From the triangle of velocities, the speed made good along the track will be

$$V_{tr} = V \cos \lambda - V_w \cos \gamma, \qquad (17.5)$$

where λ is the angle between the course and the track and γ is the angle between the wind direction and the track.

But since

$$V \sin \lambda = V_w \sin \gamma, \qquad (17.6)$$

λ may be eliminated from equations (17.5) and (17.6) to give

$$V_{tr} = V \sqrt{1 - (V_w/V)^2 \sin^2 \gamma} - V_w \cos \gamma. \quad (17.7)$$

The effective headwind component is then the difference between the speed of the glider and the speed made good along the track, i.e.

$$V_{w_{eff}} = V - V_{tr} = V[1 - \sqrt{1 - (V_w/V)^2 \sin^2\gamma} + (V_w/V)\cos\gamma].$$ (17.8)

A consequence of this expression is that a wind at right angles to the track reduces the speed made good along the track, although it has no component in the direction of the track. This effect arises because the glider must proceed on a course which is slightly into wind in order that its resultant track shall be in the desired direction.

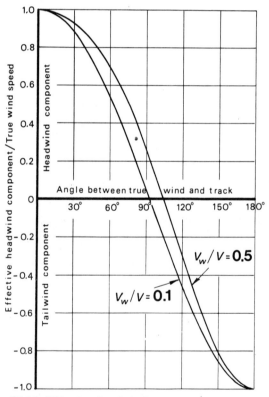

Fig 17.10 Effective headwind component for various wind directions and two wind strengths

Fig. 17.10 shows plots of $V_{w\,eff}/V_w$ against γ for two values of V_w/V. It will be seen that when $V_w/V = 0.5$, the effective headwind only becomes zero when γ is about 104°.

A consequence of this situation is that, in closed-circuit tasks, the effects of wind are never self-cancelling. For straight out-and-return flights conducted at a constant average true airspeed, the direction of the task relative to the wind has very little influence on the total time if the wind is light. But if the wind is strong, the highest average speed is attained when the task is cross-wind. Fig. 17.11 is derived from Fig. 17.10 and shows average speeds for the case $V_w/V = 0.5$, relative to the zero-wind case, for various orientations of the task. The cross-wind task is about 15% faster than the up- and downwind task.

For closed-circuit flights consisting of equilateral triangles, the orientation of the triangle relative to the wind direction has no effect although, of course, the average speed is always less than in the zero-wind case.

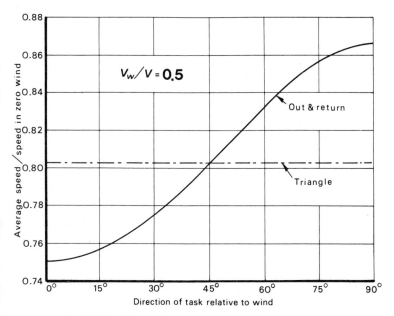

Fig 17.11 Effect of task orientation on average speed

So far, it has been assumed that the average true airspeed is constant throughout the flight. If the thermals are of constant average strength, the final leg of a closed-circuit flight will be the fastest because such tasks are usually started at a height of 1000 m above the ground. In effect, the final glide from 1000 m down to ground level can be regarded as a bonus and, since it is flown at the optimum gliding speed – appreciably faster than the average speed for the previous part of the flight – the overall average speed for the final leg is thus increased. This effect has some influence on the optimum orientation of a task in the presence of a wind.

Consider a flight of 300 km in which the optimum gliding speed between thermals is 75 knots and the corresponding average speed is 42.1 knots. If the wind is 12.6 knots, then the average value of V_w/V will be 0.3 and, when gliding at 75 knots, it will be 0.17. From the foregoing theory, the effective headwind can be found for the part of the flight for which V = 42.1 knots, V_w/V = 0.3 and for a glide from 1000 m to ground level for which V = 75 knots, V_w/V = 0.17, taking into account the directions of the various legs relative to the wind direction. The times for the various sections of the flight can therefore be obtained and the overall average speed deduced.

For an out-and-return flight, the average speeds are as follows:

(*a*) First leg downwind: 40.26 knots
(*b*) First leg upwind: 39.38 knots
(*c*) Both legs cross wind: 41.85 knots
(*d*) In zero wind: 43.81 knots.

It will be seen that a downwind final leg leads to the lowest average speed.

Triangular flights can be analysed in a similar fashion, whereupon it appears that the overall average speed is slightly affected by the orientation of the course. For the same conditions as considered above the average speeds are:

(*a*) First leg downwind: 41.60 knots
(*b*) First leg upwind: 40.57 knots
(*c*) First leg crosswind: 41.26 knots
(*d*) Last leg downwind: 40.33 knots

(*e*) Last leg upwind: 41.37 knots
(*f*) Last leg crosswind: 40.80 knots
(*g*) Zero wind: 43.81 knots

A downwind final leg leads to the lowest average speed and an upwind final leg to the highest. The difference is not very great (1.04 knots), but worth having.

In practice, as discussed in Appendix 9, the orientation of a closed-circuit task depends on many considerations other than achieving the maximum theoretical speed. Also, the presence of cloud streets can lead to speeds along down – or into–wind legs far higher than those calculated above.

FLAPS

So far, the implicit assumption has been that the glider wing is of fixed geometry. The profile drag of a wing is largely determined by the properties of the two-dimensional sections, as displayed in Figure 16.1. In the absence of novel developments in boundary-layer theory, the opportunities for further reduction in profile drag are extremely circumscribed: it can be reduced slightly by making the section thinner but this process involves the penalty of reducing the range of lift co-efficients over which the profile drag has a low value. As the discussion on page 5.10 suggests, such a penalty has undesirable consequences at both low and high speeds.

By the use of a relatively small trailing-edge flap, the best of both worlds can be achieved. A relatively thin section can be used but, by altering the flap angle, the low-drag 'bucket' can be shifted in the direction of higher or lower lift coefficients. By using the best flap setting at each lift coefficient (downwards at high lift coefficients, upwards at low values), a low profile drag can be obtained over a wide range of conditions. The use of small camber-changing flaps in such a fashion represents one of the outstanding recent developments in glider design. If flap deflections up to 90° are provided, they also function as a useful landing aid. Figure 17.12 compares the unflapped Wortmann Section FX61-168 with the flapped section FX67-K-150. The final three figures of the designation give ten times the maximum thickness in percent of the chord, so the flapped section is the thinner of the two.

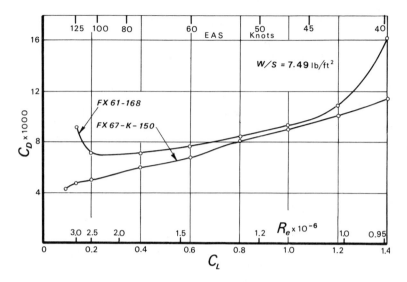

Fig 17.12 Comparison of the properties of the plain wing section FX 61-168 and the flapped section FX 67-K-150. The speeds and Reynolds numbers correspond to a wing loading of 7.49 lb/ft²

Professor Wortmann has shown that the best flap chord is quite small: in this case about 17% of the total chord.

The lower curve is that for the flapped section: it assumes that the flap deflection is the optimum at each lift coefficient, so it is really the envelope of a whole series of curves. This curve also takes into account the effect of Reynolds number varying with lift coefficient and applies to the wing of the Kestrel 19 at a wing loading of 7.49 lb/ft².

The upper curve relates to the unflapped section, assuming the same relationship between lift coefficient and Reynolds number. It is immediately apparent that the thinner flapped section has a lower profile drag at all lift coefficients and is markedly superior towards both low and high speeds.

The individual curves of profile drag coefficient against lift coefficient for a series of fixed flap angles show considerable overlap, so there is rarely much point in providing an infinitely variable flap setting. For example, at a Reynolds number of 1.5 x 10⁶ and a lift coefficient of 0.6, the drag coefficients at flap settings of 0° and 4° degrees down are indistinguishable. So it is usual to find that four or five settings at intervals of 4° or 5° are entirely adequate. A consequence of deflecting the flaps in discrete steps is that the lower curve of Figure 17.12 should strictly show some small kinks, which will produce corresponding kinks in the glider's performance curve. Such kinks are very small and are usually omitted from performance plots.

From the point of view of the foregoing performance analyses, the glider can be regarded as having a series of overlapping performance curves, each corresponding to a different flap angle. The pilot is only interested in the envelope of these curves and all the previous tangent-drawing constructions will apply to the envelope.

As implied on page 236, glider design normally involves making a compromise between low-speed and high-speed performance. Another type of flap enables this compromise to be circumvented, at least to some extent. For climbing in thermals, a low wing loading would be advantageous together with the ability to fly at high lift coefficients without an undue increase in profile drag. When gliding between thermals, the higher the wing loading the better and, since the lift coefficient is in the low-to-medium range, a fairly conventional wing section of modest camber is appropriate. Figure 17.13 shows the wing section FX67-VC-170 designed by Professor Wortmann and used on the Sigma glider. The flap, which is housed inside the wing, extends the chord by 35% and greatly increases the camber. Also, a small flap is hinged on the trailing edge of the main flap and is used as a camber-change flap to adjust the low-drag 'bucket' when the main flap is retracted.

Sigma had a wing-loading of 8.5 lb/ft^2, flap out, and 11.4 lb/ft^2, flap in. Even with the flaps out, the wing loading was quite high but the large camber meant that it was possible to circle at quite a low speed, around 45 knots.

The mechanical difficulties associated with this type of flap are obviously considerable and, in the case of Sigma, leaks and gaps prevented the achievement of the calculated performance. The basic idea worked surprisingly well and ex-

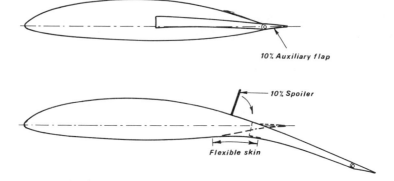

Fig 17.13 The variable-chord, variable-camber wing section used on Sigma. The main flap extension is 35% of the flap-in chord

tending or retracting the flaps introduced no particular piloting problems, once the pilot became accustomed to the marked attitude change.

There are, of course, other types of area-increasing flap, such as the Fowler. But the Sigma flap has the unique merit that the profile drag coefficient of the flap-out section remains remarkably low whereas the drag rise associated with Fowler flaps is so great as to render them of dubious value.

The experience of Sigma suggests that the variable chord and camber concept shows promise and is one of the few remaining ways of improving glider performance. Whether the enormous expense and complexity is worthwhile is a matter for debate: perhaps we may never see the like of Sigma again.

DESIGNING FOR PERFORMANCE

So far, this chapter has been mainly concerned with the problem of obtaining the best performance from a given glider. The same ideas can also be applied to the converse problem of deciding the configuration of glider which will give the best cross-country performance in certain thermal conditions. By now, it will be apparent that one cannot decide which is the 'best' glider simply by inspecting performance curves.

A comprehensive investigation involves the use of a computer, since the volume of calculation is very great. The computations involved in considering Standard Class gliders using 'parabolic' thermals, start by devising a family of 15-m gliders of various aspect ratios and generally realistic proportions. A variety of weights are chosen for each aspect ratio. The computer works out in detail the straight flight and turning performance in each case, taking into account the effects of Reynolds number. A variety of parabolic thermals are then considered and the cross-country speed is calculated for each combination of thermal, aspect ratio and weight assuming that the maximum rate of climb is achieved in all glider/ thermal combinations. For each thermal, it is then possible to pick the optimum combination of aspect ratio and weight.

A remarkable conclusion from such calculations is that the aspect ratio is of surprisingly little consequence provided that the weight is always the optimum. However, some optimum combinations are impracticably light: in weak thermals, the optimum aspect ratio is about 26 combined with all up weights as low as 380 lb. In practice, one would have to settle for a much lower aspect ratio. Both pilots and manufacturers are often interested in the best all-round glider. It would appear that an aspect ratio of 18 would be about optimum in weak thermals and, when ballasted, in strong thermals also. The current generation of Standard Class gliders with aspect ratios around 20 are also close to optimum, particularly in thermals with core strengths of about 6 knots. The main lesson to be learned from such an investigation is the importance of being able to carry a very large amount of ballast, perhaps as much as 250 lb in a Standard Class glider.

Such investigations can, of course, be made as elaborate as desired. Various thermal profiles, different spans and the effect of flaps can all be considered. Sadly, perhaps, there is little room for intuition in modern glider design.

Chapter 18

The Variometer

The whole of soaring is concerned with extracting energy from the atmosphere and using it to fly high or fast or far. The ordinary airspeed indicator and altimeter provide measures of the kinetic and potential energy of the glider, respectively, but the pilot also desires a direct, accurate and sensitive indication of the rate of change of the energy. The variometer performs this function and is therefore an essential aid to the efficient operation of the glider.

THE BASIC VARIOMETER

All variometers work by detecting a rate of flow as shown schematically in Fig. 18.1

In the simplest situation, one side of the instrument is connected to the static pressure system of the glider, the other a vacuum-insulated capacity of about half a litre (420 cm³ is a common size). When the glider ascends, the decreasing outside pressure causes air to flow out through the instrument; the flow direction is reversed when descending. The rate of flow is then measured either by observing the pressure drop as the air passes through an orifice or by the differential cooling

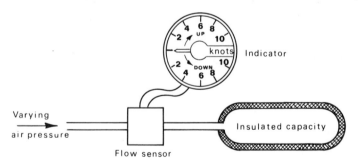

Fig 18.1 The basic variometer

284

of a pair of thermistor beads. All mechanical variometers employ the former principle, the orifice being either the clearance between a pellet and a tapered tube (Cosim type) or between a vane and the case, the vane being restrained by a hair-spring and directly connected to the indicator pointer (Winter and PZL types). Any variometer of this type applies a restriction to the flow of air and hence the reading at any particular instant depends on the history of the outside pressure changes over the previous few seconds, as explained later. When thermal-soaring, this lag is a disadvantage, since the pilot has to think about 90° out-of-phase with the glider heading (see Chapter 3), but when cruising between thermals it helps to even out the effect of minor disturbances. Those with a dial presentation and a linear scale are thus well-suited to fitting a best-speed-to-fly scale, as described in Chapter 16.

Electric variometers apply a much smaller constriction to the flow and thus have very little lag. Indeed it may be necessary to incorporate additional electrical or pneumatic damping to prevent excessive and rather irrelevant oscillations of the indication in turbulent conditions. It is simple to arrange any desired degree of sensitivity, or to incorporate different sensitivities in the same instrument. Due to their rapid response, electric variometers are particularly useful for accurate flying in thermals. The output may also be used to operate an audio device, which incorporates an audio-oscillator driving a small loudspeaker. The frequency of the sound increases with increasing rate of climb, and the threshold at which the sound starts can be adjusted as desired. Those unfamiliar with this device may be inclined to view it with some suspicion: they may feel that it destroys the peace of soaring flight, and merely adds to the mental confusion generated by the radio. But after a few flights one comes to regard it as an essential aid to soaring, particularly since it leaves the pilot free to scan his surroundings without frequent visual recourse to the instruments.

Under steady-state conditions, the rate of flow through the variometer at a certain height will depend on the rate of change of static pressure, dp_s/dt. From the usual hydrostatic equation for the atmosphere, this quantity can be related to the rate of change of height:

$$dp_s/dt = -g\,\rho(dh/dt), \qquad (18.1)$$

where ρ is the local air density and g is the acceleration due to gravity. The indication will therefore be a measure of *dh/dt,* the vertical velocity. At first sight, equation (18.1) might seem to suggest that the reading will also be directly proportional to air density. Not so, for this equation does not take into account the characteristics of the flow sensing device. For mechanical variometers, the reading is very close to true vertical speed at all heights whilst for electric variometers, as noted in Chapter 17, the reading tends to be proportional to ρ^n, as shown in Fig. 18.2. Laboratory calibrations suggest that the index n lies between 0.8 and 1.2. So if a variometer is calibrated to read true vertical speed at sea-level, a mechanical type will be correct at all heights whilst an electric type will under-read at height (See also the observations on page 261 about 'equivalent' vertical speeds).

TOTAL–ENERGY VARIOMETERS

If the pressure applied to the variometer is the static pressure minus the dynamic head of the airstream, the indication of the variometer will now depend on $d(p_s - \frac{1}{2}\rho V^2)/dt$. This expression can be expanded as follows:

$$d(p_s - \tfrac{1}{2}\rho V^2)/dt = dp_s/dt - \tfrac{1}{2}\rho dV^2/dt - \tfrac{1}{2}V^2 d\rho/dt$$
$$= -g\rho[d(h + V^2/2g)/dt] - \tfrac{1}{2}V^2 d\rho/dt$$
$$= -g\rho(dh_e/dt) - \tfrac{1}{2}V^2 d\rho/dt, \qquad (18.2)$$

where h_e is called the 'energy height'.

The final term in this expression may be shown to have the approximate value $0.57\,M^2(dh/dt)$ in the troposphere or $0.70\,M^2\,(dh/dt)$ in the stratosphere, where M is the Mach number of the aircraft. Since glider Mach numbers rarely exceed 0.2, this term can be neglected. The indications of the variometer will now depend not on the rate of change of true height but on the rate of change of the energy height, h_e. Since $h_e = h + V^2/2g$, it is clear that it represents the total energy per unit weight of the glider, i.e. the sum of the po-

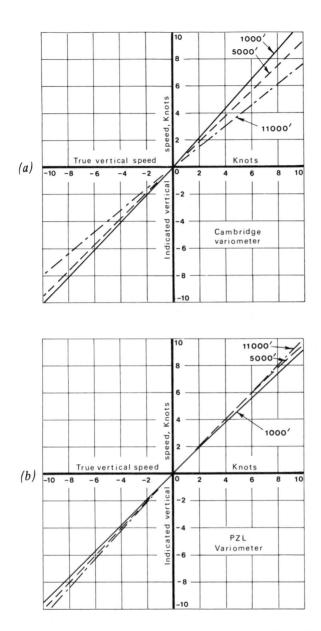

Fig 18.2 (a) Laboratory calibration curves for a PZL variometer. (b) Laboratory calibration curves for a Cambridge electric variometer

tential and kinetic energies.

If a glider is flying at a steady speed in calm air, a vario-meter connected to the static pressure source will show a steady rate of sink. If the pilot now causes the speed to vary by, say ±5 knots, the variometer will show a varying rate of descent. As the speed increases or decreases, the rate of descent will increase or decrease due to the interchange of potential energy. The effect of the varying speed on the variometer reading is largely eliminated by the total-energy arrangement.

Qualitatively, the total-energy effect can be simply explained. As the speed is increasing, the static pressure increases more rapidly than when flying at a steady speed. But the suction $(-\frac{1}{2}\rho V^2)$ is also increasing and cancels out the augmented rate of increase of static pressure. So, if the speed is varying somewhat, the total-energy variometer will show an almost steady reading: although potential and kinetic energies are being interchanged, the overall rate of loss of energy is very nearly that appropriate to the rate of sink in steady flight at the instantaneous speed. There will, of course, be small changes, since the overall rate of energy dissipation, equal to the drag times the forward speed, varies with the speed.

The advantage of the system when circling in a thermal is now apparent. 'Stick thermals' – transient variometer readings due to speed changes – are largely eliminated and the indication of the variometer is equal to the local rate of ascent of the air less, very nearly, the rate of sink of the glider at the average speed at which it is being flown. It is therefore much easier to achieve a clear picture of the variations of thermal strength around the circle without superimposed confusions due to the inevitable fluctuations in forward speed.

Likewise, as indicated in Chapter 16, a total-energy variometer is essential for the proper control of the gliding speed between the thermals. Ignoring the instrument lag for the moment, it will indicate the total of the vertical velocity of the air plus the steady-state rate of sink of the glider corresponding to the speed at the moment under consideration, even if the speed is changing.

The suction required to produce the total-energy effect may be obtained in a variety of ways: by bulges on the fuselage sides, or a small venturi, or by the 'Brunswick tube'. The first two devices are fairly self-explanatory, although a venturi which is insensitive to yaw is a rather odd-looking device with an external ring around the outlet. The Brunswick tube depends on the fact that, at the right Reynolds number, the pressure over most of the downstream side of a circular cylinder at right angles to the airflow is close to $(p_s - \frac{1}{2}\rho V^2)$. The right Reynolds number is about 10,000, corresponding to a $\frac{1}{4}$-in. diameter tube at about 45 knots at sea-level. Higher Reynolds numbers provide slightly more suction, so it would be advantageous to use a slightly smaller tube if it is not to overcompensate at the higher speeds. This effect has been known since the 1920s but this particular application is quite recent. The region of nearly constant pressure extends over a total angle of about 160° on the rearside of the tube. A typical arrangement is shown in Figure 18.3: the end of the tube is plugged and one to two slots are cut on the downstream side extending over a total angle of about 110°. Provided this angle is not exceeded, the tube will be insensitive to angles of yaw up to about 25°.

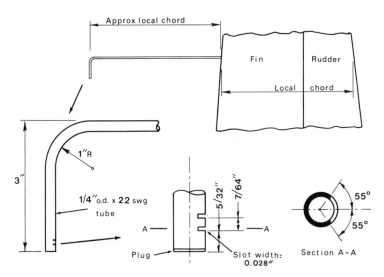

Fig 18.3 The Braunschweig tube

Insensitivity to yaw is obviously important and venturis or Brunswick tubes should equally obviously be mounted in a region where the local flow is unlikely to be disturbed by adjacent parts of the glider. In this particular context, small steady errors in the local flow velocity are not of undue consequence, but changes in velocity induced by an altering flow pattern, in turn produced perhaps by transient yawing motions, can introduce noticeable effects. Fin-mounted total-energy heads are therefore usually to be found about one chord-length ahead of the leading edge.

A totally different method of achieving total energy compensation is shown in Fig. 18.4.

A diaphragm is connected on one side to the pitot, and on the other to the capacity side of the variometer circuit. Effectively, the volume of the capacity is varied by the pitot pressure. The variometer functions in the normal fashion at a steady forward speed, since the diaphragm deflection remains constant. Suppose that the pilot again causes variations in speed to occur. As the speed is increasing, so is the rate of descent and the external air pressure. The rate of flow into the capacity through the instrument therefore tends to increase. However, the increasing pitot pressure deflects the

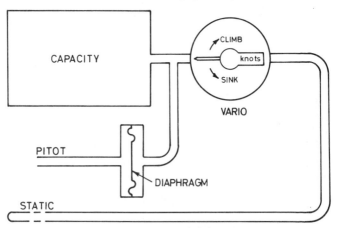

Fig 18.4 A total-energy arrangement. Effective volume of the capacity is altered by deflections of the diaphragm produced by the pitot pressure

diaphragm in the sense of decreasing the capacity. This tends to cause an outflow through the instrument which can be arranged to cancel the increased inflow if the diaphragm stiffness is suitably chosen.

Whereas the venturi system is inherently correct at all altitudes, the diaphragm can only be precisely right at one height, although the errors over the normal range of operating heights are small. For a system with a half-litre capacity, the theoretical diaphragm stiffness is about 1 cm^3 of volume change for a pressure difference of 25mm of water. However, this figure should only be regarded as an order-of-magnitude guide and the actual stiffness must be determined by flight trials or the calibration process described below. An insufficiently stiff diaphragm is very trying indeed: the pilot arrives at a thermal and performs a climbing turn with the variometer showing a large rate of descent. Slightly excessive stiffness is preferable to this state of affairs.

Diaphragm units are commercially available, some incorporated in the capacity complete with damping devices. They

Type	Advantages	Disadvantages
Fuselage bulges	Not subject to damage.	Difficult to calibrate. May be yaw-sensitive. Produce drag.
Venturi	Accurate. Correct at all heights. Can be insensitive to yaw.	Needs accurate manufacture or calibration. Produces drag. Prone to icing and water ingress.
Brunswick tube	Reasonably accurate. Correct at all heights. Insensitive to yaw. Simple to make. No calibration required.	Produces drag. Prone to icing and water ingress. Easily bent.
Diaphragm	Can be quite accurate. No drag: entirely internal.	Only accurate at one height. Difficult to calibrate and adjust. Calibration may change with age.

Table 18.1 A comparison of total energy systems.

should be mounted in the glider in the attitude specified by the manufacturer so as to avoid errors due to normal accelerations.

Table 18.1 summarizes the advantages and disadvantages of the various types of total-energy systems. A reliable total-energy system is quite essential for serious soaring: there is no point in having a variometer which simply shows rates of change of actual height.

VARIOMETER CALIBRATION

The object of the procedure described below is to calibrate the variometer and to ensure that the degree of compensation provided by a total energy diaphragm is correct. The method is based on that devised by H.C.N. Goodhart.

The relevant parts of the instrument panel assembly are shown in the left-hand part of Fig. 18.5. This is drawn as if only one mechanical variometer and total-energy unit is installed (e.g. PZL). In practice there will often be a second variometer of the electrical type, in which case the section enclosed within the dotted line is, for all practical purposes, duplicated. Additional equipment comprises (a) a stop watch

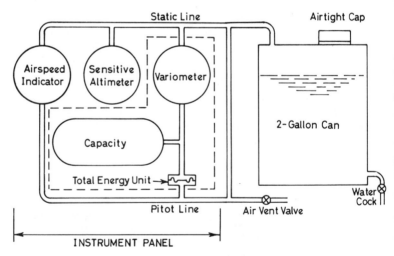

Fig 18.5 Diagrammatic layout of apparatus for calibrating a total-energy variometer

and (b) a two-gallon can with an airtight filler cap. Two pipes are soldered into the can as shown in Fig. 18.5: that from the bottom of the can is fitted with a small valve so that after the can has been partly filled with water, it can be allowed to trickle out at a controlled rate. A glass cock of the type used in chemical laboratories would be suitable. The pipe from the top of the can is fitted with T-pieces so that it can be connected to the instrument panel and to a further valve which controls the inflow of air into the system. A needle valve of the type used for model aircraft engines would be suitable.

The can should initially be about three-quarters full of water. Allowing water to trickle out of the water-cock lowers the pressure in the air space above the water and in the parts of the instrumentation connected to it. Turning off the water and opening the air vent valve causes the air pressure to rise again.

It is essential to avoid overloading the instruments. All adjustments to the valves should be made with great care, to avoid excessive indicated rates of climb. Likewise, the altimeter reading should not be allowed to exceed 500 ft. In Test 3, this corresponds to about 105 knots ASI reading. In Test 2, no reading should appear on the ASI, but it could be damaged if a failure of the plumbing occurred whilst the altimeter read, say, 1500 ft.

Test 1. This is simply a leakage test. Connect the top pipe from the can to both the pitot and static connections. Close the air vent valve. Allow water to trickle gently out of the water-cock until the altimeter reads, say, 200 ft. The cock is then closed, whereupon the variometer should return to zero, the ASI should read zero and the altimeter reading should remain steady. If it does not, locate the leaks and rectify. It is useless to attempt the subsequent tests until the system is free from leaks.

Test 2. This is a test to calibrate the variometer. With the same connections as for Test 1, the air vent valve is closed and the water-cock is gently opened until the variometer shows a steady reading, say 5 knots. When the cock has been suitably adjusted, the altimeter is timed over a height range of, say, 400 ft. By closing the water-cock and gently opening the air vent valve a similar descending run can be made. Knowing that 1 knot = 101.4 ft/min (100 ft/min in round figures), the true figure can be compared with the variometer indication.

Throughout this test the same pressure is applied to both sides of the total-energy unit, which thus has no effect on the variometer reading. The test is therefore solely concerned with the variometer indicator, as a device for measuring rate of change of pressure. By the same token, no indication will appear on the ASI.

Test 3. This is a test to calibrate the total energy unit. The pipe from the top of the tank is attached only to the static line from the instruments and to the air vent valve. The pitot line from the instruments is left open to the atmosphere. Decreasing the static pressure not only increases the indicated height but also produces an apparent increase in airspeed, since there is now a pressure difference across the ASI and the total-energy unit. If the instruments and the total-energy unit were all perfect, the indication of the variometer should now be twice the rate of climb or descent obtained by timing the altimeter indications.

This arises as follows:

A perfect total-energy variometer should show rates of change of energy height at low Mach numbers as explained on page 286.

So,

$$\text{Variometer indication} = \frac{dh_e}{dt} = \frac{d}{dt}(h + V^2/2g) \qquad (18.3)$$

where h_e is the energy height.

In this particular case, a pressure difference q is applied across the total energy unit. This is equivalent to the dynamic pressure produced in flight at a true airspeed V, i.e.:

$$q = \tfrac{1}{2}\rho V^2 \qquad (18.4)$$

where ρ is the air density at the operating height.

Combining (18.3) and (18.4)

$$\frac{dh_e}{dt} = \frac{d}{dt}\left(h + \frac{q}{\rho g}\right). \qquad (18.5)$$

But since the pressure q is also applied to the altimeter in this case (in fact as an increasing suction if the altimeter indication is increasing), timing the altimeter will give a rate of change of indicated height dh/dt such that

$$\rho g \, \frac{dh}{dt} = \frac{dq}{dt}. \qquad (18.6)$$

This is a consequence of the way in which an altimeter is calibrated. Finally, combining (18.5) and (18.6)

$$\frac{dh_e}{dt} = 2 \frac{dh}{dt}. \qquad (18.7)$$

This, of course, only applies to the conditions imposed by this method of calibration.

All of the above assumes that the instruments are perfect. In practice, we adjust the rate of outflow of water until a steady reading is obtained on the variometer, say 5 knots. From Test 2, we know the corresponding corrected figure, which might be 4.6 knots. Timing the altimeter ought to give half of this figure, i.e., 2.3 knots, or 233 ft/min. If timing the altimeter gives *less* than this figure, then the total-energy unit is over-compensating. In other words, its diaphragm is too flexible, and is exaggerating the effect of the apparent speed changes. The diaphragm should therefore be adjusted until the desired agreement is achieved. In the case of total-energy units with rubber diaphragms, the effective stiffness can be increased by putting slightly more tension on the rubber. Other types with metal capsules can only be returned to the manufacturer for correction.

The above test procedure assumes that the altimeter has been separately calibrated beforehand, although in practice any reasonably good instrument which does not tend to stick will be sufficiently accurate for this purpose. Ideally, the whole instrument panel should be gently vibrated throughout the tests.

If the total-energy device is a venturi or Brunswick tube, test 3 above is obviously inapplicable. The accuracy of any suction-type total-energy device can easily be checked in

flight by connecting a second airspeed indicator to the glider
static pressure source (to the instrument 'P' connection) and
to the total-energy device (to the 'S' connection). This airspeed indicator should read the same as the normal aircraft
instrument connected to the pitot and static pressure sources.

THE 'NET' VARIOMETER

The simple variometer arrangement shown in Fig. 18.1 will
indicate the vertical velocity of the glider (or the rate of
change of energy height) due both to the rate of sink of the
glider relative to the air V_s and to the vertical motions of the
atmosphere V_a. As explained in Chapter '16, the use of the
MacCready ring for regulating the best speed to glide between
thermals then involves a process of successive approximation.
If the variometer could be arranged so as to indicate only the
motions of the atmosphere, V_a, the MacCready ring would
display directly the optimum speed, regardless of whether or
not the glider was actually being flown at that speed. The
presence of small up-currents would also be readily apparent
to the pilot.

Suppose that a connection is interposed between the variometer and capacity which allows air to leak into the system
via a fine capillary tube, one end of which is connected to
pitot pressure. (See Fig. 18.6). If the variometer is also connected to the static pressure source, the pressure difference

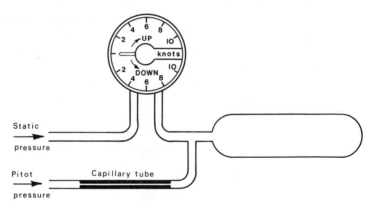

Fig 18.6 The 'net' variometer

between the ends of the capillary will be equal to the dynamic head, for all practical purposes, since the pressure drop across the variometer sensor will be relatively very small. The rate of flow through the capillary will then be proportional to the square of the equivalent airspeed. In still air, at a certain speed V_{i_1}, the glider will be sinking at a certain vertical velocity V_{si_1} and there will be a certain rate of flow into the capacity. Now suppose that the resistance of the capillary is arranged so that it produces exactly the rate of flow into the system which corresponds to the rate of sink V_{si_1}. In these circumstances, the capillary will supply all the flow required and none will pass through the variometer, which will therefore read zero. If the rate of sink of the glider were always proportional to V_i^2, the variometer would then read zero at all speeds. As noted in Appendix 7, this relationship is formally incorrect but if V_{i_1} is chosen appropriately it represents quite a good approximation to the actual performance curve over the range of speed likely to be of interest. Since the effect of the capillary leak is to remove the rate of sink of the glider relative to the air from the variometer reading, the reading gives a direct indication of any vertical motions of the atmosphere. Such a system was proposed by Paul MacCready about 20 years ago and re-invented recently by Dipl.Phys. E. Brückner.

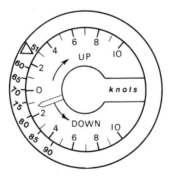

Fig 18.7 MacCready ring for a 'net' variometer. The datum is set to a rate of climb of 2.7 knots. The glider is in air which is sinking at 1.3 knots and should be flown at 77 knots. (Calibration for Standard Libelle at $W = 695$ lb)

The calibrations of the MacCready ring now correspond to figures such as those in Table 16.2, that is to say, with the ring datum opposite a rate of climb figure, the appropriate best gliding speed, in the absence of downdraughts, should appear opposite the variometer zero mark (See Fig. 18.7). Suitable values for V_{i_1} and V_{si_1} are suggested in Appendix 7.

An approximate expression for the length of the capillary tube is

$$L = 2.28 \times 10^6 \; [r^4 \; V_{i_1}^2 \; / \; V_{si_1}]. \qquad (18.8)$$

This expression applies to the following system of units:

r = radius of tube (in),
V_{i_1} = equivalent airspeed at the chosen datum point on the glider performance curve (knots),
V_{si_1} = equivalent rate of sink corresponding to V_{i_1} (knots);
L will then be in inches.

The above expressions apply at sea level. For any other height, the length must be scaled by a factor

$$(p/p_0)(\rho_0/\rho)(\mu_0/\mu). \qquad (18.9)$$

where p, ρ and μ are the pressure, density and viscosity of the air respectively at the height in question and suffix 'o' refers to sea-level values. A capillary which is correct at sea level will be about 5% too long at 3000 ft.

Since the length is proportional to the fourth power of the tube radius, quite small manufacturing tolerances have a large effect. A standard size of hypodermic tubing in the UK is 23 SWG outside diameter, whose bore diameter can be anything from 0.0125 in to 0.0145 in. Taking V_{i_1} = 90 knots and V_{si_1} = 4.79 knots for the Libelle, the smallest diameter gives a length of 5.9 in and the largest 10.65 in. Such small diameter tubes are easily blocked by dust particles, so about twice the above diameter is often used. In any case, the above expressions are not really exact, so each tube must be individually calibrated. One method is to connect the capillary as shown in Figure 18.6 to the variometer system of the glider and fly it in still air, when the variometer should show zero over a large range of speed. If it shows a rate of sink, the capillary is too long and should be shortened. An alternative system is to mount a pitot-static tube in a wing-tunnel or any other convenient source of airflow at about glider speeds. An airspeed indicator is connected to the pitot and static connections. A variometer in series with the capillary tube is also connected to the pitot and static connections. When the ASI reads V_{i_1}, the length of the capillary is adjusted until the variometer reads V_{si_1} (Caution: do not disconnect the variometer or capillary with the tunnel running). Both of these systems have their drawbacks: the first is accurate but very inconvenient whilst the latter is simple, but assumes that the glider performance is accurately known.

All of the above explanations, and the expressions for L, suppose that the pressure difference across the capillary is equal to the dynamic head. If the variometer is connected to a source of $(p_s - \frac{1}{2}\rho V^2)$, so as to display rate of change of energy height, the pressure difference across the capillary will be twice the dynamic head and its length must therefore be doubled. In principle, there is no reason why this system with the shorter tube length should not be used in conjunction with a total-energy capsule, as shown in Fig. 18.8.

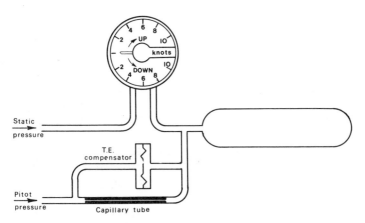

Fig 18.8 The 'net' variometer combined with a diaphragm total energy compensator

Apart from the errors due to altitude, as indicated by equation (18.9), there is a further inherent source of error in unsteady flight. As shown by equation (18.2), the simple total-energy variometer indicates rate of change of energy height, regardless of the mechanism whereby the changes occur. The capillary system effectively subtracts a quantity which should represent the rate at which the glider is dissipating energy under the prevailing conditions but in fact represents the rate of energy loss at the same speed under steady flight conditions. If the load factor differs from unity, these two quantities are not the same. For example, whilst performing a pull-up, the increased load factor will increase the induced drag, compared with that in steady flight, and the capillary compensation will therefore under-estimate the rate of energy loss.

All of these sources of error could be eliminated by a suitable electronic variometer but only at considerable cost. In practice, the errors in the capillary leak system appear to be acceptable and it represents an elegant improvement to the ordinary variometer. Since its primary application is to optimising the glide, a cock should be provided to turn off the flow through the capillary when climbing, so that the variometer then works normally.

THE FLIGHT PATH INDICATOR

An extension of the previous principle, devised by Brückner, enables the variometer to be used as a flight path indicator. If the capillary tube is shorter than that appropriate to the 'net' variometer then, when the glider is descending, the rate of flow through the capillary will be greater than the rate of flow into the bottle. There will therefore be an outflow through the variometer sensor and the instrument will show some 'climb' reading. It is possible to arrange the capillary leak so that, whatever may be the motions of the atmosphere, the glider is being flown at the correct speed if the climb reading is kept constant.

Suppose that in Figure 16.15, the average rate of climb V_c is zero and the glider is being flown at its optimum speed V_{opt} in the presence of a downdraught V_a. A 'normal' variometer would then read ($V_s + V_a$), where V_s is the rate of sink at V_{opt}.

A good approximation to ($V_s + V_a$) is given by equation (A7.16) of Appendix 7. Since the pressure difference across the leak depends on V^2, the rate of flow through it cannot be made to stimulate ($V_a + V_s$) but it can simulate ($V_a + V_s + V_k$). Since the flow entering the capacity corresponds to ($V_a + V_s$), there will have to be an outflow through the variometer sensor corresponding to V_k, which will therefore be displayed as a rate of climb. So, if the capillary leak is correctly adjusted and if the glider is always being flown at the optimum speed corresponding to $V_c = 0$, the variometer will always show a constant climb rate V_k. If it is being flown too fast, the outflow through the variometer will increase and it will show an increased climb, so the pilot should slow down. Putting it rather crudely, the pilot follows the variometer pointer with the nose of the glider.

Comparing the constants k_1 and k_2 in equations (A7.15) and (A7.18), the length of capillary required for the flight path director system is about 0.3 times that for the 'net' variometer system. Also, from equation (A7.18), the climb indication corresponding to V_k will be about 2.35 V_{so}, or about 3.5 knots for the Libelle at $W = 695$ lb. It can easily be deduced from the usual MacCready considerations that if the average climb rate is V_c, then the variometer indication at the optimum speed will always be ($V_c + V_k$). The MacCready ring is now a very simple affair: it is provided with a datum mark which can be set to the assumed V_c and a single mark at a circumferential distance from the datum corresponding to V_k on the variometer scale (see Figure 18.9).

This system is subject to the same errors as the 'net' variometer arrangement but has an additional snag: it cannot deal with large rates of climb. In the example quoted above, the mark will be at the end of the normal variometer scale if the rate of climb is about 7 knots.

Calibration of this arrangement is rather difficult since it depends on a good choice of V_k. In still air, one could fly the glider at the speed for $(L/D)_{max}$ and the variometer should indicate V_k. When flying at the speed appropriate to a rate of

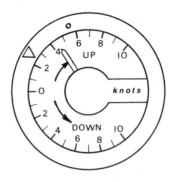

Fig 18.9 MacCready ring for a flight path indicator. The datum is set to 2.7 knots. As shown, sinking air has been encountered and the needle, being below the mark on the ring, is telling the pilot to fly faster. (Calibration for Standard Libelle at W = 695 lb)

climb V_c, as calculated from the usual MacCready construction of Fig. 16.15, the variometer should show a climb reading of $(V_c + V_k)$. If the variometer under-reads, the capillary is too long. Using a wind tunnel, a pressure difference of one dynamic head across the variometer and capillary should produce a reading of $\frac{1}{2}(V_a + V_s + V_k)$, assuming that it is to be used with a total-energy head, where $(V_a + V_s)$ corresponds to the speed of the airflow according to the Mac-Cready construction of Figure 16.15.

Various improvements are possible by the use of an electric variometer: for example, the reading of the instrument can be adjusted electrically so that it always reads zero when the glider is being flown at the correct speed, instead of showing a climb indication. It can also be arranged to produce an audio signal to tell the pilot to fly faster or slower.

COMPUTERS

All of the above explanations relate to pneumatic systems, even if the variometer sensor is an electrical device whose output, suitably amplified, is displayed by a meter. In principle, it is entirely possible to produce a system which senses, by suitable transducers, the pitot and static pressures, their rates of change, and the load factor. Thereafter, the system is entirely electrical. By suitably combining the various signals

and, in effect, by performing the MacCready type of calculation, such a device can be made to function as a normal total-
energy variometer, a 'net' variometer or a flight path indicator.
It could use the actual performance curve, as opposed to the
parabolic approximations implicit in capillary leak systems
and it could be provided with adjustments to take the actual
glider weight into account. The load factor input would
permit accurate internal calculation of the total drag power
loss under unsteady conditions. It could also be arranged to
function accurately at all altitudes. Finally, if the pilot can
insert information about the wind, it can calculate the best
height to leave the last thermal. Indeed, it is quite possible to
perform any of the calculations involved in presenting the
pilot with the information he requires in a convenient form.

Since sensitive pressure transducers are expensive objects,
most of the existing 'air data computers' are somewhat less
elaborate than the ideal device. Generating functions such as
those involved in equation (16.17) also tends to be expensive
so, in practice, they tend to use much the same approximations as the pneumatic systems. Load factor is not normally
sensed and they are unlikely to take proper account of altitude effects. Given these limitations, the cost-effectiveness of
such an elaborate system seems questionable.

TUNING OF VARIOMETER SYSTEMS

Variometers are required to measure continually changing
vertical velocities, so the dynamic response of the system is
important. On the one hand, it should not be so slow that the
instrument only shows a figure averaged over tens of seconds
but on the other hand, it should not be so rapid that its indication is obscured by 'noise', i.e., very short-term signals, possibly quite large, due to the effect of atmospheric turbulence
and gusts on the pitot and static pressures.

From this point of view, any variometer system which
does not use diaphragm total-energy compensation consists
simply of a capacity and a restriction, due to the variometer
sensor and the resistance of the piping, connected in series to
the source of input pressure (See Fig. 18.1). Such a system
has a roughly exponential response: a steady rate of pressure

change, corresponding to a steady climb or descent, will produce a certain steady rate of flow through the system but, if the rate of climb or descent is suddenly altered, the rate of flow takes some while to settle at the new steady value and the instrument reading lags behind the real situation. Suppose the rate of climb, initially zero, suddenly becomes V_c. Then, t seconds later, the indication of the variometer will be something like

$$(V_c)_{\text{ind}} = V_c \left[1 - \exp(-t/T) \right], \qquad (18.10)$$

where T is a time constant for the system. For a mechanical variometer, T would typically be about $3\frac{1}{2}$ sec. From the pilot's point of view, this time-constant is a rather abstract quantity. Although equation (18.10) suggests that the variometer never quite reads V_c, the pilot is interested in how soon it reads something close to the correct value and his impression of the lag of the system more like the time for the indication to achieve 90% of V_c. This time is about 2.3 T, or about 8 sec for the mechanical variometer. Not all of this lag is due to the resistance of the piping and the sensor: some of it is a consequence of heat transfer effects within the capacity. As the pressure of the air in the capacity falls, it cools. The walls of the capacity cool less rapidly so, if the rate of climb suddenly becomes zero, the air in the capacity absorbs head from the warmer walls. If the outside pressure stays constant, this warning will produce a continued outflow from the capacity, giving a false 'up' reading. One way of reducing this effect is to reduce the cooling of the air by filling the capacity with loosely-packed wire wool, preferably of a non-corrodible metal, and with some sort of filter to prevent odd loose bits getting into the instrument. Although its volume will be small compared with the air volume, its relative heat capacity will be large and the air temperature stays almost constant as the pressure changes. It is said that this arrangement will reduce the time constant to about one-fifth of its initial value.

Electric variometer sensors introduce very little pneumatic resistance into the system so the response tends to be rapid, perhaps to the extent of displaying sundry transient indications of no real value. In such a case, it may be necessary to increase the time constant by inserting a short length of capillary tube between the pressure source and the sensor. If the bore of the capillary is 0.020 in and the capacity has a volume of 420 cm^3, the time constant is increased by about 1 sec per inch of capillary at sea-level. The time constant is inversely proportional to the fourth power of the capillary diameter.

With any 'straight-through' system such as that shown in Fig. 18.1 only the overall time constant can be modified. However, if diaphragm-type total energy is used, the circuit has two branches whose time constants need to be matched if transient errors are to be avoided.

In the system shown in Fig. 18.4, suppose that the variometer is a mechanical type with a time constant of a few seconds. The glider is being flown at a steady speed in still air and is therefore descending steadily at the appropriate rate, which will be displayed as a constant variometer reading. If the pilot now increases the speed to a new steady value the variometer, in the absence of total-energy compensation, would show a greatly increased rate of sink whilst the speed was increasing before eventually settling down to the new steady reading. There will, of course, be the appropriate lag in its reading. The object of the total-energy compensation is to eliminate the large transient sink indication, as explained on page 290. Even if the steady-state calibration of the diaphragm is correct, it is likely to respond much more rapidly to the changing speed than the variometer-plus-capacity responds to the changes of static pressure. A premature deflection of the diaphragm would momentarily reduce the flow through the variometer, which would initially show a diminished rate of sink. The various responses are shown diagrammatically in Fig. 18.10.

The time constant of the pitot-plus-compensator system should therefore be about the same as that of the static-variometer-capacity system if the desired smooth response is to be obtained. In order to achieve this result, a capillary resistance R_1 must be added to the circuit such that

$$R_1 C_1 = R_2 C_2 \qquad (18.11)$$

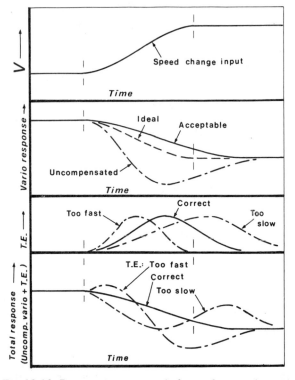

Fig 18.10 Response to a speed change by a variometer
with diaphragm total-energy compensation, showing the
effect of various response rates

where C_1 is the volume of the compensator and the connecting pipe between R_1 and the compensator, R_2 is the resistance
of the variometer and C_2 is the volume of the capacity (See
Fig. 18.11). This reasoning suggests that R_1 needs to be quite
large, since C_1 is likely to be small. In the absence of an elaborate dynamic test rig, R_1 is best decided by trial and error
in flight.

The pilot would really like an instrument with a fast response but with spurious signals due to turbulence filtered
out of the system. To some extent, this is accomplished by
the resistance R_1, but a more sophisticated approach due to
W.C. Schuemann is shown in Fig. 18.12. Here the variometer
is electric and is assumed to have negligible resistance.

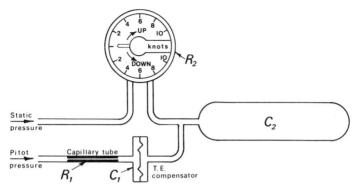

Fig 18.11 Adjustment of the total-energy compensator response rate by a constriction in the pitot connection

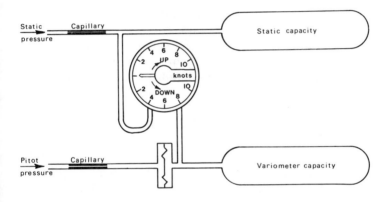

Fig 18.12 The Schuemann scheme for filtering-out unwanted high frequency signals

The scheme is based on the analogous electrical circuit and effectively places matched filters in the pitot and static circuits. In the original system, the 'static capacity' was about the same size as the variometer capacity. The filters strongly attenuate high frequency gust signals while having an insignificant effect on the response of the variometer to the lower-frequency inputs which are of real interest. The restrictions appear to consist of short lengths of hypodermic tubing and are best adjusted by trial and error.

Chapter 19

Other Instruments and Equipment

This chapter is written primarily for those owners who like to devise their own cockpit arrangements and for those concerned with the maintenance of instruments. Many owners of factory-built gliders prefer to design their own instrument panels and other cockpit fittings, partly because they think they are likely to be more competent than the factory, coupled with a desire to tailor them to their personal requirements. There is also, quite legitimately, a wish to display some individuality in an otherwise standardized machine. In this last respect it is important to exercise restraint: the cockpit is a place where the pilot receives information and exercises control of the machine, and neither of these functions is facilitated by an array of instruments seemingly installed to impress onlookers at the launch point. The machine should be equipped with the minimum instrumentation which conveys to the pilot that information required for convenient operation. Additional, irrelevant, information merely adds weight to the glider and confusion to the mental processes of the pilot.

It should be apparent that the instrumentation should be of the utmost reliability: cheap instruments from dubious sources often represent false economy, and can be dangerous.

CHOICE AND LAYOUT OF INSTRUMENTS

Quite apart from the above considerations, the space available for the instrument panel is often very restricted, even to the extent that there may be difficulty in fitting the minimum instrumentation in a convenient fashion.

The usual selection of instruments is as follows:

Altimeter
Airspeed Indicator
Compass
Variometer
Turn-and-slip Indicator
Artificial Horizon

Pilots who are really competent at blind flying on primary instruments may be happy to omit the artificial horizon, but most ordinary mortals find it an invaluable aid. It may well be desirable to fit two variometers: an electric type, with a rapid response and an audio output for climbing in thermals, and a mechanical type with a slower response, equipped with a speed-to-fly ring and perhaps some of the elaborations described in Chapter 18 for cruising between thermals. Furthermore, two compasses may be useful, one of the normal aircraft standby variety and the other a Cook or equivalent type. With the installation of an accelerometer and a clock, one is verging upon luxury, although the former is required when training for aerobatics. But beyond these, there must be very convincing reasons for fitting more. Of course, there is always the possibility that new instruments will be invented and pilots will naturally use them if they are of proven value. A reliable thermal-locating device would rapidly become extremely popular.

The area and shape of instrument panel into which the desired instruments are to be fitted is usually determined by a mixture of geometrical consideration (width of fuselage, adequate view over the top of the panel, location of mounting points, etc.) and those relating to convenience and safety (ease of entry to the cockpit, baling-out, clearance for knees, ability to reach switches, etc.). It will often be useful to make a cardboard mock-up to determine a suitable shape.

Having fixed the outlines of the panel, the layout of the instruments within it is determined by the following considerations:

1 For convenience when cloud-flying, the airspeed indicator, artificial horizon, turn-and-slip indicator, and a variometer (electric if fitted) should form a compact group near the centre of the panel.

2 To facilitate accurate cruising, the airspeed indicator and the variometer fitted with the speed-to-fly ring should be adjacent.

3 Compasses should be as far away as possible from electrical instruments and wiring.

4 Instruments which are observed only intermittently (compass, altimeter, clock, etc.) can be placed in the outer corners of the panel.

5 Gyro instruments, panel-mounted compasses and the accelerometer must be mounted with the face of the instrument very nearly vertical when the glider is in a normal flying attitude.

Taking all these requirements into account, it will usually be found that there is relatively little freedom for manoeuvre, and possible arrangements rapidly become apparent.

The available panel space being usually very restricted, the precise location of the instruments is correspondingly a matter of some difficulty. This is one of those situations in which time spent on the drawing board is well worthwhile in avoiding subsequent frustration in the workshop. Perhaps the simplest way of proceeding is to make cardboard templates to represent the instruments, and to shuffle them about within the outline of the panel. The templates should be quite accurate and detailed, since one discovers that in real life surprisingly few instruments have a really 'standard' case, even if the locations of the fixing screws are conventional. Many of them (e.g. altimeters, some ASI's, accelerometers, etc.) have bulges and control knobs superimposed on the 'standard' outline. It should also be remembered that the problem is often less two-dimensional than it looks on the drawing board: for example, if the panel hinges forward about its lower edge, clearance may have to be provided between the instruments and the fuselage structure, ventilation ducts or mounting brackets.

The arrangement of the panel may also be further complicated by the incorporation of switches and other minor controls, or attachment brackets for fittings such as total-energy capsules. It is a mistake to suppose that these can all be added as afterthoughts in the interstices between the main instruments, because they often require more space than one might at first suppose. Finally, one may have to take into account clearances for bend radii and the provision of clips for attaching wiring and brackets for electrical sockets.

Some thought should be given to the strength and stiffness of the panel and its attachments. A fully equipped panel weighs 15 – 20 lb, so when the appropriate load factors are applied (see Chapter 20) the forces on the mountings are by no means small. In practice, transitory loads during landing and take-off may be even more severe unless some form of flexible mounting is fitted. In any case this is helpful to avoid damage to the bearings of gyro instruments. The panel often relies on the instruments themselves to provide much of its strength and stiffness, since in their absence it consists largely of holes. But it cannot be too flimsy, and 16 swg dural is usually just adequate.

It is difficult to prevent the instrument panel producing reflections in the perspex canopy. Those due to the instruments themselves are almost inevitable since a cowl long enough to prevent them would be of inordinate size and a possible source of hazard. All other sources of reflection should be reduced to a minimum by painting the panel itself matt black and using fixing screws with a black oxidised finish.

WIRING AND PLUMBING

Good wiring is an important aid to serviceable instrumentation. The wires themselves should be of the flexible variety with pvc insulation, since single conductors are prone to break off at soldered joints and rubber insulation tends to perish. Soldered joints should be made with a non-corrosive resin flux. Where connections have to be made to screws or terminals, a proper end-tag should be attached to the wire, and a spring washer should be incorporated to prevent the connection working loose. Spring connectors clipping on to blades (e.g. on switches of the automotive variety) are convenient and reliable. Colour coding is often useful, and the complexity of wiring has now become such that it is essential to work out a circuit diagram before seizing the soldering-iron. Wires should be attached to the structure by proper clips and junctions should be made at suitable terminal strips or tag boards. Plugs and sockets tend to excite strong emotions in those who frequently grapple with them: most of the aeronautical variety seem to have been designed by committees. Miniature Jones plugs, or the equivalent, seem very satisfactory provided that they are fitted with retaining blades to hold them positively in place. Some thought should be applied to their arrangement, so that live pins cannot cause accidental short circuits when plugs are removed. It may also be advisable to screen most of the circuits to avoid interference on the radio and audio variometer from gyro instruments and inverters.

The circuits should be arranged so that even if the main accumulators become exhausted, the turn-and-slip indicator and electric variometer can continue to operate from an alternative dry battery supply. It is also useful to fit a battery master-switch, to reduce the possibility of leaving unobtrusive instruments, such as the variometer, switched-on after landing. Circuits connected to the accumulators should incorporate suitable fusing arrangements, since the accumulators contain enough energy to start a dangerous fire if short-circuited. A 5-amp fuse will normally suffice. Connections to batteries and accumulators should be arranged to prevent inadvertent reversal of polarity, since incorrect polarity can cause wrong rotation of gyro instruments and damage to transistors. Pressure instruments are generally connected by means of flexible tubing. Thick-walled rubber tubing (e.g., DTD 251D) does not kink easily and is very satisfactory except for a tendency to perish in time. Thick-walled medical PVC tubing is equally satisfactory provided that it is of the soft and flexible variety. It also tends to age, but more slowly than rubber. Shiny PVC tubing is unsatisfactory since it takes a permanent set; initially, it is extremely difficult to remove from instrument connections but eventually creeps and falls off very easily. On the balance, medical PVC seems most satisfactory. Any tendency to kink can be discouraged by inserting a wire spiral, as used for hanging curtains, inside the tube. The obstruction is normally of no significance.

A useful attachment, which enables an instrument panel to be removed without disturbing the tubing, is a four-way plug and-socket connector. Suitable types are manufactured in Germany and the UK.

INSTRUMENTS IN DETAIL

This section deals with instruments other than the variometer which has already been described in the previous chapter.

Altimeter. The altimeter is simply a sensitive device for measuring the air pressure, in which deflections of a suitable capsule operate the pointers through a train of gears. The instrument is calibrated in terms of height, using the standard atmosphere pressure/height relationship. There is also provision for adjusting the zero-setting and a small sub-scale is provided which indicates the ambient pressure when the instrument reads zero.

New altimeters are very expensive, so it is usual to fit a government surplus instrument. It is advisable to have the accuracy and freedom from friction checked before fitting, and the reading of the sub-scale should be checked against a mercury barometer. It should be accurate to within 3 mb (equivalent to about 100 ft) or better, to facilitate compliance with laws relating to airways, in which flight levels are defined in relation to an altimeter set to 1013.2 mb.

In theory, pressure errors in the static system of the glider can introduce a corresponding error in the altimeter reading but in practice such errors are usually negligible. The static system is often simplified by leaving the altimeter open to the cockpit static pressure.

This arrangement is only satisfactory if the cockpit ventilation system does not produce much pressure or suction. If the cockpit were at pitot pressure, the altimeter would read more than 400 ft low at 100 knots.

Airspeed Indicator. The airspeed indicator is a very sensitive differential pressure gauge, indicating the difference between the pitot pressure and the static pressure. In a perfect installation, this pressure difference would be $\frac{1}{2}\rho V^2$ (at low speeds) where ρ is the local atmospheric density and V is the true airspeed. The instrument is calibrated in terms of speed, corresponding to the sea-level density ρ_0. Ideally, therefore, the instrument would indicate V_i, the equivalent airspeed, defined by the relationship

$$\tfrac{1}{2}\rho V^2 \;=\; \tfrac{1}{2}\rho_0 V_i{}^2 \tag{19.1}$$

The true airspeed can therefore only be deduced from the equivalent airspeed by knowing the local atmospheric density. The accurate TAS is rarely of much interest when flying a glider, except perhaps when flying at a great height in a wave, and since all the characteristic speeds of a given glider at a certain weight are fixed values of equivalent airspeed (see Chapter 16), the pilot is really interested in the actual readings of the ASI. In this context, characteristic speeds refer to the various placarded limitations and important speeds from the operating point of view, such as that corresponding to best glide angle.

In practice, the indicated airspeed, as displayed by the instrument, differs from the equivalent airspeed on account of (*a*) errors of the instrument itself and (*b*) pressure errors introduced by the pitot and static systems. Instrument errors can be eliminated by comparing the instrument with a suitable standard, such as a water manometer calibrated in terms of airspeed (see Appendix 3). Such a calibration should be performed at each annual overhaul, and the error should not exceed about 2 knots over the whole range.

Pressure errors arise as a consequence of the pressures picked up by the pitot head and static source being different from the correct values due to the airflow being affected by the glider itself. The errors introduced by a pitot *tube* are generally negligible unless it is mounted at some appreciable angle to the flow, or gets into the wake of some other part of the glider in certain conditions of flight. Normally, it will pick up the true total head to a high degree of accuracy. The same cannot always be said for a flush pitot mounted on the nose of the glider, which may be subjected to considerable errors as the point of maximum pressure moves about at various speeds. Such errors can be greatly reduced by fitting a lip projected about one inch ahead of the nose, but the fuselage drag may be increased by this device, and consequently there is now a tendency to revert to a pitot-tube mounted on the fin. It should be remembered that this location may be encompassed by the wing wake near the stall.

Flush static vents, consisting of a pair of holes suitably located on opposite sides of the fuselage, are generally preferred to a static tube since they cause less drag. The pressure along the fuselage is generally slightly different from the true static pressure of the atmosphere, but it is usually possible to find a location for the holes where the error, in terms of speed, is very small. Some error must sometimes be accepted in the interest of reducing effects due to small angles of sideslip. Static errors can only be determined by a process of calibrating the installation in the course of the prototype flight trials. The aircraft ASI reading is compared with that of another instrument connected to a pitot head and a suspended static head — a device like a small finned bomb suspended about one wing-span below the glider. Speed limitations, calculated in terms of equivalent airspeed, are then corrected for pressure error so that the placard shows the corresponding readings of the airspeed indicator (assuming no instrument error).

Pitot tubes, as opposed to large-diameter 'pot' pitots, require electric heating to prevent icing and both the pitot and static systems should be arranged so as to prevent the water entering and obstructing the pipes.

If the maximum reading of the ASI is less than the placarded never-exceed speed, it is possible to go too fast without knowing it. The maximum reading should therefore be about 10% above the never-exceed speed. It is also desirable that the scale should be well spread-out in the normal operating region, 35 – 80 knots, say. Very satisfactory instruments are made by Smiths (UK) and PZL (Poland).

Turn-and-Slip Indicator. The rate of turn is indicated by means of a gyro which normally has its axis of rotation lying athwartships. The gyro is mounted in gimbals whose axis runs fore-and-aft, and is restrained against pivoting about the gimbal axis by a spring. When the glider is turning, the gyro wants to turn about the gimbal axis, but the spring restrains it and its eventual angular displacement, as shown by the indicator needle, is a measure of the rate of turn. The direction of rotation of the gyro is such that its deflection about the gimbal axis is opposite to the angle of bank in turning flight. The gyro therefore stays nearly vertical, and indicates something close to the rate of turn of the aircraft about a vertical axis. The rotor is, in effect, a permanent-magnet DC motor. In order to render its rate of rotation independent of supply voltage (above a certain minimum) it is fitted with contacts which open when the centrifugal force on them exceeds a certain amount.

Government-surplus instruments are inexpensive but can rarely be used without some modification. They are designed for aircraft use, where the rates of turn are lower than in gliders: a normal turn in a glider will cause such an instrument to deflect fully. It is then necessary to increase the force of the restraining spring, which can be done quite easily by shortening it one turn at a time until a rate of turn of about 30°/sec gives full deflection. Aircraft instruments are normally intended for a 24/28-volt supply, and will run at less than their design speed on the usual 12-volt glider supply. Even so, the above adjustment to the spring stiffness is usually necessary. At the lower rotational speed, the governor becomes inoperative, but this is of little consequence provided that the batteries are not allowed to become too exhausted.

The slip indicator consists either of a ball in a curved tube, damped with fluid, or a pointer geared to a pendulum and damped magnetically. The former system is simpler and much more reliable. It should be noted that the slip indicator does not actually show the angle of side-slip (the angle between the direction of the relative airstream and the fore-and-aft axis of the aircraft), but rather the angle between the yawing axis of the aircraft and the apparent direction of gravity.

Indicators are manufactured specifically for gliders, either in a $3\frac{1}{2}$-in. case using a 12-volt supply or, more elegantly, in a

2½-in. case using a 4½-volt supply. The latter instruments are somewhat prone to reluctance in starting, since small amounts of oxide on the governor contacts or armature produce enough resistance to frustrate the low supply voltage. If this happens, the contacts should be carefully cleaned with *very* fine abrasive paper and anointed with a *very* small amount of silicone contact lubricant.

Artificial Horizon. The artificial horizon contains a gyro whose axis of rotation is normally vertical. It is mounted in gimbals so that the gyro assembly is free to rotate both in roll and pitch. These movements of the gyro, relative to the case of the instrument, are displayed by a fixed aeroplane silhouette against a moving horizon bar. Due to small amounts of friction in the gimbals, the orientation of the gyro axis of rotation would tend to depart from its initial setting as the aircraft moved in pitch and roll. It is maintained vertical (i.e. along the earth's gravitational field) by means of an erection mechanism, a device which senses the difference between the orientation of the gyro axis and the apparent direction of gravity at any instant. It then causes a corrective torque to be applied to the gyro. If the error is in pitch, the corrective torque must be applied about the rolling gimbal axis, and vice-versa. Since the whole system has a very long time-constant, it averages out the apparent directions of gravity over a period of some minutes and hence for all practical purposes aligns itself truly vertically. It is important to appreciate that it averages out the apparent directions of gravity in space, and not with respect to an aircraft datum. So, if the aircraft is performing a continuous steady turn, the instantaneous apparent direction of gravity is inclined to the true vertical as a consequence of the angle of bank. The mean direction in space of apparent gravity after an integral number of complete turns is vertical and, for all practical purposes, this is what the instrument shows. It will not, as might be thought, show a steadily decreasing angle of bank. Of course, if the aircraft turns through an angle which is not an integral number of complete turns, in theory there will be a small residual error at the end of the manoeuvre. For example, a U-turn of 180°

should leave a small error in the pitch indication. In practice, the errors involved are not noticeable, and in any case instruments embody various subtle arrangements designed to reduce them to even smaller values than might be deduced from the above discussion.

Artificial horizons suitable for use in gliders are electrically operated, the actual rotor being an induction motor driven by three-phase alternating current, at about 400 Hz. This type of motor avoids the use of a commutator, and enables high rotational speeds to be attained without the use of rubbing contacts. The erecting mechanism may be either electrical or mechanical: in the former case there is a circular vessel partly filled with a conducting fluid or mercury beneath the gyro axis. Apparent tilt immerses contacts which supply current to a coil in such a sense as to provide a torque about a gimbal axis so as to correct the tilt. The mechanical system is simple enough in principle, but not easily explained in a few sentences. Neither system is perfect: the electrical one is subject to high contact resistance and the mechanical one to friction and dust.

Since horizons are very expensive instruments, almost all of those to be found in gliders are government-surplus. When cloud-flying, most pilots place great reliance on the horizon, so any government-surplus instrument should be overhauled and adjusted by an aircraft instrument organisation before installation.

There are too many different types to mention individually. In general terms, the most desirable variety is a straightforward artificial horizon with a standard $3\frac{1}{4}$-in. case, not cluttered with other indications, and with electric erection. Instruments with mechanical erection, such as the Bendix J8, do not seem to take kindly to the landing shocks transmitted by most glider instrument panels.

Most modern horizons require a 115-volt, 3-phase, 400-Hz supply, usually provided by a transistorized inverter operating from the glider batteries. When running steadily, the battery drain is likely to be about 1.0 to 1.5 amps. Attempts to reduce the current consumption by reducing the voltage supplied to the instrument tend to be unsatisfactory.

Some types of horizon have a 'fast-erect' facility: this must only be used when the instrument has run up to full speed and it requires a greatly increased current. The inverter must obviously be capable of dealing with the demand.

Most modern instruments are fitted with an 'OFF' flag which disappears when the current is switched on, assuming that it is correctly connected so as to give the proper direction of rotation. Reversal of rotation can be achieved by changing over any two AC wires.

Horizons also exist with the inverter built into the case so that they are effectively DC instruments. A recent development, highly desirable but unlikely to be generally available for a long time, is the miniature instrument in a $2\frac{1}{2}$-in. case.

Compass. Various panel-mounted aircraft compasses are available from government-surplus sources, either in the standard $3\frac{1}{4}$-in. or $2\frac{1}{2}$-in. case or the smaller E2 variety. These are all quite reliable instruments, although the markings tend to become obscure with age. They are fitted with corrector magnets, and should be adjusted after installation. Some good instruments for use in cars are also available, but often have no means of correction. These should be calibrated after installation, since the errors may be appreciable.

All of these conventional instruments suffer from turning errors; such errors are discussed in detail in the standard references and need not be considered further here except to note that the practical result at glider rates of turn is to cause the compass to swing so wildly that straightening-up on a desired heading in cloud becomes almost impossible. In aeroplanes, a directional gyro or a gyro-stabilized magnetic compass is used to eliminate such effects, but these devices are usually excessively heavy for glider use. A very satisfactory substitute is the Cook compass, in which the magnetic element has a high magnetic moment and small inertia. It is not pendulously mounted as in the normal compass card, but fixed in rigid bearings. In order to give accurate indications of heading, its axis must be vertical, so the whole instrument is free to swing in the pitch sense, and the pilot must set it vertical in the roll sense by reference to the artificial horizon. It is then substantially free from turning errors and indicates the correct heading at all times.

A compass indicates the direction of the component of the earth's field in the plane of rotation of the needle or card. In regions where the angle of dip is large (it is about 67° in the UK), quite small departures of the axis of rotation from the vertical introduce large errors into the indicated heading. It is therefore important that the axis of a Cook compass be vertical to quite a high degree of accuracy. It also follows that compasses such as the Magnesyn, in which the sensing element is rigidly attached to the airframe, will tend to suffer from large errors when the glider is banked. They do not suffer from oscillations due to turning errors, and the indicated heading will vary smoothly in continuous turns, but nevertheless the indication at any instant may be greatly in error.

The Cook principle is taken a stage further in the Bohli compass. Here, the needle is mounted on a transverse pivot through its centre of gravity and is also free to rotate about a vertical shaft carried in bearings rigidly fixed to the case. The needle therefore aligns itself with the local direction of the Earth's magnetic field: it aligns itself North-South and tilts at the angle of dip. The top of the case is a segment of a sphere made of transparent plastic and is engraved with radial lines to indicate direction and a series of concentric circles centred on the vertical axis of rotation.

The upper end of the needle (i.e., the south-seeking pole in the northern hemisphere) carries a red blob, which lies just beneath the spherical top of the case and the fixing of the whole instrument is arranged so that, when the glider is turning, the vertical axis of rotation can be aligned with the true vertical.

With this arrangement, the needle points accurately N-S, even if the vertical axis is not quite true. Also, if the axis is correctly aligned and the glider is flown in a steady turn, the red blob will describe a circle concentric with those engraved on the top. It is said to be so good in this respect that it can be used as a blind-flying instrument. It is expensive, bulky, and generally needs to be viewed through a mirror. Different versions are required for use in the northern and southern hemispheres.

Compasses should not be installed in positions subject to magnetic fields due to parts of the glider or other instruments. The control column, for example, should be of light alloy rather than steel. Turn-and-slip indicators and the meters used with electric variometers can produce appreciable fields, although these fields can be reduced by the use of mu-metal screening. If two compasses are fitted, they should not be too close together.

EQUIPMENT

Radio. The authors of this book would certainly not claim any detailed knowledge of the working of a modern VHF radio: they have simply been involved in its use in gliders long enough to have developed strong and possibly prejudiced views about it. Its use is considered in Chapter 12 and here we are only concerned with its engineering aspects in the glider. It is axiomatic that no radio at all is better than a semi-serviceable one, and it follows that the products of electronically-minded amateurs should be eschewed unless the constructor is a veritable genius at the art and, moveover, has enough self-restraint to refrain from fiddling with it once it is built. Producing a VHF radio which is really reliable and which will receive approval from the appropriate government agency, as is demanded in most countries, represents a major piece of R. and D., which is best left to the professionals.

Requirements for numbers of channels, and frequencies to be used, vary so much from one country to another that there is little point in discussing them at any length, except to note that 'progress' seems synonymous with more channels. Legal requirements should be studied before fitting a radio. In the UK, the set itself requires type approval by the Civil Aviation Authority, and an annual licence fee must be paid to the Home Office. An operator's licence is not required if transmissions are confined to the frequencies allocated for glider use.

It goes without saying that the set should be small, light, compact, reliable and economical in current consumption. Solid-state circuitry represents a great advance in all these respects. It should also have enough audio output to drive a loud-speaker: earphones are an unmitigated nuisance. It is a convenience if the set is small enough to be mounted on the instrument panel. Mounting the 'transmit' switch on the control column is helpful.

The set should be connected to the antenna by means of coaxial cable of the correct impedance: an arbitrary piece of 'coax' from the local TV shop is unlikely to be suitable. In wooden or glass fibre gliders, the antenna can be mounted internally and a quarter-wave aerial and groundplane forming a 'T' can often be accommodated within the depth of the fuselage. A position somewhat aft of the wing trailing-edge is often satisfactory, but adjacent push rods can lead to a very poor polar diagram with little forwards radiation. Better results may be obtained by fitting a centre-fed half-wave aerial along the fin-spar, where it is usually remote from metal fittings and the pilot. The elements of the aerial are usually made from thin-walled brass or aluminium tubing, with suitable plastic insulation. It is inadvisable to fix the tubing directly to a bare wooden structure, since moisture in the wood can absorb some of the energy. Further information on aerials is given in Appendix 11.

The simplest antenna on metal glider is an external quarter-wave whip, using the adjacent structure as a groundplane. Even quite a thin wire produces a significant drag, so the ideal installation would consist of a flush aerial built into the skin of the fin.

Oxygen. Whilst some individuals can function happily at great heights without oxygen, the effects of anoxia are dangerous and insidious, and oxygen should be fitted and used when flying at heights in excess of 10,000 ft or so. The most desirable oxygen system is of the diluter-demand type, in which the oxygen is turned on and then an automatic regulator ensures that the pilot breathes air enriched with a proportion of oxygen appropriate to the ambient atmospheric pressure. However, this system is somewhat bulky, and the regulator must be serviced at regular intervals and considerable expense.

Much simpler and lighter is the constant-flow system. A regulator delivers oxygen to the face mask at a constant rate: there are usually two settings, of 2 and 4 litres/min. The oxygen flows into a rubber balloon and a very slight resistance in the outlet from the mask ensures that the first part of the pilot's exhalation flows into the balloon, and his initial inhalation is drawn from it. Part of each breath thus consists of air enriched with oxygen. The balloon provides temporary storage for the oxygen whilst the pilot is exhaling. Except perhaps under extreme conditions, such as prolonged wave-flying at very great heights, this system is quite satisfactory. It is, however, important to use a suitable face mask: the lightweight plastic emergency variety are prone to freeze-up at low temperatures and are not approved for use below $-5°C$. Various alternative types are available with satisfactory characteristics, and the advice of the manufacturer should be sought.

Oxygen cylinders should be handled carefully and should never be emptied completely, otherwise moist atmospheric air may enter and cause internal corrosion. They should only be refilled with dry aircraft oxygen. Ordinary medical oxygen contains more moisture, and can cause internal icing of the reducing valve. Most filling organizations demand that they be tested at regular intervals, and this schedule should be carefully followed. Oxygen systems usually work at a maximum pressure of 1800 lb/in^2 up to the reducing valve, and oxygen at this pressure represents a considerable explosion and fire risk. The piping and connections should therefore consist of the appropriate aircraft components, assembled with the utmost care and tested for leaks before applying the high-pressure oxygen.

In the UK, diluter-demand systems are manufactured by British Oxygen Ltd and constant-flow systems designed for glider use by Walter Kidde and Normalair.

The quantity of oxygen carried obviously depends on the circumstances in which it is to be used. A small bottle (e.g. of the 230-litre type) is satisfactory for the occasional quick climb in cloud, but bottles of 500 or 750 litres are needed for high-altitude flights of significant duration.

The Barograph. A reliable height-recording instrument is obviously an essential part of the glider's equipment, since applications for most certificates and records must be supported by a barograph chart. It is well worth making a habit of carrying on every flight a barograph sealed by an official observer, to avoid missing unexpected opportunities.

Above all, the instrument must be reliable and robust. The aneroid mechanism should be properly temperature-compensated and the clockwork which moves the chart must work in all attitudes and at the lowest ambient temperatures likely to be encountered (say $-40°$C for an 8-km instrument). Subject to these requirements, the barograph should be as simple as possible: experience shows that complicated types, or those in which efforts have been made to reduce the size of the mechanism, tend to be unreliable.

The record may be made in various ways: (*a*) Ink on paper, (*b*) a scratch made by a fine stylus on smoked paper, smoked aluminium foil, or a specially coated foil or (*c*) small holes pricked in a paper chart at frequent intervals. Ink on paper tends to be unsatisfactory, since the friction of the pen on the paper may introduce an appreciable error, and the record may be blotchy unless great care is taken. The ink must be of a non-freezing type specially prepared for such instruments. The friction is greatly reduced by using a stylus which just touches the chart, but a smoked surface is messy to prepare and is easily spoilt by handling. For permanent preservation, a chart must be fixed by soaking in dilute shellac-in-alcohol solution (French polish). The Peravia Barograph, which indicates the height by pricking holes in a continuous strip of prepared paper, has the advantage that the effective friction between the stylus and the chart is zero.

The barograph should be carefully calibrated at intervals of one year or so.

Power Sources. As a re-chargeable power source, the lead/acid battery is still the most satisfactory. A 12-volt, 12-amp-hr installation, using batteries with plastic cases, will weigh about 10 lb. Much lighter batteries exist, such as the silver/zinc type, but they are expensive, have a relatively short life and require very carefully-regulated charging.

The lead/acid batteries commonly used in the UK are of a type manufactured for motor-cycle use. Whilst not suitable for use under sustained negative loading, they are sufficiently spill-proof for normal purposes. Methods of charging and maintaining batteries are so well known that it would be tedious to repeat them here, save to observe that they should not be charged in situ in the aircraft, since they may produce a highly corrosive aerosol of acid from the vents. Spillage of battery acid can cause severe damage to any structural material including glass fibre.

Dry batteries are a useful stand-by source of power, or for working devices such as the audio unit of the variometer, which consumes little power. They should be of reasonably generous size.

It is worth repeating the warning about reversed polarity: radios and transistor devices dislike it intensely.

Undercarriage Warning Systems. It goes without saying that pilots should always carry out a meticulous cockpit check before approaching to land, ensuring that the undercarriage is lowered, the flaps are at their correct setting, and so on. It is surprising how many pilots, some of great repute, have forgotten to lower the wheel after the excitement of a final glide. Very often, little damage is done to the glider (as opposed to the pilot's self-esteem) but such occurrences are potentially expensive. Since few manufacturers fit warning devices, it is well worth indulging in the modest extra cost involved in fitting one's own: it may save many times the outlay.

The usual arrangement involves fitting microswitches to the airbrake and undercarriage controls, wired to a buzzer and the power supply as shown in Fig. 19.1.

The sense of operation is that, if the undercarriage is in any position other than down and locked, unlocking the airbrake lever causes the buzzer to sound. This arrangement also acts as a warning that the airbrake lever is not fully locked, although it only works in this sense when the undercarriage is up. The most suitable buzzer is the solid-state type of warn-

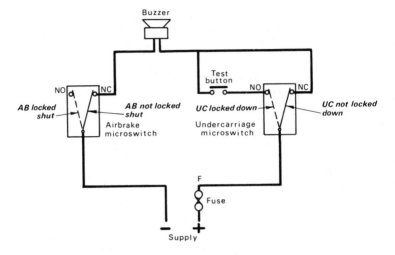

Fig 19.1 Circuit diagram of an 'undercarriage-up' warning device

ing device which produces a penetrating tone at about 2500 Hz.

It is also prudent to fit a test switch, which simulates the effect of raising the undercarriage. The warning circuit should be permanently live when a battery is installed in the glider with, of course, protection by a suitable fuse. If the pilot can switch the warning off in flight, or has to remember to switch it on before take-off, the whole purpose of the warning system is defeated.

Chapter 20

Flight Limitations

As flying machines go, gliders are surprisingly strong. In their own element, they will withstand very large forces, sometimes to the extent that the pilot gets frightened long before he is in any danger. But there are limits to the loads and speeds they can withstand, because they have to be reasonably light to fulfil their primary function of soaring, and they must therefore be handled with some discernment. Circumstances may often arise, particularly in championship flying, when one wishes to operate the machine quite close to its limitations. Most people are unaccustomed to treating machines intentionally in such a fashion — they rarely take the family car near its design limits. The competent pilot who wishes to exploit his machine to the full in safety should have a thorough knowledge of its characteristics and limitations, and of the hazards involved if he accidentally presses it too far.

It is important to remember that the limitations given on the placards in the glider cockpit represent the minimum information which the pilot needs for safe operation. Different airworthiness authorities have various ideas as to what should be placarded, but Fig. 20.1 which shows the standard BGA placards for a Standard Libelle, illustrates good conventional practice. In point of fact, there are plenty of ways of breaking a glider, apart from disobeying these notices. Some, such as heavy landings, do not need specific mention: it is assumed that ordinary good airmanship prevails. Others are rather more subtle: one can cause damage by applying full control deflections at high speeds, for example. Short of papering the whole inside of the cockpit with extracts from airworthiness requirements, one can scarcely explain every limiting feature to the pilot. It is assumed that he is sufficiently well-trained not to indulge in eccentric behaviour in the air or, that if he has invented a new aerobatic manoeuvre, he will have the

B.G.A. 1688 **Flight Limitations**

MAXIMUM SPEEDS KTS/~~MPH/KPH~~

Pitot-static installation Fin pitot, rear fuselage statics.

Never Exceed	123
Air Brakes Open	123
Rough Air	90
Aerotow	80
Winch/Auto Tow	65

WEAK LINK to break at 1000 **lbs.**

CLOUD FLYING (T/S fitted) Yes

AEROBATIC MANOEUVRES: LOOP, SPIN, STALL TURN, TIGHT TURN $3\frac{1}{2}$ g

Permitted

LOADING LIMITATIONS

GLIDER No. B.G.A. 1688

Empty Weight	453	lb.
Max. All-up Weight	695	lb.

Weight and C.G. limits meet the loading as follows:

MAX. COCKPIT LOAD ..	229	**lb.**
MIN. COCKPIT LOAD ..	137	**lb.**

Ballast must be carried forward/~~aft~~ if cockpit load is less/~~more~~ than 137 lb., but the Max. All-up Weight must not be exceeded.

Fig 20.1 Speed and loading limitation cards, Standard Libelle

common sense to seek better-informed advice before trying it.

The limitations which the pilot must observe depend on the aerodynamic and structural characteristics built into the glider by the designer. Broadly speaking, the aerodynamic characteristics are determined by the need to achieve a high performance, coupled with reasonable stability and control. The limitations will depend to some extent on these latter qualities. The structure will depend partly on the aerodynamic characteristics and the geometry of the glider, and the operating conditions to which it is to be exposed. These conditions are not normally chosen by the designer, but are described in whatever Airworthiness Requirements he uses, as laid down by the national airworthiness authority or, failing this, by OSTIV (Organisation Scientifique et Technique de Vol à Voile, an international body concerned with technical aspects of gliding). In the present context, we will be mainly concerned with OSTIV requirements, since they bear a close similarity to many national requirements. Mention will also be made of British Civil Airworthiness Requirements (BCAR). However, it is important to remember that the remarks of this chapter do not apply to all types of glider and the reader should not be surprised to find that the limitations given for his own machine differ from those indicated below.

The extreme operating conditions to which a glider is likely to be exposed arise as a consequence of speeds and loads applied by the pilot, and loads applied by atmospheric gusts. These two sets of conditions, which obviously overlap, and may be present simultaneously in actual operations, are expressed in terms of the *Manoeuvring Envelope* and the *Gust Envelope* respectively. There are also various other situations, such as winch or aerotow launching, which have to be taken into account. As is usual in flying machines of any sort, the assumed conditions represent a compromise: on the one hand they must not be so severe that the glider becomes too heavy to soar satisfactorily, but nevertheless they must not preclude operation under quite severe conditions.

THE MANOEUVRING ENVELOPE

This is a diagram showing the extreme conditions of load-factor and speed for which the glider must be designed, as applied by deliberate actions of the pilot. The load factor is defined as the ratio of the lift to the weight, and in a steady glide is therefore equal to the cosine of the angle of glide (see Fig. 20.2). The angle of glide of modern gliders, with the air-brakes shut, is so flat that the value of the load factor is substantially equal to 1.0 under these conditions. When manoeuvring, the load factor is no longer 1.0. For example, when turning (Fig. 20.3) the vertical component of the lift must equal the weight, and the total lift is therefore greater than the

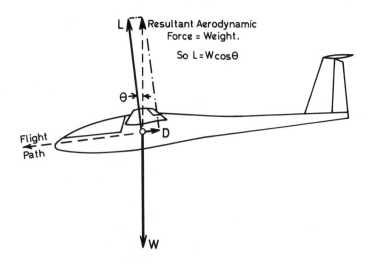

Fig 20.2 Forces on a glider in straight flight

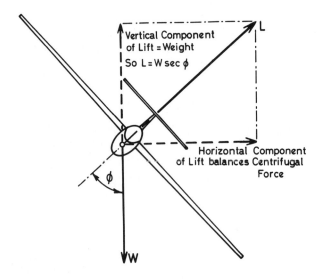

Fig 20.3 Forces on a glider in turning flight

weight. From Fig. 20.3, it will be seen that in a turn with 60° of bank, the load factor will be 2.0. The variation of load factor with angle of bank is given in the following table:

Angle of bank	0°	15°	30°	45°	60°	75°	80°	85°	90°
Load factor	1.0	1.04	1.15	1.41	2.00	3.86	5.76	11.47	∞

Table 20.1   *Variation of load factor with angle of bank.*

The load factor may also be increased by pitching manoeuvres. When the flight path is curved (e.g., when pulling out of a dive), there is an acceleration towards the centre of curvature of the flight path, of magnitude V^2/r (see Fig. 20.4). The force required to produce this acceleration is (the mass of the glider) x (V^2/r), i.e., (W/g) x (V^2/r). This force is supplied by the difference between the lift and the appropriate component of the weight, so that at the bottom of a pull-out, or when starting a loop,

$$L - W = \frac{W}{g}\frac{V^2}{r} \qquad (20.1)$$

or

$$n = \frac{L}{W} = 1 + \frac{V^2}{gr} \qquad (20.2)$$

and is therefore greater than 1.0. In a well-conducted loop, the initial load factor is usually about three.

It is also possible to apply negative load factors. When in steady inverted flight, the lift is again equal to the weight but is in the opposite sense to that prevailing in normal flight, so the load factor is -1.0. Push-overs and manoeuvres such as outside loops (bunts) can produce load factors less than $+1.0$, down to some appreciable negative values. Negative load factors beyond about -2.0 are rather dangerous physiologically although the body can stand positive load factors in the neighbourhood of $+5.0$ for a few seconds with only temporary results such as a reduction of vision.

The accelerometer, now compulsory for gliders used for teaching aerobatics in the UK, is really a load-factor meter

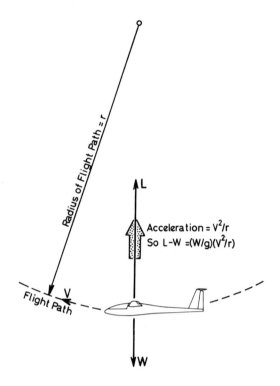

Fig 20.4 Forces on a glider during a pull-out

and its indications correspond to the figures mentioned above.

Corresponding to each load factor, there is a certain stalling speed. If the stalling speed in steady flight is V_{s_1}, then

$$W = C_{L\,\max}\tfrac{1}{2}\rho\,V_{s_1}^2\,S \qquad (20.3)$$

At a load factor n, the stalling speed will be V_{s_2}, where

$$L = nW = C_{L\max}\tfrac{1}{2}\rho V_{s_2}^2 S \qquad (20.4)$$

so

$$\frac{V_{s_2}}{V_{s_1}} = \sqrt{n}. \qquad (20.5)$$

Let us now refer to the manoeuvring envelope shown in Fig. 20.5. If we consider positive load factors, we can draw a line on the left-hand side of the diagram, if we know the stalling speed in level flight. If it is 37 knots, then the stalling speed

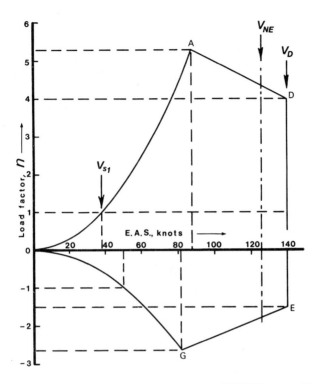

Fig 20.5 The manoeuvring envelope (OSTIV airworthiness requirements) for a typical modern glider

in a 60°-banked turn, with a load factor of 2.0, is 37 x $\sqrt{2}$, i.e., 52 knots, and so on. This stalling line represents one boundary to the diagram: we cannot fly at lower speeds. Similarly, towards the lower left-hand side of the diagram, there will be a line representing the inverted stall. The stalling speed for a certain negative load factor is higher than for the same positive load factor because the wing section has a lower maximum lift coefficient when working inverted.

There must obviously be a limit placed on the maximum load factors which the glider is designed to withstand: it would be ludicrous to make the maximum positive load factor +20, say, for it would be impossible to provide a sufficiently strong structure and nobody wants to apply this sort of load anyway. Equally, it would be folly to make it only +2: the glider would be far too weak for normal use. The usual compromise is around 5.0 (5 in BCAR, 5.3 in OSTIV). In the case of negative load factors, about half of this value is sufficient, since it represents roughly the maximum the pilot can take.

It is also necessary to define a maximum speed, which forms the right-hand boundary of the diagram. This speed, the *design dive speed* V_D, is defined in terms of both the wing loading and the minimum drag coefficient of the glider: the higher the wing loading and the cleaner the glider, the faster the pilot will want to go. The OSTIV formula for the minimum value of V_D is

$$V_D = 16.5 \sqrt[3]{w/C_{D\,\text{min}}}, \qquad (20.6)$$

where V_D is in knots and w is the wing loading in lb/ft^2. The minimum drag coefficient may not be known very accurately in advance but the effect of the cube root is to make the effect of errors in its estimation fairly small.

For example, if $w = 6.8$ lb/ft^2 and $C_{D\,\text{min}} = 0.011$, then V_D will be at least 141 knots but the designer could choose a higher value.

To put in the remaining boundaries, the assumption is made that pilots are less likely to apply large loads at high speeds. The maximum positive load factor therefore tapers off from 5.3 on the stalling line to 4.0 at V_D, and the negative factor from -2.65 to -1.5. If the glider is designed to withstand the conditions at any corner of the diagram then it will withstand those anywhere else within it.

At the boundaries of this diagram, some parts of the structure will attain their 'Limit Loads', i.e., the maximum loads anticipated in normal conditions of service. The limit loads on different parts of the structure normally occur under conditions corresponding to different points on the diagram: for example the main spar in bending will probably attain its limit load at point A, whilst the wing torsion box may attain its limit load at point E. On the other hand, some other condition, not shown on this diagram, may produce the limit load which determines the strength to be provided in a particular component: perhaps a gust, for example. The 'Proof Load' is defined as the product of the Limit Load and a quantity, defined in Requirements, termed the 'Proof Factor'. For most parts of glider structures, the Proof Factor is 1.0, so Proof Loads and Limit Loads are usually the same. The 'Ultimate Load' is the Limit Load multiplied by the 'Ultimate Factor' or 'Factor of Safety', as it is called in OSTIV Requirements. This latter factor is usually 1.5, quite a low value by most engineering standards. The point of these definitions is that – to quote BCAR – 'The structure shall not fail before the ultimate load is reached and it shall not suffer from detrimental deformation or minor failure during loading, and after having been loaded, to the proof load.' OSTIV Requirements contain a slightly more elaborate statement.

So, if the glider is just strong enough to meet the Requirements, flying it slightly outside the manoeuvring envelope could produce small permanent deformations of the structure and, if loads exceeding 1.5 times those produced at the boundaries of the envelope were applied, something fundamental is likely to break. In practice, parts of a glider may have a reserve of strength: if the 'Reserve Factor' of the mainspar in bending at the wing root is 1.1, it will withstand loads 10% higher than those specified in the Requirements. Such reserve factors may occur fortuitously, perhaps because a standard material thickness is slightly greater than is strictly necessary, or they may be provided deliberately, to permit repairs, to take account of variations of material strength or to provide for future development. Also, the ultimate factor may exceed 1.5 if, for example, fatigue is a consideration.

Exceeding the proof load factors by a small margin is unlikely to be serious in wooden or glass fibre parts of a glider structure, unless it causes minor failures of 'unstressed' parts which then cause stress concentrations in the primary structure. In metal parts, it produces a small permanent set, which again may not be very serious in itself but represents stored-up damage which will tend to hasten the onset of a fatigue failure. To take the extreme positive load case, load factors in excess of 5.3 are likely to cause minor damage, and a load factor of 8.0 is likely to cause a failure. In practice, other requirements such as gust loads may result in the glider being stronger than these figures indicate, and the material used in a particular machine may have a higher strength than that assumed by the designer when performing his stressing calculations. Also, a certain amount of concealed strength may be built into the machine, arising from parts of the structure which are not taken into account in the calculations. It is obviously very unwise to assume that any of these possible sources of extra strength are in fact present. Exceeding the proof loads can be a very serious matter, and any pilot who suspects that he has done so should report the occurrence and have the machine inspected by a qualified person: it is all too easy to cause damage which is not readily visible but which might have unfortunate future consequences to another pilot.

Exceeding the limit loads can also be due to flying at excessive speeds. Placarded in the cockpit is a 'never-exceed' speed, V_{NE}. This speed, according to OSTIV Requirements, is 0.95 times the speed demonstrated in flight tests, V_{DF}. V_{DF} shall not exceed V_D, but must not be less than 0.9 times the minimum value of V_D specified above. So, if the designer settles for a V_D of 141 knots as in the example above, V_{DF} could be as low as 0.95 x 0.90 x 141 knots, i.e. 121 knots, or as high as 0.95 x 141 knots, i.e., 134 knots. In practice, V_{NE} is often about 0.9 V_D, or 127 knots in this case.

In practice, the indicated air speed may differ from the EAS, due to pressure errors as explained in Chapter 19, so the placarded IAS may be slightly more or less than 127 knots. The reason for allowing this margin between V_{NE}, the tested speed V_{DF} and V_D, is that it is relatively easy in modern gliders to overshoot some desired speed, and provision is therefore made for pilots to exceed V_{NE} unintentionally by a small margin. It is obviously unwise to attempt to take deliberate advantage of this margin, even in calm air, since it is quite small. Exceeding V_{DF} takes one into untested regions, even if the calculated strength of the glider is adequate up to V_D.

Forces are applied to the glider structure as a consequence of speed as well as of load factor. Increasing speed applies larger torsional loads to the wing, and greater down-loads to the tail. Since, in broad terms, these loads depend on the square of the speed, the safety factor of 1.5 applied to the stresses implies a factor of about $\sqrt{1.5}$ applied to V_D. So, at about 1.22 V_D, one would expect a failure to occur. There is, however, an alternative source of failure due to excessive speed known as flutter, when bending and twisting oscillations of the wing occur at such frequencies and phasing as to reinforce one another.

The wing may break almost instantly or, as is not unusual in glass-fibre structures, may indulge in large oscillations which are limited in their amplitude by non-linear effects such as the ailerons stalling. Even so, severe damage is likely to occur. The minimum critical flutter speed is usually 1.25 V_D or 1.3 V_D, and is therefore about the same speed as that at which one would expect a straightforward breakage due to excessive stress. However, flutter has been known to occur at lower speeds than the theoretical value, due to

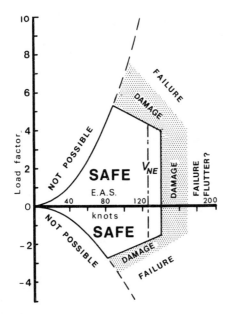

Fig 20.6 Safe and unsafe conditions of flight as determined by the manoeuvring envelope

effects arising from poor maintenance, such as loose aileron mass-balance weights or slack aileron cables. There are various other interesting possibilities such as tail-flutter, which may also be encouraged by slack control circuits or backlash in linkages.

Fig. 20.6 summarizes the above remarks in diagrammatic form but it must be emphasized that, in practice, the boundary between damage and failure is likely to be less sharply-defined than the diagram would suggest.

THE GUST ENVELOPE

Loads are also applied to the glider as a consequence of atmospheric gusts. The pilot is unable to control the intensity of the gusts lurking unseen ahead of him, but he can often foresee the presence of rough air if Cu-nbs or dust-devils are present, and he can usually control the speed at which he traverses a gusty region. Gusts may come from any direction —up, down and sideways. Side-gusts may design the fin structure of large aeroplanes, but are seldom of much consequence to gliders. Up- or down-gusts are of great consequence to most aircraft, including gliders, since they produce additional bending loads on the wing of such magnitude that they often determine the design of the main-spar. Fig. 20.7 illustrates

EFFECT OF VERTICAL GUSTS

Extra lift is proportional to $\Delta C_L V^2$, i.e. to $\Delta\alpha V^2$

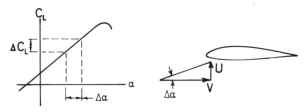

So Extra Load Factor = Extra Lift / Weight

and is proportional to $(U/V) \times V^2$, i.e. to UV.

Fig 20.7 How an up-gust increases the load factor

the mechanism whereby an up-gust produces an increased up-ward bending load on the wing: the increase in incidence produces more lift, the overall effect being proportional to the strength of the gust U and to the forward speed V. This diagram has been drawn as if the gust were sharp-edged, in other words, as if the glider had passed instantaneously from a motionless region of the atmosphere to one in which there was an upwards air velocity U. Obviously, real gusts will not behave in this way: there will be a transition region between the still air and the maximum gust velocity. Moreover, even if a sudden change of incidence is applied to a wing, it does not instantaneously provide the increase of lift one might expect.

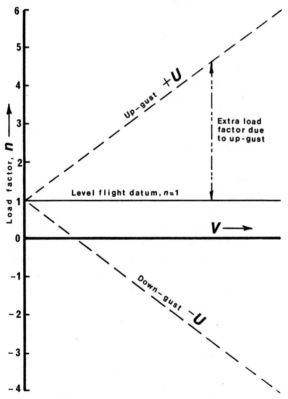

Fig 20.8 Effect of speed on the load factor due to up-or down-gusts

These effects mean that the actual increase in load due to a gust U is less than that based on a simple sharp-edged calculation for this strength of gust. One therefore applies an alleviation factor, F, to take these effects into account, and then calculates the loads as if the glider had encountered a sharp-edged gust of strength FU. The values of F are given in design requirements and have been derived by methods which are too complicated to explore here. The consequence of Fig. 20.7, as modified by these considerations, is that a gust U produces an additional load factor proportional to UV, superimposed on the steady load factor which the pilot is applying at the particular instant in question. Normally, one superimposes gust loads on a steady level flight condition, when the initial load factor is 1.0. A gust of a given strength will therefore produce load factors shown by the upper sloping line of Fig. 20.8. Similarly, down-gusts cause a decrease in load factor, shown by the lower sloping line in the diagram.

One can therefore draw a series of lines, each applying to a certain gust velocity, as shown in Fig. 20.9. If the gust is sufficiently strong, the increase in wing incidence will be so great that it stalls, and the attainable load factor will then depend only on the maximum lift which the wing can produce at a given forward speed. If the machine is just at the stall in level flight, the load factor cannot increase beyond 1.0 because any up-gust will increase the incidence beyond the stall. Similarly, if the speed is $\sqrt{2}$ times the normal speed, there exists a gust which will just stall the machine at a load factor of 2.0, and the load factor will not be increased further by stronger gusts. The foregoing assumes that the wing, when subjected to an up-gust, stalls at the same incidence as in normal flight, when the stall is supposed to be approached very slowly. Although this assumption is not strictly true, it is the basis of some gust requirements. Just as there is a lag in the wing attaining the lift corresponding to the increased incidence, so also is there a lag in the onset of the stall. For a brief period, the wing can achieve an appreciably higher lift than that normally achieved at the stall. In OSTIV Requirements, it is assumed that the transient maximum lift coefficient is 25% higher than under steady conditions, so the stalling boun-

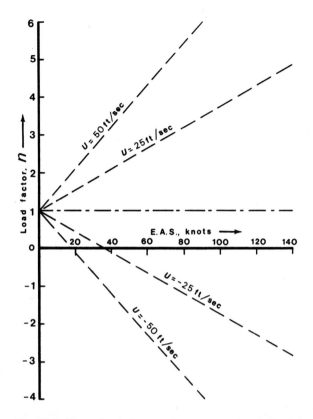

Fig 20.9 Extra load factors due to gusts (as defined in OSTIV airworthiness requirements) for a typical glider

daries in Fig. 20.10 correspond to load factors which are 25% greater than those used in the manoeuvring envelope.

The maximum gust strengths and the speeds at which they are assumed to be encountered are specified in OSTIV Requirements as follows:

(a) Strong gusts with a nominal intensity of ± 15m/s(50ft/s) at V_B.
(b) Weak gusts with a nominal intensity of ± 7.5m/s(25ft/s) at V_D.

V_B, the 'Design Strong Gust Speed' must not be less than V_A (the speed corresponding to point A in Figure 20.5) but

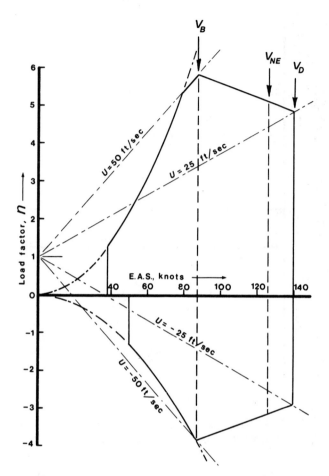

Fig 20.10 The OSTIV gust envelope for a typical glider

the designer can choose a higher value. The 'Rough Air Speed' placarded in the cockpit must not exceed V_B.

Such data as exists seems to suggests that the OSTIV strong gust will be encountered about once per million miles of flying in clear air at moderate altitudes in medium latitudes. A pilot flying a glider for 200 hours per year would therefore meet one, on the average, about every century. He may be inclined to dismiss such gusts as being so infrequent as to be of no concern—except that the once-per-century occasion may be tomorrow afternoon. Weaker gusts occur much more fre-quently: about every 1000 miles for the 25 ft/sec gust. At V_{NE}, a glider would withstand a gust of about 29 ft/sec, which occurs about every 3000 miles so, if a pilot habitually started and finished every task at V_{NE}, flying say a total of 5 miles at this speed, he would meet such a gust, on the average, every 600 tasks and would apply something close to the limit load to the structure on such occasions. For the individual pilot engaged in vigorous competition, this may seem to be an acceptable risk, but the picture looks rather different when seen through the eyes of championships organisers. A moder-ately successful meeting might produce 200–300 task flights and hence, on the average, somebody is going to be badly frightened in every two or three meetings – assuming that all the pilots behave so imprudently. Moreover every 100 meet-ings, somebody's glider is likely to fall apart. Reducing the speed to 0.9 V_{NE} increases the strength of the gust required to produce the limit load to about 35 ft/sec, which occur with a frequency about one-seventh that of the 29 ft/sec gusts. These gust statistics may not be particularly exact but it is worth noting that they are compatible with British standard thermals every 10 miles.

Whilst flying at the rough air speed or less provides almost complete safety, whatever the gusts, consistent flying at V_{NE} produces a level of risk which is by no means negligible. At intermediate speeds, the pilot can select an acceptable level of risk. These observations are not intended to encourage pilots to fly at high speeds in unsuitable conditions: the figures are very rough indeed, they do not apply to flight in clouds, and they will vary from one glider to another. In par-ticular, one should be more conservative when considering gliders designed to the 1961 issue of BCAR, for which the ability to withstand negative gusts at high speeds may be more limited than that of gliders designed to OSTIV Require-ments. Nor should they supersede the use of common sense and foresight in recognising, for example, that it would be unwise to ignore a large Cu-nb sitting above a start line.

The loads produced by gusts are again limit loads, and the ultimate loads which may cause failure are – as for the manoeuvring envelope—normally 1.5 times the limit loads. So, small excursions outside the gust envelope may cause small permanent deformations or damage, but if the loads are exceeded by more than 50%, failure is likely. The gust envelope is solely concerned with loads and speeds: it does not guarantee that a pilot of inadequate skill will retain control of the glider after encountering a gust strong enough to stall it when flying in a rough cloud.

In the case of the manoeuvring and gust envelopes illustrated in Figs. 20.5 and 20.10, which apply to a realistic glider with a wing-loading of 6.8 lb/sq ft, superposition of the diagrams should show them to have nearly the same shape. This situation will not always occur, but in this typical case it means that there is little concealed strength available for manoeuvring purposes arising from the ability to deal with gust loads.

All of the above remarks relate only to the gust loads on wings when flying in the en-route configuration. Requirements also state gust loads with flaps in various positions and during launching. When designing a glider, gust loads on tail surfaces must also be taken into account.

PERMITTED MANOEUVRES

The placarding of most British cloud-flying gliders permits loops, spins, stall-turns and steep turns up to $3\frac{1}{2}g$. Implicitly, inverted manoeuvres such as inverted loops, slow rolls and rolls-off-the-top are not permitted. The design of soaring gliders does not normally make specific allowance for aerobatics, and the ability to perform the permitted manoeuvres should be regarded as bonus, arising as a by-product of the strength implied by the manoeuvring and gust envelopes.

Since the stick force per g of most gliders is fairly low, between about 3 and 10 lb/g, it is by no means difficult to apply an excessive load factor to the structure. It is therefore advisable to fit an accelerometer if aerobatics are to be carried out since, without a great deal of experience, it may not be easy for the pilot to estimate the load factor he is applying, particularly if the seat is of the reclining type. In a well-conducted loop, the initial load factor would typically be about

3.0, with a speed of about 2.5 times the stalling speed. In a genuine spin, the load factor will be about 2.0 with a height loss of about 300 ft per turn. It should be remembered that many gliders will not perform a genuine spin, particularly with the centre of gravity well forward. Attempts at spinning result in a spiral dive, with the speed and *g* increasing rapidly. It is prudent to initiate recovery when the speed attains 2.5 times the stalling speed, or the accelerometer reads 2.5 *g*. In the recovery from both loops and spins, there is a moment at which the glider is pointing steeply nose-down and accelerating rapidly. Care should be taken not to get too fast, nor to pull-out sharply, and the airbrakes should be used if necessary.

Stall turns in gliders should be performed with care. The full-blooded aeroplane manoeuvre, in which the machine is climbed almost vertically and full rudder is applied when the speed has fallen almost to zero, relies to large extent on the rudder continuing to function in the slipstream. If the same manoeuvre is attempted in a glider, the rudder will have practically no effect, and a tail-slide is likely to occur with considerable risk of damage to control surfaces. So the glider manoeuvre is generally somewhere between that described above and a chandelle – a very steep U-turn, with the plane of the whole manoeuvre inclined to the horizontal. The glider is flown round the top, usually with rather more than 90° of bank, using ailerons and rudder. When done accurately, the minimum speed is rather less than the normal stalling speed, but by no means zero. The loads applied are fairly low.

The mention of '$3\frac{1}{2}$ *g*' in the context of steep turns may seem to be excessively conservative when the manoeuvring envelope extends to about 5.0. There are two reasons for this cautious limitation:

1 The fitting of an accelerometer is not usually mandatory, so the pilot has to rely on his own judgement to decide when he has achieved $3\frac{1}{2}$ *g*. Different pilots may have very various ideas on this matter. In theory, the load factor is directly related to the angle of bank, so it might be thought that a visual assessment of this angle would be a good guide. Unfortunately, it requires a fair amount of experience to assess steep angles of bank with any accuracy and, at this sort of load factor, small changes in the angle of bank have a large effect on the load factor (see the table on p. 331).

2 The effect of gusts is superimposed on the manoeuvring loads applied by the pilot. For example, a gust of 24 ft/sec at 87 knots will apply 2.3 *g* to the typical glider of Fig. 20.10, bringing the total load factor up to the maximum gust envelope value.

WINCH LAUNCHING

This represents a much more severe stressing case than is commonly realized, and the speed limitation is correspondingly low, particularly for older types of glider. Many modern machines have a maximum winch-launching speed of about 70 knots, which is not only very adequate but often unattainable with the average winch. But some machines are still in use with a limitation of 50 knots or even lower.

Winch launching produces higher bending moments at the wing root than might be imagined, as shown in Fig. 20.11. The top diagram represents a glider in normal, nearly level, flight. The lift is distributed across the wing in a roughly elliptical fashion, and the total lift (ignoring any tail lift) will equal the weight of the wing and the weight of all the other components, including the pilot. The wing weight of a glider is quite a high proportion of the total (typically about 35%), and this will be distributed across the span more or less as indicated whilst the remainder of the weight is concentrated on the centre line. The bending moment at the wing-root is less than that due solely to the lift forces, as a consequence of the downward bending due to the wing weight.

If the glider is now performing a steep turn or pull-out at a load factor of *n* (second diagram), to a first order one can simply multiply all the forces in the upper diagram by *n*. The effective weights of the wing and all the other parts are increased by this factor and hence the lift must also increase correspondingly to maintain equilibrium.

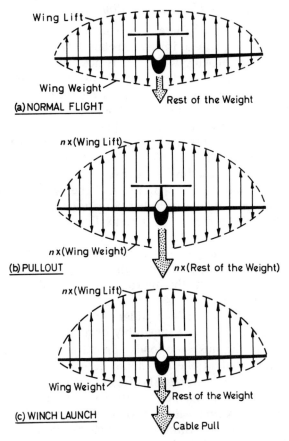

Wing Lift

Wing Weight

Rest of the Weight

(a) NORMAL FLIGHT

$n \times$(Wing Lift)

$n \times$(Wing Weight)

(b) PULLOUT

$n \times$(Rest of the Weight)

$n \times$(Wing Lift)

Wing Weight

Rest of the Weight

(c) WINCH LAUNCH

Cable Pull

Fig 20.11 Loads on glider wings in (a) normal flight, (b) a pull-out, and (c) a winch launch

Suppose now that the glider is being winch launched with the same total wing lift as when performing the tight turn or pull-out. (See the bottom diagram of Fig. 20.11.) The effective weights of the wings and other components will now have their normal values (in fact, rather less from the present point of view, as a consequence of the angle of climb). But the tow cable is now applying a downwards force to the fuselage, and the total wing lift, of n times the weight, now balances the total weight, plus the force in the tow cable. The upwards bending moment at the wing root, due to the lift, is also *n* times its normal value, but whereas in the middle diagram it was relieved by a downwards bending moment due to *n* times the normal wing weight, it is now offset by roughly the same downwards bending moment as in level flight. The bending moment in a winch launch is therefore greater than in a pull-out, both with the same wing lift.

For the purpose of stressing the glider, the design requirements now superimpose a surge load in which the tow cable force is suddenly increased to 1.2 times the ultimate strength of the cable or weak link. The overall loads are therefore quite severe, and it is apparent that the winch-launching speed limitation is to be regarded with respect. Nor can one assume that the presence of a weak link in the tow cable means that, even if limitations are exceeded, the weak link will break before the glider structure. This might be roughly true in the absence of gusts, but gusts apply additional loads conveyed directly from the air to the glider without passing through the weak link.

When being launched in a glider whose maximum winch-launching speed is almost inevitably exceeded, the pilot can take action to diminish the loads applied to it. The requirements assume that at the maximum design winch-launching speed, the glider is in horizontal flight, with the cable at 75° below the horizontal. The load in the cable is either 1.2 times the nominal weak-link value or that appropriate to full up elevator, or to the maximum lift which can be produced at that speed. (Again, individual national requirements may be slightly different in detail, but their intention is much the same.) By refraining from applying full up elevator, and by endeavouring, via the stick force, to sense the loads applied to the machine, the pilot can avoid imposing excessive stresses. But this process is somewhat uncertain, and the only real safeguard is to observe the limitations.

AERO TOWING

Pilots who are skilled in flying on aerotow may be tempted to wonder why any particular limitation is imposed for this condition of flight, since it only seems to differ from free flight in that a fairly small load is applied to the towing hook.

However, the requirements have to cater for the extreme conditions which may arise both from piloting techniques which are less than perfect and the effects of rough air. Towrope angles between 20° up and 40° down, and at 30° sideways are prescribed, with a moderate gust of 10 m/s (33ft/s) superimposed, leading to a condition which applies appreciably greater loads than in free flight, and having a corresponding speed limitation. If one is carrying out a long cross-country tow in the calm of the evening, when the glider pilot can guarantee to keep within 3 or 4 ft of the correct position behind the tug, these rather pessimistic conditions will not apply and there is no harm in flying at quite high speed provided that the control forces required to fly the glider do not become excessively tiring. In modern gliders, the maximum aerotowing speed usually exceeds the best climbing speed behind most tugs by a handsome margin, and there is no point in flying at high speeds during the normal launch.

Under rough conditions, the requirements can acquire a distinctly realistic air. The self-esteem of one accustomed to being launched on a pleasant summer's day over the gentle countryside of northern Europe can be greatly deflated by towing through the rotor of a lee wave, or along the side of an Alpine valley. In brief, the limitation is one to be observed, with the possible exception that really skilled pilots can exercise discretion under calm conditions.

INVERTED MANOEUVRES

Although there are some notable exceptions, most cloud-flying gliders are not permitted to perform inverted manoeuvres. Inverted manoeuvres in the present context means those manoeuvres involving the deliberate application of negative load factors: inverted flight, slow rolls, half-loops, rolls-off-the-top and so on. Loops do not come into this category since, although the glider is temporarily upside down, the load factor remains positive – or should do so.

Since the manoeuvring envelope extends to negative load factors, it is by no means clear why inverted manoeuvres are not usually permitted. The basic reason is that the manoeuvring envelope only provides fairly small negative factors, particularly at high speeds. In drawing up the requirements, it is recognized that even if the pilot only intends to operate at positive loadings, he will occasionally apply negative loads, and the glider must be strong enough to withstand them. The most obvious example is the push-over following a cable break during a winch launch. If, however, the glider is in steady inverted flight at, say, 100 knots, the corresponding point on the manoeuvring envelope is well into the bottom right-hand corner, and there is little margin to deal with fortuitous loads and gusts. The situation is rather worse when the glider is built to the 1961 British Civil Airworthiness Requirements, where the bottom right-hand corner of the diagram corresponds to a load factor of zero. It is then quite possible to get outside the envelope by flying inverted at a high speed. This situation leads to a high lift force on the tail ('downwards' so far as the glider is concerned, but actually pointing towards the sky), and the tailplane or its attachments may well fail first. Moreover, gliders have a poor rate of roll by aeroplane standards, so there is a tendency to start a roll at a high speed in an endeavour to get inverted as quickly as possible and the speed may increase further if the nose is allowed to drop whilst rolling. Another effect of the poor rate of roll is that very large sideslip angles may occur whilst rolling, leading to sideways loads on the fin and rudder far higher than those applied by ordinary side slips. Finally, if inverted flight is entered by means of a half loop, to avoid the effects of the poor rate of roll, one is still faced with operation close to the bottom right-hand corner of the envelope.

To summarize, inverted manoeuvres are usually forbidden in ordinary cloud-flying gliders because they may only have a small reserve of strength when inverted at high speeds and the ability to withstand gusts is then very limited indeed. There may also be difficulties in control, particularly in avoiding large angles of sideslip and consequentially high sideways tail loads.

A further complication, which is not placarded in the cockpit, relates to control surface loads. Ignoring gust loads, the machine is only designed to deal with loads due to full control deflections at speeds up to the manoeuvring speed (corresponding to point A in Fig. 20.5), and due to only one-third of maximum deflection at the design dive speed. Rolling manoeuvres often require greater control deflections, assuming that the pilot is strong enough to apply them. This consideration should also discourage pilots from inventing 'new' manoeuvres, based only on a superficial acquaintance with the manoeuvring envelope. Antics such as figures-of-eight in the vertical plane are very prone to apply excessive loads to the ailerons and wing structure.

WEAK LINKS

It is customary to include amongst the placarded limitations the maximum strength of weak link to be fitted to the towing cable near the glider. This limitation is of great importance since the weak-link strength determines some of the winch-launching stressing cases.

In the past, there has been some diversity of practice in defining weak link strengths. In the UK, 1000 lb has been standard for a very long period, but in some countries different strengths are specified for different sorts of gliders: a single-seat elementary training machine would use a weaker weak link than a heavy two-seater. This practice may be theoretically ideal, but it introduces more hazard than it avoids since it is inevitable that the primary trainer will eventually be launched using the two-seater weak link. The current tendency is to standardize on 1000 or 1100 lb (500 kg) for all types of glider.

The glider is designed to withstand a surge load 20% higher than the nominal weak link strength. This allowance recognizes that, under dynamic conditions, the breaking load of the weak link may exceed the static value. It is not intended as a let-out clause to condone the use of over-strength weak links.

There are numerous types of weak link, ranging from the somewhat inconsistent piece of thin rope to mechanical assemblies designed to litter the site with bolts and shackles which then lie waiting to damage grass-cutter blades. It would be tedious to discuss their design in detail, but it is worth defining the properties of the ideal device:

1 Its breaking load should be within 5% of the nominal value.
2 It should not increase in strength after a few applications of load (as a consequence of work-hardening, for example). Nor should it show a large decrease in strength in similar circumstances, since failures then become frequent and the operator is tempted to fit a link of excessive initial strength.
3 It should not be significantly affected by moisture, corrosion, or abrasion on the ground over a reasonable period.
4 Replacement of the breakable component should be rapid and cheap, preferably without using tools. Nuts and bolts, or other components which can easily be lost, should be avoided.

One design which has been found satisfactory uses a 12-swg (0.104-in.) steel nail as the shear pin and breaks at 1100 lb. The British figure of 1000 lb is obtained with mild steel wire of 0.098-in. (2.5-mm) diameter. This material, surprisingly enough, is used in this country for making the wire coat-hangers used by dry-cleaners.

COCKPIT LOADS

In most gliders the cockpit is well forward of the centre of gravity position of the laden machine, so the smaller the cockpit load, the further aft is the laden CG position. The minimum cockpit load is determined by the aftmost permitted CG position which, in its turn, depends on maintaining acceptable stability or spin recovery characteristics. In this context cockpit load refers primarily to the pilot, plus parachute (18−20 lb) and any other items (cameras, etc.) which the pilot carries with him.

As the centre of gravity of the laden glider is moved further aft, so the longitudinal stability worsens. In a rather rough fashion, the effect can be seen from Fig. 20.12. In the upper

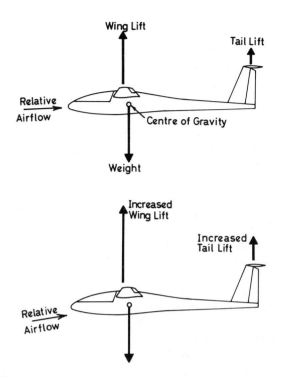

Fig 20.12 Diagram to illustrate longitudinal stability

diagram, the glider is flying in equilibrium. It is then disturbed
so that the angle of attack increases and consequently the
wing and tail lifts both increase. At the same time, the wing
centre of pressure moves further forwards. It is clear that the
increase in wing lift, coupled with the forward shift of the
centre of pressure, gives rise to an additional nose-up pitching
moment about the centre of gravity, whilst the effect of the
extra tail lift is to provide an additional nose-down moment.
If the glider is to have a tendency to revert to its original angle
of attack, the overall effect should be a nose-down moment;
in other words, the stabilizing effect of the tail should exceed
the destabilizing effect of the wing. As the centre of gravity
is moved further aft, the effect of the tail decreases slightly
whilst that of the wing increases appreciably. When they just
cancel out, the glider has neutral stability and the correspond-

ing CG position is appropriately called the *Neutral Point.* If the CG is forward of the neutral point, the glider will be stable, whilst if it is aft, the glider will be unstable.

The above explanation is, to say the least, lacking in mathematical rigour and does not entirely correspond to the state of affairs which aerodynamicists envisage when performing static stability calculations. The term 'static stability' indicates that interest is concentrated on the tendency to return to the original steady condition of flight after a disturbance, it being assumed that the vertical forces are in equilibrium at all times. In the lower diagram, this condition is not satisfied. However, the above explanation indicates the general trend.

In considering the tendency of the glider to revert to the original condition of flight, the changes of tail lift with angle of attack are obviously important. For a given change in the angle of attack (at a certain speed) the changes of tail lift obviously depend on what is happening to the elevator. If it is held fixed, the whole tail behaves like a rigid wing. If, on the other hand, it is allowed to float freely, it usually tends to move upwards when the angle of attack is increased. The increase in lift is therefore less than in the elevator-fixed case, and the stabilizing effect of the tail is correspondingly reduced. These two situations, referred to as 'stick-fixed' and 'stick-free' respectively, obviously represent extreme conditions, neither of which necessarily corresponds to a real condition of flight. Incidentally, the above explanation only relates to a glider with a fixed tailplane and a separate elevator. In the case of gliders with all-moving tails, the stick-free stability may be equal to or even greater than the stick-fixed stability.

Now, the stability of a glider is not only related to its behaviour after meeting a disturbance but also, as one might intuitively expect, to the actions which the pilot must take when he wishes to alter the conditions of flight. A very stable machine will not only tend to revert rather quickly to its original angle of attack after a disturbance, but will also tend to resist the efforts of the pilot when he wishes to introduce a deliberate disturbance. Such intentional disturbances may be visualized as changes in angle of attack, which ultimately appear as changes of speed if the lift is always equal to the weight. As it turns out, the stick-fixed stability is associated with the change of stick position required to alter conditions from one steady speed to another, whilst the stick-free stability is associated with the corresponding stick forces, assuming that the trimmer position is left unaltered. Whilst the pilot is not very conscious of the stick positions corresponding to various steady speeds — as opposed to the movements required to initiate the changes — he is very aware of the stick forces. If he has to pull by 2 lb to reduce speed by 5 knots, he will declare the elevator control to be very heavy and will become irritated by the need to make incessant adjustments to the trimmer to cancel out the stick forces.

The main interest, so far as the pilot is concerned, is therefore associated with stick-free stability. If the glider becomes unstable, stick-fixed, the effects may not be very noticeable, although the stick-fixed instability should not be too great. On the other hand, stick-free instability can be very unpleasant and even dangerous: if the pilot increases the speed above some trimmed value, he finds himself pulling on the stick to prevent the speed increasing still further.

The minimum cockpit load is such that the centre of gravity of the laden glider is sufficiently far forward to provide reasonable stick forces. If this limitation is ignored, the forces become excessively light and the glider feels distinctly twitchy, or the forces may even become reversed.

So far, only the stick force required to alter the speed by a certain amount, from one steady value to another, has been considered. Stick forces are also involved in pitching manoeuvres. For example, if a glider is trimmed to fly at, say, 85 knots and a loop is started, it might require a pull-force on the stick of 10 lb. The initial load factor might be about three, of which one is due to the ordinary force of gravity and two are due to the upwards acceleration. In this case, the resultant upwards force, due to the extra lift, would be twice the weight of the glider, and the resulting acceleration would be twice that due to gravity, or $2g$. So the stick force per g would be 5 lb/g in this case. The stick force per g is a measure of the manoeuvrability of the glider and is also associated with the pilot's subjective impression of the lightness of the elevator. Values around 10 lb/g feel distinctly heavy, whilst 3 lb/g is quite light—to the extent that some practice is required before the average pilot feels entirely happy. Again, as the centre of gravity is moved further aft, the stick force per g decreases, but the glider will always run out of stick-free stability before the stick force per g becomes zero. However, one could visualize a situation in which the aftmost acceptable centre of gravity position depended on maintaining a reasonable stick force/g.

The nature of the spin, and spin recovery, are both influenced by centre of gravity position. With the centre of gravity well forward, many gliders will not perform a genuine spin. Attempts to spin result in a spiral dive with most of the wing unstalled and with the speed and load factor increasing rapidly. As mentioned above, recovery should be made before excessive speeds or loads are attained, and there is no particular problem in recovery except that of accidentally going too fast whilst still pointing nose-down.

When the centre of gravity is moved further aft, a point is reached at which a genuine spin can be performed. All or most of the wing is thoroughly stalled and the rate of rotation and rate of descent are more-or-less steady. Further aft centre of gravity positions produce a flatter spin, and the motion may sometimes be rather oscillatory. Most gliders have to be held into a spin by keeping the rudder fully deflected and holding the stick fully back, and recovery often starts immediately either control is moved from its extreme position. However, there is a standard procedure, as follows:

1 Apply full opposite rudder (i.e., against the direction of rotation of the spin);
2 pause;
3 ease the control column forward until the rotation ceases;
4 centralize rudder and allow the glider to dive out.

In many cases, the spin stops immediately one starts (*1*), but one occasionally encounters situations in which (*1*) and (*2*) have no effect, and the spin only stops as a consequence of (*3*). The further aft the centre of gravity, the more reluctant is the glider to recover, as a rule. So the aftmost acceptable centre of gravity position may well be determined by spin recovery. If this is so, an excessively aft centre of gravity position is very dangerous: even if the glider will eventually respond to action (*3*), a pilot accustomed to more usual characteristics is likely to find this situation very disconcerting indeed.

The maximum cockpit load is very often simply the difference between the maximum all-up weight of the glider, as determined by stressing considerations, and the empty weight. Exceeding the maximum all-up weight means that proof stresses will be attained in various parts of the structure at load factors lower than those shown in the Manoeuvring and Gust Envelopes, so the glider is effectively weakened. Since the extra load is in the cockpit, and not uniformly distributed over the structure, the effect is rather like the towing cable load during a winch-launch, as in Fig. 20.11. The effective reduction in strength is appreciably more than the percentage by which the glider is overweight.

Occasionally, the maximum cockpit load is determined by the most forward permitted centre of gravity position. This may be fixed either by stressing considerations (usually the tail-load at high speeds), or by the ability to flare-out for landing after a slow approach.

To summarize this section, the minimum cockpit load may depend on one or more of the following:

1 Minimum acceptable stick-free stability (and hence changes of stick force with speed);
2 Minimum acceptable stick force per *g* (rather unlikely);
3 Spin recovery.

The maximum cockpit load may be determined by:

1 Maximum permitted all-up weight (from the stressing point of view), or
2 Most forward acceptable centre of gravity position (either as it affects stressing or ability to flare-out).

BALLAST

Many modern gliders are designed with provision to carry water ballast in the wings to improve the performance when the thermals are strong (Chapter 12.). The ballast is usually contained in tanks, either integral or of rubberized fabric, fitted ahead of the main shear web. The additional load is therefore distributed over part of the span and leads to a downward bending moment at the wing root which partly cancels out the extra upward bending moment due to the increase in overall lift. On the other hand, the bending moment outboard of the tanks is not subject to any such relief so the carriage of water ballast invariably leads to increased stresses somewhere along the wing. In many gliders, the tank capacity is such that the machine may be overweight if the pilot is heavy and the tanks are completely filled: it cannot be said too loudly that the maximum weight stated by the manufacturer must not be exceeded. If necessary, the tanks should be only partly filled. Even more dangerous than pouring in too much water is the practice of carrying lead weights in the fuselage to increase the total weight still further on days of strong thermals. The effect is analogous to the winch launch situation shown in Fig. 20.11, in that the wing-root bending moment is increased by appreciably more than the proportional increase in total weight.

In the case of a typical Libelle, the maximum water ballast (110 lb) can always be carried if the cockpit load is between 134 lb and 198 lb. If the cockpit load is more than 198 lb the water ballast must be reduced and only 80 lb can be carried with maximum cockpit load of 228 lb. The minimum and maximum cockpit loads correspond to the aft and forward CG limits respectively.

In principle, more complicated situations can arise. The water ballast is usually slightly ahead of the most forward permitted CG position, so the maximum cockpit load may be limited by this consideration when full ballast is carried. In German practice, it it not unusual to state a maximum weight for the non-lifting parts (i.e., everything other than the wings). This limit may determine the maximum cockpit load, rather than the maximum all-up weight or the forward CG limit, which in turn may have repercussions on the ballasting.

Whatever the limitations may be, there is a good reason for their existence and they should not be exceeded.

CONCLUDING REMARKS

The Design Requirements for gliders are framed so that there is usually little difficulty in observing the limitations even under severe operating conditions. They confer a very high degree of safety, but the penalty for exceeding them can be severe. Unless a pilot is deliberately foolhardy, they are only likely to be exceeded as a consequence of some untoward occurrence, such as loss of control in cloud coupled with failure to use the airbrakes. In such a case, the pilot should report the occurrence and have the machine inspected.

Appendix 1

A Note on Units

This book is primarily written for those who use the English system of units and hence the units which occur in the text are those most likely to be encountered by practising pilots for some time to come, notwithstanding the intention to convert the UK to the metric system. However, it is an international convention in sporting aviation that flights for records and badges are reckoned in metric units, and consequently one tends to think of total flight distances in kilometres.

In the UK, the convention is to calibrate airspeed indicators, in all types of aircraft, in knots and it is then logical to use nautical miles for horizontal distance. Feet are the normal units of height and are likely to remain so as long as aeronautical maps give spot heights in feet. Vertical speed can be expressed in ft/s, ft/min or knots: knots are most convenient since the gliding ratio can be calculated mentally when both vertical and horizontal speeds are in the same units. Another advantage is that calculations of time to gain or lose a certain height can be done very simply in conjunction with an altimeter calibrated in feet, since one knot is very nearly 100 ft/min.

From the pilot's point of view, using knots for both vertical and horizontal speeds, nautical miles for horizontal distance and feet for height, forms a reasonably coherent system. One may wish to convert distances into kilometres, but there is little point in using units such as statute miles, mile/h or ft/min, since they complicate the arithmetic. Throughout this book, miles have been taken to be nautical miles (6080 ft).

Countries using metric units invariably express distances in kilometres, forward speed in km/h, height in metres and vertical speeds in m/s. This usage conforms with standard practice in such countries and the conventions of SI units (see below) but is inconvenient in two respects: calculation of glide angle involves multiplying the rate of sink by 3.6, and the calibration of sensitive altimeters becomes somewhat awkward. One either has one revolution per 1000 m, which gives a rather coarse scale, or sometimes one revolution per 500 m which, despite a sub-scale, can lead to dangerous confusion. In these respects, an altimeter having one revolution per 1000 ft is a much more satisfactory instrument. Ultimately the metric system could be improved by expressing vertical speeds in km/h and by using digital altimeters.

The above is written from the pilot's viewpoint, but we must also consider the designer who, in gliding, tends to enjoy a close rapport with pilots. For aeronautical engineering purposes, the English system of units is based on the foot for distance, the second for time and the slug for mass. A slug is a mass of 32.174 lb. Hence the unit of air density, for example, is $slug/ft^3$. Using such units in expressions for aerodynamic force (e.g. equations **16.1, 16.2, 16.3, 16.5** and **16.8** of Chapter 16) in conjunction with areas in ft^2 and velocities in ft/s gives forces in pound-force (lbf) units (the force due to standard gravity acting on a mass of one pound). This is convenient when one thinks of the weight of the aeroplane expressed in pounds – strictly pounds-force. Provided that consistency is maintained, this system presents no difficulties if one remembers that moment of inertia should be expressed in $slug.ft^2$ and viscosity (see Appendix 6) in slug/ft sec.

However, this country is committed to 'metrication' and will ultimately use the Système International d'Unités (otherwise known as SI units). This is based on the metre for distance, the second for time and the kilogramme for mass; The unit of density is therefore kg/m^3. On this basis, the standard sea-level air density (in English units, 0.002377 $slug/ft^3$) becomes 1.225 kg/m^3. The unit of force is that which produces an acceleration of 1 m/s^2 on a mass of 1 kg and is called the newton, symbol N.

It therefore follows that if, in the equations mentioned above, density is in kg/m^3, areas are in m^2 and velocities are in m/s, the aerodymic forces will be in N. This system is entirely logical in that forces are not *defined* with respect to the effect of some rather arbitrary gravity on a given mass. In practice, we must consider forces due to gravity since, for example, in steady level flight, the aerodynamic lift force balances the weight. Since the international standard gravity value is 9.807 m/s^2 it follows that the force due to gravity acting on a mass of 1 kg is 9.807 N. Hence, if we have a glider whose mass is 360 kg and whose wing area is 13 m^2, its weight will be 3530 N, and its wing loading, being strictly a force per unit area, will be 272 N/m^2. In dealing with SI units, one is encouraged to use multiples or submultiples obtained by multiplying the basic unit by 10^3, 10^6, etc., or 10^{-3}, 10^{-6}, etc., respectively. The above weight then becomes, more briefly, 3.53 kilonewtons or 3.53 kN. It may be useful to remember that 1 N = 0.2248 lb force, or roughly the weight of an apple.

It should also be remembered that SI units do not always correspond with current usage in 'metric' countries. For example, a common unit of force is the kilopond (kp). This is the force due to gravity acting on a mass of one kilogramme. It is sometimes called the kilogramme-force and is analogous to the English pound-force.

One often finds the weights of aircraft expressed in kp and wing loadings in kp/m^2.

There is, however, an increasing tendency to refer to 'mass' rather than 'weight' (e.g., Empty mass = 230 kg), to quote forces in newtons (e.g., Maximum weak link strength = 5000 N or 5 kN) and to indulge in even more esoteric SI units, such as tyre pressures in bars (1 bar = 10^5 N/m^2, slightly less than standard sea-level atmospheric pressure).

At present, most pilots will find these units unfamiliar and so this book has been written in terms of current English usage. SI units are finding increasing favour in technical writing, including Airworthiness Requirements, and there is no doubt that, eventually pilots and designers will have to make use of them.

SI units are explained fully in *Changing to the Metric System,* 3rd Ed., HMSO, 1969.

Conversion Factors

Distances, Areas and Volume

1 in = 2.54 cm, exactly	1 cm = 0.3937 in
1 ft = 0.3048 m	1 m = 3.2808 ft

1 statute mile = 5280 ft = 1.609 km
1 km = 3281 ft = 0.622 miles
1 nautical mile = 6080 ft = 1.151 statute miles
$\qquad$ = 1.853 km

1 in^2 = 6.452 cm^2	1 ft^2 = 0.0929 m^2

1 Imperial gallon = 4.546 litres

Masses and Forces

1 lb = 0.4536 kg	1 kg = 2.2046 lb
1 N = 0.2248 lbf	1 lbf = 4.4482 N

Wing Loadings and Pressures

1 lb/ft^2 = 4.88 kg/m^2	1 kg/m^2 = 0.2048 lb/ft^2
1 lbf/in^2 = 0.07 kp/cm^2	1 kp/cm^2 = 14.2 lbf/in^2
1 bar = 10^5 N/m^2	1 millibar = 100 N/m^2

Map Scales

1/250,000 = 0.253 in. to the statute mile (approx $\frac{1}{4}$ in. to the mile)
$\qquad$ = 0.292 in. to the nautical mile
1/500,000 = 0.127 in. to the statute mile (approx $\frac{1}{8}$ in. to the mile)
$\qquad$ = 0.146 in. to the nautical mile.

Miscellaneous

Standard gravitational acceleration, g = 32.174 ft/s^2
$\qquad\qquad\qquad\qquad\qquad\quad$ = 9.807 m/s^2

1 Radian = 57.29°   1 ft^3 of water has a mass of 62.4 lb
To convert temperatures in °C to °F, multiply by 9/5 and add 32°.

Some Round Figures

π = 22/7   1 in.= $2\frac{1}{2}$ cm   1 m = $3\frac{1}{4}$ ft
1 km = 5/8 mile   1 m^2 = 10 ft^2
1 kg = $2\frac{1}{4}$ lb   1 lb/ft^2 = 5 kg/m^2

Appendix 3

Conversion Scales and Equivalents

Table A3.1 Speed conversion scales

V_i knots	W.G. in.	V_i mile/h	W.G. in.
10	0.07	10	0.05
20	0.26	20	0.20
30	0.59	30	0.44
40	1.04	40	0.79
50	1.63	50	1.23
60	2.35	60	1.77
70	3.19	70	2.41
80	4.18	80	3.15
90	5.28	90	3.99
100	6.52	100	4.93
110	7.89	110	5.96
120	9.40	120	7.09
130	11.02	130	8.33
140	12.78	140	9.66
150	14.68	150	11.08
		160	12.61
		170	14.24

Table A3.2 Airspeed-water gauge equivalents for A.S.I. calibration

The right-hand table gives the dynamic pressures corresponding to equivalent airspeeds in knots and mile/h, expressed in inches water gauge. The figures are obtained from the following relationships, which do not include the effect of compressibility of the air.

Water guage, in. $= 0.000652 \ (V_i \ \text{knots})^2 = 0.000493 \ (V_i \ \text{m.p.h.})^2$

366

Appendix 4

The ICAO Standard Atmosphere

Height	Temperature	Speed of sound	Pressure (p)		Density (ρ)	$\left(\dfrac{\rho}{\rho_0}\right)^{\frac{1}{2}}$
ft	°C	knots	lb/ft^2	mb	slug/ft^3	
0	15.00	661.3	2116.2	1013.2	0.002377	1.0000
1000	13.02	659.0	2040.9	977.2	0.002308	0.9854
2000	11.04	656.8	1967.7	942.1	0.002241	0.9710
3000	9.06	654.5	1896.6	908.1	0.002175	0.9566
4000	7.08	652.2	1827.7	875.1	0.002111	0.9424
5000	5.10	649.9	1760.8	843.1	0.002048	0.9283
6000	3.11	647.5	1695.9	812.0	0.001987	0.9143
7000	+ 1.13	645.2	1632.9	781.9	0.001927	0.9004
8000	− 0.85	642.9	1571.9	752.6	0.001868	0.8866
9000	− 2.83	640.5	1512.7	724.3	0.001811	0.8729
10,000	− 4.81	638.2	1455.3	696.8	0.001755	0.8594
11,000	− 6.79	635.8	1399.7	670.2	0.001701	0.8459
12,000	− 8.77	633.5	1345.9	644.4	0.001648	0.8326
13,000	− 10.76	631.1	1293.7	619.4	0.001596	0.8193
14,000	− 12.74	628.7	1243.2	595.2	0.001545	0.8062
15,000	− 14.72	626.3	1194.3	571.8	0.001496	0.7932
16,000	− 16.70	623.9	1146.9	549.1	0.001447	0.7804
17,000	− 18.68	621.5	1101.1	527.2	0.001401	0.7676
18,000	− 20.66	619.0	1056.8	506.0	0.001355	0.7549
19,000	− 22.64	616.6	1013.9	485.5	0.001310	0.7424
20,000	− 24.62	614.2	972.5	465.6	0.001266	0.7299
25,000	− 34.53	601.8	785.3	376.0	0.001065	0.6694
30,000	− 44.44	589.2	628.4	300.9	0.000889	0.6116
35,000	− 54.34	576.3	498.0	238.4	0.000737	0.5567
36,089	− 56.50	573.4	472.7	226.3	0.000706	0.5450
40,000	− 56.50	573.4	381.7	187.5	0.0005851	0.4962
50,000	− 56.50	573.4	242.2	116.0	0.0003618	0.3902
60,000	− 56.50	573.4	149.8	71.7	0.0002238	0.3068

Barometric Pressure

1013.2 mb. = 760 mm. Mercury = 29.92 in. Mercury = 14.7 lb/in.^{2}

Appendix 5

Lift Coefficients, Wing Loading and Speeds

As explained in Chapter 16, the lift of an aircraft may be written in the form

$$L = C_L \tfrac{1}{2} \rho_0 V_i^2 S \qquad \text{(A5.1)}$$

where
L = lift (lb)
C_L = lift coefficient
ρ_0 = standard sea-level air density (slug/ft^3)
V_i = equivalent airspeed (ft/s)
S = wing area (ft^2)

In steady level flight, the lift is equal to the weight W, and the above equation then becomes:

$$w = C_L \tfrac{1}{2} \rho_0 V_i^2 \qquad \text{(A5.2)}$$

where
w = wing loading, W/S (lb/ft^2)

Inserting the value of ρ_0 (0.00238 slug/ft^3), and putting V_i in knots instead of ft/s, equation (A5.2) becomes

$$w = 0.0034 \, C_L \, (V_i \text{ knots})^2 \qquad \text{(A5.3)}$$

The curves of Fig. A5.1 have been derived from this expression using values likely to be appropriate to gliders.

If the true airspeed is required when flying under conditions other than standard sea-level, it may be obtained from the expression

$$V = V_i / \sqrt{\sigma} \qquad \text{(A5.4)}$$

where
$\sigma = \rho/\rho_0$

and
ρ = local air density (slug/ft^3).

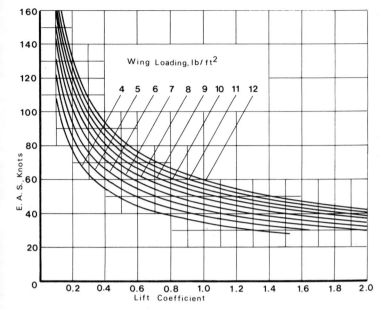

Fig A5.1 Relationship between equivalent airspeed and lift coefficient for various wing-loading

The lift coefficient is a dimensionless quantity which depends on the geometry of the wing (strictly, of the complete aircraft), the angle of attack, the Reynolds number and the Mach number. The last quantity is unlikely to be of any significance in gliders. If the equivalent airspeed and height are given, for a machine operating at a certain wing loading, then the Reynolds number (see Appendix 6) and lift coefficient are fixed. These quantities then determine the angle of attack at which it must be flown.

Example. A Standard Libelle has a wing area of 102 ft^2. What will be its lift coefficient when it is flying at an equivalent airspeed of 60 knots and an all-up weight of 670 lb?

Wing loading = 670/102 = 6.57 lb/ft^2. Interpolating between the 6 and 7 lb/ft^2 lines of Fig. A5.1, C_L = 0.54.

Appendix 6

Reynolds Number

As mentioned in Chapter 15, Reynolds number is a dimensionless quantity which expresses the ratio of the inertia forces to the viscous forces in the flow of a fluid. It is an important parameter in determining the behaviour of the boundary layer on the surface of a wing or body. In the case of a wing section, the curve of drag coefficient against lift coefficient depends on the Reynolds number, as do various other section properties such as the maximum lift coefficient. When considering wing section data, it is therefore essential to use figures relating to the correct Reynolds number. Unfortunately, glider wings operate in the range 0.5×10^6 to 5×10^6, where the section characteristics are often fairly sensitive to Reynolds number.

Reynolds number is defined as:

$$R_e = \frac{\rho V l}{\mu} \qquad \text{(A6.1)}$$

where
ρ = air density (slug/ft^3),
V = true airspeed (ft/s),
l = a characteristic length (ft) (the chord in the case of wings),
μ = viscosity of the air (slug/ft s).

An alternative way of writing the above expression is:

$$R_e = \frac{V l}{\nu} \qquad \text{(A6.2)}$$

where $\nu = \mu/\rho$, and is called the 'kinematic viscosity' of the air. Its units are ft^2/s.

If equivalent airspeed V_i is to be used in preference to true airspeed, V

in the above expressions must be replaced by $V_i/\sqrt{\sigma}$, where σ is the density of the atmosphere relative to sea-level conditions. Moreover, if V_i is expressed in knots, instead of ft/s, equation (A6.2) finally becomes

$$R_e = \frac{1.69\,V_i l}{\nu\sqrt{\sigma}} \qquad (A6.3)$$

For the purpose of the curves in Fig. A6.1, l is taken as 1 ft. Hence, to obtain the actual Reynolds number of a wing section, the value obtained from the curves must be multiplied by the chord in feet.

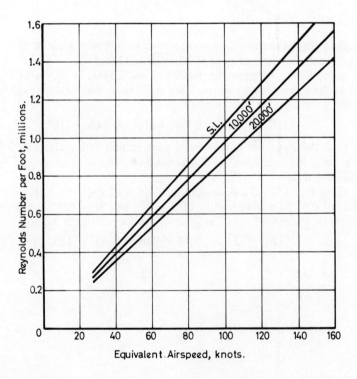

Fig A6.1 Relationship between Reynolds number per ft and equivalent airspeed at various heights

Values of $\sqrt{\sigma}$ and ν relating to the I.C.A.O. Standard Atmosphere have been used, as follows

Height (ft)	ν (ft²/s)	$\sqrt{\sigma}$
0	1.576×10^{-4}	1.000
10,000	2.015×10^{-4}	0.8594
20,000	2.624×10^{-4}	0.7299

In round figures, the Reynolds number at sea level is given by:

$$6,400 \times \text{chord (ft)} \times \text{speed (ft/s)}$$

or

$$10,800 \times \text{chord (ft)} \times \text{speed (knots)}.$$

Examples

1. Find the Reynolds number of a wing section with a chord of 3 ft 6 in. at an equivalent airspeed of 80 knots at 12,000 ft.

Interpolating between the 10,000 ft and 20,000 ft curves of Fig. A6.1, the Reynolds number per foot at 80 knots and 12,000 ft will be 0.765×10^6. So, for a chord of 3.5 ft,

$$R_e = 3.5 \times 0.765 \times 10^6 = 2.68 \times 10^6.$$

2. Find the Reynolds number of a wing section with a chord of 3 ft 6 in. at a lift coefficient of 0.8 at sea-level. The wing loading of the glider is 5 lb/ft².

From Fig. A5.1, the equivalent airspeed is 43 knots for a lift coefficient of 0.8 and a wing loading of 5 lb/ft². The Reynolds Number per foot is therefore 0.47×10^6 at sea-level. So, for a chord of 3.5 ft,

$$R_e = 3.5 \times 0.47 \times 10^6 = 1.65 \times 10^6.$$

Appendix 7

Analysis of Performance Curves

Equation **16.16** showed that, with the lift equal to the weight, the rate of sink of a glider is theoretically given by

$$WV_{si} = AV_i^3 + B/V_i \qquad (A7.1)$$

More generally, if the load factor is n, the second term of this expression should be multiplied by n^2 but, for the present purposes, the above expression is sufficiently accurate. For most modern fixed-geometry gliders, the shape of the polar corresponds remarkably well to such an expression except, perhaps, at low speeds.

Differentiating **(A7.1)** shows that the glide angle (V_{si}/V_i) will be a minimum, at an equivalent airspeed V_{i_0}, where

$$V_{i_0} = \sqrt[4]{B/A}. \qquad (A7.2)$$

The equivalent rate of sink at V_{i_0} will then be V_{si_0}, where

$$WV_{si_0} = 2A^{\frac{1}{4}}B^{\frac{3}{4}}. \qquad (A7.3)$$

Combining these three expressions enables **(A7.1)** to be written in dimensionless terms as follows

$$V_{si}/V_{si_0} = \tfrac{1}{2}[(V_i/V_{i_0})^3 + (V_{i_0}/V_i)]. \qquad (A7.4)$$

Also, with the lift substantially equal to the weight, it follows from equation **(16.14)** that the best gliding angle condition also corresponds to the maximum lift/drag ratio, i.e.,

$$V_{i_0}/V_{si_0} = (L/D)_{max}. \qquad (A7.5)$$

Equation **(A7.4)** therefore suggests that the performance curves of all fixed-geometry gliders are basically of the same shape.

373

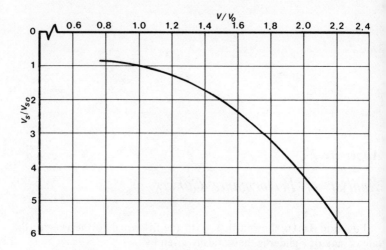

Fig A7.1 The 'universal polar' in which rate of sink is plotted against forward speed, both quantities being divided by the value appropriate to $(L/D)_{max}$. The speeds may either be 'true' as shown here, or 'equivalent', as in the equations of the text

If, from equation **(A7.4)**, V_{si}/V_{si_0} is plotted as a function of V_i/V_{i_0}, we have a 'universal polar' applicable to any fixed-geometry glider (Fig. A7.1). The ordinates of this curve are as shown in Table A7.1.

V_i/V_{i_0}	0.76	0.80	0.90	1.00	1.10	1.20	1.40	1.60	1.80	2.00	2.20	2.40
V_{si}/V_{si_0}	0.877	0.881	0.920	1.000	1.120	1.281	1.729	2.361	3.194	4.250	5.551	7.120

Table A7.1 Ordinates of the dimensionless performance curve

To find the polar of an actual glider, one simply multiplies the top row of figures by V_{i_0} and the bottom row by V_{si_0}. The complete performance is therefore defined by these two quantities, or by V_{i_0} and $(L/D)_{max}$.

This method of presenting glider performance is ultimately based on the earlier assumption that a plot of C_D against C_L^2 gives a straight line. As Fig. 16.3 indicates, this is often quite a good assumption except at high lift coefficients.

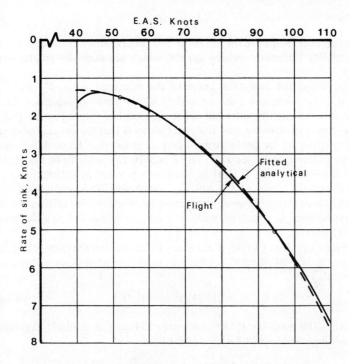

Fig A7.2 A fitted analytical curve from Fig A7.1 compared with the measured polar of the Standard Libelle at W = 695 lb

For reasons which are explained below, it is often convenient to fit an analytical curve corresponding to equation (**A7.4**) to the measured performance of a glider. In general, such a curve can only be made to pass through two measured points. Substituting the two sets of values of V_i and V_{si} corresponding to the chosen points in equation (**A7.4**) gives two simultaneous equations which can be solved for V_{i_0} and V_{si_0}, thus enabling other points on the analytical curve to be calculated. Applying this process to the measured performance of the Libelle is illustrated in Fig. A7.2. In this case, the points chosen corresponding to speeds of 52 knots and 94 knots, leading to V_{i_0} = 51.36 knots, V_{si_0} = 1.489 knots. It will be seen that the agreement is remarkably good at speeds above about 50 knots. The greatest discrepancy in rate of sink is of the order of 0.1 knots, probably within the limits of the original experimental error. The analytical curve tends to be optimistic at low speeds and is not of much value near minimum sink. This is not of great consequence, since the usefulness of this process arises in the context of calculating optimum cruising speeds, which are normally greater than V_{i_0}.

In fitting the analytical curve to the measured polar, V_{i_0} and V_{si_0} need to be calculated quite accurately by the method explained above and may be slightly different from the nominal values for the glider. The object of deriving this analytical curve is that the process of drawing tangents to the performance curve as in Chapter 16 to derive optimum gliding speeds (see Figs. 16.13 and 16.15) tends to be inaccurate and time-consuming. It is often simpler to proceed by calculation, having found the values of V_{i_0} and V_{si_0} which give fit the actual performance curve reasonably well. From now on, the 'i' in the suffices will be dropped since, in equations such as (A7.4), all speeds can be either equivalent or true.

From equation (A7.4), it can easily be shown that the relationship between the rate of climb V_c (or $V_c + V_a$) and the optimum speed between thermals V is

$$V_c/V_{s_0} = (V/V_0)^3 - (V_0/V). \qquad (A7.6)$$

Also, the quantity $V_c + V_b$ (see page 254) can be similarly expressed by adding equations (A7.4) and (A7.6):

$$(V_c + V_b)/V_{s_0} = \tfrac{1}{2}[3(V/V_0)^3 - (V_0/V)]. \qquad (A7.7)$$

A convenient procedure is then as follows: Having found V_0 and V_{s_0} as described above, convenient values of V (to be engraved on the MacCready ring) are chosen. The corresponding values of V/V_0 are then inserted in (A7.6) and (A7.7) to give V_c/V_{s_0} and $(V_c + V_b)/V_{s_0}$. Knowing V_{s_0}, V_c and $(V_c + V_b)$ can then be found.

Using the above values of V_0 and V_{s_0} for Libelle, the calculation is as tabulated in Table A7.2. opposite.

Tables 16.2 and 16.3 were obtained in this fashion.

When a glider is fitted with flaps, each flap-setting will correspond to slightly different values of V_0 and V_{s_0}. However, a good approximation to the envelope of the performance curves can sometimes be obtained from a single pair of values. For example, taking $V_0 = 57$ knots, $V_{s_0} = 1.313$ knots, gives a very good fit to the manufacturer's curve for the Kestrel 19 at $W = 1040$ lb at speeds between 55 and 110 knots. The maximum error is only 0.08 knots rate of sink. The above method of calculation can therefore be used with considerably accuracy.

Effects of speed errors. Equation (A7.4) is also useful in deriving various generalised conclusions about glider performance which serve

V knots	V/V_0	V_c/V_{s_0}	V_c knots	$(V_c + V_b)/V_{s_0}$	$(V_c + V_b)$ knots
51	0.993	0	0	1	1.49
55	1.071	0.294	0.44	1.375	2.05
60	1.168	0.738	1.10	1.962	2.92
65	1.266	1.237	1.84	2.649	3.94
70	1.363	1.798	2.68	3.431	5.11
75	1.460	2.429	3.62	4.326	6.44
80	1.558	3.137	4.67	5.352	7.97
85	1.655	3.929	5.85	6.498	9.68
90	1.752	4.810	7.16	7.781	11.59
95	1.850	5.788	8.62	9.227	13.74
100	1.947	6.868	10.23	10.814	16.10

Table A7.2 MacCready calculations for the Libelle

to show that one should not attach too much importance to the above calculations or the devices explained in Chapters 16 and 18. Indeed, they cannot provide precise information since one important quantity, V_c, cannot be assessed with any great accuracy.

First of all, suppose that V_c is accurately known but the pilot glides at a speed which differs from the appropriate optimum value. If the effect of downdraughts is ignored and if the performance curve corresponds to equation (A7.4), it may be shown that the deficit in average speed, $\delta \bar{V}$, is given by

$$\delta \bar{V}/\bar{V} = -[\delta V/V]^2 [3V^4 + V_0^4]/[3V^4 - V_0^4].$$

$$(A7.8)$$

Here, V is the optimum gliding speed corresponding to the rate of climb V_c, δV is the error in gliding speed and V_0, as usual, is the speed for $(L/D)_{max}$. In this expression, all of the speeds can be either true or 'equivalent'. This expression can also be written

$$\delta \bar{V}/\bar{V} = -E[\delta V/V]^2,$$

$$(A7.9)$$

where E depends on V/V_0, as shown in figure A7.3.

For the Libelle at $W = 695$ lb, $V_0 = 51.4$ knots. If the optimum gliding speed should have been 75 knots, $V/V_0 = 1.46$ and hence $E = 1.158$. If the actual gliding speed is 65 knots, $\delta V/V = 0.133$, and hence $\delta \bar{V}/\bar{V} = 0.021$. So the loss in average speed will be about 2% of the theoretical figure of 42 knots which corresponded to 75 knots gliding speed (see Figure 16.14).

Another, and much more usual possibility, is that the actual value of V_c is not the same as the assumed value to which the datum of the

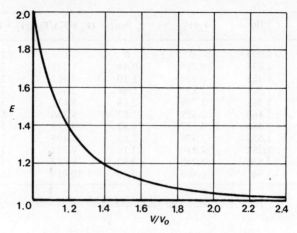

Fig A7.3 E plotted as a function of V/V_0

MacCready ring has been set. If the error in the datum setting is δV_c, it follows from equation **(A7.4)** that the gliding speed displayed by the MacCready ring will be in error by δV

$$\delta V/V = [\delta V_c/V_c][V^4 - V_0^4]/[3V^4 + V_0^4]$$

(A7.10)

Here, V is the optimum gliding speed corresponding to the correct value of V_c.

This can also be written

$$\delta V/V = G[\delta V_c/V_c]$$

(A7.11)

where G is a function of V/V_0, as shown in Figure A7.4.

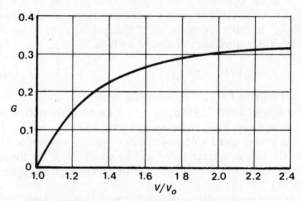

Fig A7.4 G plotted as a function of V/V_0

Again, taking the Libelle as an example, suppose V_c was actually 2.5 knots. The corresponding V is then 69 knots, V/V_0 is 1.342 and G is 0.21. If the ring had been set to 3.5 knots, $\delta V_c/V_c$ would be 0.4 and hence $\delta V/V$ would be 0.084. The pilot would therefore be told to fly too fast by $0.084 \times 69 = 5.8$ knots, or say 6 knots.

From Figure A7.3 and equation (**A7.9**), this error in gliding speed relative to a correct value of 69 knots will reduce the average speed from 35.4 knots to 35.1 knots, or by less than 1%.

These considerations show that quite large errors in gliding speed or in MacCready ring datum setting can be tolerated because their effects on the achieved average speed are second-order. There is therefore little to be gained by trying to control the glide very accurately, particularly since the whole basis of such control is likely to be in error. It is much more profitable to cultivate skill and judgement in the pursuit of improved rate of climb since this quantity has a first-order effect on the average speed.

It may be shown from the foregoing equations that, under optimised conditions, an increase in the rate of climb δV_c improves the average speed by $\delta \overline{V}$, where

$$\delta \overline{V}/\overline{V} = [\delta V_c/V_c][V^4 + V_0^4]/[3V^4 - V_0^4]$$

(**A7.12**)

This can be written

$$\delta \overline{V}/\overline{V} = F[\delta V_c/V_c]$$

(**A7.13**)

where F is a function of V/V_0 as shown in Figure A7.5

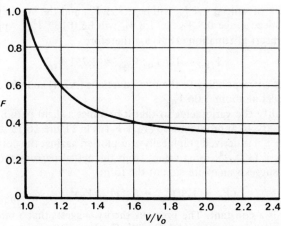

Fig A7.5 F plotted as a function of V/V_0

An improvement in V_c from 2.5 knots to 2.7 knots will increase the average cross-country speed of the Libelle from 35.4 knots to 36.8 knots, a gain of about 4%.

Approximation to the performance curve. In order to modify the variometer reading in ways which are explained in Chapter 18, it is necessary to make the assumption that the rate of sink of the glider is roughly proportional to the square of the speed over the speed range likely to be of interest when gliding between thermals. This is equivalent to assuming that the form of the performance curve is

$$V_s/V_{s_0} = k_1(V/V_0)^2. \qquad (A7.14)$$

It is clear that k_1 must be determined by some ad-hoc process so that equation (A7.14) is a reasonably good fit to the performance curve. The method suggested by Bruckner is to plot values of V_s against V^2, using the actual performance curve of the glider. One then draws the 'best' straight line through the plotted points and the origin. The slope of the line effectively determines k_1.

A more general result can be obtained by noting that, in a typical case, the straight line would intersect the accurate curve of V_s against V^2 at about 1.7 V_0. The constant k_1 can then be found by equating the right-hand sides of equations (A7.4) and (A7.14), having put V/V_0 equal to 1.7. The value of k_1 is then 0.952, so equation (A7.14) becomes

$$V_s/V_{s_0} = 0.952 (V/V_0)^2. \qquad (A7.15)$$

The rate of sink at 1.7 V_0 will be 2.751 V_{s_0} and the maximum error over the speed range 0.9 V_0 to 1.8 V_0 will be 0.137 V_{s_0}. Appropriate values to insert in equation (18.8) are therefore:

$$V_{i_1} = 1.7 V_0 ; V_{si_1} = 2.751 V_{s_0}.$$

The curves corresponding to the two equations (A7.4) and (A7.14) will also intersect at about 1.06 V_0.

To modify the variometer so that it becomes a flight path indicator, it is necessary to approximate to $(V_a + V_s)$ as in Figure 16.15 with $V_c = 0$. If $(V_a + V_s)$ is derived graphically and plotted against the corresponding values of $(V_{opt})^2$, using values from the actual performance curve, the result suggests an expression of the form

$$(V_a + V_s)/V_{s_0} = k_2(V_{opt}/V_0)^2 - V_k/V_{s_0} \qquad (A7.16)$$

where V_k is a constant. The previous theory suggests that a more accurate expression is equation (A7.7), with $V = V_{opt}$:

$$(V_a + V_s)/V_{s_0} = \tfrac{1}{2}[3(V_{opt}/V_0)^3 - (V_0/V_{opt})].$$

$$(A7.17)$$

If these two expressions are to have the same value at $V_{opt} = 1.06\ V_0$ and $1.7\ V_0$, then $k_2 = 3.26$ and $V_k = 2.35\ V_0$, so equation (A7.16) may be written

$$(V_a + V_s)/V_{s_0} = 3.26\ (V_{opt}/V_0)^2 - 2.35 \quad (A7.18)$$

Appendix 8

Thermal Velocity Profiles

It is a matter of common observation that, in a real thermal, there is a core where the strength of the upcurrent is greatest and the strength diminishes as one moves away from the core. This situation is implicit in the diagrams and explanations of Chapter 3, whilst the calculations of Chapter 16 assume a parabolic distribution of upcurrent velocity with distance from the centre. Such models assume that the thermals have an axis of symmetry whereas, in the real atmosphere, the shape is often much more irregular. Nevertheless, designers, handicappers, and others interested in performance calculations require some mathematical model which should, so far as possible, provide a reasonable idealisation of an "average" real thermal. The simplest requirement of such a model is that there should be a smooth gradation of upcurrent velocity with distance from the axis since, in a real atmosphere, the effects of turbulence and viscosity will tend to prevent the occurrence of sharp steps in both the velocity and the velocity gradient. A more elaborate requirement is that the velocity distribution should be such that the principle of continuity is satisfied (i.e. there should be regions of downwards velocity associated with the upcurrent so that there is no net transport of the atmosphere into outer space or through the Earth). The vertical velocity will then taper off to zero at large distances from the thermal. If one is only interested in conditions fairly close to the core, the latter requirement need not necessarily be simulated.

Power-Law Velocity Distributions. These are purely mathematical idealisations, with no physical justification except that they satisfy the first of the above requirements and can be made to provide reasonably realistic results if the numbers are appropriately chosen. They assume an expression of the following type:

$$V_T/V_{T_0} = 1 - (r/R)^n \tag{A8.1}$$

where V_{T_0} is the vertical velocity on the axis, i.e., where $r = 0$, and R is the "thermal radius", i.e., the value of r at which $V_T = 0$. The index n is conveniently taken to be an integer. If $n = 1$, the thermal profile is triangular: it therefore has a discontinuity in velocity gradient at $r = 0$ which, for reasons explained above, is unlikely to be realistic. However, such a thermal is not too different from one type postulated by Konovalov. Putting $n = 2$ gives a parabolic profile, a form commonly adopted for relatively simple analyses. For example, as explained in Chapter 16, the standard BGA thermal for handicapping purposes is parabolic with a core strength of 4.2 knots and a radius of 1000 ft. It therefore corresponds to

$$V_T = 4.2 \left[1 - (r/1000)^2 \right]. \tag{A8.2}$$

This may be regarded as the simplest plausible thermal profile provided that one is only interested in values of r appreciably less than R. At large values of r, the velocity gradient becomes very steep and, if $r > R$, there is a downdraught velocity which continues to increase as r increases.

If greater values of n are chosen (3 or 4, say), the thermal profile becomes more nearly rectangular and the velocity gradients near R begin to look unrealistic.

Spherical Bubbles. One concept of a thermal corresponds to an isolated bubble of warm air ascending through the atmosphere. If, for the moment, the bubble is assumed to be spherical and no mixing occurs at its surface, then the vertical velocity profile will be given by

$$V_T / V_{T_0} = \left[1 - (r/R)^2 \right] / \left[1 + 2(r/R)^2 \right]^{5/2}. \tag{A8.3}$$

This idealisation of the thermal looks fairly plausible but leads to a large region of low vertical velocity towards the outer regions. The velocity profile, up to $r/R =$ about 0.5, is fairly close to a parabolic shape, a situation which imparts some justification to the use of the latter profile. The expression given above corresponds to the flow produced by a 'doublet' located at the centre of the spherical bubble.

The above expression only defines the shape of the vertical velocity distribution and is independent of height relative to the centre of the bubble. Strictly, it does not apply in the equatorial plane of the bubble, since the vertical velocity becomes infinite just at the centre. Also, R is *not* the radius of the bubble at the section under consideration nor is V_{T_0} the rate of ascent of the bubble as a whole. A more detailed examination of the flow, beyond the scope of this Appendix, is required to explain such matters.

Another type of spherical bubble corresponds to 'Hill's spherical vortex'. This is somewhat akin to the vortex ring concept, as explained below, except that the vorticity is distributed over the whole interior of the spherical bubble according to a particular law. In the simpler bubble, considered above, all the vorticity is effectively concentrated at the centre. Here, the vertical velocity distribution within the bubble is parabolic, again lending credence to this simple distribution. The flow outside will be the same as for the previous spherical bubble and the tangential velocities inside and outside must match at the surface. This condition leads to a discontinuity in the velocity gradient at the surface.

Both of these types of spherical bubble thermals satisfy the principle of continuity.

A Modified Parabolic Distribution. A velocity distribution proposed by Gedeon, for the purpose of analysing 'dolphin' flying is

$$V_T/V_{T_0} = [1-(r/R)^2] \exp [-(r/R)^2]. \tag{A8.4}$$

This expression gives a distribution rather similar to that of the spherical bubble, and also satisfies the continuity requirement. It has no particular theoretical or experimental basis but is simply a plausible-looking mathematical expression.

For any distribution which satisfies continuity, any number of such thermals may be supposed to occur with arbitrary distances between the cores. This consideration is useful in the analysis of cloud-street flying.

Vortex Rings. Experiments have indicated that a likely structure for an isolated thermal is similar to the vortex ring, in which the vorticity is distributed throughout a doughnut-shaped region. If the diameter of the ring section is small compared with the diameter of the aperture, the result looks like a smoke ring. The annulus of air transported with the ring is appreciably larger than the ring itself. If the diameter of the ring is increased somewhat, the hole in the middle of the annulus closes and the volume of air transported with the ring, which may be regarded as the bubble, becomes somewhat spherical, but flattened in the vertical sense. The result looks rather like Fig. 3.1. The two types of spherical bubbles previously considered may be regarded as extreme cases of the vortex ring.

It can be argued that in a real bubble, the vorticity cannot be concentrated at the centre, as required in the simple spherical bubble. The vortex ring or Hill's spherical vortex therefore represent more likely situations, in which the vorticity is distributed over a finite volume. The velocity distributions associated with vortex rings are calculable in principle but do not lead to simple analytical equations. Such calculations do not necessarily provide an insight into the properties of real thermals since the criteria which decide the geometry of the vortex ring and the distribution of the vorticity are not known.

Laboratory 'Thermals'. Numbers experiments have been made in which a bubble of one fluid is released in a vessel full of another fluid of slightly different density, the bubble being rendered visible by ink or solid particle. Usually, the experiment is inverted compared with the real atmosphere: e.g., the bubble might be of salt solution sinking through fresh water. The results of such experiments look remarkably like time-lapse films of growing cumulus clouds.

Detailed observations and measurements tend to give credence to vortex-ring theories. In particular, Betsy Woodward's measurements of vertical velocity agree reasonably well with those calculated within a Hill's spherical vortex although agreement with velocities predicted outside the bubble is rather poor. The relevant part of the velocity profile is therefore approximately parabolic.

Elementary theory applied to such bubbles indicates that, if the total buoyancy remains constant, the size of the bubble will increase linearly with height above some datum, not necessarily at ground level. The vertical velocity of the whole bubble will be inversely proportional to the height above datum.

Real Thermals. The practical glider pilot will be inclined to think that arbitrary formulae, hydrodynamic theory and small-scale experiments are all very well, but why not go and measure what happens in real thermals? Unfortunately, such measurements are extremely difficult to make, due to the variability and invisibility of thermals, instrumentation problems and — almost worst of all — the organisation required. Konovalov has published results based on 377 traverses of thermals, reduced to averaged dimensionless plots of vertical velocity. He identifies two types: one with multiple cores and one with a single core. The latter has a velocity profile which appears to be somewhere between triangular and parabolic. The plot of the multi-core thermal is difficult to interpret and has some unconvincing features.

Other Features of Thermal Bubbles. All of the foregoing has been devoted to the distribution of vertical velocity along a horizontal line implicitly passing through the axis of the thermal. The actual velocities and the radii at which they occur will also depend on the vertical location of the line relative to the centre of the bubble. For example, at the centre, the vertical velocity will be about twice that at the uppermost point on the bubble.

As explained in Chapter 3, a sailplane encountering a thermal may either sink out of the bottom of the bubble or eventually find a position which is at a constant height above the centre of the bubble assuming, of course, that the thermal is strong enough and the rate of sink of the glider is not too great. In the latter case, the rate of climb of the glider will be the same as the rate of ascent of the bubble, whatever the performance of the glider. If there are several gliders of differing performances in the same thermal, they will all ascend together but with those of better performance at the top of the stack.

The remarks above are concerned only with vertical motions of the air: except at the equatorial plane of a bubble, there will also be inflow or outflow velocities, as indicated in Fig. 3.1. Suppose a glider has climbed to its equilibrium position above the centre of a thermal bubble. Then it will be flying in a region of outflow and, if the pilot keeps the sideslip angle zero, he will have to crab the machine inwards. If the bubble corresponds with Hill's spherical vortex, the maximum outflow velocity he encounters is half the rate of rise of the bubble so, in thermals of moderate strength, the crabbing angle is unlikely to exceed $2° - 3°$.

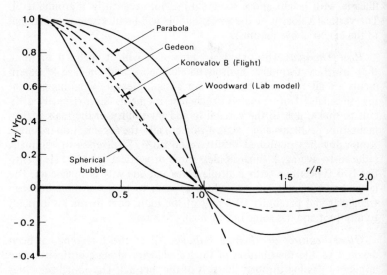

Fig A8.1 Comparison of various theoretical and measured thermal velocity profiles, scaled to give the same core strength and radius

Fig. A8.1 shows some of the velocity profiles mentioned above plotted so that they all have the same core strength and all pass through zero at the same radius. The shapes look appreciably different. However, if the radii are varied so that they all have the same core strength and the same local strength ($0.75\ V_{T_0}$) at $r = 500$ ft, the curves are very close together up to $r = 600$ ft. This suggests that, for the purposes of calculating climb performance, the parabolic profile is quite accurate enough.

Appendix 9

Selecting Tasks for Gliding Contests

A competition will not be successful unless the tasks are satisfying to the pilots. Gliding is unlike many sports in that the action for the day cannot be decided in advance; until detailed weather information is available neither the type of task nor the route can be determined. If the wrong task is set good soaring weather will probably be wasted, and competitors may be frustrated or even hazarded. Bad tasks will affect the final results by introducing an unreasonable degree of luck.

WEATHER AND PLANNING

Arrangements should be made in advance to obtain the fullest and most up-to-date weather information as early as possible each morning. In addition to the general synoptic situation, information is needed on wind strength and direction, thermal strength and distribution, cloud cover and cloud base height, and the likely period of convection for the probable task area. If there is any doubt about the timing of the expected weather this should be checked by telephoning one or two places well upwind for their actual conditions. If necessary, briefing should be postponed.

In addition to meteorological information the following will be needed:- Half million, quarter million, and 1:50,000 (or 1-inch maps), ruler or scale, pocket calculator, the Rule book, and data on turning points and goal airfields, if possible with photographs.

THE TASKS

The majority of tasks should be closed circuit speed flights in which the pilot has a good chance of returning home. Speed tasks are well liked because they are more of a direct contest with the pilot able to quickly calculate whom he has beaten, and who has beaten him. They save tedious and expensive retrieving, and enable the organisers to get out the results quickly.

Speed tasks challenge most pilot skills except the selection of route in relation to the weather. Distance tasks give the pilot more choice and decision making, but also increase the luck element. If there are long overnight retrieves it may not be feasible to set a task on the following day, which would then be a day lost. Nevertheless, in certain circumstances, and particularly in junior or training competitions, downwind distance may be all that is possible. When selecting a task route the proximity of controlled airspace especially downwind must be taken into account, as also must be busy airfields, parachute competitions, or other hazards. It also has to be decided whether the task course shall conform to international (CIVV) record requirements, or whether the needs of providing the best possible contest course shall be paramount.

TASK CONSIDERATIONS

1 Speed over a Triangular Course

Purpose. Speed around the course with return to base.

Weather. This is a 'racing circuit' task at its best in really good weather. Thermals should be at least moderate, preferably strong. They should be uniformly distributed and there should be little or no over-development of cumulus. The wind is best light or moderate. This task can be unsatisfactory when there is a real risk of thunderstorms obscuring turning points.

Considerations. Triangles come in multiples of 100 km. A good competition pilot is able to complete 300 km in weather that is unexceptional. The strength of the head wind on a long leg may be the determining factor on the size of the triangle. 100 km is the minimum for other than training competitions. If it is necessary for some reason to keep gliders in the local areas a triangle of suitable size and shape may be lapped more than once to give a total distance of 100 km or over.

2 Out-and-Return Speed

Purpose. Speed to a turning point with a return to base.

Weather. Thermals moderate to strong. Overdevelopment of cumulus or isolated thunderstorms can be accepted as there is only a single turning point. Wind is not critical, but if strong the lift should not be sporadic or weak. This can be a useful task when the good weather area is limited.

Considerations. If thermal or cloud streets are expected the course should be parallel to the wind, even though this will give a big speed discrepancy between into and down wind. A first leg downwind is encouraging, allows the task to be started earlier, and reduces overcrowding early in the flight. If there are no streets the route should be set across wind. An out-and-return should be avoided in poor visibility because of the increased risk of collision.

3 Straight Race

Purpose. Speed with an away landing at a goal.

Weather. Even thermal distribution is more important than strength. It can be flown in winds up to operational limits.

Considerations. The biggest disadvantage of this task is that all gliders have to be retrieved. If set downwind speeds may be high and the task completed in an unsatisfactorily short time. It is not a very effective task and achieves little towards finding the best pilot, but may be useful when the task area is limited by air traffic prohibitions or to escape fast approaching bad weather.

4 Out-and-Return Speed to Alternative Turning Points

Purpose. To give some choice to the pilot in doubtful weather. It can also be used on triangular courses for one or both turning points.

Weather. Moderate to good thermals when there is doubt about the wind strength and direction, or in a known wind when there is doubt about thermal strength or distribution.

Considerations. The alternative courses should be of similar expected difficulty within an angular spread of 30°. This task should be used only when a triangle or ordinary out-and-return are unlikely to be successful.

5 Distance along a Predetermined Course

Purpose. Maximum distance when limited in direction by air traffic or other reasons, and ending with an outlanding.

Weather. Anything that provides reasonable lift.

Considerations. The predetermined course may have one turning point and is useful for making use of a narrow flight corridor. The probable length of the flight can be selected by adjusting the length of the first leg and the angle to the wind of either or both legs. A substantially downwind flight may end at the coast and provide little except retrieves.

6 Free Distance

Purpose. To achieve maximum distance

Weather. The poorest weather in which it is possible to set a task.

Considerations. Free Distance is fine if the purpose is to beat a record, but if given in a contest in any but weak weather it will produce a great retrieve problem. It is not a very competitive task as pilots may take quite different routes and fly in weather not foreseen by the organisers. Under some circumstances it is a useful task for training competitions.

7 Prescribed Area Distance (Cats Cradle)

Purpose. Pilot selection of route over a multi-leg course for distance.

Weather. Moderate to good thermals, moderate wind. Because the pilot can select his route as he goes along this task can be successfully flown when the air is severely unstable, being less critical to storms and squalls. *Considerations.* With 4–7 turning points spread over a large area of country the task will provide interesting and varied distance flying without much in the way of retrieving. The course area should preferably be upwind of base. Crosswind of base is acceptable, but downwind will result in numerous outlandings. Very big distances can be achieved.

SELECTING THE TASK

(*i*)   The weather should be studied and any task which is obviously unsuitable eliminated. If conditions look very good only speed tasks should be considered.

(*ii*)   The intended degree of difficulty should be decided, depending on the type of competition, pilot skill, and glider performance. The size of a triangle or out-and-return should be such that a predetermined proportion of the competitors should be expected to complete it. This might be, say, $\frac{3}{4}$ in a Regional competition to less than $\frac{1}{2}$ in a World Championship so as to provide a tough challenge. If many fewer get back than was expected and the weather was as forecast, the task was too difficult.

(*iii*)   The length of the task should be calculated in terms of expected flight duration. Less than 2 hours is wasteful of weather and increases the luck element; more than $4\frac{1}{2}$ hours may be too long in terms of the convection period available. After a number of consecutive contest days pilot fatigue should be considered.
Fig. A9.1 should now be used to determine the length of course for triangles or out-and-returns.

(*iv*)   Every effort should be made to find the best possible course for the weather. Standard 'milk run' courses should not be used simply because they exist and are familiar. Where possible a leg into a strong wind should not be immediately followed by one downwind, because it will produce a big step in the marks, since those who are able to round the point will then go much further without difficulty.

(*v*)   Finally, the forecast and the task that has been set should be carefully reviewed to ensure that no relevant factor has been omitted. Setting tasks in good weather is usually easy, but in poor weather it can be very difficult. After several days of no flying there is always a tendency to send pilots off on some flight that the weather does not justify. On the other hand, nothing succeeds like success; several days of good tasks will have pilots flying better, whereas a run of tasks that do not come off leave them frustrated and the task setter underconfident.

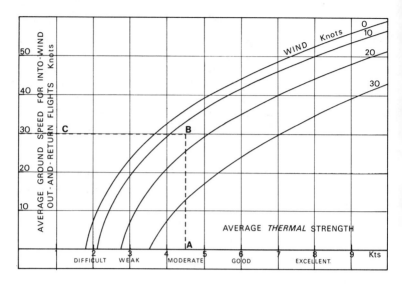

Fig A9.1 Course Length Calculator

TO USE:

1 Determine thermal strength, say 450 fpm (4.5 knots). Enter at A.

2 Determine wind speed, say 15 knots. Go vertically up from A to hit 15 knot wind line (point B)

3 Read average ground speed over closed circuit by going left from B to C

4 Multiply speed by desired flight time in hours (say 3) to obtain length of circuit. Therefore 30 × 3 = 90 nautical miles (167 km)

NOTES

This chart assumes uniform thermal distribution without streets on an out-and-return along the wind for a Libelle. Streets will increase the average speed

THE START

Part of the job of setting a task is deciding the time at which launching shall take place. If too early a high proportion of gliders will land back and the overall period needed to get competitors away will be lengthened. If the start is late soaring weather will be wasted. If the period of good lift is expected to be short all gliders should be off tow *before* the peak conditions arrive.

If a glider is used for thermal snifting as a check on thermal development the pilot should be directed to explore out along the intended route as soon as he is able to stay up, and to report back frequently by radio. It has to be accepted that one small patch of lift will not support 40−50 gliders, but equally that once started thermal development may be rapid. Every effort should be made to get the timing right.

Appendix 10

Compass Swinging

The reading of a compass installed in a glider is affected by steel components and magnets in other instruments. It may also be affected by electrical currents flowing in adjacent wiring. The latter effect can be largely eliminated by using twin flex so that the field generated by one wire is cancelled out by that due to the return circuit in the other wire.

Most compasses are provided with supplementary magnets to cancel out the influence of these stray magnetic fields. In order to adjust these magnets correctly, it is necessary to determine the errors when the aircraft is pointing in different directions; this process is known as swinging the compass.

The following method is simpler than that normally used for light aircraft. It has the advantage that it is not necessary to make use of another compass nor to know the magnetic bearing of any reference point. Whilst it gives acceptable results, it must be realized that it will be accurate only if the following two conditions are satisfied: that the compass is correctly made and that it is installed in the aircraft with the proper alignment.

The procedure is as follows.

1 Take the glider to a flat area remote from metal objects, reinforced concrete, etc.

2 Install all the usual equipment. If the stick is made of steel fix it in the approximate flying position. Shut the airbrakes. An idealist would also retract the undercarriage.

3 Align the glider so that the compass reads exactly East (090°), with the wings level. Sight along the fuselage to some distant object which can be easily identified again.

4 Turn the glider to face the other way, and sighting along the fuselage in the opposite direction to that used previously, realign the glider on the distant object.

5 Observe the compass reading and see how much it differs from West (270°). (For example, suppose the compass reads 290°. The discrepancy is therefore 20°.)

6 Adjust the compass correcting magnets so that this discrepancy is halved. (In the example it would be necessary to make the compass read 280°.) The method of making the adjustment depends on the type of compass; it may be by means of a screwdriver in a slot marked E-W, or by using a special key in a hole facing either fore or aft, or by adding little magnets pointing fore and aft.

7 Turn the glider until the compass reads North. Observe another distant object in line with the fuselage axis.

8 Turn the aircraft around to face in the opposite direction by sighting on the distant mark, and observe the new compass reading. (For example, suppose that it is 170°.)

9 Adjust the compass to halve the discrepancy. (In our example, make compass read 175°.) Use screwdriver slot marked N-S, special key in athwartships hole, or little magnets inserted athwartships.

10 If large errors have been corrected, the whole procedure should be repeated.

Appendix 11

Radio Notes

Specific channels in the VHF aeronautical communications band 118 MHz–132 MHz are allocated for glider use. These vary in different countries. In Great Britain in 1976 the allocated frequencies were 130.1 and 130.4 MHz.

FREQUENCY-WAVELENGTH CONVERSION

$$\lambda \text{ (wavelength in metres)} = \frac{300}{f\text{(frequency in MHz)}}$$

Therefore a frequency of 130 MHz corresponds to a wavelength of 2.308 metres.

ANTENNAE

Normally, vertically polarized antennae are used to give omni-directional coverage. Typical antennae are shown in the diagram (Fig. 11.1). The theoretical lengths of the elements shown in the diagram are $\lambda/4$. In practice this figure has to be corrected for the diameter of the antenna and its method of mounting. For example, the theoretical length of a quarter wave antenna for 130 MHz is 0.577 metres (22.7 in.). For an antenna of type A mounted on the metal roof of a motorcar, or externally on a metal glider, the actual length should be 21.6 in. if it is made of wire 0.10 in. in diameter.

Since the efficiency of a radio depends to a marked extent on the suitability of the antenna, its installation and its wiring, it pays to go to considerable trouble over these details, and consult the manufacturer or a competent radio engineer.

396

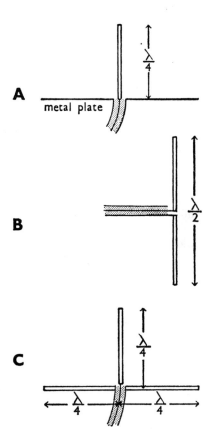

Fig A11.1 Suitable types of radio antennae

A External quarter-wave whip on metal ground (roof of car or fuselage of metal aircraft)

B Half-wave dipole in fin or fuselage

C Quarter-wave whip with quarter-wave elements in fuselage

Internal antennae (B and C) can only be used if the surrounding structure is non-metallic (e.g. of wood or glass-fibre). They should be mounted as far as possible from push-rods, control cables, substantial metal fittings and the pilot

PROPAGATION

The communication range using VHF is essentially confined to 'line of sight' but refraction in the atmosphere effectively increases the earth's radius by a factor of 4/3.

In the absence of obstructions, stations with antennae at heights H_1 and H_2 (in feet) are in radio line of sight provided the spacing in statute miles is less than $\sqrt{2H_1} + \sqrt{2H_2}$.

THE INTERNATIONAL PHONETIC ALPHABET

Alfa	Hotel	Oscar	Uniform
Bravo	India	Papa	Victor
Charlie	Juliet	Quebec	Whiskey
Delta	Kilo	Romeo	X-ray
Echo	Lima	Sierra	Yankee
Foxtrot	Mike	Tango	Zulu
Golf	November		

Appendix 12

Rules of the Air

Converging. When aircraft are converging at approximately the same altitude, the aircraft which has the other on its *right* shall give way.

Head on. When two aircraft are approaching each other head on, or approximately so, each shall alter course to its *right*.

Overtaking. The overtaking aircraft shall normally keep out of the way of the aircraft being overtaken by altering course to the *right*. Legally a glider is allowed to overtake another glider on either side. The object of this regulation is to permit the common-sense rule of slope soaring, which is to overtake on the downwind side of the other glider.

> *Note*: With converging and overtaking, the aircraft which has the right of way shall maintain its course and speed.

Landing. The lower aircraft has right of way.

Appendix 13

OSTIV Requirements for Pilot's Controls

COLOURS AND OPERATION

Control	Colour	Direction of operation	Location
Release	yellow	pull to release	for left hand operation
Air Brakes	blue	pull to open	for left hand operation
Trimmer	green	forward = nose down	preferably for left hand operation
Canopy Opening*	white	direction of operation for opening to be clearly marked	
Canopy Jettison*	red		
Wing Flaps		forward = up or retract	preferably for left hand operation
Landing Gear		pull to retract	
Other Controls	not yellow blue, green, white or red	to be clearly marked	

* If canopy opening and jettison are combined in one handle, the colour shall be red.

General Remarks: (a) The shape and size of control knobs and handles shall be suitable for their intended use.

(b) Marking by means of symbols and pictures is preferred to marking by words.

(c) In sailplanes fitted with dual controls, towing hook release, air brakes, trimmer, canopy, flaps, and landing gear shall be capable of being operated by either pilot.

OSTIV, the Organisation Scientifique et Technique Internationale du Vol à Voile, is advisory to the Fédération Aeronautique Internationale. This Appendix is reproduced from the 1976 edition of the OSTIV Airworthiness Requirements for Sailplanes.

Appendix 14

Trailer Reversing

It is easy to get confused when reversing a car and trailer, particularly if the driver has ever been told, 'Turn the steering wheel the wrong way.'

One simple way of looking at the problem is to forget about the car completely and to imagine that you are trying to push the trailer backwards by its towbar. Then you can just drive the car so that the towbar goes in the right direction.

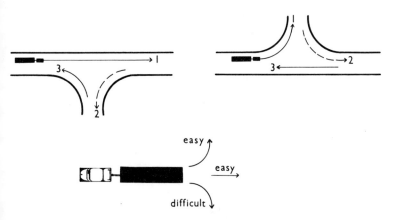

Fig A14.1 *It is difficult to reverse the trailer on a path curving away from the driver's side, because he cannot see its rear end. This point should be borne in mind when planning how to turn the car and trailer round. The diagram shows the easiest methods of turning round when using side roads. It is drawn for the British rule of the road, with the driver in the right-hand seat*

401

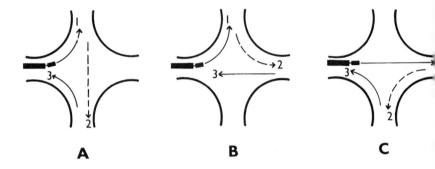

A   **B**   **C**

Fig A14.2 When turning at cross-roads the same prin-
ciples apply. Since it is usually easiest to reverse straight
back, most drivers find method (A) the simplest. How-
ever, there may be reasons for not doing this, in which
methods (B) and (C) are satisfactory since, when
reversing, the trailer can be seen
  The rule for turning round at any road junction is
therefore as follows: Initially, either drive straight on and
reverse so as to keep the trailer in view or turn in the
direction away from the driver's side and then reverse
straight back

A long reverse, particularly around a curved path, or at night, can be
made more easily if a crew member walks beside the trailer and gives
information in a clear way. One simple method, which works well, is
for him to shout out soundings of the trailer wheel from the edge of the
road. He tells the driver that he should keep, say, two feet out, and
then shouts the distances as the trailer goes back – '2, 2, $2\frac{1}{2}$, 3, $2\frac{1}{2}$, $2\frac{1}{2}$,
2,' etc. The driver can go on indefinitely, continually correcting so as to
keep near his target figure of 2. He knows that if the soundings get near
4 or 0 he must be prepared to stop.
  If there is no clearly defined edge to the road, as for example across
a side entrance, the crew member can select an imaginary line and guide
the driver in relation to this.
  The reasoning behind this method is that a driver finds it much easier
to work on information, rather than instructions. In the same way,
when directing someone who is reversing a trailer straight backwards up
to an obstruction, he would prefer to be told, '20 feet, 10, 5, 3, 2, 1,'
rather than 'Come on, come on, come on, stop, too late!'

Appendix 15
List of Symbols

A	Aspect ratio.
A	A constant $(C_{D_0}\frac{1}{2}\rho_0 S)$ for a particular glider in a given configuration [Equations **(16.11)**, **(A7.1)**, etc.] .
A_s	Cross-sectional area of a stream tube.
B	A constant $(kW^2/\frac{1}{2}\pi\rho_0 b^2)$ for a particular glider in a given configuration at a certain weight [Equations **(16.11)**, **(A7.1)**, etc.] .
b	Wing span.
C_1	Volume of total-energy compensator.
C_2	Volume of variometer capacity.
C_D	Drag coefficient.
$C_{D_{min}}$	Minimum value of C_D for a complete glider.
C_{D_0}	Profile drag coefficient of a complete glider.
C_L	Lift coefficient.
$C_{L_{max}}$	Lift coefficient at the stall.
C_{Lms}	Lift coefficient of a complete glider at the minimum sinking speed condition.
D	Total drag of a glider.
D_i	Induced drag.
$D_{i_{min}}$	Minimum induced drag, corresponding to an elliptical spanwise lift distribution.
D_p	Profile drag.
E	A function of V/V_0 [Equation **(A7.9)**] .
F	A function of V/V_0 [Equation **(A7.13)**]
G	A function of V/V_0 [Equation **(A7.11)**] .
g	Acceleration due to gravity.

403

H	Height above the ground (for photography).
h	Height.
h_A	Minimum height for leaving the last thermal of a cross-country flight.
h_e	Energy height, $h + V^2/2g$.
k	Induced drag factor.
k_1	Constant in equation (**A7.14**).
k_2	Constant in equation (**A7.16**).
L	Lift.
L	Length of a capillary tube [Equation (**18.8**)].
l	A characteristic length associated with Reynolds number.
M	Mach number.
n	Load factor.
n	Index in equation (**17.1**).
n	Index in equation (**A8.1**).
p	Atmospheric pressure.
p_0	Standard sea-level atmospheric pressure (1013.2 mb).
p_s	Static pressure applied to instruments (usually taken equal to p at the height of the glider but may differ slightly in practice).
q	Dynamic pressure, $\frac{1}{2}\rho V^2$.
R	Radius of a thermal (i.e. the value of r where $V_T = 0$).
R_1, R_2	Pneumatic resistances due to capillary tubes in variometer circuits.
R_e	Reynolds number.
r	Radius of turn.
r	Radial distance from the axis of a thermal.
r	Radius of curvature of the flight path in pitching manoeuvres.
r	Radius of the bore of a capillary tube [Equation (**18.8**)].
S	Wing area.
T	Time constant of a variometer system.
t	Time.
t_c	Time spent climbing.
t_g	Time spent gliding.
U	Vertical gust velocity (EAS).
V	True air speed (TAS). [EAS in airworthiness requirements]

NOTE: True airspeed (TAS) is the actual speed of the glider relative to the air. As explained in Chapter 16, equivalent airspeed (EAS) is obtained by multiplying true airspeed by the square root of the relative density of the atmosphere:

$$V_i = V\sqrt{(\rho/\rho_0)}$$

In this expression, ρ is the local air density in the region of the atmosphere where the glider is flying and ρ_0 is the standard sea-level value of air density (0.002377 slug/ft³ or 1.225 kg/m³).

It is often convenient to use an 'equivalent' rate of descent, defined in an analogous fashion:

$$V_{si} = V_s\sqrt{(\rho/\rho_0)}$$

V_A	Manoeuvring speed (EAS).
V_a	Vertical velocity of the air in downdraughts (TAS); "air mass movement".
V_B	Design strong gust speed (EAS).
V_b	The total vertical velocity of a glider in the presence of a downdraught (TAS).
V_c	Rate of climb (TAS).
V_c'	See Fig. 17.2 and associated text.
V_D	Design dive speed (EAS).
V_{DF}	Speed demonstrated in flight (EAS).
V_i	Equivalent airspeed (EAS).
V_{i_1}	Equivalent airspeed at the chosen datum point on the glider performance curve (knots). See equation (18.8).
V_{i_0}	EAS corresponding to $(L/D)_{max}$.
V_k	An effective rate of climb associated wth the use of a variometer as a flight path indicator (see Chapter 18 and Appendix 7).
V_{opt}	The optimum speed to fly between thermals, to maximize $\bar{V}$ (TAS).
V_{ms}	The value of V corresponding to $V_{s\,min}$ (TAS).
V_{NE}	Never-exceed speed (EAS).
V_s	Rate of descent of the glider in still air (TAS).
V_{si}	'Equivalent' rate of descent, $V_s\sqrt{\sigma}$.
$V_{s\,min}$	Minimum rate of descent (TAS).
V_{s_0}	Rate of descent at the speed V_0 corresponding to $(L/D)_{max}$ (TAS).
V_{si_0}	'Equivalent' rate of descent at V_{i_0}, i.e., $V_{s_0}\sqrt{\sigma}$.

V_s	Stalling speed (TAS or EAS).
V_{s_1}	Stalling speed at $n = 1$ (TAS or EAS).
V_{s_ϕ}	Rate of sink at angle of bank ϕ.
V_T	Vertical velocity of the air in a thermal (TAS).
V_{T_0}	V_T on the axis of the thermal (TAS).
V_w	Wind speed component (TAS).
V_ϕ	Speed when circling with an angle of bank ϕ (TAS).
V_0	Speed corresponding to $\phi = 0$ (TAS). [V_ϕ and V_o relate to the same C_L].
V_0	Speed corresponding to $(L/D)_{max}$ (TAS).
V_1 , V_{si_1}	Values of V and V_s at a certain point on a glider's performance curve (TAS).
V_{i_1} , V_{si_1}	'Equivalent' speeds corresponding to V_1 , V_{s_1} .
V_1 , V_2	See Fig. 17.2 and associated text.
$\overline{V}$	Average cross-country speed (TAS).
$\overline{V}_{max}$	Maximum average cross-country speed (TAS).
W	All-up weight of a glider.
w	Downwash velocity [Equations (16.3), (16.4)] .
w	Wing loading, W/S.
X	Horizontal distance between the point of leaving the last thermal on a cross-country flight and the goal.
α	Angle of attack.
γ, λ	Angles defined in Fig. 17.9.
ϕ	Angle of bank in circling flight.
μ	Viscosity of the air.
μ_0	Standard sea-level value of μ.
ν	Kinematic viscosity, μ/ρ.
ρ	Air density.
ρ_0	Standard sea-level value of ρ.
σ	Density ratio, ρ/ρ_0 .
θ	The attitude of the glider in pitch. Also, in steady flight, the flight path slope.

NOTES ON SYMBOLS

Speeds. It would be very convenient if all true speeds could be denoted by V with, if necessary, suitable subscripts to indicate which particular speed was under consideration. Thus V alone would be the true airspeed of the glider, V_s would be the true rate of descent of the glider and so on. 'Equivalent' speeds could then be denoted by the further subscript '*i*' or '*e*', giving V_i, V_{si}, and so on. Unfortunately, this neat scheme is confused by the tendency of airworthiness authorities to imply equivalent airspeeds at all times unless specifically stated otherwise and without any distinguishing subscript. So V_D is the equivalent design dive speed.

Moreover, many of the speeds listed above as true airspeeds can be either true or equivalent airspeeds provided that they are used in self-consistent groups. Thus, the analysis relating to $\overline{V}_{max}$ and V_{opt} in Chapter 16 is written as if all speeds were 'true' but it is equally valid if all speeds are 'equivalent', admittedly with some qualification if the height ranges involved are large. Specific remarks are usually made in the text when such a situation occurs.

Heights. Throughout this book 'height' is used rather loosely. Strictly, one should distinguish between tape-measure height (e.g. in the context of final glides) and pressure height (the height corresponding to a certain pressure in a Standard Atmosphere: for all practical purposes, the indications of an accurate altimeter). In a non-standard atmosphere, the two are not the same: indeed, to be really pedantic, they are not quite the same in a Standard Atmosphere. From the point of view of the glider pilot, practical differences are unlikely to be apparent even on a very non-standard day.

Index